Praise fo

THE VIRAL UND

Long-listed for the 2023 PEN/John Kenneth Galbraith Award for Nonfiction
Long-listed for the 2023 Andrew Carnegie Medal for Excellence in Nonfiction
Winner of the 2022 POZ Award for Best in Literature

"Steven Thrasher has written the book we urgently need. Putting a compelling and human face on the millions of people affected by the course viruses like HIV and COVID take in the human population, he shows us how race, class, gender, and sexuality combine to help some survive pandemics and even profit from them, while others experience pandemic through their bodies in the form of illness, death, death of loved ones, shame, stigma, and financial insecurity. His analysis of the viral underclass should be required reading for everyone concerned with transforming unequal access to health care in a world where pandemic heightens the brutality of inequality."

—Michael Eric Dyson, *New York Times* bestselling author of *Tears We Cannot Stop* and *What Truth Sounds Like*

"At once precise and sweeping, rigorous and inviting, *The Viral Underclass* fearlessly crosses the policed borders of academic disciplines and literary forms, creating an irresistibly readable and humane exploration of the barbarities of class. Through the sheer force of his storytelling, Thrasher challenges us to abandon our fatal illusions of separateness in favor of an embrace of our place in a collective entanglement of bodies. Readers are gifted that most precious of things in these muddled times: a clear lens through which to see the world."

—Naomi Klein, *New York Times* bestselling author of *This Changes Everything* and *The Shock Doctrine*

"An important new book . . . [showing] we are all more vulnerable and intertwined than we realize."

—*The Washington Post*

"A genre-defying work of journalism, memoir, and cultural critique, *The Viral Underclass* is underpinned by a theoretical model for understanding why certain populations are in consistently more danger of getting sick. It also reveals how deeply Dr. Steven W. Thrasher, a journalist and professor at Northwestern University, believes in community care and mutual aid, in the interconnectedness of living beings and the importance of acknowledging it. Really, though, this is a book about people and the ways they care for one another in the face of governmental and social neglect."

—Ilana Masad, *Them*

"The perfect book for this moment in time. Using his years of studying the effects of the HIV epidemic, Thrasher shows how viral epidemics expose the flaws in the modern American social system in the forms of racism, homophobia, classism, and ableism. Combining years of research with the personal stories of people living with these diseases or fighting for justice for those who are, this book speaks perfectly to the intersection of virology and activism."

—*Vulture* (9 Great Books About Navigating Viruses Throughout History)

"The pandemic brought America's health inequities into stark relief, but *The Viral Underclass* illustrates that the problem isn't new, and that it is embedded more deeply than many of us realize. . . . Thrasher, a gay Black man, brings figures from the viral underclass to life in this engaging, enraging read."

—*The Boston Globe*

"Brilliant . . . Stunning."

—Jonathan Van Ness

"A remarkable book."

—Amy Goodman, *Democracy Now!*

"Throughout this insightful and unflinching book, Thrasher is unafraid to let his anger shine, but he also consistently deploys love and compassion. In a text marked by mistreatment and loss, the author encourages hope. . . . Powerful and revelatory, this is an essential, paradigm-shifting book."

—*Kirkus Reviews* (starred review and a Best Nonfiction Book of 2022)

"I fully expected to encounter rigorous research and a full accounting of the relevant history in Dr. Steven W. Thrasher's *The Viral Underclass*. But what excited me and kept me rapt the entire time was the astonishing level of craft and depth of compassion with which the book was written. More than just sets of facts, Dr. Thrasher illuminates truths, all of which implore us to live by the grandest, most liberating of all principles: love. *The Viral Underclass* is journalism and journey, science and sermon, astute articulation of grievance and pathway to healing. It is vital reading."

—Robert Jones Jr., *New York Times* bestselling author of *The Prophets*

"[The] last great book someone recommended to me: My friends know me so well that when I ask about what I should read they always send me au courant nonfiction recommendations, and *The Viral Underclass* is certainly that. The book is about systems that make certain people more likely to contract and spread viruses, and is told through the lens of HIV and COVID. Thrasher doesn't go into the science of the illnesses, but rather the social and political constructs that increase the likelihood that marginalized groups of people (Black, queer, disabled, etc.) will get sick, have their lives radically altered, and/or die from these diseases. The book is smart and covers a lot of ground. And now, I'm recommending it to everyone I know."

—Traci Thomas, *She Reads*

"*The Viral Underclass* marks the beginning of a new epoch in cultural work. Steven Thrasher has utilized and finely crafted theory, memoir, and reportage to show us what we've been doing the first few years of this century." —Kiese Laymon, bestselling author of *Heavy* and winner of an Andrew Carnegie Medal

"A compelling and compassionate analysis of health disparities that delivers both wake-up call and gut punch." —*Booklist* (starred review)

"It's hard to imagine that one single book could truly speak to the moment that we're in. But that's exactly what Steven Thrasher has achieved in *The Viral Underclass*. . . . It's truly a riveting book. I almost had to devour it in one sitting. I just did not want to put it down. . . . One of the most beautiful kind of pieces of craft I've encountered in a long time."

—*Slate*

"[A] beautifully written account illustrat[ing] the complex and textured relationship between disease and inequality." —*Science*

"In *The Viral Underclass*, through a combination of broad and deep reporting and narrative storytelling, Steven Thrasher examines the ways HIV/AIDS and other viruses strike people and communities with deliberate intention. His book is essential reading for our current moment—and a signpost for understanding epidemics to come."

—Linda Villarosa, author of the Pulitzer Prize finalist *Under the Skin* and contributor to the *New York Times* bestselling *The 1619 Project*

"Rigorous scholarship and intimate portraits of life and death on the margins make this a must-read."

—*Publishers Weekly* (starred review and a Best Politics and Current Events Book of Fall 2022)

"A page-turner. An intimate view of how stigma and class inequality produce suffering at the hands of our two emblematic viruses: COVID and HIV. Thrasher tells a complex story of social stratification and injustice through very well-drawn portraits of individuals in his life and in the world. Moving and compelling."

—Sarah Schulman, author of *Let the Record Show: A Political History of ACT UP New York, 1987–1993*

"*The Viral Underclass* is remarkably insightful for spotlighting the profound health inequities in the United States." —Eric Topol, MD

"[A] wide-ranging examination of how our society's ills exacerbate those of our bodies . . . [with] a sense of poetry." —*Jezebel*

"*The Viral Underclass* is wonderful." —Maris Kreizman

"Thrasher is an excellent investigator. The reader sees how and why the narratives develop in particular ways, and feels fury and despair, as well as occasional glimmers of hope." —*Nature*

"A remarkable quality of Thrasher's book is his attentiveness to injustice on a large scale as well as in its most intimate forms . . . [making] the case for urgent change, envisioning a society that doesn't force people to expose themselves to sickness in order to survive."

—*The New Republic*

"Groundbreaking LGBTQ scholar, social critic, and journalist Steven W. Thrasher, PhD, has spent his career studying HIV criminalization and how the virus has been policed in marginalized communities. This vital and potent book explores how viruses can expose the vast inequalities in our society, something we witnessed all too recently during the COVID-19 pandemic. Friends, activists, and teachers shared their heartbreaking stories of navigating the coronavirus, HIV, and other viruses with Thrasher, uncovering the devastating effects of privilege.

The Viral Underclass is a powerful book that helps us to understand more fully the differences that determine who receives care when society is facing the deadly effects of a mysterious virus." —*POZ*

"In this sometimes shocking, always fascinating book, Thrasher reveals how politics, money, and cultural scapegoating have cost lives throughout modern history. Along with solid reporting and impressive research, Thrasher introduces us to people who've been caught in the web of viral disease or are fighting to protect others—and his warm, compassionate character studies remind us of the human beings behind the statistics. You may be outraged by *The Viral Underclass*, but it's a gripping read and a powerful call to action." —Apple Books (Editors' Pick)

"An essential work . . . sweeping and profound." —*Shondaland*

"[*The Viral Underclass* is] an articulation of illness politics as a practice of love. . . . The portraits here are deeply moving. Thrasher has a way of capturing community activists in action by providing touching details about their characters and work along with careful analysis of the structural violence they are up against."

—Lisa Diedrich, professor of women's, gender, and sexuality studies at Stony Brook University

"Journalist and LGBTQ scholar Thrasher, who exposed and fought the criminalization of HIV, offers a bold new COVID-19–era study on the societal inequalities exposed by viruses, and how their spread and toll are shaped by social structures." —*USA Today* (Editors' Choice)

THE VIRAL UNDERCLASS

The Human Toll When Inequality and Disease Collide

STEVEN W. THRASHER

CELADON BOOKS
NEW YORK

 Printed in the United States of America. For information, address Celadon Books, a division of Macmillan Publishers, 120 Broadway, New York, NY 10271.

www.celadonbooks.com

Designed by Steven Seighman

The Library of Congress has cataloged the hardcover edition as follows:

Names: Thrasher, Steven W., author.
Title: The viral underclass : the human toll when inequality and disease collide / Steven W. Thrasher.
Description: First edition. | New York : Celadon Books, 2022. | Includes bibliographical references and index.
Identifiers: LCCN 2021060451 | ISBN 9781250796639 (hardcover) | ISBN 9781250796653 (ebook)
Subjects: LCSH: Social status—Health aspects. | COVID-19 Pandemic, 2020– —Social aspects. | Viruses—Social aspects. | Equality—Health aspects.
Classification: LCC RA418.5.S63 T47 2022 | DDC 362.1962/414—dc23/eng/20220411
LC record available at https://lccn.loc.gov/2021060451

ISBN 978-1-250-79664-6 (trade paperback)

First Celadon Books Paperback Edition: 2024

10 9 8 7 6 5 4 3 2 1

for

Syed Ali, Eli Pollard,
Tanya McKinnon,
Christopher Statton,

and

Matt Mager

The world is one big petri dish.

—Alice Wong (王美華)

CONTENTS

FOREWORD

The sirens with which Steven Thrasher opens this tragic, beautiful, erudite book announced what seemed at the time to be a common threat to shared humanity.

It was late March 2020. He was in Brooklyn, as was I. The world as we knew it was upside down. The novel coronavirus had sickened and killed people in places like China and Italy. Now it was here, among us, in our air.

Those early days of the COVID-19 pandemic saw a range of responses in New York and then elsewhere that in many ways presaged what was to come. Denial was chief among them. For many people, viral pandemics happened overseas or over *there*, places with mosquitoes or dirty water, or where people ate or did the wrong things. Surely America was protected by the nature of our capitalist spirit, our resolve, our scientific advances. People who felt this cast the response to the pandemic as overblown—*this thing will be gone in two weeks, it's no worse than the flu*—and went on with their daily lives.

At the other end of the spectrum sat terrified doomsayers, people glued to their news feeds for developments or information who left their apartments only long enough to rush to bodegas or supermarkets to load up on ever more toilet paper, Clorox wipes, boxes of pasta, and other everyday items whose utility they had never fully appreciated until now.

In the middle were the confused, the I-don't-care-ers, the what's-going-on-ers, and those who felt that whatever was coming down the pike was inevitable.

This range surely represents the gamut of responses to many tragedies, from wars to 9/11, and the vastly different ways people process threats. But the sirens put an end to all that. The sirens, inescapable and penetrating in those early days, weeks, and months, piercingly announced that social psychology was irrelevant to the new apex predator in our city. It didn't care how you felt, who you were, what sports team you liked, or what you ate for lunch that day. It just wanted to infect humans.

The sirens announced that the virus, and not human minds, would set the narrative. And for one brief moment COVID seemed an equalizer. No one was safe until everyone was safe. Infection anywhere was a threat to people everywhere.

But just as quickly, that moment was gone. More sirens, then even more. The crescendo of it all revealed that though we were all equally vulnerable to the novel pathogen by nature of our earthly humanity, some people were more vulnerable than others by nature of preexisting fault lines, not of biology but of society.

As the virus traveled down streets and into subways and then through towns and communities, its suffering tracked along layers of disparity. It quickly became clear that illness and death reflected existing, mutually reinforcing systems of discriminatory housing, education, employment, earnings, health care, and criminal justice. Paths of COVID suffering and loss illuminated centuries of support systems that America did not build, investments it did not make, opportunities it did not allow.

As but one example, it was soon evident that early rates of COVID death in cities like New York mapped onto socioeconomic neighborhoods, leaving white populations with higher income and wealth relatively unscathed while decimating neighborhoods with lower-income and lower-wealth Black and Latinx populations. And the sirens that blared through days and nights topped ambulances that disproportionately carried people who already suffered from housing insecurity, or lived in multifamily or multigenerational housing where social distancing was not an option, or worked essential jobs that exposed them to the virus without necessary protective equipment. Many of these people did not even make it into ambulances at all. Among the din, they died in silence.

The sirens, in other words, portended not just doom but decision for people in cities like New York and in countries like the United States. Did we, the safely distanced, hear the noise and think *we* were dying? We, humans. We, citizens. We, neighbors, workers, parents, friends of friends. Or did we breathe relief and autonomically think *they* are dying? They, the deserving. They, the disposable. They, the viral underclass.

The former response is what should have happened. If *we* were at risk, then *we* could have taken collective action to seriously address inequity, build vibrant common structures, and create ever more of the kinds of social capital or social cohesion through which healthy societies survive in pandemics. Building social capital based on common ground, in turn, would move us closer to what economist Amartya Sen calls *better societies*, which can emerge from moments of crisis—in which peril sparks appreciation of our shared humanity and a renewed drive toward building mutually beneficial infrastructures that persist well after the crisis has subsided. National health care systems, for instance. Or reformed police, more vibrant food distribution networks, protected climates, and closed wealth gaps. Or wider roads. As Sen explains it, societies that react to moments of crisis by democratizing access to resources, health, and decision-making power come out ahead in the long run.

Instead, despite profound individual moments of bravery and heroism, we as a nation responded to the sirens via the latter reflex, and in the ways that Steven Thrasher powerfully exposes in this remarkable book. As he rightly puts it, we responded, as so many others have responded in the global instances he also tracks, by magnifying

> the divisions already present in our world. In 2020, it quickly became apparent in the United States that the novel coronavirus may not consciously discriminate, because viruses have no consciousness. Similarly, water and fire do not discriminate; they also have no sentience. Yet their effects *do* discriminate against the bodies of the

underclass, because those bodies have been placed in proximity to danger by the structural design of powerful humans.

"The cracks in our society" widened, as Thrasher rightly describes it. We failed to expand Medicaid or access to quality masks or information, or to build better bridges and repair historic wounds. We failed to become structurally competent. Some people got filthy rich off of the instability of it all (a report by the Swiss bank UBS "found the world's billionaires' wealth soared to upward of ten trillion dollars. This has given militaries and governments cover to enforce borders and police populations more harshly"), while others were cast into ever more precariousness and instability. And thus the pandemic, like so many before it, highlighted the effects of what sociologist Whitney Pirtle, adopting a term from Cedric Robinson, calls *racial capitalism*, a system that constructs the harmful social conditions that fundamentally shape biologies, diseases, and pandemic patterns.

This searing book, this forever book, forces us to look and hear and feel the human costs of our decisions and indecisions and indifferences. With power, empathy, and deep insight, Thrasher tells the stories of people left to fend for themselves, people we made vulnerable long before the virus arrived. People who thought their country, their leaders, or their ideologies would save them. These are stories of people whose vulnerability is "manufactured," and stories of how such exposure "spreads through society more broadly—with the economy, media, and law acting as potent modes of transmission for the infection of inequality." And they are stories of resilience and compassion, of survival, of love in the time of cholera and the time of COVID-19.

Listen to these stories. Pay deep attention to the masterful way Steven Thrasher tells them. Then think, again, about your place in it all, about what you have done and what more you can do. About how, despite the veneer, risk at the end of the day is communal, and safety the same.

And, hopefully, you will never listen to a siren the same way again.

Jonathan M. Metzl
Nashville, Tennessee

I'm revising my position on viruses living in *bodies;*
they live briefly in spaces where bodies interface,
making the war against the virus also a
war against moments and spaces of connections.

—Adia Benton

AN INVITATION

Sirens, Silence, Standby

In the waning days of March 2020, it felt like the sirens in Brooklyn would never stop.

At first, the noticeable uptick in their frequency had felt worrisome. But perhaps, I tried to convince myself, I was hearing sirens so often only because there wasn't much else to hear. After the mayor and the governor ordered everyone indoors, much of the foot and vehicular traffic of Bed-Stuy had disappeared. An eerie silence descended upon the neighborhood I'd long imagined to be bustling years before I ever lived there, from its depiction in Spike Lee films like *Crooklyn* and *Do the Right Thing*, which I'd watched repeatedly on VHS tapes as a teenager in Oxnard, California.

Absent from the Brooklyn soundscape were the sounds you'd normally hear during the spring thaw: of motorcycle mufflers and SUV horns, of music blasting from stoops and basketballs bouncing on pavement. Instead, in the middle of a sunny day, it was so uncharacteristically quiet on Malcolm X Boulevard that you could hear birds chirping—until, that is, the birdsong began to be drowned out by the screeches of the sirens piercing the unsettling urban quiet with their urgent cries.

Like the Greek mythical figures for whom they are named—who lured sailors away from safety so that their ships would crash on rocks as they approached the shore—the sirens began wailing hourly in Brooklyn and then many times each hour. Occasionally, they belonged to fire trucks, but usually they almost undeniably belonged to ambulances and (strangely, for such a policed neighborhood) almost never to cop cruisers.

Given the reduction in traffic and the subsequent drop in calls to 911 about automobile, bicycle, and pedestrian collisions, there should have been fewer sirens, not more. And yet the sound of sirens increased, as many people worried they would after hearing news reports from Wuhan, China, and the Lombardy region of Italy. Day by day, hour by hour, their wails increased until they formed one overlapping, screaming, inescapable dirge around the clock. It didn't matter how much you might have wanted to escape thinking for just one moment about the horror unfolding nearby. The sirens would not let you avoid the crisis.

Though gentrifiers had been moving in for years, our corner of Bed-Stuy was still largely composed of working-class Black people. As during three-day holiday weekends of years past in the neighborhoods of brownstone Brooklyn, Bed-Stuy had become almost entirely Black and brown again by late March 2020. The white gentrifiers had largely skipped town. But unlike during those idyllic summer weekends of yesteryear, the white people hadn't left the city "to summer" as a verb. Rather, they'd fled to second homes that were not even meant to be inhabited in the winter. Or to their suburban families of origin. Or to suddenly *very* expensive country rentals—all to try to avoid a pandemic that was rapidly taking on and taking over the bodies of the New Yorkers who weren't allowed or able to work from home.

While many white Brooklynites fled the city in this moment—perhaps afraid of the rationing of medical care, the possibility of social unrest, decreasing accessibility to certain foods, an inability to hoard toilet paper, or the epiphany that they'd have to start scrubbing their own toilets as they no longer felt safe with "the help" coming into their homes—I had just returned.

New York City had been my home for a quarter century since I moved to the Village when I was seventeen in 1995. But in 2019, I'd moved to Chicago to become a professor of journalism, public health, and queer studies. And yet, I had returned to New York City in early March 2020 because of *another* virus, one I had been studying for a long time: the human immunodeficiency virus (HIV). I was staying in Bed-Stuy, in the very brownstone that had been my last New York home, with dear friends.

Over the course of a single week, I was supposed to present field research I had recently completed in Greece to a philanthropic foundation in New York. Then I was supposed to travel to Boston by train to attend the annual Conference on Retroviral and Opportunistic Infections (CROI) to learn about the newest research on HIV. Finally, I was supposed to travel back to New York by train to present my research to another philanthropic foundation, before flying back to Chicago.

But I made only the first of these three dates. The organizers of CROI retrofitted the event to primarily become an emergency conference about the one and only virus that was suddenly on everyone's mind: severe acute respiratory virus (SARS-CoV-2), or the dreaded novel coronavirus. Then CROI moved online entirely. I never made it to Boston, and my second foundation presentation in New York City was canceled—along with all the basketball games at Madison Square Garden, performances at the Metropolitan Opera, and shows on Broadway. As the world began to shut down, stalked by a virus moving rapidly and microscopically through societies around the globe, I had to decide whether I would stay in New York with my friends or return to Chicago, where I'd be isolated and alone in a new apartment, in a city I didn't yet know well.

If I remained in New York, I could help create and receive care within my well-established mutual aid network. But I didn't know when, or even if, I would be allowed to leave again.

I decided to stay. Somewhat by accident, I had become obsessed with viruses years before. As the writer Sarah Schulman first taught me, you can't understand the history of the United States without understanding how viruses shaped the development of this country in general or how HIV shaped the last forty years of American politics specifically. By the time coronavirus disease 2019 (COVID-19) deaths began overwhelming New York City's hospitals, I'd been studying HIV and the acquired immunodeficiency disease syndrome (AIDS) in the city for a decade. I could sense that, in New York, there was going to be another big moment in American viral history that would be worth seeing up close. And as I had lost my father, birth mother, and stepmother in my twenties, before losing one of my sisters in my thirties, I had come to appreciate how, while painful, witnessing death can be a blessing. Even when there is nothing to be done to stop or postpone death, just being with someone in the last moments of their life can be very meaningful—for the person left behind holding the deceased's hand and, I suspect, for the person leaving the land of the living.

Besides, New York City had been one of the truest loves of my life. I had breathed its deadly smoke on September 11, 2001; ridden its financial crash in 2008; and weathered Hurricane Sandy in 2012. Many of the people I loved most lived in the Big Apple's five boroughs. And even though the sights of a U.S. Navy hospital ship pulling into New York Harbor and a field hospital going up in Central Park were alarming, the resources were flowing toward New York, not from it. If I was going to get sick, I had as good a shot in that city as in any.

I didn't yet know that by the end of the summer, more than 33,000 New Yorkers would be dead, including people I loved—a similar loss to the city as the one wrought by the influenza pandemic of 1918 and the equivalent of eleven 9/11s. I didn't know if I would be among them.

If I am going to die, I thought, *I'd rather die in New York*.

* * *

I think it was my friend Stephen Molldrem, a scholar of critical HIV data, who pointed out to me that we were experiencing the first viral pandemic also to be experienced via viral stories on social media. These viral stories *about* viruses created a kind of squared virality.

I learned of the first COVID-19 death in my extended social circle on Twitter on March 30, 2020. It would be the first of many instances in which I learned via social media about the death of people who were loved by someone I loved. The friend of a friend who died had lived near a jail and a hospital in New York that were both epicenters of this new epidemic. "Look at the map of COVID-19 rates," our mutual friend had tweeted. "It is a map of poverty, racism and overpolicing. People are dying in jail and because they have been to jail."

They were articulating something I had been working through for a few days: people were getting sick from this new virus because of where they lived, and they were dying disproportionately from it because of the bodies they had been living in their whole lives. Their bodies had repeatedly been pushed into contact with danger.

I'd done much of my reporting and research over the years in St. Louis. And so, when I read that of the first dozen confirmed coronavirus deaths in St. Louis, all twelve of them were of Black people, I was sad but not at all surprised. All over the United States, early data showed that Black people were dying of COVID-19 at alarmingly high rates. Research was also showing that Latinx people and Native Americans were dying disproportionately from the disease, as well.

And as the maps began to emerge showing where in New York the people being infected by and dying from the novel coronavirus lived, I realized that they were very familiar maps to me. The maps showing where people were most likely to become HIV positive (and to be harassed by police, or be killed by police, or be incarcerated, or have their HIV progress to an AIDS diagnosis, or have their AIDS diagnosis proceed to death) were maps of the same spaces where people were most likely to get the coronavirus and die of COVID-19.

When we follow the virus—any virus, really—we follow the fault lines of our culture. Like all pathogens, the novel coronavirus was not a "great equalizer," as some initially called it, but a magnifier of the divisions already present in our world. In 2020, it quickly became apparent in the United States that the novel coronavirus may not consciously discriminate, because viruses have no consciousness. Similarly, water and fire do not discriminate; they also have no sentience. Yet their effects *do* discriminate against the bodies of the underclass, because those bodies have been placed in proximity to danger by the structural design of powerful humans. In a hurricane, water drowns the underclass not because two molecules of hydrogen and one of oxygen discriminate by income or race. Rather, the inequitable drownings happen because the built environment of society makes it so water will physically be kept away from the rich, while stormwaters will flow through the cracks in flimsy barriers to flood the poor.

Similarly, viruses show us where the cracks in our society are; they offer a stark revelation of inequality. In times of mass crisis, those cracks get wider and more people fall into them. For instance, within months of the first coronavirus case in the United States being confirmed, more than 40 million people had lost their jobs (ironically, including nearly a million and a half health care workers). Meanwhile, approximately 27 million people lost their health insurance. All these people were then at higher risk for a host of disasters, including eviction, which, researchers soon discovered, alarmingly increased the likelihood of novel coronavirus infection and COVID-19 death.

For the poor, this precariousness and instability affect people's financial, spiritual, mental, and biological health. The people living in these valleys are dwelling in the kinds of metaphysical spaces the ancient Greeks might have referred to as Hades or the underworld. *Get Out* filmmaker Jordan Peele might describe the psychological and physiological dimensions of this domain as "the sunken place."

I call it the viral underclass.

I did not come up with this phrase, but first heard it in the summer of 2018. I was at a conference called the HIV Is Not a Crime National Training Academy, in Indianapolis, Indiana, where activists from around the United States and other countries had gathered to strategize about repealing laws that criminalize HIV transmission. Some activists did not like that efforts were underway to reform but not abolish HIV laws. They argued that people who had access to HIV medication that made their viral loads "undetectable," and thus unable to be transmitted to others, should not be liable under HIV laws, while people who had detectable viral loads should still be vulnerable to prosecution.

What the activists recognized was that people living with HIV who have detectable viral loads are disproportionately Black and unhoused and often can't get access to the medication needed for viral suppression. Leaving these people behind, the activists argued, created a viral divide, with a privileged white set above it and a Black underclass below—a viral underclass.

Sean Strub, a white man and one of the main organizers behind the training conference, had coined the term *viral underclass* with a slightly different emphasis in 2011, writing, "Nothing drives stigma more powerfully than when government sanctions it through the enshrinement of discriminatory practices in the law or its application. That is what has happened with HIV, resulting in the creation of a viral underclass of persons with rights inferior to others, especially in regard to their sexual expression. After nearly 30 years of the AIDS epidemic, people who have tested positive for HIV continue to experience punishment, exclusion from services, and a presumption of guilt or wrongdoing in a host of settings and for a host of practices that are, for those who have not tested positive for HIV, unremarkable."

I have built on Sean's phrase to develop a theory of the viral underclass. Like all theories, this one doesn't definitively prove only one outcome, nor is it meant to shut down conversation or prevent further inquiry. Rather, theories are helpful for thinking about our world. They are helpful for finding better ways to understand the social, physical, biological, and cultural forces around us. They can help us identify and interrogate a dynamic.

If we were to look through a powerful microscope, physics and biology might help us to *see* subcutaneous viruses inside a group of disadvantaged people. But a theory of the viral underclass can help us think about *how* and *why* marginalized populations are subjected to increased harms of viral transmission, exposure, replication, and death. And it can help us to understand not only why viruses reside where they do, and in whom they do, but also why the underclass has formed in the first place. It can help us to understand that the dynamic works in both directions: that just as marginalized people are made vulnerable to viruses, viruses are also used as justification for the policies and systems that marginalize people in the first place.

Just as Naomi Klein's "shock doctrine" and Michelle Alexander's use of the concept of a "new Jim Crow" have done, a theory of the viral underclass can serve as a framework for understanding how vulnerability is manufactured for certain kinds of people and how it spreads through society more broadly—with the economy, media, and law acting as potent modes of transmission for the infection of inequality.

The COVID-19 pandemic has made both the capital held by the world's wealthiest and the number of people in the viral underclass expand dramatically. Globally, the World Bank has estimated that as many as one hundred and fifty million people were pushed into extreme poverty by the COVID-19 pandemic by 2021. At the same time, a report by the Swiss bank UBS found, the world's billionaires' wealth soared to upward of ten trillion dollars. This has given militaries and governments cover to enforce borders and police populations more harshly. As climate change compels more interactions between humans and microscopic pathogens, these dynamics will likely grow more severe in the coming decades.

How can we survive in such an underclass, or maybe even shrink its scope, if we don't learn to recognize it and think about it communally? Viruses are all around us. "Biologists estimate that 380 trillion viruses are living on and inside your body right now—10 times the number of bacteria," infectious disease pathologist David Pride wrote in *Scientific American*. We humans are vastly outnumbered by them (though we are going to consider what it means to think about *us* and *them* on our journey in this book). This creates thorny difficulties when it comes to fighting viruses—which brings me to an additional dynamic we'll explore. As my colleague, anthropologist Adia Benton, has written, viruses "live briefly in spaces where bodies interface, making the war against the virus also a war against moments and spaces of connections." The fear of such connections is that viruses expose how the social divisions imposed upon humanity (nationalism, race making, capitalism) by hard wars or softer ones (like policing) are fictions. The truths that viruses reveal could topple the systems meant to divide us. We, the people, are connected to one another—and so, war metaphors are not helpful ways to think about public health.

Like airplanes dropping bombs on residents too poor to flee the city that the pilots are ostensibly liberating, waging war on viruses will often kill humans in the viral underclass, but not *only* them. For viruses are *wherever* any of us meet—and how can we declare war on where we meet? Hug? Make love? Where our lips touch and our hearts beat? Where we sing, dance, laugh, and pray together?

Without romanticizing them too much, viruses have been some of my greatest teachers. Even in avoiding them, we find them pulling our consciousnesses down out of our minds, don't we? (*There's cloth over my mouth! Ow—a needle in my arm! Rubber on my genitals?!*) They've forced me to learn and unlearn not just with my brain, but with my heart, my lungs, my skin, and with my embodied relationship with others. They have led me to seek out and better know some of the people I most dearly love on this planet and some I never would have known otherwise. They have continuously shown me how dangerous vulnerability is *and* how necessary it is to the very meaning of our lives as social animals. And in the ways they've drawn me around the world and even taken human lives, they've taught me that I could love (and mourn) more deeply than I ever knew was possible.

* * *

Around a half million people died of COVID-19 in the United States alone over the first year of this pandemic, ten times the number who ever died of AIDS in a single year (about fifty thousand in 1995, some fifteen years into *that* pandemic). Before the second year of American life under COVID was over, the death toll reached seven hundred thousand—surpassing more than forty years of AIDS deaths in the United States of America.

But this book is not a story of numbers, at least not primarily. It is mostly a story about just a few of the people in the viral underclass I've gotten to know over a decade of reporting on viral epidemics—in person or as ghosts, sometimes up close, sometimes from afar—and of the people who loved them in various ways.

This book is also a story of the guides I've learned from as I've traveled through the viral underclass on five continents: of the doctors, condom-mongers, syringe-exchange volunteers, lovers, librarians, colleagues, boyfriends, sex workers, journalists, bathhouse attendants, friends, activists, bartenders, maps, movies, dogs, doulas, and drag queens who have pointed me in the right direction. By hearing a few of their stories, we will learn together about the structures that ensnare most of us who live in what the late anthropologist David Graeber first called "the ninety-nine percent."

And while these stories will be narrated by me, an American trying to make sense of the particular cruelties of the American empire, the viral underclass is a global phenomenon. This is *not* a book about or for only the United States of America.

While we will follow, on our journey, people in the viral underclass encountering or negotiating life around a number of pathogens, such as hepatitis B (HBV), hepatitis C (HCV), West Nile virus (WNV), influenza, and smallpox, we will see them dealing mostly with two viruses: HIV and SARS-CoV-2, the novel coronavirus.

We will follow these two viruses for several reasons. First, even though there are effective medications for HIV and good vaccines for SARS-CoV-2, both these viruses still power two of the world's most dangerous ongoing pandemics. They are both also likely viruses that humans will not be eradicating anytime soon and will probably be living with for a good long while. The risks of both of these viruses can be mitigated with simple prophylactic barriers (masks for the novel coronavirus, condoms for HIV)—both of which have spawned intense international culture wars—but also, more conceptual forms of prophylaxis (like access to safe housing, stable employment, and the collective medication of populations) can protect against both. This broader idea of prophylaxis, and the elusiveness of these measures for many, reflects a commitment to care that many societies persistently resist; adopting them would mean changing the notions of inequality, manufactured scarcity, and hoarded abundance that currently organize our world.

This brings us to the main reason we will mostly be following these particular pathogens' dance with humanity. Despite the fact that these are very different viruses, with *very* different properties, lifespans, and modes of transmission, they afflict alarmingly alike populations, especially in the United States: Black people, Native Americans, Latinx people, queer and trans people, migrants, poor people, and people who are unhoused or incarcerated. Viruses impact a disturbingly similar group regardless of the properties of any particular pathogen.

And while virology plays a role in all human interactions with viruses, a viral underclass is produced by all the isms: racism, ableism, sexism, heterosexism, cisheterosexism, nativism, anti-Semitism, and the biggest social vector of them all, capitalism.

In his 1943 book, *Being and Nothingness*, existentialist philosopher Jean-Paul Sartre wrote about *mauvaise foi*, or "bad faith." This occurs, as a viral YouTube video explains it, when "we lie to ourselves, in order to spare ourselves short-term pain, but thereby suffer from long-term psychological impoverishment." Viruses offer us the opportunity *not* to engage in this collective delusion of bad faith. Because they are not merely cerebral ideas but, rather, inseparable components of our anatomy, viruses can push us toward reckoning with an embodied honesty that can't be ignored. They are so intimately a part of us—altering our DNA, even—that they can force us to deal, in some way, with short-term pain we might want to avoid in order to create long-term societal health and well-being.

Viruses demand something more of us than the bad-faith argument of "going back to normal"—as if *normal* were not itself plagued by social ills. They invite—no, command, really—that when we interrogate our relationship with them honestly, we can clearly see an equation:

(HIV) [or (SARS-CoV-2) or (HBV) or (HCV) or (H1N1)]
+ racism [or ableism, or sexism, or heterosexism, or capitalism]
= a viral underclass

In other words, viruses interact with the power structures already at play in our society so that those who are already marginalized are left even more susceptible to danger, exacerbating existing social divides. But more important, of the variables in this equation, it is social structures that are the *drivers*, while viruses merely amplify. If we remove the viruses without dealing with the isms in a population, the underclass will remain, plaguing the people whom public health campaigns purportedly want to help and leaving conditions intact for future viral outbreaks.

Some reductive public health and economic approaches to epidemics see humans only as *hosts* of viruses. But it is *whole human beings*, in all our wonderful complexity, whom we want to keep in mind. If a society tells someone with cancer, "You're on your own to deal with it," and tells the same person, "You're on your own if you get evicted," that person might not respond well if they're also told, "You must get vaccinated to protect others in society."

A theory of the viral underclass acknowledges the people most susceptible to viruses not as hosts, but as whole people. It can help us understand that if we care about people, we need to care about them as much when they face cancer or eviction as we do when they pose a viral risk to more privileged members of society. And it can help us to understand that if we eliminated the conditions of the underclass as a whole (viral or otherwise), the health of the society overall would be so much better. Vectors of transmission for viruses could be mitigated before those viruses even had the chance to reproduce and cause harm.

* * *

A viral underclass is produced through twelve major related social vectors that enable the relationship between viruses and marginalization. Sometimes, these vectors produce the material conditions for unequal viral transmission; sometimes, they turn the presence of viruses into discrimination or economic ruin, leading to compounding harms. These social vectors are:

1. Racism
2. Individualized shame
3. Capitalism
4. The law
5. Austerity
6. Borders
7. The liberal carceral state
8. Unequal prophylaxis
9. Ableism
10. Speciesism
11. The myth of white immunity
12. Collective punishment

The twelve chapters of this book will dramatize, mostly through the stories of people, how each of these dozen vectors operates. All the vectors are interconnected: racism is tied up with the courts and with access to prophylaxis; austerity is tied up with ableism and shame; policing bolsters many of them. And these vectors are intrinsically connected to other social ills, such as homophobia, sexism, and transphobia. So, in chapters foregrounding one of the vectors, we'll see shades of others, for these conditions, like our identities, are always intertwined.

Viruses don't move across time and space in neat, predictable lines. But they *do* move in patterns, and following their trajectories can often reveal fascinating (if depressing) echoes and rhymes. In this book, I have broken these beats into four waves of understanding.

The story of Michael "Tiger Mandingo" Johnson and his prosecution for transmitting HIV is the main story we will keep returning to, as it was through reporting it that I came to understand the tenets of what would become my theory of the viral underclass. Each act will begin with a chapter circling back to Johnson's life every two years or so.

Act I, "Blame," explores how and why marginalized people are made into scapegoats for viruses via some of the biggest isms of the modern era: racism and capitalism. In chapter 1, "Mandingo," we will meet Michael Johnson shortly after he was arrested for HIV transmission and exposure in 2013. We'll also travel from Missouri back in time several centuries, to the galleys of ships carrying people who were enslaved (and many pathogens) across the Atlantic, to see how racism creates viral conditions. In chapter 2, "The Infinite Weight of Zero," we will meet a gay French actor named Olivier, explore how news "goes viral," and consider the consequences of reporting (and misreporting) on an individual person (often called "patient zero") as being at fault for a newly recognized virus. In chapter 3, "Parasite," we will compare pandemic responses in the Republic of Korea and the United States and look at how capitalism operates in both countries to create viral conditions—through the lens of Bong Joon-ho's 2019 film, *Parasite*.

Act II, "Law and Order," will show us how policing, prisons, and legal structures create a viral underclass. Chapter 4, "Guilty Until Proven Innocent," will take us into the courtroom drama of Michael Johnson's 2015 HIV trial. In chapter 5, "From Athens to Appalachia," we'll meet a gay Greek American activist named Zak Kostopoulos (drag name: "Zackie Oh") and learn about the relationship among viruses, addiction, and austerity, from the Aegean Sea to the coalfields of West Virginia. In chapter 6, "Borderlands," we will meet Lorena Borjas, the "mother of the trans-Latinx community" in Queens, New York, and travel with migrants throughout the Americas. And in chapter 7, "Cages," we will trace how the liberal carceral state has plagued people in the viral underclass over decades, particularly through the ways Democratic politicians have augmented incarceration and homelessness.

Act III, "Social Death," explores how even those members of the viral underclass who avoid or even survive viral encounters are still often not considered completely alive or fully human. In chapter 8, "One in Two," we'll reconvene with Michael Johnson circa 2017, as he appeals a thirty-year prison sentence. We'll learn about prophylaxis and the different kinds of protection various populations receive. In chapter 9, "Disability as Disposability," we'll meet Ward Harkavy, a seventy-two-year-old former *Village Voice* editor who winds up in a nursing home during COVID-19, and Asian American disability rights activist Alice Wong, as she tries to avoid COVID-19. And in chapter 10, "Ride-Along," we'll meet my police officer cousin in Nebraska and follow bats in China, seagulls in the Philippines, police dogs on two continents, and pigs on three to see how zoonotic viruses travel; we will also see how treating nonhuman animals with the disdain of speciesism presents a danger to all human animals, too.

In "Reckoning," our fourth and final act, we will circle back around to learn about the fate of several members of the viral underclass we will have met over the course of the book. This will include examining, in chapter 11, "Release" and, in chapter 12, what happens to communities afflicted by viruses when they are subjected to "Compound Loss."

In the epilogue, "Why Am I 'Me' and You Are 'You'?" we will consider what pandemics can teach us about our need to think communally rather than individually—especially if we humans want to survive the *next* viral pandemic, not to mention the climate crisis.

A theory of the viral underclass provides a map for a kind of worldwide liberation. In a similar way to how the Combahee River Collective believed that "if Black women were free, it would mean that everyone else would have to be free since our freedom would necessitate the destruction of all the systems of oppression," I believe that creating a world where the conditions that create the viral underclass are abolished would improve life on earth for nearly everyone.

* * *

Like the COVID-19 and AIDS pandemics, this book would likely not exist without modern air travel. Because I reported much of it right after getting off jets, dreamed so much of it in cheap motels at the end of airport runways, and sketched so much of it on airplanes—and yet was largely grounded in the year I wrote it—I have been dreaming a lot about flying.

The night before he was assassinated in 1968, Martin Luther King Jr. invited his final congregation to join him on a "mental flight by Egypt through, or rather across the Red Sea, through the wilderness on toward the promised land." As he described a journey from the time of the pharaohs to contemporary Memphis, King narrated a multigenerational understanding of humanity's interconnected sojourn toward justice. I now invite you to come on a similar mental flight with me, as we explore how a viral underclass can offer a multigenerational, multinational, multiracial understanding of humanity's interconnected sojourn toward justice.

First, a word about class, which we are going to be talking about a lot, because this theory is of a viral under*class*, after all. In the United States, many of us who have ever been poor often tend to think, as the saying goes, that we're just temporarily down-on-our-luck millionaires. We are taught that it is shameful to be of a certain class, or even to acknowledge class at all. But naming the existence of an underclass is not an insult to anyone. Being poor is not a reflection of one's character; it's just a function of how capitalism works. With capitalism, there will always be a group on the bottom. Class is a reality, but in no way a judgment. So, we will keep naming how class shapes interactions between humans and viruses.

Also, a question you may have: Am I, your narrator, a member of the viral underclass? Like most of my relationships with humans, the relationships I have with viruses and class are complicated. For the first six years of my life, I lived with my birth mother in very precarious, itinerant housing situations, including sharing a rented bedroom with her and my sister (in the kind of home a virus could rip through, because it housed far more people than it was meant to). We were at times homeless—without a permanent, safe home—though never unsheltered. I didn't receive my standard series of MMR shots in childhood, a fact that left me at heightened risk for measles, mumps, and rubella (and caused logistical problems into my adulthood). I stabilized a lot when I moved in with my dad and stepmom, who became another mother to me. But I went without health insurance for most of my twenties, forgoing flu shots during that time. As I did as a young child, I've experienced periods of hunger in my adulthood. By the time I began reporting on Michael Johnson's case in my midthirties, I was a freelance journalist who'd recently been laid off from my only staff writing job, lost my insurance, and been evicted from my apartment (my seventeenth home in eighteen years). My economic condition has improved a great deal since then. I also now have a PhD, a steady job, and good insurance—well, as "good" as predatory private health insurance plans in the United States can be. But I'm still a Black gay man who dates mostly other men of color, which makes me about as likely to become HIV-positive as not. Before I got vaccinated against COVID-19, my race and gender placed me at elevated risk of serious illness or death if I contracted SARS-CoV-2.

So, it's complicated. But though I've certainly been highly at risk for viruses throughout my time on this earth, no one needs to be in the viral underclass to learn from it or try to create a world where it doesn't have to exist. Nor are the boundaries for who is or isn't in it fixed over time. Sean Strub, who introduced the phrase *viral underclass*, is a well-off white man and the mayor of his town. Yet his being HIV-positive has made him more susceptible to criminal prosecution. He's also one of the people most committed to helping others less privileged than he whom I've ever had the honor to meet.

When it comes to the viral underclass, we just need to listen to the people in it—and that's what we will be doing in this book. I'll be the primary narrator, but this story belongs to those we'll meet along the way. As viruses try to move between them and others, we will see a quilted tapestry of the world and think in new ways about how to live together in better global solidarity.

All right. Before you fasten your seat belt, please consider grabbing some tissues. While not everyone we meet on our journey is going to die in these pages, a lot of them will—and regardless of viruses, we'll all pass away eventually. For, as John Irving wrote, "in the world according to Garp, we are all terminal cases."

Now, stand by for takeoff with me—or, rather, *us*: that would be this reporter and the 380 trillion viruses living in our shared body—on a journey around the world. And learn from the often painful, sometimes pleasurable, and always fascinating experiences of the viral underclass. May their stories guide us toward a world with better health politics and help us let go of our most deeply held assumptions.

For, if we listen to them closely enough, they might just lead us toward a better understanding of the universe, of our species, and—dare we dream?—of a better way of life itself.

I

BLAME

I think maybe there is no borderline between countries now because we all live in the same country, it's called capitalism.

—Bong Joon-Ho (봉준호)

1

MANDINGO

(Racism)

On May 25, 2020, a white Minneapolis police officer named Derek Chauvin violently pressed his knee into the neck of a Black man named George Floyd, crushing him into the ground for some eight minutes and forty-six seconds.

This ended Floyd's life at just forty-six years of age, about thirty years younger than the average age a white man like Chauvin might expect to live in the United States. Floyd's fatal encounter with the police began after he was accused of using a counterfeit twenty-dollar bill at a convenience store. The store clerk had effectively been deputized as an enforcer of currency law; and even though he offered to pay for the counterfeit bill, he was compelled by his manager to call the police anyway, which would lead to Floyd's being executed by the state of Minnesota without so much as a trial.

But long before a jury would take the unusual step of convicting Chauvin of murder—which happens in only about one out of every two thousand police killings—an autopsy revealed another way Floyd might have prematurely died.

Though it got only passing mention in the news at the time, George Floyd died with SARS-CoV-2 antibodies in his system. This meant he had recently contracted the virus that was a leading cause of death in the United States that summer, especially among Black men. When we find viruses, we are going to find them residing among people who are plagued by many painful, lethal manifestations of racism.

Before his gruesome, horrifying death, Floyd had endured a difficult life marked by racism at various turns. He had served several jail terms, including one where the sole accusations against him came from a police officer who was later charged with falsifying evidence and murder. Floyd had done itinerant work as a truck driver and guard, once working security at a homeless shelter. And in 2020, he had already lost one part-time driving job for being in a minor crash. Then he had lost his other part-time security job at a club closed by the COVID-19 pandemic.

The cops came for him that fateful day in May because he was poor and using counterfeit money (either out of desperation or, maybe, unwittingly because someone else had passed the phony bill on to him). But if he'd survived his arrest, he might have gone to jail, where he still might have died, though perhaps more slowly, or out of the view of a camera—like Sandra Bland, the Black woman who died in a holding cell after being arrested in Texas in 2015.

Or Floyd might have gotten out of jail only to die of COVID-19, as so many Black people did that month.

Or—given that his girlfriend would later testify how they both suffered from addiction—he might have survived his arrest and COVID-19 only to later die of a drug overdose.

We will never know what might have happened with George Floyd, because Derek Chauvin calmly murdered him. What I do know for sure, though, is that throughout his life, Floyd was repeatedly plagued by the vector of racism—and in one way or another, racism was going to get him.

When he died, the City of Minneapolis had been spending more than a third of its annual budget on policing—*far* more than it spent on public housing or health care. This is what structural racism looks like; it allows viruses to seep into a city's cracks and efficiently transmit and reproduce among Black people. When people don't have access to health care, they are more likely to be susceptible to all diseases, including infectious ones (and more likely to transmit those diseases to their kinfolk, especially if they live in crowded households). If people don't have stable housing, they are much less likely to get access to health care of any kind.

The budget priorities of Minneapolis increased the odds that its police would have a deadly encounter with someone like Floyd *and* increased the odds that Floyd would encounter the novel coronavirus. At the same time, the Minneapolis budget decreased the odds that a Black man like Floyd would encounter the social support he needed to avoid poverty, addiction, or pathogens in the first place. It was no coincidence that in the summer of Floyd's murder, the United States represented less than 5 percent of the world's population, but was home to about 25 percent of global COVID-19 deaths *and* 25 percent of the world's incarcerated people. And it was no coincidence that the people in America getting arrested, going to prison, and dying of COVID-19 were disproportionately Black.

Apart from the external forces that shorten the lives of Black people (prisons, policing, poverty), the stress of racism has its own insidious effect on Black men's bodies in particular. The epidemiologist Sherman James has identified a medical condition he calls *John Henryism* (after the American steel-driving folk hero) to describe the quantifiable biological effects of the stress of racism, in the form of conditions like hypertension and kidney disease. These form a basis for why Black men die years younger than other demographic groups.

Similarly, it was viruses that taught me to see how racism manifests physiologically in Black bodies, consigning people to health disparities and premature death. Viruses also revealed to me how and where Black people are ensnared by poverty and the criminal justice system.

But while George Floyd's murder demonstrated the link between racism and viruses with stark clarity, I first learned about this dynamic years before, when a trusted editor sent me to a city I'd never visited to report on a disturbing story involving HIV and a young Black man known as "Tiger Mandingo."

* * *

In May 2014, I found myself staying in a miserable efficiency motel in a suburb of St. Louis, Missouri. It was the kind of place where desperate people rented rooms by the week. Illuminated by stark, depressing fluorescent lights and staffed by people who seemed embarrassed to be seen there by the guests, these joyless dwellings were where people (like me) engaged in shady work and were economically stretched to their breaking point.

I was in St. Louis to investigate the story of Michael "Tiger Mandingo" Johnson, a twenty-three-year-old student wrestler. I had been paid a flat fee for my assignment, and I had already put in many weeks of work and spent most of my budget on plane fare and expenses. I still didn't know if I'd even get to interview the main person I'd come to meet. This dingy motel was all I could afford.

The story I was there to report was a salacious one. Michael Johnson had been arrested the previous October in a classroom at Lindenwood University. He was one of the few Black students at the private school located in the "white flight" suburb of St. Charles. With its 91 percent white population, St. Charles has radically different racial demographics from nearby St. Louis, which many white suburbanites had fled.

Yet, despite being in the minority, Johnson had been a well-liked and popular student athlete on campus. Prior to enrolling at Lindenwood, he'd been a national star on the junior college wrestling circuit. And though wrestling was his main sport, social media posts showed him hanging out with cheerleaders and working out with athletes in all sports at Lindenwood. Johnson, with his infectious smile, was photographed with men and women, students and coaches who were Black and white, gay and straight.

But in the fall of 2013, he was accused of having sex with five men without telling them he'd been diagnosed with HIV before they hooked up. For this, he'd been charged with "recklessly" transmitting, or exposing someone to, HIV, and under Missouri law, he now faced the possibility of life in prison.

A couple months before I first landed in Missouri, Pulitzer Prize–winning editor Mark Schoofs (who had been covering HIV/AIDS for decades and who'd just started an investigative unit at BuzzFeed News) invited me out to dinner to pitch Johnson's story to me. Mark was concerned that, except for stories about the initial arrest, a case of HIV transmission being treated as akin to murder wasn't getting much media coverage. He knew about my interest in the criminalization of interracial desire, as I'd written about my deceased parents, an interracial couple who were legally barred from marriage in Nebraska, where they'd met, in 1958. Mark also correctly predicted that at least some of this "Mandingo's" sex partners were white, and he told me that when news of Johnson's arrest went viral, it consisted of news stories that had merely repeated the prosecutor's press releases.

No one had actually interviewed Johnson or his partners. Mark wanted to send me to St. Louis to find them and to interview Johnson himself in the St. Charles County Department of Corrections facility where he awaited trial—and that's how I wound up in that awful motel a few months later.

One of the first conversations I had while reporting Johnson's story had been with a white male college student who, in January 2013, noticed a profile on a gay mobile hookup app for a Black guy with ripped abs and a chiseled chest. The guy's username was "Tiger Mandingo."

"I am more into white guys, but I like Black guys, and there were certain things about him," the student told me over the phone. "His body was gorgeous, and he had great legs, and he was well endowed."

When they met, the student at Lindenwood University quickly recognized that, in real life, Tiger Mandingo also attended his school and was a recent transfer student on the wrestling team. They hooked up later that month in Johnson's dorm room, where, the student said, Johnson told him he was "clean."

Johnson invited the white student to go out again sometime, but the student got busy and "didn't have time for that." They didn't hook up again until early October, this time without using a condom. But the white student wasn't worried, he said, because Johnson had told him yet again that he was "clean."

To declare oneself "clean," in these scenarios of gay parlance, is akin to saying, "I don't have any viruses, bacteria, or sexually transmitted infections." It's an absurd claim—who can really know at any time which microorganisms are inside them? But it's a claim that gay men ask one another to make all the time.

The white student told me he had "barebacked" (had unprotected intercourse) with multiple "friends and ex-boyfriends," situations in which "we trusted each other. I mean, I don't just let anybody do it." He said that knowing people well made them trustworthy.

Yet he also said he had bareback sex "with people I barely knew." In those cases, he said, "I knew they were clean," sometimes just "by looking at them." The student's nonchalance changed when he described a call he got from Johnson a few days after their second hookup.

"He calls me and he said, 'I found out I have a disease.' And I asked, 'Is there a cure?' and he said, 'I don't know.' And I was like, 'Are you fucking kidding me?' I got pissed. I had asked him several times, and he'd said he was clean, and I trusted him! And I got mad at him, and then he got mad at me for getting mad, and then he said, 'I gotta go.'"

Neither of them said aloud the three letters that were on their minds.

That same day, October 10, 2013, Johnson was pulled out of a Photoshop art class and led away in handcuffs by St. Charles Police. He was later charged with one count of "recklessly infecting another with HIV" and four counts of "attempting to recklessly infect another with HIV," felonies in the state of Missouri.

Johnson pleaded not guilty. News of his arrest, coupled with reports that he possessed more than thirty videos of sexual encounters on his laptop, rocked St. Charles, lit up local broadcasts, and made international headlines as far away as Australia—as if Johnson posed some kind of transcontinental global menace, even though tens of millions of people around the globe were already living with HIV.

Lindenwood University urged anyone who'd had "intimate contact" with Johnson to get tested for HIV, and many did. The student Johnson had had sex with who first spoke to me went to Saint Louis Effort for AIDS for an HIV test, which came back negative, as did subsequent tests. He didn't press charges himself. Still, he said, Johnson "infected someone with HIV. Without medication, that person could get AIDS, so he's slowly killing someone. It's a form of murder, in a sense. I hate to say it, since he's a nice guy." The white student assumed either that HIV was untreatable or that a person like Johnson wouldn't have access to medication, that his infection was a death sentence, and that it would be a death sentence for anyone who came into contact with him. (None of this need be true, but in this country and in this society, we have decided that these are acceptable realities for many Black people.)

With few exceptions, judgments across the internet concurred with the white student: Johnson was a predatory "monster" who was intentionally "spreading HIV/AIDS." Overtly racist blogs, like Chimpmania .com, labeled him an "HIV Positive Buck." A typical comment on Instagram proclaimed him to be the "Worst type of homosexual: a strong one with HIV."

My initial thought was that Johnson did not know his HIV status prior to these sexual encounters. After all, many people living with HIV simply don't know they are living with the virus. The year before his arrest, the Centers for Disease Control and Prevention found that among young people between the ages of thirteen and twenty-four who were infected with HIV, more than half did not know the virus was replicating inside their bodies. As recently as 2019, the U.S. government estimated that of the 1.1 million people living with HIV of all ages, about one in every seven—or 165,000 people—did not know they were HIV-positive.

But even if Johnson *had* knowingly had sex without telling his partners of his HIV diagnosis, he would hardly have been the only one keeping such information to himself. A review of fifteen studies on disclosure conducted over a dozen years in the United States found a wild variation in how often people living with HIV disclosed their status to partners, ranging from as much as 89 percent of the time to as little as 42 percent. Research from 2016 published in the journal *AIDS and Behavior* shows that there is a "high level of anxiety about sharing one's HIV-positive status," which dissuades people living with HIV from having open conversations about it.

As I've learned over the years, this isn't because people living with the virus are trying to cause harm. Sometimes, they are afraid of rejection and losing love; sometimes, they assume if the other person isn't asking questions, they must also be positive; sometimes, they are on treatment and know there is, therefore, no way they can transmit the virus to their intimate partners. Johnson's partners also carried responsibility, because relying on someone to say they are "clean" is a foolhardy and dubious strategy to avoid contracting any virus.

Indeed, the community around Johnson (his sexual partners, many of his fellow students, and his college) ignored HIV until it had the perfect scapegoat: a gay, Black, sexually active wrestler with learning disabilities who went by the nickname "Tiger Mandingo." But up until his status became known in a very dramatic way, Johnson's body had been quite popular, for myriad uses, in that very community.

As Carolyn Guild Johnson (no relation), then the prevention director of Saint Louis Effort for AIDS, put it, "Everyone wanted a piece of him, until he had HIV."

* * *

In 2020, the CDC showed that Black people in the United States were more likely to live with much higher rates of many pathogens and diseases, including HIV/AIDS, gonorrhea, chlamydia, syphilis, hepatitis

(B and C), tuberculosis, and the novel coronavirus. But despite the racist myths that say otherwise, Black folks are not the cause of viruses. Rather, they have been historically subjected to them by structural racism. These disparities can be imagined as what scholar Dorothy Roberts calls "racial diseases," conditions "tied to the original use of biology in inventing the political category of race."

There is nothing essentialist about race, and these conditions are not due to inherent physiological differences or individual moral failings of Black people. They have less to do with race than with racism and with a notion of white health being dependent upon Black people being unwell, which writer and medical ethicist Harriet Washington calls "medical apartheid." Similarly to how South African apartheid segregated nonwhite people by law, medical apartheid segregates access to health and wellness on the basis of race. Racial differences in viral and bacterial rates are not simply due to bad decisions made by someone like Michael Johnson. Rather, they are rooted in the historical structures of white supremacy, which can be traced back to European colonists arriving in northwestern Africa and the Americas.

The model for European colonialists was a straightforward, if genocidal, cycle: sail boats from Europe to Africa; convert money into enslaved people by buying them; move the enslaved across the Atlantic (the Middle Passage) on ships to the Americas; clear land in the Americas of indigenous people, who could use language and culture to fight back; bring in enslaved Africans, who have been broken of language, family, culture, and place, to work the cleared land and create raw goods (cotton, tobacco, sugar); ship those goods back to Europe to be sold, manufactured, and converted into money; and sail back to Africa to start the whole process over again.

Colonization has been, and continues to be, responsible for the movement of viruses across the world, and every stage of this process has created race *through* racial health disparities in general and viruses in particular. The beginning of the slave trade brought together bodies from different (and often previously isolated) cultures and, along with them, different viruses and bacteria. The humans who had not yet developed effective biological protections against the microorganisms they encountered paid a very high price. (While colonizers initiated the risk and thus bore its responsibility, the risk itself was not always unidirectional; both the colonized and the colonizers could be killed by contact with pathogens that were new to them.)

From West Africa, European enslavers spread viruses at sea, in ships packed belowdecks with 250 to 600 enslaved people per voyage. Humans were kept chained to their neighbors throughout their defecation, vomiting, and even death. Of course, viruses moved freely in these fetid conditions, making the slave ship one of the most potent disease vectors in human history. Estimates vary, but about 15 percent of enslaved Africans died in the Middle Passage crossing. And many of those who didn't perish at sea, as historian Elise Mitchell has written, died in quarantine just shy of shore: "If enslaved Africans appeared to be ill with smallpox or other contagious diseases, colonial officials" quarantined them on islands. Then, even if they survived the initial disease, the quarantine's longevity "enabled comorbid infections, parasites, and dysentery to spread."

During the colonial period in the United States, the trade in human cargo exported smallpox, hepatitis B, yaws (a chronic skin infection akin to syphilis), measles, and influenza from Europe to the Americas. Genocidally clearing the land of indigenous people through biological warfare, sometimes intentionally and sometimes by accident, white settlers used enslaved Africans to work in what became the United States, keeping them in appalling conditions that facilitated viral transmission up until the Civil War and beyond. Because racism and colonialism (a) spread diseases around the world, (b) created living conditions for Black and indigenous people in which diseases spread, and (c) devalued Black lives such that illness wasn't treated or prevented, white settlers—and, later, white Americans—associated sickness with Blackness and their own health with distance from it.

Indeed, racial health disparities have been maintained over time in ways that make white health dependent on people of color being, inversely, unwell. For example, in the nineteenth century, the "father of gynecology," James Marion Sims, experimented upon enslaved Black women (without anesthesia) to develop the cesarean section, which improved birthing for white people (even as high rates of Black maternal mortality persist to this day). During the yellow fever plague of the mid-nineteenth century, as historian Kathryn Olivarius has written, immigrants actively *tried* to get the disease so that *if* they survived, they'd be immune and thus employable; meanwhile, Black "enslaved people who'd acquired immunity increased their monetary value to their owners by up to 50 percent. In essence, black people's immunity became white people's capital." The forty-year-long "Tuskegee Study of Untreated Syphilis in the Negro Male" in the early twentieth century studied Black men for the effect of syphilis in their bodies without their consent or even their knowledge that they were being denied treatment for decades after they could have been receiving it. And in the COVID-19 pandemic, white people's ability to work relatively safely at home was possible only because disproportionately Black and brown delivery drivers, food workers, and shoppers made it possible—too often sacrificing their own health and lives in the process.

(Sometimes, as we will learn more about in chapter 11, the attempt to suppress Black health harms poor white people, too. For instance, present-day U.S. fights over universal health care are rooted in white supremacists stymieing a smallpox campaign during Reconstruction because they didn't want Black people getting medical treatment "for free"—even if that meant millions of poor white people had to go without health care, too.)

In the media coverage of Johnson before I started reporting on his case, I saw a familiar trope: the irresponsible Black body as a vector of disease. But people should never be considered vectors; vectors are situations, buildings, conditions, *isms*. And while reductive stereotypes of Black health are common in American culture, they are not reflective of why Black people suffer from health disparities.

Indeed, throughout their history in the Americas, Black people have had limited to no control over their bodies. Black bodies have repeatedly been made more vulnerable to viruses by way of slavery, squalid housing, evictions, dangerous working conditions, incarceration, substandard education, manufactured illiteracy, food deserts, and outright medical fraud. Fittingly, much of this dynamic is encapsulated in the history of the word *mandingo*, which has come to mean a fetishized sense that white people project onto Black bodies, mixed with a fear of how the boundaries between white and Black bodies might break down biologically and financially. And the nasty racial tone Johnson's story took was not surprising in the United States, given his charged nickname and the overwhelmingly white press amplifying it.

The eight letters making up the "Mandingo" half of Johnson's nickname sum up centuries of America's racist anxiety (and titillation) over interracial sex. The word conjures up the 1957 novel and 1975 film *Mandingo*, about an enslaved man of West African descent named Mede. During antebellum times, Mede is coerced into having sex with Blanche, the mistress of the plantation where he is owned. (For this, he is murdered by his owner and, in the novel, cooked into a soup.) But more important, *mandingo* has become an American shorthand for unfairly imagining Black men as rapacious, violent, and sexually insatiable. Scholar Ann duCille calls these white projections of sexual licentiousness upon the Black body "mandingoism." This kind of understanding of brute Black masculinity has been used to justify lynchings as punishment even for consensual interracial sex, and it formed the basis for criminalizing interracial unions from the 1660s to the 1960s.

With Johnson's story, I realized that while interracial sex was technically no longer illegal in America, sex was criminalized for people living with HIV. Because Black people were far more likely to be living with HIV, the kinds of laws being used to prosecute people like Johnson were a manifestation of an American tendency once again to criminalize Black sexuality in general and interracial sex in particular.

And so, through this, I began to understand *mandingo* also to encapsulate the fear of how viruses and diseases move between and among white and Black bodies. But such fear obscures a racist reality that is reflected in empirical data. Research conducted in Tennessee and published the year of Johnson's arrest had shown that the law punishes Black men more often, and more severely, for crimes related to HIV than it does white men. In the years since Johnson's arrest, multiple studies and journalistic investigations examining racial disparities involving HIV and the law across the United States and around the world have found that people who are immigrant, indigenous, Black, or a combination thereof are disproportionately punished.

* * *

For nearly a week after I arrived in St. Louis, I tried to see Johnson. But even though I had filled out the right paperwork, and even though the correctional facility's authorities were supposed to make available anyone who wanted to speak to a journalist, they didn't make it easy. The chief guard, a man in a white shirt who reminded me of Boss Hogg on *The Dukes of Hazzard*, made it clear that he would not help speed up any such meeting to ensure that I spoke to Johnson before I left town. So, I went to the jail daily, spending many hours across the street from it in the county courthouse—close in case they called to tell me I could come in—watching arraignments and sentencing hearings. And I spent my nights finding people who'd known Johnson when he was free.

The cases appearing before Judge Jon Cunningham were all remarkably similar: one drug case (usually meth) after another, each one featuring poor people, often lured into stings. They were facing the prospect of spending years of their lives behind bars over small amounts of fentanyl, opioids, or crystal methamphetamine. Of different races, most of the defendants were men, and none was ever found not guilty. They often faced losing custody of their children, who sometimes were in the courtroom for a glimpse of the parent they hadn't seen in months. (Once, the custodial grandmother of a child asked Judge Cunningham if the child could hug her father, whom she hadn't seen in a year; the judge said yes, but told her to make it brief.)

Right before my last business day in town, I still didn't know if I'd get to talk to Johnson. But at the last minute, his public defender, Heather Donovan, agreed to use her right to meet with her client to take me along so that I could interview him in jail, as long as I didn't ask him about the factual details of his pending charges. I agreed.

In a small visitation room at the St. Charles County Department of Corrections, I finally met Michael Johnson. He walked in wearing an orange jumpsuit but no handcuffs; I was still wearing a tie and felt out of place. Though I felt nervous about meeting him and guilty about being so hypermobile, probing into the most personal details of his sex life while he was stuck in a cell, he was grateful I'd come to see him. He had a broad smile and an easygoing manner. In person, he didn't seem like the predator portrayed in the news. But after seeing his own mugshot in the media, even Johnson admitted to me, "If I didn't know that person, I knew I would be very shocked and scared."

Johnson was born in 1991 in Indianapolis. He was the youngest of his single mother's five sons; he didn't know his father. Both Johnson and his mother said that he had dyslexia and had been enrolled in special education.

Johnson knew from a young age that his best shot for success was via his athleticism. While he flirted with other sports, he liked wrestling partially, he said, because, unlike "a team sport, you can't point the finger at another person—you can only point the finger at yourself." Sports was also an arena where his learning disabilities wouldn't matter. By high school, Johnson dreamed of parlaying his successful wrestling career into a ticket not just to college, but to the Olympics and professional wrestling.

"I always identified as gay," Johnson said, but "my mom wasn't ready," and she urged him to stay in the closet. Johnson added that his Christian "faith made me want to fight to be straight," and he said he "wasn't sure whether I would be accepted in the wrestling community" if he came out, given all the grinding and pinning of sweaty teen boys eager to prove their masculinity.

So, as a teenager, Johnson presented as straight, becoming "Tiger" the wrestler after he started wearing what he called his "lucky tiger shirt" to matches. But he also started publicly exploring his identity as a gay man by walking in drag balls in Indianapolis.

Drag balls are parties where queer and trans people, in teams known as houses, come together to compete in various categories. Made known to the wider world by the 1990 film *Paris Is Burning* and the TV show *Pose* (2018–21), drag balls have long been places where queer people of color have affirmed (and thrown shade at) one another. Some balls are occasions for peer-to-peer education about HIV, and some even have on-site testing.

In going to balls, Johnson found a world that was as Black as his campus life was white. Joining the House of Mizrahi, he was very "butch" and walked a style known as BQ ("Butch Queen") Body, which looks more like a bodybuilding competition than the kind of drag shown on the TV show *RuPaul's Drag Race*.

He also found a sense of family. "Being in a house, you got a mother and a father," said Johnson, his smile lighting up more than usual as he recalled how his house family gave him the support he craved and that everyone there knew what it meant to be gay. Johnson said that in all his years of health education, even in college (where he was pursuing a physical education teaching career), he "never had a class mention homosexuality," which he took to mean that "it's wrong to be gay."

It was in this era of his life when "Tiger" became "Tiger Mandingo."

Johnson was not the only person who enjoyed the "Mandingo" roleplaying, but he was the only one facing the law because of it. That was because prosecutors had in their possession what they considered a smoking gun. On January 7, 2013, Johnson signed a form from the state of Missouri acknowledging that he had been diagnosed with HIV. From that date forward, anytime he had sex with someone without disclosing his HIV status, he would have been committing a felony. Johnson's status was reported to the state under what's known as mandatory reporting.

Asking someone to sign their status assumes, first, that they will not go into a period of self-denial, which is common with HIV diagnoses; and second, that they can read. But when I met him, Johnson could barely read. "No one told him, 'Before you sign this legal document, you need to get counsel,'" his mother, Tracy Johnson, told me. She said he wouldn't have understood that "this is a legal document, and if you go against this legal document, you can be incarcerated."

Johnson's defense, already difficult because of his being semiliterate, poor, and represented by a public defender, was shaping up to be all the harder because, while the state had a signed statement from him, Johnson didn't have signed statements from any of his sex partners saying that they knew he was HIV-positive. It may sound preposterous, but there are so many people who have taken or considered taking such steps that HIV activist Josh Robbins developed two smartphone apps for people living with HIV to use to record their partners' consent prior to sexual encounters. (The popular gay hookup app Grindr began allowing people to disclose their HIV status in their profile. But after my colleagues at BuzzFeed News broke a story on how Grindr was letting third parties see its members' status, it became hard for many users to trust the platform.)

Some found it easy to blame Johnson for not being smart enough to understand the dilemma he had found himself in. But accessing literacy has often been a historically difficult, if not outright lethal, enterprise for Black American students, and accessing special education has come with its own particular challenges. Heading into the gears of the criminal justice system, Johnson was like many defendants before him who were unable to navigate the laws being used to prosecute them; he also didn't yet understand the virus multiplying inside his body, nor know how to navigate a complex medical system.

* * *

While Johnson kept "Tiger Mandingo" and his BQ Body wins on the down-low, his body was quite visibly successful in the wrestling world. He won the Indiana High School Athletic Association wrestling championship in 2010, his senior year of high school. "Many colleges would have liked to have had him but academically it was not possible," Jim Ledbetter, who coached Johnson in high school, wrote to me in 2014. "Therefore, he ended up at Lincoln Junior College in Lincoln, Illinois."

Johnson got his associate's degree at Lincoln College and came in first place at the National Junior College Athletic Association Wrestling Championships in 2012. He then was recruited to wrestle for the Lindenwood Lions, at Lindenwood University in St. Charles. Lindenwood was an academically lackluster institution that shone in Division II collegiate athletics. Johnson was recruited by the award-winning wrestling program and enrolled in the university with a sports scholarship, despite the fact that everyone I interviewed who knew him well (including his mother) expressed their concern that he could barely read or write.

"Reading is very hard, and spelling is very difficult," Johnson said. "When I look at a chapter book, I get more sleepy the more I read." He was painfully aware of his learning disabilities. He told me he would stutter when he tried to "read off a paper" in class, worried that he'd "miss words" and "people would look at me and say, 'Oh, he's so big, and he can't read.'"

Akil Patterson, a Maryland-based wrestling coach who volunteered with the National Black Justice Coalition, had seen Johnson wrestle once in person, at a meet. They had never spoken, but Patterson, who is Black and gay, also struggled with reading disabilities as a student. After Johnson's arrest, Patterson organized letters of support, flew to Missouri to visit Johnson at his own expense, and talked to him on the phone regularly.

"Sometimes," Patterson told me, "I imagine what I might have been able to do to help this kid before he got into this situation." It was an extraordinarily intimate gesture of support, unlike anything I had ever seen in years of covering activism. Patterson was empathetically aware of the ways Black athletes were more likely not just to be affected by HIV, but to have their bodies used up by collegiate or professional sports. Collegiate teams care little whether Black athletes can read or are set up for success in life, just as professional leagues care little for what happens to Black athletes after their careers (which usually last only a few years) are over. (Years later, in 2021, the Associated Press reported that the National Football League had agreed to "halt the use of 'race-norming'—which assumed Black players started out with lower cognitive functioning—in a $1 billion settlement of brain injury claims. The practice had made it harder for Black players to qualify" for compensation.)

Johnson said he considered his fellow wrestlers to be his closest friends at Lindenwood, yet not a single teammate ever made the one-mile trip to visit him in jail. "That does show, I think, some poor character on our team," one of Johnson's former teammates told me. After the Lions were told of Johnson's arrest, they "focused on the year ahead," the teammate said, and it was as if Johnson "had never been here." (Asked about this, Johnson said, "I don't blame anybody. I just think it's sad." He has not seen or talked to any of his teammates since.)

The former teammate said, "There was much more to Michael than the current light the public has upon him," but he did think Johnson should be prosecuted. Why do "people around the poverty line," he pondered, "continually choose to infect one another? It's because they get selfish pleasure in one aspect, they're selfish and greedy for that short pleasure that takes them to another place, because of all the pain they've had to deal with." Johnson, he said, must have had a lot of demons. But he could have "kept the HIV to himself. Instead, he decided to be selfish and to infect others."

The wrestler's belief that viruses move among and between poor people because those people are selfish and greedy is a common, if inaccurate, assumption. It is rooted in how racism (originally as a vector of disease transmission in the trade of enslaved people) and capitalism (as a vector of pushing poor people together) created conditions of illness as a *justification* for treating Black and other poor people as deserving of untouchable status. When one lives in conditions that create disease, it is hard to keep anything to oneself—and touch itself can become deadly.

But being touched and experiencing intimate contact is an inherent human need, as much of humanity experienced while billions of people struggled to address this during the COVID-19 pandemic. Humans manage this need by negotiating various levels of risk. This need doesn't disappear among people who have been predetermined by design to be the most at risk for viruses, though they're the ones most likely to be punished for it.

Two of the most important tools for preventing communicable diseases are communication and testing, so that the people affected can get the help they need (which, in turn, will prevent onward transmission to others). HIV laws make both harder, because *if you don't know your status, you can't be prosecuted*. A high-profile prosecution for HIV like Johnson's, then, incentivizes people *not* to learn their status, which further consolidates viral risk among a racialized underclass. Indeed, the HIV prevention professionals I interviewed in St. Louis told me their work to convince the young Black people most vulnerable to HIV to get tested got even harder after they'd seen Michael Johnson's arrest on TV. Learning that testing could lead to their finding out they were positive—and thus to risking, for the rest of their lives, someone's saying they hadn't disclosed their status—they concluded it was better off not to know.

This is one reason "HIV criminalization does not produce positive health outcomes for individuals or populations," as Fred Rottnek, the medical director of corrections medicine for the St. Louis County Department of Health, explained to me around the time the House of Delegates of the American Medical Association adopted a resolution against HIV laws. In the years since, more medical associations and even some legislatures have repealed or called for the repeal of HIV laws; and yet, other legislators still keep trying to criminalize infectious sickness, which is a way of criminalizing Blackness.

* * *

When I left Johnson and completed my first reporting trip to St. Louis, Johnson had already been waiting for eight months for a trial (and he'd wait a year more before one was held). I had come to understand, from his story, that the paths of viral transmission can be heavily predicted by the weight of history and the grooves of racism already etched into the bedrock of society. A few months after I published my first story about Johnson in the summer of 2014, much of the entire world would learn something similar via another young Black man *also* named Michael, near St. Louis.

On August 9, 2014, a white police officer named Darren Wilson shot eighteen-year-old Michael Brown Jr. in the heart of the Canfield Green Apartments in Ferguson, Missouri. Michael Brown was unarmed, and his bloodied body was left lying in the street for hours. While it lay there, something unusual happened in the media history of dead Black victims of police killings. Instead of the police feeding their narrative of events to traditional media outlets for them to repeat—a narrative in which the victim would be described as a "thug" who needed to be put down—Mike Brown's friends and neighbors created a counternarrative on social media of an innocent dead child. They painted him as their friend, their neighbor, and a beloved member of a community worthy of the world's empathy.

The week Mike Brown was killed, I had just started a new job as a columnist for the British newspaper the *Guardian*. I wasn't supposed to travel or do much on-the-ground reporting for this job, particularly as I was about to start a full-time, funded PhD program a month later. But an editor heard I had gotten to know the St. Louis region while covering Michael Johnson and told me to get on a plane to cover the uprising.

Before heading to the airport, I asked one of the HIV prevention experts I'd come to know what I should be looking for in this town of Ferguson. And they told me their colleagues had recently been in the Canfield Green Apartments because there had been new HIV transmission in the area and that Ferguson was located in St. Louis's heavily Black "North County," which suffered from higher rates of HIV and AIDS than other parts of the region.

Learning this zapped me with the sharpest physical sensation I've ever had in my life as a reporter and scholar, while helping me to understand something about life in America: *Of course, the HIV folks know the area where Michael Brown was killed*, I thought. *Wherever you find police violence and racism in the United States, you're bound to find Black people living with viruses and dying of disease.* Though I didn't yet know the term, this was the first time I was beginning to see the manifestation of the viral underclass.

In the coming months and years, many white people in the United States looked to St. Louis as if looking through a prism for understanding truths about America that Black America had long known. Ferguson showed the world how the cartography of systemic racism meant that the maps revealing dense concentrations of poor Black people and the maps showing lethal police violence nearly always overlapped. Locating one of these injustices could easily reveal the other. But I started using a third metric as my guiding cartography, viral transmission—and I found that wherever you find people living with viruses and dying of disease, you're bound to find Black people dying of police violence or poverty, too.

The fallout from Ferguson led many people to see how health disparities plagued heavily policed Black communities. The Ferguson Commission, convened in 2015, found that "life expectancy differed by nearly 40 years depending on zip code" in St. Louis County, reaching 91.4 years in "mostly White, suburban Wildwood" and just 55.9 years in "the mostly Black, inner ring suburb of Kinloch." And while such health disparities existed throughout the United States, there was something extreme about the disparities in Ferguson. For instance, in a

2015 *New York Times* article, researchers illustrated how for every one hundred white women in the United States, there were ninety-nine white men; yet for every one hundred Black women, there were just eighty-three Black men. Nationally, this resulted in about a million and a half fewer Black men than women, because so many Black men are disappeared from society by way of prison or premature death. And the city with a notable Black population with the largest differential of all—only sixty Black men for every one hundred Black women—was Ferguson. This was a biological reality manifested from centuries-old roots of colonialism, genocide, the slave trade, and policing.

Journalists and politicians have a difficult time narrating how broadly such systemic scenarios indict every element of U.S. society and, indeed, many societies on earth. They prefer a simpler narrative, like the myth of a convenient scapegoat. I've long thought that Michael Johnson is not free of any responsibility in his own story; he himself has told me about wanting to take responsibility for his own life. But I have also long thought it unfair that he carried *all* the responsibility in his story—for his actions, for his partners' actions, and for the deep anxiety America has about race, homosexuality, and disease.

America prefers a less complicated, ableist story, one where everyone is healthy until one bad actor comes along. And that's where the "patient zero" narratives come in.

2

THE INFINITE WEIGHT OF ZERO

(Individualized Shame)

On Sunday, June 29, 2009, I walked into a party on Fifth Avenue in Manhattan, high above New York City's annual Gay Pride Parade. I was wearing a tutu, hiking boots, and a cowboy hat (and feeling myself) when, from across the room, I locked eyes with Olivier Le Borgne. We looked at each other flummoxed, as if each was seeing an old friend he just happened never to have met before.

Then, he crossed the room immediately and walked into my heart, where he'll firmly have a special place for the rest of my days on this earth (and, who knows, perhaps beyond). A slender Frenchman, he tilted his head slightly to the right when he looked at me and had the kind of laugh lines around his eyes that made me relax a bit, despite how disarmed I was by his radiance (and how self-conscious I was about not having any pants on).

We talked that entire afternoon at that raging house party as if no one else were there, even though his English was only slightly better than my terrible French—and even though I was at the party with my then boyfriend.

We talked as the party spilled out onto the street and headed west, toward the Stonewall Inn, where the queer uprising against police violence forty years to the day before had triggered so much of the modern gay rights movement.

We talked as our party tried, in vain, to find a place to sit down and have dinner. Olivier smoked cigarettes as we walked under the light of fireworks, and he told me about how he'd come to New York City that summer to work with the theater director Robert Wilson.

And when my boyfriend took the subway home to Queens, Olivier and I rode the Q Train together toward Brooklyn, as he was staying just one train stop away from me. We didn't plan to sleep together—I was very committed to monogamy back then—but we exchanged numbers and agreed to meet up again before he returned to France.

When I got off the train, we shared a kiss so sweet that, a dozen years later, I still smile thinking about it. I couldn't wait to see him again.

Then he left town without saying goodbye—ghosting me.

That first conversation would be one of only four times we'd meet in real life in the nearly seven years of our friendship. Still, Olivier taught me more about viruses than just about anyone I've ever known, except maybe Michael Johnson. But while Michael taught me about the manifestation of the viral underclass via racism in a professional way, Olivier taught me how it manifests via individual shame very personally.

And to this day, every time I see news stories unfairly putting the weight of pandemics on the shoulders of individuals, I think of Olivier and the tragic harm that befalls those who bear such stigmas.

* * *

On the morning of July 1, 2020, ABC News anchor Robin Roberts asked the audience of *Good Morning America*, in a stentorian voice, "Are you ready for this?"

ABC News had a sensational COVID-19 scoop: college students at the University of Alabama were "intentionally trying to get sick, even *gambling* on who gets the virus first." According to interviewee Sonya McKinstry, a Tuscaloosa City councilmember, "College kids are having COVID-19 parties where they're getting tickets—to come to the party, and they will invite a couple of people who have tested positive" for SARS-CoV-2. "If you are the first person testing positive for COVID" after being exposed at the party, McKinstry said, "then you win the money." It was an outrageous claim—mostly because it wasn't true.

As I first read the story circulating online, I cringed, hoping it would not hype up the idea of irresponsible, calculating, virus-spreading monsters too much. (I had seen enough of that in Michael Johnson's case.) I found the idea—that college students would advertise a party, find someone who had COVID-19, sell tickets, collect money at the door, make sure all participants were exposed to the sick partier, have all the attendees get tested in the days after the party (when it was still *really* hard to get a test), and *then* distribute the prize money to whoever first produced a positive result—laughable.

Such contests never happened. Sure, young people had parties where social distancing wasn't respected, though these weren't happening very often near closed college campuses in the summer of 2020. But even when parties happened the next fall at or near colleges, students were *not* intentionally trying to get one another sick for money. The crisis of community spread of SARS-CoV-2 in the United States from New York to Alabama could no more be blamed upon any one college kid intentionally trying to spread it than the tens of millions of cases of HIV on earth could be blamed on a college wrestler in Missouri.

And yet, that was the message the ABC News story was trying to convey—as were other news outlets (like CNN and the Associated Press), when they unethically and uncritically repeated their competitor's story without doing any original reporting of their own: COVID-19 was being driven by the solipsism of genocidal college students. The story was a case of moral panic, meant simplistically to assign blame for complex social problems that were politically inconvenient for the ruling class.

Stories like the one about COVID-19 parties aren't just shoddy journalism; they are useful mythmaking for the ruling class agenda. As Americans fell into poverty and begged for relief in the pandemic, the federal government could have taxed the wealthy more, taxed corporations (whose wealth is built by workers), and printed money to send to people to keep them from falling into starvation or homelessness. This largely did not happen, and mainstream media *could* have told stories that explained this failure.

Instead, the news media created myths (like COVID parties) steeped in a shame-inducing ideology for the masses to consume. In this mythology, the villains were not CEOs, or senators blocking relief, or landlords threatening evictions, but reckless young people.

This myth also obscured an epidemiological crisis of the young: that their COVID-19 rates rose with the reopening of businesses, because it is young people who staff public-facing, low-paying retail and service jobs. These jobs often lack health care benefits. Retail workers are more likely to be Black, Latinx, and impoverished than the workforce overall. And in the United States, the fault for this cannot be placed upon those workers, nor even fully on an American public who has been told since September 11, 2001, that the proper response to any crisis is to go shopping.

When the City of Chicago's official Twitter account quoted the ABC News story about COVID parties, I knew we were stuck in a dangerous and inescapable feedback loop—one in which a small-town official's unsubstantiated claims were deemed legitimate by news organizations and then further laundered by a larger city's propaganda arm repeating the news, which dulled the public into believing something that wasn't true.

In their propaganda model of journalism, Noam Chomsky and Edward Herman identified five filters of mass media: ownership, advertising, sourcing, flak, and fear. Before making its way to an audience, all information reported by mainstream news outlets must pass through these five filters, and only the least controversial information can trickle through the filters to reach mainstream audiences. The COVID party hoax was an illustration of the use of several of these filters—perhaps most prominently, the third, sourcing (which overly relies upon officials, whose words are distributed far *more* often than those of people without state power and with far *less* scrutiny), and the fifth filter, fear (which hypes up hysteria over a common enemy).

Media stories and the metanarratives they conjure in the zeitgeist often personify the common enemy not in the form of viruses themselves, but in a marginalized group afflicted *by* a virus. Indeed, those most likely to be harmed by viruses are contorted into being the *source* of viruses—or even depicted *as* viruses. The teenager working in McDonald's who is sick with COVID-19, the Black gay man in Mississippi who is infected with HIV, the Jewish girl forced into a Warsaw ghetto by the Nazis who is plagued with typhus, the Palestinian boy who is stuffed into cramped quarters in Gaza and whose diarrhea is filled with norovirus—all these people deserve *compassion* for how viruses affect them, not *blame.* And all have been vilified as "the other" at some point in various media ecosystems, by journalists doing the bidding of the ruling class. While many successful journalists fancy themselves "objective," there is nothing objective about scapegoating someone who is suffering and making them seem unworthy of care, so that the ruling class can run off with the resources necessary for *everyone* to be safe. It is a subjective ideology.

As with the COVID party story, it's a hoax to think of a virus magically appearing in any one person who can be neatly blamed. Just as we can never think of a baby alone without invoking parents, grandparents, sperm, eggs, or caretakers, viruses are *socially* produced and reproduced. Like humans, viruses exist within social relationships formed within an economic reality that is rarely discussed in the news.

Yet viruses are often described as being the *opposite* of social—as being the fault of one singular actor who negligently (and sometimes even purposefully) infects other would-be healthy people. We in the United States tend to think about such a person as a "patient zero," but nearly everything about such framing is a lie. These individualized shame narratives not only work to shift the blame from the state and society to the individual, but also isolate individuals, both through policy and socially. Stories like that of my friend Olivier—who, I would soon learn, had been made to feel alone because of media-fueled (and state-endorsed) stigma—are a necessary counternarrative.

* * *

In late June 2010, Olivier friended me on Facebook.

"Hello Olivier," I wrote, accepting his request. "I was just thinking about you last night. So nice to hear from you. It has been a year since that Pride party where I met you. That was the best conversation I have ever had at a party, ever. I had never fallen so quickly and momentarily for someone. Maybe I never will again. But what a thrill it was to meet you."

"Thanks for this message," he responded, "i really felt something strong when i met you, but i was feeling your love for your boyfriend; and last year i was a little 'fragil' for this kind of relation!!"

He had reached out from Paris to tell me the reason he had not wanted to see me again before he left New York: he was HIV-positive. In the years since his diagnosis, he had been hurt so many times by people who couldn't handle his status, and he had felt so strongly toward me upon our meeting, that he was scared about the possibility that I might reject him when he told me.

So, he'd just left.

I am ashamed I said some stupid things that were puritanical and holier-than-thou when we first talked about our sexual practices ("I only have very safe sex. Very safe"). I regret placing this burden on Olivier, and I am grateful for the grace he showed me in our too-short time knowing each other. Despite having negotiated HIV risk with my then boyfriend, I hadn't yet dated anyone who knew he was HIV-positive (though I now have many times).

"My life was never the same after meeting you," I wrote Olivier, to express my overall gratitude but also my sadness that we hadn't gotten to hang out again when we'd been on the same continent. If we'd wanted to have sex, we could have managed that safely, though my ignorance and his trauma had made that impossible. And stigma had kept us from even hanging out.

"You offered me a great kiss too!" Olivier wrote me, adding that "now you understand better why i didnt call you back fast . . ."

Later, he told me of growing up in a small village by the sea. His sexuality had already been so challenging for his parents that he decided he couldn't allow them to be burdened with his HIV status. And so, he'd never told them.

It hurt me to see such a lovely person afraid that the virus in him could hurt his parents—not because they were at risk of catching it, but because its mere existence inside him would cause them anguish (which hurt him). Stigma is contagious; even when someone living with HIV doesn't tell the people around them, the stigma spreads to everyone in their social sphere, isolating the person with the virus from the very people they love when they may need them the most.

Those early exchanges were the start of a yearslong correspondence, of messages filled with mutual love and affection, expressed across the Atlantic. "whats happening on the other side to the ocean?" he'd message me, and I'd tell him. For four years, we messaged each other often, about things big and small—him, in charmingly blunt English; me, sometimes in oddly formal French. (I'd use an online translator, but because I couldn't figure out how to turn on the informal mode, I used too many instances of *vous* when I should have used the familiar *tu*.)

He'd tell me about the shows he was doing, and I'd tell him about what I was writing. Sometimes we'd ask for affirmation. Me, in 2013: "Do you still think about me?" Him: "yes, i was very touched by our meeting, truly."

Sometimes we'd tell each other about our sex lives. He told me how he wanted to have sex only with other HIV-positive men, to avoid judgment. I stupidly wondered if he could be having unprotected sex with them, in a way in which they could infect each other anew, and he very patiently explained to me how this wasn't possible, due to the medication he was taking. "I'm HIV for 22 years," he wrote, adding his life was "pretty good!"

But when we'd talk about our fantasies of sleeping together, he was very nervous. "will u be afraid to make love with me??" he once asked me so tenderly. Even in the domain of fantasy, there was wounded shame. I told him about a new drug called Truvada. I could take that *and* use a condom. But it wasn't even an issue in our reality. In the first years we knew each other, I was too poor to consistently afford stable housing and food, let alone to board airplanes at will.

Still, our banter went on for years—sometimes by video calls, but mostly by texting and, occasionally, sexting. When I started carrying a smartphone, Olivier was one of the first people I felt happy knowing was always in my pocket, just a message (and an ocean) away.

* * *

When it first began to circulate in the 1980s, patient zero etymologically invoked *ground zero*, a term coined near the end of World War II to describe the point on the ground closest to a nuclear explosion. In the summer of 1945, this referred to the sandy ground beneath the Los Alamos National Lab, in New Mexico, and to Japanese soil beneath Hiroshima and Nagasaki, where the United States dropped nuclear bombs that led to about a quarter million deaths. And decades later, after hijackers flew two 767s into the World Trade Center's Twin Towers, the heaping pile of burning steel wreckage left behind was dubbed Ground Zero.

When the term *patient zero* was first used in relation to a person living with AIDS, it contained in its four syllables all the violence of a nuclear detonation—as if that first person contained in their body all the kinetic energy and evil of an atomic weapon. And when *patient zero* was invoked to describe the first person imagined to be living with SARS-CoV-2 in various communities decades later, the term infected any person living with that novel coronavirus with all the malevolent intent of hijackers who had purposefully killed thousands of people. This association between nuclear and biological bombs increased when, many decades after the atom bomb was developed there, the Los Alamos National Laboratory became the home of the U.S. Pathogen Research Databases, which tracks the genetic sequences of HIV, HCV, and Ebola as carefully as Manhattan Project scientists once split the atom.

Of course, people living with viruses or bacteria are *not* bombs or terrorists. Ebola, *Enola*—there is nothing about a person living with Ebola or HIV engaging in normative life activities that can be equated with the violence of pilots Paul Tibbets and Robert Lewis flying the *Enola Gay* toward Hiroshima on behalf of the U.S. government, nor of Mohamed Atta flying American Airlines Flight 11 toward Manhattan on behalf of Al Qaeda.

It is grotesque and irresponsible for news media to equate, even linguistically, people living with viruses with some of the most violent seconds in human history. It is similarly unfair how often journalists and researchers continue to breathlessly refer to the "hunt for patient zero," in language that either conjures up an enemy on the battlefield (*The Hunt for Red October*) or equates a sick person with a wild animal needing to be stalked and butchered.

The first popular use of *patient zero* was largely predicated upon a mistake. In the blockbuster 1987 book *And the Band Played On: Politics, People, and the AIDS Epidemic*, journalist Randy Shilts identified and vilified Gaëtan Dugas, a French Canadian flight attendant who died of AIDS in Quebec City in 1984, as the infamous "Patient Zero" who had spread AIDS around North America. But in 2016, scholars published a study in the journal *Nature* that showed how a method of "jackhammering" ribonucleic acid (RNA) helped reveal that HIV had been circulating in North America since at least 1970. One of the most newsworthy aspects of this discovery was that the study cleared Dugas.

In Shilts's book, and according to Dugas's friends, the flight attendant *was* a very sexually active gay man. By his own count, he had sex with at least hundreds of partners. Yet, in the years after the Stonewall riots of 1969, when many gay men felt free to express their sexuality for the first time, having so many sexual partners was not considered unusual or necessarily even unhealthy. In the 1970s and early '80s, when thousands of horny gay men just like Dugas were having sex with thousands of other horny gay men in New York City and San Francisco, condoms were something straight people used to prevent pregnancy. (And, depending on the availability of birth control pills, straight people often preferred to bareback, too, even though birth control pills didn't offer protection from sexually transmitted infections.) Syphilis and gonorrhea were easily treatable with cheap antibiotics.

This all changed when doctors, nurses, and journalists began noticing in the early 1980s that gay men were dying of an unusual cancer. No one (gay, bi, or straight) knew that a relatively inefficient virus—HIV needs a high number of humans to repeatedly swap blood, milk, or semen with many other people—had begun circulating among them. In one of the great peer-to-peer public health campaigns of modern medicine, many gay men *did* eventually grow to use condoms widely during sex, without government mandates. But it took time. As any person who struggled not to shake hands, hug their friends, kiss their kin, get closer than six feet from people they loved, remain indoors with others, or touch their face during the COVID-19 pandemic can tell you, adjusting behaviors takes a bit of time.

Like many people, gay and straight, Dugas had a lot of sexual encounters in his life in the pursuit of pleasure without the intention to procreate. This is a common human activity and nothing to be ashamed of. In a black-and-white photo of him, Dugas has a slight, youthful build and a mustache evocative of 1970s frivolity. He made it around the sun only thirty-one times before he died.

In his book, Shilts frames the HIV crisis as a detective story in which the key to understanding the epidemic required crusaders to hunt down "Patient Zero." While Shilts writes, "Whether Gaetan Dugas actually was the person who brought AIDS to North America remains a question of debate and is ultimately unanswerable," he answers that question just a few lines later when he writes that "there's no doubt" that "Gaetan played a key role in spreading the new virus from one end of the United States to the other." As my friend, scholar Anthony Petro, once put it to me, Shilts frames "the epidemiological spread of the epidemic as very much a moral failing on the part of this flight attendant."

And the Band Played On is a book-length work of journalism, and like a lot of journalism, it suffers from an inherent bug: it reported the story before the ending was known. There is nothing evil about this. Shilts, who died in 1994, didn't live to see the development of antiretroviral medication. He never got to reexamine the story he helped set in motion with the benefit of time passed. But he did bear responsibility for framing and marketing the book as he did. Long before the *Nature* article showed, at a microscopic level, that Dugas could not have been the first person with HIV in North America, Shilts's overwrought emphasis on Dugas's alleged promiscuity had been widely criticized by historians, social scientists, and public health researchers.

What I found most newsworthy about the *Nature* study was not how genetic material proved something I already knew to be true, but that Shilts had simply made a mistake: Dugas was *never* supposed to have been known as a numeric Patient Zero at all, but as Patient *O*. Dugas was just one of many men whom investigators were looking to when tracking the movement of a new virus they didn't understand. And when contacted by tracers, Dugas was cooperative, giving them the names of 750 men he'd had sex with. One investigator, who was primarily researching men who lived in California, labeled Dugas "Patient *O*," for being "outside" California.

Subsequent people who read that capital letter *O* as a zero weren't the only ones to make the mistake. In his 2017 book, *Patient Zero and the Making of the AIDS Epidemic*, Richard A. McKay (who coauthored the *Nature* study) wrote that "For years, several successive editions of a top-selling medical dictionary—a type of publication frequently considered to be the ultimate imprimatur of authority—contained an entry for Patient Zero which read: 'an individual identified by the Centers for

Disease Control (CDC) as the person who introduced the human immunodeficiency virus in the United States. According to CDC records, Patient Zero, an airline steward, infected nearly 50 other persons before he died of acquired immunodeficiency syndrome in 1984.'"

As a gay journalist, Shilts gave an enormous boost to this framing, while also granting cover to many straight journalists and scientists to frame the crisis not as an ethical failure of the society to support a marginalized population being devastated by an epidemic, but instead to blame one horny gay man. According to the *New York Times*, "in a 1993 interview, Mr. Shilts said he had heard C.D.C. investigators use the term Patient Zero and thought, 'Oooh, that's catchy.'" The *Times* also said that Shilts had "said he was initially horrified that his publisher, St. Martin's Press, focused his book tour on Patient Zero instead of the government's slow response to the epidemic, but he went along."

Shilts's choices were not unusual; they were common throughout media and society. When Dugas was scapegoated, it made it all the easier for governments to say that AIDS was a failure of gay people to behave responsibly. (Gay people, it should be noted, created pandemic-slowing health models that have helped a great deal to address COVID-19.) It deflected blame that should have been directed at the federal government for the economic and homophobic conditions that allowed HIV to reproduce so quickly. It made it harder for groups like the AIDS Coalition to Unleash Power (ACT UP) to force the government to treat people dying from AIDS with dignity.

I believe it helped people like Olivier internalize a sense of failure about the very normative process of becoming infected by a virus after having sex. And it primed an American response to COVID-19 in which Americans would look less readily at the economic forces fueling the pandemic and spend more time blaming nonexistent "COVID parties" or people going to the beach—probably the safest place to be during an airborne pandemic.

Douglas Rushkoff, the media theorist who conceived of the phrases *viral media* and *media virus*, has said, "People are duped into passing a hidden agenda while circulating compelling content." The "Patient Zero" stories circulating during Shilts's publicity tour in 1993 and the "COVID party" hoax in 2020 are both mutations of viral news. Such stories can spread through traditional media with a high level of focused distribution (ABC News, St. Martin's Press) and social media with a more diffuse level of distribution (Twitter, Facebook, interpersonal gossip) alike, inflaming the body politic the way influenza might trigger inflammatory responses within humans.

As puns and visual jokes making fun of these COVID parties (as if they were real) proliferated on my social media feeds, I thought about how the term *meme* was originally coined as a neologism by biologist Richard Dawkins. In his 1976 book *The Selfish Gene*, Dawkins—who has been widely criticized for statements he's made about women and Muslims—argues that a story or an "idea-meme" can mutate and evolve in a mode similar to genetics. Like literal viruses, and especially when it is *about* viruses, viral news does not transmit in a neutral manner. It mutates and infects along lines of race, class, and sexuality, making the most defenseless people ever more vulnerable as it reproduces.

While stories of COVID parties cast aspersions upon millions of young people, media-generated stigma against any group creates countless cases of individual shame, whether or not someone is singled out publicly as a patient zero.

I saw this in a most catastrophic way with Olivier.

* * *

When I met Olivier at Café Beaubourg in Paris in 2014—just days after I'd published my first story on HIV criminalization—we kissed each other on both cheeks before ordering coffee.

It had been five years since we'd last been together. He was so nervous seeing me after all this time that he was shaking. I was nervous, too, but I couldn't figure out why *he* was nervous. (He was one of the most gorgeous men I'd ever seen; why was *he* acting nervous with *me*?)

We caught up on our lives—though, was that the right term? We were always texting. But here, each of us could just enjoy staring into the other's irrepressibly smiling face as he savored his presence.

He had a new boyfriend, who made him happy. He was going to Athens for part of the summer, a city he loved and which I'd never been to. I told him about my anxiety over being a student again at age thirty-seven. And he had read my reporting on Michael Johnson, which horrified him. While Johnson's arrest frightened me as a Black gay American, Olivier was frightened by it differently, as someone living with HIV. (France does not have specific HIV laws, but according to the HIV Justice Network, at least forty people with HIV have been prosecuted in France for exposing others to the virus, under "poisoning" or "administration of harmful substances" laws.)

After our coffee, Olivier and I took a walk from the place Georges Pompidou, wandering through the Fourth Arrondissement. When we came to an alley wall covered in colorful graffiti, we held hands briefly, then took two selfies. Before we parted, he told me his theater company was going to do a major tour of North America, and he'd pass through New York City in October to perform the work of Luigi Pirandello. Could I come?

Yes, I assured him.

We texted constantly that summer. I sent him my dispatches from Ferguson. Olivier expressed alarm when he saw the tanks and tear gas on TV.

On the night of Halloween 2014, I went to the Brooklyn Academy of Music's Harvey Theater to see Olivier in the Théâtre de la Ville's sold-out production of *Six Characters in Search of an Author*. Olivier was hilarious and physical, and I felt sneaky sitting in his comped seat, knowing I shared such an intimate bond with an actor onstage who was performing in front of hundreds of people.

Afterward, he introduced me to his company. Then Olivier and I had dinner alone at a tiny restaurant around the corner and got drunk on red wine. He convinced the owner to crank up the music, then Olivier pushed back the tables, grabbed me by the waist, put his hand on the small of my back, and (while looking me in the eyes and sensing my bashfulness) just held my gaze as he said, "Stay with me. Stay with me." Then, we danced. As the room spun around us, I felt both in danger and safe in this gorgeous Frenchman's arms.

It was the closest I would ever feel to him physically.

The morning after, Olivier texted me that he loved me, right before I got word that my sister Sharron's long journey with cancer was coming to a close and that I needed to travel that day to be with her in hospice care.

"I love you too," I wrote back. "My sister will die soon so I will not come back to NYC for a while, so I am glad I saw you last night."

"Bon courage, you are strong, i love love you," he wrote.

* * *

Around the time *And the Band Played On* came out in 1987, an article in the *Chicago Tribune* was published under the screaming all-caps headline "CASE SHAKES THEORIES OF AIDS ORIGINS." The article brought into question not just Randy Shilts's misguided obsession with his Patient Zero, but the entire American understanding of HIV's time line.

In late 1968, according to the *Tribune*, a fifteen-year-old Black teenager named Robert Rayford was hospitalized at Barnes Hospital in St. Louis with pneumonia. He had been in and out of the hospital for a couple of years with mysterious ailments, often perturbed by doctors' questions. His body was riddled with various pathogens. When he "finally entered the hospital" for the last time, the *Tribune* reported, Rayford's "lower legs and genitals had been swollen," and "the black teenager had grown thin and pale, fatigued and short of breath—his bloodstream swarmed with the microbe called Chlamydia."

Rayford told doctors he had been having symptoms since 1966, when he was just thirteen years old. He had perhaps been the victim of child survival sex; his rectum had signs of severe anal bruising. Short of breath, he had an immune system that was incomprehensibly failing. He was discharged, but readmitted a few months later. When he died on May 15, 1969, at age sixteen, the official cause was listed as pneumonia. During an autopsy, doctors found a small purple lesion on one of his thighs and another inside him. These were Kaposi sarcoma tumors, which had been known to affect primarily older men living around the Mediterranean Sea.

Rayford's death was so unusual that tissue samples were saved from his corpse. As HIV/AIDS was first beginning to be understood years later, the tissue from Rayford's body were thawed and tested in 1984 for HIV antibodies, organic material produced by the body to ward off infection. They were present.

In his brief life, Rayford not only developed cancer, genital edema, proctitis, and bruising in his rectum, but he also lived with viruses such as herpes, cytomegalovirus, Epstein-Barr, and, the posthumous test highly suggests, HIV.

There is often a dehumanizing quality to the pieces written in news media and scientific research about people living with viruses. In a 2020 *New York Times* article on coronavirus "superspreaders," Carl Zimmer crudely wrote that "some people become virus chimneys, blasting out clouds of pathogens with each breath." The term *superspreader* evokes *superpredators*, the racist term then–First Lady Hillary Clinton infamously evoked in 1996 to describe youth as not "just gangs of kids anymore" but as "the kinds of kids that are called superpredators—no conscience, no empathy," and who needed to be brought "to heel."

It is hard to feel empathy for someone described linguistically as a chimney, an object erupting pathogens. They sound pathological. Similarly, Robert Rayford, a child who was likely a victim of rape, was described after his death as possibly a "male prostitute" by one of his doctors and as "a bag producing Chlamydia" by another. I once went to a panel discussion in St. Louis meant to compassionately inform Black people in St. Louis who cared about local history about Rayford's life. His body was so devalued, however, that during the presentation, naked autopsy photos of the child, including of his swollen penis, were shown.

"How did Rayford contract the virus more than a decade before HIV/AIDS was identified and reached epidemic proportions in the 1980s?" a National Park Service website about him asks, adding, "How many people suffered and died from the mysterious illness before it was identified?"

According to AIDS scholar and activist Theodore Kerr, who has done extensive research on Rayford, the child wasn't the right fit for a patient zero archetype. "We can be so cruel," Kerr told me, saying that storytellers of early AIDS history "could just, like, eat Dugas alive, in a way that we wouldn't have done to Robert Rayford." As a child, Rayford fortunately couldn't be pathologized like the adult French Canadian flight attendant. And while he was sexually demonized by his doctors, Rayford was mercifully not old enough to be cast as a global menace like Michael Johnson would be. But as a Black child, Kerr said, Rayford was subjected to cruelty of a different kind: "We just ignored him instead, neglected him."

The first people who are affected by viruses are often so deep in the underclass that most of society ignores them. Think of the people who injected drugs who likely died of AIDS in the 1970s. There was little collective concern over the people suffering from "junkie pneumonia," "the dropsies," or "the dwindles." (Similarly, as we will see in chapter 10, people who collect bat or bird feces for fertilizer from caves may have caught and died from SARS-CoV-2 prior to 2019, but they were socially isolated, and likely no one ever knew why they died.) To members of the news media, those living without homes can be ignored in general, even if a pandemic is more likely to be felt by them before the more telegenic fictional partygoers.

Still, while it's important not to ignore viral deaths, with the National Park Service overstating Rayford as "the first HIV/AIDS patient in the United States," there is a real danger of inscribing upon him the patient zero myth. It would be wrong for anyone, let alone a dead Black child, to carry by himself the stigma and weight of a social disease.

We *all* share the burden and responsibility of life on a planet with viruses. But those of us living without the most lethal types of them must shoulder the responsibility *more*. For the media heap a tremendous weight upon people living with pathogens, making them feel like they're a burden or some kind of individual failure—and the toll of this can be deadly.

* * *

"how are you? life, sex? heart? Job?" Olivier asked me during our last exchange, in 2016. He was a little stressed about money, but had just been cast in a new theater production. "are u working on a book????????" he wanted to know.

"No, the PhD first," I told him, "then a book." Then: "Send me a picture of your smile."

It had been about a year and a half since we'd danced in that café, just before my sister died, and though we'd talked about meeting up, we had been unable to see each other again. But we texted all the time.

"I don't get one now. . . . I will." He didn't have a picture of his smile, he meant, but he'd send me one soon. "i miss you," he wrote, "very much. . . . it is 2:19, i need to sleep . . . hope to feel you very soon, not in 3 years."

"XO," I replied.

When I learned of his death by suicide a few weeks later, I sent "him" a short burst of messages immediately—as I immediately had messaged him about all kinds of news for so many years.

NOOOOOOOOOO!
I can't believe I am sending this to you
but I am
Where are you?

Where *was* he? This time he had really ghosted me—ghosted *everyone*—though, unlike with other suicides I had experienced, I had no temporary sense of anger. Just an immediate sense of sadness and disbelief.

How could the world go on without someone whose light shone so brightly?

In the coming weeks, after the shock turned to numbness, I went through the six years of our messages, seeing what we'd said to each other. (This posthumous scroll through digital correspondence with the dead became all too common as a way of mourning during COVID-19, though it was helpful when physically gathering to grieve with others wasn't possible.)

In our old texts was tenderness in English and French, lots of "I love you"s and "je t'aime"s. And every year around Pride, messages of awe that we'd even met.

June 30, 2013. Me: "Happy Pride Sunday. I always think of meeting you on this day, 4 years ago"; him: "Yes, this meeting was very special, like a beginning of something sweet or sexy or wet . . ."

June 29, 2014. Me: "Parfois, vous vous souvenez-vous d'une journée, une seule personne." ("Sometimes you remember one day, one person.") Him: "Je m'en souviens parfaitement, j'avais envie de te caresser." ("I remember it perfectly, I wanted to caress you.")

Outside my instant messages, everyone who knew Olivier on Facebook was shocked. He was a popular, extroverted, and beloved actor in Paris. On his page, I connected with an elderly friend of his, an Englishman in his eighties who lived in Paris. Later in 2016, when I was in Europe to work at the *Guardian* headquarters for a week, I traveled to Paris just to meet the octogenarian gentleman to talk about our late mutual friend. I wanted to see if I could learn any more about what had so plagued Olivier that he'd taken his own life.

This elderly man, an early and long-term survivor of HIV, had always been open about his trials with the virus; he said Princess Diana had intervened at one point to get him care. He had seen Olivier just a few days before the suicide, when Olivier had come by his frail friend's flat to help him procure a new set of shoes and take him to lunch.

But even *he* did not know Olivier was living with HIV until I told him. That's how secretive Olivier had felt forced to be about it. I couldn't find anyone else who seemed to know about his HIV status. Was it a secret he mostly took to his grave? Like a patient zero, did Olivier feel that his viral status made him a zero, a nothing?

I am not sure why Olivier told me. Maybe it was because I lived so far away from his life in France. Maybe it was because we really did love each other, and he wanted me to know him in a way that many others did not. But I am glad he did, and I hope I was able to give him a little respite from the stigma of the world, even though that stigma had still played a large part in keeping us from achieving the physical intimacy we might have had.

Suicide is complicated. Several people close to me have taken their own lives, including my biological mother, and I would never presume to know why exactly it happens with anyone. I certainly would never assume that any single factor causes suicide. It would be simplistic to say that being closeted about his HIV status alone drove my friend to end his life.

But it is true that while "suicide rates have decreased substantially among people living with HIV in the last three decades," as a large study conducted over twenty years and published in 2019 found, they "have remained about three times higher than in the general population." And it would be fair to imagine that the forces that made Olivier feel that he couldn't tell many people about his HIV diagnosis (depression, despair, stigma, viral shame, homophobia) were some of the same forces that had led to his suicide.

Olivier didn't die from HIV. But he died with the virus and likely with depression, two interlocking medical conditions made worse by the infinite weight of stigma. This can be explained as what I call *viral alienation*: the way media and government can make people feel alone, full of individualized shame, and crushed by an inability to master "personal responsibility." This makes people suffering from viruses, depression, or both feel like they are failures—when they are no such thing.

While he never got to send me a picture after our last exchange, I do have a lot of photos of Olivier. The one I love the most is of us together in front of that colorful wall of graffiti. But it's not the one I posted when we took it; rather, I love the slightly more intimate of the two selfies we'd taken that day. In this one, Olivier had leaned in at the last moment and kissed me on the cheek.

When the coronavirus lockdowns began, and I realized I was going to go days, then weeks, then a full year, without a single kiss from anyone for any reason, I started trying to conjure, as I fell asleep at night, sense memories of particularly memorable kisses I'd shared—with lovers like André or Anwar; or the one I gingerly planted on the head of my mother, Margaret, on her last day on this earth; or the one I received from my dear straight buddy Daniel, on my right cheek under some mistletoe at a Christmas party.

And often, I would think of two kisses from Olivier—our first, on the Q Train on June 30, 2009, and then Olivier's lips pressed briefly against my left cheek in that Parisian alley as I smiled goofily at the camera, beaming like the most openhearted fool in the world.

* * *

Communication scholar Daniel Hallin has theorized three spheres of influence in mass media. There's the sphere of consensus, which includes subjects that all major outlets agree upon (i.e., "terrorism is bad"; "the U.S. military is good"); the sphere of legitimate controversy, composed of the common debates (i.e., abortion rights, gay rights); and the sphere of deviance, made of topics too taboo to be discussed.

In my research, I've found that mass media place the blaming of scapegoats for sickness almost entirely in the sphere of consensus while relegating any critique of the economic structure creating such sickness almost entirely within the sphere of deviance. As the COVID-19 pandemic churned on, and as more people faced homelessness, job loss, and the risk they might be killed by suicide, COVID parties were a useful story for the ruling class. For, if everyday people were going to purposely give each other the virus, then society did not need to critique the class structure fueling transmission—and the ruling class stood a better chance of having its largesse unquestioned (and even increased).

Good Morning America is produced by ABC News. ABC News is owned by the Walt Disney Company (net value: $130 billion), which is chaired by Bob Iger (net worth: $690 million). All corporate media companies' chiefs and stockholders have a strong vested interest in paying low taxes, and they rarely have to fear an increase, even in a pandemic. But this is particularly obvious when corporations like Disney have their own venture capital firm and when ABC's advertisers include companies like Google and Apple, which *really* don't want to pay taxes.

Especially in times of unrest, it is advantageous for these corporations if the masses are angrier at one another for not masking or distancing than they are at those above them in the economic hierarchy. When this is so, viral news stories will not only deflect opprobrium *away* from conglomerate media corporations but also generate viewership, clicks, and advertising *for* those same corporations. Such an arrangement creates a world where people with viruses may feel compelled to kill themselves rather than a world where everyone has the resources they need to extend gentle care to one another.

Through news media, stigma doesn't just make some people hyperaware that they live with a virus; it tries to trick people like Michael, Gaëtan, Robert, and Olivier—and in the case of COVID-19, young people working service jobs—into believing that *they* themselves are viral parasites. And it tries to trick everyone (including, I am embarrassed to say, me at times) into feeling like we should be afraid of them.

While referring to anyone as a "zero" is a linguistic reduction, reducing anyone to *any* number dehumanizes them. In South Korea, a sixty-one-year-old woman known as Patient 31 was vilified after thousands of COVID-19 cases were traced to her having attended a church service.

But being named a number isn't really the issue. It's equally problematic that Olivier felt he couldn't share his status as it is to name people as a vector; it kept him from being fully himself with his parents and friends and with me, and it may have cost him his life.

People living with viruses need support to lead full lives, for they are too often unfairly made to feel the infinite weight of zero—that they're nothing, a drain, a parasite.

But there is an actual parasite at work, a truly powerful one that often goes unexamined in popular media. This parasite is the reason why, six months after the first ABC News reports of "COVID parties," there were, in fact, large parties at the University of Alabama. But they weren't thrown by students conniving to transmit COVID-19. Rather, they were thrown in response to that university's leaders' decision to hold classes in person, to continue the school's football program, and to send its athletes off to (win) a championship game.

This parasite is the reason why, a quarter century after effective HIV treatment has been available, somewhere between 480,000 and one million people still die each year from that virus.

This parasite is the reason why, after many COVID-19 vaccines were successfully developed, billions of humans went unvaccinated longer than they needed to, just to protect the intellectual property rights and profits of a few drug companies.

People who live with and die from viruses are *not* the parasites.

The parasite is capitalism.

3

PARASITE

(Capitalism)

In February 2020, I emailed a former boyfriend who lived in his home country of the Republic of Korea. We'd met in the southern United States many years before and had enjoyed a perfect love affair in 2007, while we were both living in the same city temporarily for work. A brilliant scientist, he had a small mouth that always produced a big smile due to his enormous, dimpled cheeks. I'd taken him for soul food, and he told me about life in Seoul. When he drove me to the airport after our last night together, I cried a little, but we visited each other a couple times and have been long-distance friends ever since.

When I emailed him, it was just a few weeks after the first cases of the novel coronavirus had been documented in the United States and in South Korea on the very same day. But that wasn't why I'd thought to touch base with him; I wrote because we shared a love of cinema and the movie *Parasite* (기생충; *Gisaengchung*) had surprisingly just won the Oscar for Best Picture.

It was an odd choice for the Academy of Motion Picture Arts and Sciences's highest honor. Just a few months prior to winning two Oscars himself, the film's director, Bong Joon-ho, was asked by writer E. Alex Jung about "the fact that no Korean film had ever been nominated for an Oscar. 'It's a little strange, but it's not a big deal,' he says, shrugging. 'The Oscars are not an international film festival. They're very local.'" The film was almost entirely in the Korean language, featured no stars who were famous in the United States, and had been directed by a man who was calling the Academy provincial.

While an armistice agreement was signed in 1953, technically, the Korean War has never ended, which means that *Parasite* is set in a region of the world where the United States has been engaged in a simmering war for seven decades. Most controversially, *Parasite* indicts the very economic system by which the Oscars are meant to earn producers a maximum return on their financial investment. When asked how a film about "the Korean class struggle" had become embraced globally, Bong told film writer Kate Hagen, "I think maybe there is no borderline between countries now because we all live in the same country, it's called capitalism."

Parasite tells the story of the family of a young man in Seoul named Ki-woo Kim (who later goes by "Kevin") and the other members of the Kim family: Ki-woo's father, Ki-taek ("Mr. Kim"); his mother, Chung-sook ("Mrs. Kim"); and his sister, Ki Jung ("Jessica"). Ki-woo, a poor young man, is not in college and has few prospects. He, his sister, and his parents are all out of work, and the entire Kim family lives in a tiny basement apartment in Seoul, where they are routinely subjected to fumigation by municipal exterminators. Early in *Parasite*, the family is seen being gassed in their own home, as if the city wants to rid itself of poor people like them, just as it might want to destroy vermin such as rats and cockroaches, or viruses infecting the city.

For older South Korean viewers, the gassing scene might recall the widespread use of dichlorodiphenyltrichloroethane (DDT), primarily in urban areas and around American military bases after World War II (and in the most active years of the Korean War in the 1950s), and of how tear gas was used on student and labor activists during the *minjung* democracy protests in South Korea of the 1970s and '80s. But when I went to see *Parasite* on the big screen three times in 2019, it reminded me of three times I had personally experienced being gassed.

The most recent memory was as a reporter in Ferguson in 2014, when

I saw residents of West Florissant Avenue ordered into their homes by a tank under Missouri governor Jay Nixon's curfew. As the police began gassing their street, elderly Fergusonians became stuck in their houses and had to make a terrible decision: *Should I stay at home and be gassed, or flee and be arrested for breaking curfew?* It also brought me back to Southern California in 1989 and to Brooklyn in 1999, two instances a continent and a decade apart, when I'd been chased inside to avoid helicopters spraying the insecticide malathion. In California, the choppers were trying to kill crop-damaging medflies, and in Brooklyn, they were trying to kill West Nile virus–carrying mosquitoes. But in both cases—as in fictional *Parasite* and very real Ferguson—regardless of their intended targets, the gas hit people at home, too.

By the time I saw *Parasite* for a fourth time, at home during the quarantine summer of 2020, I remembered seeing U.S. police tear-gas protesters in a wide variety of settings in some one hundred cities to tamp down antiracist dissent, and China spraying entire cities with disinfectant to tamp down coronavirus. The gassings are a reminder of how toxic attempts to control viruses often cause collateral damage to the bodies of the very people those viruses are most likely to infect.

In *Parasite*, when Ki-woo's friend, who is a student at university, prepares to study abroad, he asks Ki-woo to take over his job tutoring the daughter of the wealthy Park family. Helped by fake credentials forged by his sister, Ki-woo passes himself off to the Parks as college student "Kevin" and gets the job, eventually bringing his sister, "Jessica," into the Parks' home as an art teacher for their son. Eventually, Kevin and Jessica conspire to get the Parks' chauffeur fired, hiring their father in his place. Wanting a job for their mother, they go about getting the Parks' housekeeper, Moon-gwang, fired as well, by conning the Parks into thinking she has an infectious and highly stigmatized disease: tuberculosis. (Underscored by composer Jung Jae-il's unrelenting classical violins, the revelation of the fake TB diagnosis is the most wickedly funny scene in the film.)

When the Parks go camping, the entire Kim family moves into their mansion and lives it up. At that point, Bong Joon-ho seems to depict the Kims as a kind of virus, leeching off the host Parks' lives in the body of their beautiful home. But while trying to enjoy all the lovely trappings of capitalism, the Kims receive a rude surprise: the banished housekeeper, Moon-gwang, returns. Scaring the Kims into thinking they've been found out, Moon-gwang desperately reveals that, for years, ever since he took money from loan sharks he could not pay back, she's been hiding her husband, Geun-sae, in a secret subbasement below the Park mansion. (Geun-sae seems grateful for this life and even has erected an altar to Mr. Park, to whom he pays bloody homage.)

Moon-gwang and the Kims are *not* parasites, as such, of the wealthy Parks. Rather—as becomes obvious in the final act of *Parasite*—it is the Park family who is leeching off the labor of Moon-gwang and the Kims. As Karl Marx wrote in 1867, "Capital is dead labour that, vampire-like, only lives by sucking living labour, and lives the more, the more labour it sucks. The time during which the labourer works, is the time during which the capitalist consumes the labour-power he has purchased of him." (Marx was evoking not the kind of vampire in Bram Stoker's *Dracula*—that novel wouldn't be published until 1897—but likely the folktales that also inspired Stoker, which humanized the parasitic qualities of bloodsucking bats.)

With his film, Bong taps into a common feeling among lower- and middle-class workers around the globe that the "time during which the labourer works" has no boundaries; it exists around the clock, leaving workers no time for themselves, sucking their blood, and trapping them in untenable circumstances, as Geun-sae is trapped in that basement for years without light or fresh air. Indeed, this was a sentiment shared even by many real-world professional-class laborers when they began working from home in 2020.

Parasite shows how capitalism orders relationships within intimate domestic spaces. In order to have time for high-paying jobs in which they can accumulate more capital, the upper classes depend upon low-paid workers to complete an increasingly absurd number of domestic tasks.

The film points to an international system (outside white/nonwhite U.S. race relations) that structures these relationships globally. It shows how capitalism requires an underclass whose life value is depleted and sucked upward, "vampire-like," toward the ruling class. Meanwhile, because of the material conditions of the underclass, the viral risk is concentrated there, both metaphorically and in reality.

Many domestic workers in the United States were sent away during the pandemic, lest they infect those they served. And yet, more of the professional class's domestic tasks than ever were performed by newly designated "essential workers"; they were just done off-site.

Essential workers did not include just nurses and doctors. The category of folks who did not get to work from home included people cooking food for minimum wage in fast-food restaurants, delivering food via Uber Eats, and shopping for groceries. The people who performed these tasks were often not legal employees at all, but "contractors," with no guaranteed salary or benefits. Initially, these crowd-sourced human shields performed their work without personal protective gear, taking on viral risk so those above them in the class hierarchy could be safer. But the term *essential worker* is misleading: the *jobs* were considered essential, but the *workers* performing them were considered expendable. If someone died doing these jobs—and they did—they'd be replaced by someone else who couldn't afford to avoid viral risk like the people staying at home.

According to a study published by the School of Public Health at the University of California, Berkeley, the most lethal "essential" job during the first year of the COVID-19 pandemic in California was line cook in a restaurant. Line cooks died at higher rates because they performed work in poorly ventilated, crowded spaces and because they were often poorly paid, undocumented, didn't have health insurance, and lived in crowded households. During the pandemic, most people did not need to eat in restaurants; if the goal of the lockdown was to keep people distanced to prevent transmission, bulk food could have been distributed more safely to people's homes, where they could have cooked it themselves (or, if they were workers who had to leave their homes, where they could have made lunches to eat on the job without restaurants). But line cooks were justified as essential to try to keep the economy going—because capitalism demanded that fast-food chains keep operating, even if the "essential" line cooks had to sacrifice their lives.

* * *

Throughout human history there have been modes of exchange and even commerce within most societies, but they were not necessarily *capitalist*. Capitalism is often presented in educational systems, journalism, and popular culture as the pinnacle of human organizing, a system by which humans, acting rationally, bring their goods and services to a common marketplace to make logical trades with one another, lowering poverty and improving the quality of life for everyone as they do. But capitalism is not predicated upon free exchange at all; rather, it is an all-consuming system whose central incentive is to extract value, or capital, for profit. It does so by usurping the entirety of the lives of workers, including those who are enslaved.

If this sounds extreme to you, just think about how many times you've been told, by your job or by a self-help book, that your personal value is defined by your productivity. This places capitalism's economic goals at odds with human health. And because of this pressure to optimize value creation on the backs of, and at the expense of, workers at every turn in its development, capitalism has created a viral underclass.

Capitalism rose as a system intertwined with the trade in human cargo, especially in the seventeenth and eighteenth centuries. As we saw in chapter 1, this enriched those who owned enslaved humans (and all industries associated with this barbaric practice) while also exporting pathogens across the seas. As capitalism moved, in the nineteenth century, from a reliance on enslaved labor to a reliance on wage labor, it created appalling conditions in the form of dangerous factories and crowded housing, in which viruses flourished among the proletariat, or working class—anything to keep operation costs down and profits up.

And while state-sponsored medical research improved life expectancy dramatically in the twentieth century, capitalism increasingly made sure those gains were not felt by all. For example, state-funded pharmacological research created medications to stop the effects of HIV by 1996. But in order to protect the profits of the private corporations contracted to develop those medications with state monies, the drugs were manufactured in and for only wealthy countries for a long time (when they could have been produced en masse around the world to save lives faster). This meant that even as death rates in the United States declined, AIDS deaths globally continued to soar for another seven years. Shockingly, more people died of AIDS *after* there were effective medications than before, either because those people couldn't afford the medications or because the medications weren't available in their country at all.

Capitalism distorts the world so that *the* reason for human existence becomes the accumulation of value by the ruling class—even if that means the viral underclass must perish. By 2021, there were many effective vaccines to treat the novel coronavirus. However, their patents weren't freely shared globally as a way to produce as many doses as quickly as possible to save lives and tamp down the virus before it could mutate further. The reason was capitalism. Drug companies wanted to protect the intellectual property of what they had made and to treat it as a private, profit-generating good, even though their research was largely funded by state grants and even though sales were guaranteed by government purchases.

Capitalism also creates a sense of alienation, as people become separated from the means of production that make life itself possible (i.e., farmers can't eat their own goods because they need to sell them to turn a profit; carmakers learn only one part of making a car but not how to make the whole thing, in order to maximize assembly-line productivity; a housekeeper like Moon-gwang in *Parasite* doesn't get to enjoy time in her own home, and her husband, Geun-sae, learns to live without sunlight). When their countries are raided or destabilized by global capitalism, people can even be forced to leave their homelands to survive, only to be exploited again in the countries to which they flee.

Side effects of capitalism can include a sense of alienation even within one's own body. For instance, Michael Johnson's body was used as an athlete by his university, while he was a college student who couldn't really read. The wealth generated by a young athlete's enormous talent doesn't benefit the athlete as much as it does a team owner's wallet or a university coach's salary; the athlete's body becomes a vessel out of which someone else siphons capital and accumulates the value of their labor elsewhere—even at the expense of the athlete's health and well-being.

Perversely, viral infection and other illnesses can do the same. Under capitalism, pharmacological treatment isn't just an opportunity to bring healing to an afflicted person, but a business opportunity to extract value out of that person's body. The Greek drag queen Zackie Oh once referred to his HIV medication by describing "that awkward moment when you realize that the most expensive thing in your house is your antiretrovirals!"

That's capitalism. Capitalism exploits humans' best abilities and their vulnerabilities alike and their relationships with others. The system does not breed wellness; it produces widespread need that can never quite be met, leading to ongoing crises that can be exploited for profit.

* * *

Karl Marx asserted that history is driven by class conflict—by the creation of different classes and by the tension between them in gaining access to the resources necessary to live well that help define the very meaning of life on earth. Yet, until the end of *Parasite*, the conflict is mostly *intra*class conflict, not *inter*class conflict. The poor families fight one another for limited job opportunities and don't join forces to take on the upper class that is oppressing them both. Rather than trying to take resources from the wealthy Parks, the Kims and Moon-gwang and her dungeon-dwelling husband fight among themselves; the parasite of capitalism uses their bodies as a host to replicate itself. But in the final moments of the film, we do see an eruption of the class conflict Marx identified.

In the penultimate sequence, the chauffeur, Mr. Kim, is forced to dress up as an "Indian" alongside Mr. Park for the Parks' son's birthday—there is even a teepee ordered from the States—on what is supposed to be Mr. Kim's day off. This is a nod to the United States' role as an occupying force in the Korean Peninsula since the end of World War II, much as the United States had already colonized the North American continent. (Note that to pull off their deceit as they move into the Parks' lives, the Kims take on contemporary American English names.) Unknown to Mr. Kim, the housekeeper, Moon-gwang, is accidentally killed by Mrs. Kim, and his son, "Kevin," has tried (and failed) to kill Geun-sae.

As "Indians," Mr. Park and Mr. Kim, clad in war paint and headdresses, are supposed to pretend to attack the Kims' daughter, "Jessica," with a tomahawk axe as she brings out the birthday cake. Instead, Geun-sae emerges from the subbasement and mortally stabs Jessica with a real knife. Chaos breaks out. While trying to save her daughter, Mrs. Kim is attacked by Geun-sae and kills him with a kebab skewer. In his final breaths before dying, Geun-sae tells his idol, Mr. Park, that he has "respect" for him, but ironically, the confused rich man doesn't even know who Geun-sae is. Mr. Park becomes focused solely on evacuating his family from the melee, screaming at Mr. Kim to stop trying to save his bleeding daughter and give him the car keys. Mr. Park is so disgusted by Geun-sae's smell, he holds his nose (echoing a disdain he's had throughout the film for the odor all his employees share because their salaries force them to live literally among pesticides and human feces). In the end, Mr. Kim explodes, stabbing his employer to death.

But the capitalist logic that has infected the Kim family is not so easily excised. In the final sequence of the film, the theory of false consciousness (coined by Marx's *Communist Manifesto* coauthor, Friedrich Engels) is illustrated in Kevin's fantasy. The Parks have sold their home, new owners have moved in, and Mr. Kim has moved into the secret subbasement to live in exile and avoid murder charges. As he mourns his father, Kevin fantasizes about going to college, working, and becoming so rich that he can buy the Park house. Then, he, his mother, and his father will be together and whole—illustrating Engel's theory of false consciousness, which encourages workers not to see themselves through the eyes of their actual circumstances, but through the prism of aspirational fantasies the ruling class wants them to believe.

It will never happen, of course, a point foreshadowed by the final piano chords of Jung Jae-il's haunting score. Kevin will never own that house. Perhaps his American name has made him prey to the same dynamic that makes many Americans hesitant about forming unions: because we think that, someday, we will be billionaires—and when we are, we won't want any greedy unions taking our billions.

The trick of capitalism, especially since the entrenchment of neoliberalism, is that it promises individual success via individual choice and productivity, placing all responsibility on the individual. This is an illusion, of course, and it obscures the real forces at play. I think of neoliberalism as the shifting of risk from the many onto the few—when the state, corporations, and other entities of concentrated wealth do not want to share risk, but instead place it on individuals. "It's all about *you*" is how architectural historian (and my former boyfriend) André Bideau once explained it to me. Neoliberalism warps access to education, medicine, and even clean water with a market logic. It sells itself under the illusion of choice, even as it denies people access to the necessary resources of life itself. For example, in the United States, when a worker loses their job (and with it, their health insurance), they are offered the "choice" of buying into their former employer's insurance plan via the 1985 Consolidated Omnibus Budget Reconciliation Act (more often known by its sinister acronym, COBRA). Since 2011, they could also buy into a plan under the Affordable Care Act ("Obamacare"), where the onus is on the unemployed worker to make the right choice in a market exchange. But if the premiums for a family are hundreds or even thousands of dollars a month to buy into COBRA or Obamacare, how much "choice" does a newly unemployed worker actually have?

The last scene of *Parasite* helps explain why many members of the middle and underclass in societies around the globe reacted to the COVID-19 pandemic with far less fury at oligarchs than they might have. Like Kevin imagining he'll own that house someday when he won't, we find our imaginations becoming blunted by neoliberal capitalism, which prevents us from thinking outside its system. Even though COVID-19 disrupted the entire world at once more than anything at any time in modern history ever had, we largely accepted that profit *must* be a priority with vaccines, no matter how many people died. Even when tens of millions had no income, we largely accepted that rent *had* to be paid to landlords (and when financial government assistance came in the United States, it often just passed through those in distress to landlords and holders of debt). And even when the right to health care was more obvious than ever in America, during the 2020 Democratic primary, voters did not rally behind Bernie Sanders, the candidate who'd championed Medicare for All; they chose Joe Biden, who does not believe in universal health care.

Mr. Kim may have killed his boss in *Parasite*, but he also became locked in the basement as a literal member of the underclass, living beneath yet another wealthy family. Usually, being suspended in a state of false consciousness allows the ruling class to run off with the car keys and leave the underclass holding the bag.

* * *

Why is the word *viral* helpful for describing not only gossipy news and what's going wrong in networked computers, but also for understanding how capitalism perpetually creates an underclass? First, viruses have been associated in our minds, fairly and unfairly, with deviant sex, intravenous drug use, poor hygiene, and incarceration. Even though literal viruses can pass via human activity as uncontroversial as drinking water, eating food, touching surfaces, or breathing air, viruses have never shaken their historic association with vice. This has shaped how we narrate the stories of people living with viruses, which in turn shapes the medicine and politics around how we treat them.

Though they are often used interchangeably in popular media and metaphors, viruses, bacteria, and parasites are not all the same thing. Long before the medical field of virology developed over the last century or so, and for the better part of a millennium, the word *virus* had been used to refer generically to any disease or sickness. It comes from the Latin word *virus*, referring to poison, slime, or the harmful sap of plants. It also forms the root of the word *virulent*, which, over the centuries, has meant diseased, bad, or even politically illiberal.

Physically, bacteria are smaller than living cells, and viruses are even smaller than bacteria. All viruses are parasites in that they need a host to live, but not all parasites are microscopic viruses. Bacteria can reproduce outside a host, but while some viruses can live for a short while outside a host, they can't reproduce outside one.

In the late eighteenth century, English surgeon Edward Jenner developed a vaccine for smallpox, the only infectious disease in human history ever to be eradicated, and around 1880, French biologist Louis Pasteur developed a vaccine against cholera bacteria. But neither researcher pinpointed the microscopic virus we now understand as the causal agent of so much biological activity. It wasn't until Russian botanist Dmitri Ivanovsky experimented on diseased tobacco plants in 1892 that scientists began to understand viruses as we now imagine them. Ivanovsky filtered sap from the diseased plants with material whose holes were small enough to retain bacteria; when the filtered sap was found to remain infectious and could make other plants sick, he knew something smaller than bacteria was passing through his filter. When Dutch microbiologist Martinus Beijerinck independently re-created similar experiments in 1898, he named the microscopic pathogens *viruses*.

As a system, capitalism preys on human hosts and eats away at their energy in ways both metaphorical (as seen in *Parasite*) and also quite literal. This process also opens the door to how viruses enter human bodies. But we have been socialized from childhood to unfairly conflate viruses, virulence, and the people who live with viruses as uniformly toxic. Consider that in fairy tales, viruses signal wickedness. Just look at drawings of warts (caused by the human papillomavirus, or HPV) on the faces of gnomes, ogres, or the witch in the first feature-length animated film, Disney's 1937 *Snow White and the Seven Dwarfs*. Similarly, jokes about herpes simplex virus (HSV) being caused by teen promiscuity pervade American pop culture, even though two-thirds of the world lives with herpes. But rather than accept these conflations, we should pull them apart. When we define humans by their most stigmatizing biological traits at the expense of affirming their whole personhood, we create vulnerabilities—the kinds of vulnerabilities that viruses exploit and that can create a viral underclass.

Once parasitic viruses burrow inside any one person, they can sometimes move very easily between other humans. And when they do, they are able to harm not just the person physically placed in their path, but everyone in that person's social network. This is a natural by-product of a capitalist system in which the flip side of exploitation is reliance, meaning that the fates of everyone in the system are deeply intertwined—something thrown into stark relief by the sudden rebranding of workers earning minimum wage as "essential." In such a highly connected world, even the patriarch at the top of the ruling class is vulnerable and can become infected—as President Donald Trump showed in real life when he was hospitalized with COVID-19. This is why *this* virus has unnerved the ruling class around the world more than others; as the casually transmitted SARS-CoV-2 dropped a match into decades of social kindling, those rulers became aware that the blast might reach even them.

U.S. society *could* share the risks of health with universal health care. The risks of the novel coronavirus of 2019 *could* have been shared with robust state support for protection, housing, and food security. The billionaire class *could* have shared the wealth their employees earned, instead of making themselves richer and their workers poorer throughout 2020. But because the state (at the behest of the wealthy who control it) did not want to share this risk, the onus was put on every individual to figure out COVID-19 largely on their own.

This is not a bug of capitalism; it is one of its defining features.

* * *

While SARS-CoV-2 was certainly floating around before this date, South Korea and the United States both recorded their first cases on January 20, 2020. At the time, what this would portend was so unimaginable that, when I corresponded with my former lover in Seoul in February about *Parasite*, we didn't even discuss it.

In his country, the first wave of its COVID-19 outbreak peaked with 909 daily cases on February 29, five weeks after its first case and only three weeks after *Parasite* won the Oscar. By July, South Korea had just 284 confirmed deaths and about 13,000 confirmed cases in total. Meanwhile, in the United States, we were seeing three times more (40,000) new cases every *day* by that July and had already amassed about 130,000 confirmed deaths.

In the initial months of the pandemic, South Koreans benefited from having a universal health care system. (Though much of it is privatized and fee-based, the costs are low.) Meanwhile, the United States has no universal health care, and the costs of its patchwork system are very high. In the United States, millions of people who lost their jobs in the pandemic *also* lost their health care, joining the millions who never had it in the first place.

Additionally, as my friend, writer E. Tammy Kim, wrote in the *New York Times*, South Korean government, businesses, and citizens took to wearing masks earlier and more collectively than their U.S. counterparts. As Kim reported, the South Korean government coordinated the manufacturing of masks and then subsidized their sale for modest prices in pharmacies and post offices. This kind of state intervention with masks (or much of anything) simply didn't occur in the United States in the first and second COVID-19 waves, where Amazon profits soared, price gouging of essential supplies went largely unregulated, states bid against one another for medical equipment, and the Trump administration went so far as to stop a plan to distribute 650 million masks to every address via the U.S. Postal Service. (The Biden administration never took up this plan and only began distributing masks through pharmacies after the deadly Delta and Omicron surges had taken hundreds of thousands of lives.) The guiding principle in America seemed to be that the market would save us. But it wouldn't, because under the guise of American individualism, neoliberal capitalism generally organizes itself by having the poor, rather than the public state, pay for things they need (like masks in a pandemic). This keeps taxes lower and ensures that those who privately control things people need (like Amazon) can concentrate more capital.

But even in South Korea, which touts an effective, enlightened capitalism and which, early on, succeeded in containing COVID-19 for a while (and always kept death rates far lower than the United States), it was easy to shift the blame onto those living in economic precarity when politically expedient. In response to one of the Republic of Korea's first spikes after rates had fallen, press and government officials went after gay people who had been to a bathhouse where the virus spread, outing them in a culture that is deeply homophobic. In May 2020, the bulk of the country's second wave of coronavirus infections was traced to a gay club in Seoul's Itaewon neighborhood; two people at the club had also visited a gay bathhouse.

Quickly, even though the gay nightclub and bathhouse were cooperative with contact tracing, blame was heaped upon gay South Koreans for the resurgence. Because the level of the virus was low and the level of contact tracing was high, the cluster was contained. But a twenty-five-year-old man in the cluster who tested positive was arrested for lying to authorities. The exact charge was that while he cooperated in answering many questions honestly, he said he didn't have a job when, in fact, he worked as a tutor for hire. As the *Los Angeles Times* reported, the man's name isn't known; nor is his sexuality. But he seems to have been financially precarious; perhaps he depended upon his tutoring gigs in real life as desperately as Kevin/Ki-woo does in *Parasite*. Maybe he withheld certain information because he didn't want his clients to fire him because they thought he was infectious or gay.

Essential workers in the United States faced the same conundrum. One of the perverse ironies of capitalism is that it organizes everything in society around incentives to make money at the expense of everything else—but when the poor do this, they are shamed. If an undocumented worker who picks crops (that people working safely from home are eating) has a fever, what are they supposed to do? Stay home? When they are not eligible for government help and facing eviction? Can they be judged for working while sick to avoid the starvation of their children?

The Korean tutor may have faced a similar dilemma. After spending six months in jail awaiting trial, he was convicted of lying to contact tracers. According to Al Jazeera, the court ruled that he was responsible for eighty infections of COVID-19 and sentenced him to two additional years in prison. As it did with SARS-CoV-2, and as the United States has done with HIV, the Republic of Korea also prosecutes people living with HIV, though rarely. But when the 1987 AIDS Prevention Act is invoked in South Korea, the maximum penalty is only three years' imprisonment.

I have never been to South Korea, let alone sat in one of its courtrooms where people were prosecuted for transmitting viruses. But in 2015, I did get to sit through every second of such a trial in the United States, where HIV exposure can send someone to prison for *life*. And in that courtroom, I learned that when it comes to using law and order to produce a viral underclass, South Korea can't compete for cruelty with the American empire occupying it.

II

LAW AND ORDER

Then Aaron shall lay both his hands on the head of the live goat, and confess over it all the iniquities of the people of Israel, and all their transgressions, all their sins, putting them on the head of the goat, and sending it away into the wilderness by means of someone designated for the task. The goat shall bear on itself all their iniquities to a barren region, and the goat shall be set free in the wilderness.

—Leviticus (וַיִּקְרָא) 16:21–22

4

GUILTY UNTIL PROVEN INNOCENT

(The Law)

In May 2015, after a year and a half in jail, Michael Johnson was finally about to get his day in court.

Shortly after he was led into the courtroom of Judge Jon Cunningham prior to the voir dire, his handcuffs were removed before any potential jurors were ushered in for jury selection. Unlike the first time we'd met, he was not wearing a dumpy orange jumpsuit, but a crisp red tie and a bright blue dress shirt that outlined his athletic form.

Johnson was on trial for infecting two men with HIV and "recklessly" exposing four others to it. Under Missouri law, people living with HIV are required to tell all their sexual partners that they are infected, even if they practice safe sex. Long before viral videos of NYPD arrests five years later, when almost exclusively Black and brown people were violently beaten by police for failing to practice social distancing or wear masks in the early days of the COVID-19 pandemic, *State of Missouri v. Michael L. Johnson* was the highest-profile pathogen-related prosecution in the United States. Johnson was accused not merely of keeping his HIV status to himself but of willfully lying to his partners, telling them he was HIV-negative before engaging in what the prosecutor would call the most "dangerous" form of sex possible.

While particular modes of viral transmission in the case made many people squeamish, *Missouri v. Johnson* elucidated a difficult truth about virology: viruses move in messy ways. Disease spreads between humans when a virus burrows into the cells of one person, replicates, then hitches a ride out of that person's body in some gaseous, solid, or liquid form (through breath, semen, stool, milk, blood, skin, or vaginal secretion) and enters the body of another. Some modes should require active consent (sex); some, passive consent (handshakes); some, no consent at all (breath). Even though some modes are more stigmatized than others, viruses move among us through *normative* life activities—when parents and children share natal blood, when friends share a hug, when believers pray together, when lovers share semen, when strangers share the same sharp puncture of a mosquito's bite.

Viruses remind us that we are not autonomous individuals, and they pass through barriers more porous than we perceive them to be. Attempting to prevent their spread via punitive law is an ineffective way to stop transmission. And yet, that is and has long been a major state response to viruses.

"For centuries," my friend, sociologist Trevor Hoppe, has written, "quarantine was a staple of public health efforts to combat such scourges as the plague and Spanish flu" and the punishment for breaking it could be severe. As French philosopher Michel Foucault wrote of the plague in seventeenth-century Europe, breaking "a prohibition to leave the town" could result in the "pain of death."

Quarantine *was* widely used around the globe during the COVID-19 pandemic before there was a vaccine. But as Trevor notes, for the most part, the crude use of quarantine law largely disappeared over the course of history as "improved nutrition and sanitation, and then the advent of vaccines, antibiotics, and new treatments—effectively put an end to diseases that had once killed or maimed millions, such as polio and smallpox. In this context, public health practitioners in the mid-twentieth century began to view quarantine and coercive public health tactics as retrograde approaches of yesteryear."

But instead of being a tool of last resort in an emergency, contemporary public health laws, particularly in North America, have also been used to punish sick people, stigmatize minoritized groups, and justify eugenic population-control measures. In the early twentieth century,

Mary Mallon, often disparagingly known as "Typhoid Mary," was kept in quarantine as an asymptomatic carrier of typhoid fever for more than twenty-six years; her incarceration was, in part, because she was a single woman and an Irish immigrant, two groups that frightened the ruling class. Similarly, the fear of the bubonic plague in San Francisco in the late nineteenth century led to the quarantining of the city's Chinatown. A century later, the National Park Service acknowledged that this was "motivated more by racist images of Chinese as carriers of disease than by actual evidence of the presence of bubonic plague." Still, this helped justify a decades-long extension of the federal Chinese Exclusion Act of 1882, which forbade mostly male Chinese workers in the United States from bringing their families to join them (and, when paired with antimiscegenation laws, kept them from reproducing). And while about seventy-five countries have HIV-specific laws, a working paper by the Global Commission on HIV and the Law found that "Canada and the US have, in absolute terms, convicted more people (a disproportionate number from minority ethnic, especially African and Afro-Caribbean communities) for HIV exposure and transmission offences than all the other countries of the world combined."

In response to viruses, the law does not only attempt to manage disease; in the spectacle of a courtroom, it can warp the public's understanding of science itself. And with the weight of the law behind it, a trial's outcome can legitimize ideas that are detrimental to public health and not scientific at all—ideas that create and perpetuate a viral underclass.

* * *

Days before he was scheduled to stand trial, as his lawyer tried to negotiate a plea deal, the then-twenty-three-year-old Johnson rejected the idea—even after a friend visited him in jail and begged him to reconsider and despite how Johnson said he had spent months in solitary confinement due to his HIV status, not even allowed to attend church services. He was innocent, he said, and had confidence in the American criminal justice system. But it was statistically unlikely that he would be found not guilty. While data in Missouri were scarce at the time, the year *Missouri v. Johnson* went to trial, the Williams Institute at the UCLA School of Law analyzed 390 HIV cases that went to court in California. Of those, 389 resulted in convictions—a conviction rate of 99.74 percent.

Before any potential jurors entered, I took a seat near the rear of the courtroom, opened my laptop (which was allowed, though I couldn't record audio), and began taking notes. The prosecutor, Philip Groenweghe, addressed Judge Jon Cunningham, who was, coincidentally, the same judge I'd seen preside over many drug arraignments while I waited to interview Johnson. The opening moments of the trial revealed a presumption of guilt upon Johnson and, oddly, upon me.

"Some of the so-called journalists, from what I've read of their articles, are more activists, and they have a right to be here, of course, but I have concerns about them making statements under their breath[,] and if they're elbow to elbow with the jurors[,] I'll never know if they made those comments," Groenweghe told the judge. "Frankly, you know, why anyone wants to see jury selection is beyond me," he added, before asking that I be preemptively admonished.

Judge Cunningham declined to admonish me specifically, but he did reasonably say, "Whether or not you're a member of the press, same difference, during the process I just want to make sure that you don't speak about the case anywhere where a juror could hear you." Still, the prosecutor's request was meant to intimidate me. From that point forward, during the weeklong trial and multiple hearings in the years after, the same bailiff would watch me intently in that courtroom, often with his hand resting on his gun as he stared me down. Outed to the court officers as a "so-called journalist" (who would later have to sue that court to obtain public documents), I began to feel, with *Missouri v. Johnson*, a bit like I was on trial as a nosy Black gay man.

Meanwhile, Johnson was subjected to a foreshadowing of how things would go for him that morning. As jury selection began, it was clear that no one had shown up to support him. His own mother wasn't there—she would arrive late and leave before the trial ended—and his only ally that morning was his public defender, Heather Donovan, a petite white woman in a gray suit. When she stood up in front of the pool of potential jurors for the first time, she told them, "An arrest is a mere accusation. So, does everybody understand that as we're sitting here today, given that the State has not presented any evidence, if we took a vote right now, that everybody would have to vote Mr. Johnson guilty of all the offenses; does anybody have a problem with that theory?"

The courtroom groaned.

"Not guilty. I'm sorry," Donovan corrected herself.

But the damage had been done. The fifty-one potential jurors thought even Johnson's *own lawyer* didn't think he should be considered innocent until proven guilty.

Over the next five days, as a procession of sex partners, police, and medical experts, and Johnson himself, testified, what unfolded was a courtroom drama that, on the surface, pitted an aggressive prosecutor against a hapless public defender, but that, in a deeper sense, pitted Johnson against America's deeply entrenched attitudes about race and sexuality. Characterized by his sexual partners as being "large" and "too tight" for condoms, Johnson's penis would be described in unusually graphic and at times almost absurd detail in police reports and, later, on the stand. It would even be shown to jurors in still images from a sex tape that he and one of his partners made.

And just as important, *Missouri v. Johnson* would also show how the law could distort both the science regarding a virus in a courtroom and scientific understanding of virology (and people living with viruses) in wider society. This is exactly how activist Sean Strub first conceived of the term *viral underclass.*

Sean once told me one of the main reasons that HIV criminalization concerned him was because it meant that the "government was creating a different law based on an immutable characteristic," which relegated people living with HIV to second-class citizenship. On paper, U.S. laws do not generally discriminate explicitly against people for things they cannot change about their bodies, like race. But people living with HIV, including children born with the virus, are permanently consigned to explicit legal discrimination. And prior to when the Affordable Care Act banned the practice, laws governing health insurance allowed people with many preexisting medical conditions to be discriminated against by being denied coverage.

Consider how the Missouri AIDS law allowed prosecutions for actions, according to the HIV Center on Law and Policy, "posing no or negligible risk of HIV transmission, such as spitting and biting" as felonies, with up to fifteen years in prison. The law doesn't take into account that people living with HIV who are on medication and with undetectable viral loads will not transmit the virus to others.

Yet, when a prosecutor is able to land a conviction for someone for HIV exposure despite these untruths, the law leads the public to believe that spitting *does* transmit HIV, and that people on meds *can* transmit the virus. It leads the public to believe that those with HIV are inherently dangerous to society. And this, in turn, shapes public opinion, future legislation, and the kinds of medical policies that get funded.

* * *

Of the fifty-one potential jurors in *Missouri v. Johnson*, only one appeared to be nonwhite (a retired African American woman nurse), and all identified as straight. Most looked to be in their fifties or older.

During questioning, about half the would-be jurors said being gay was a "choice." Only a third agreed that being gay was "not a sin."

No potential juror acknowledged having HIV. All said they believed that people living with HIV who do not tell their sexual partners that they have the virus should be prosecuted.

When asked, not a single person said they had any distrust of the police, even though the Ferguson uprising had occurred thirty miles away just a few months before, after Darren Wilson's shooting of Michael Brown exposed the systemic racism of law enforcement. Across the United States, even white people were questioning the role of police in society—and yet everyone in that jury pool testified that they trusted the police. It is hard to imagine that these views did not influence the way they approached testimony from police, or that the opposite view, a healthy skepticism of law enforcement, appropriately informed the jurors' deliberations.

The difference between the prosecutor, Groenweghe, and Donovan, Johnson's defender, was stark. Much of the time Groenweghe spoke eloquently and persuasively and without any notes at all. He stalked the courtroom, never asking the judge for permission to approach the bench. He would drop his voice to sound reasonable while addressing jurors, but he sometimes yelled and jabbed his finger at witnesses.

By comparison, Donovan, who appeared to be many years Groenweghe's junior, clutched her notes, the papers sometimes shaking. She routinely asked Judge Cunningham for his permission to approach the bench. When she spoke, she often stumbled over her words.

Groenweghe was backed up at all times by another attorney, Jennifer Bartlett, and by an omnipresent paralegal, along with a rotating cast of four or five police detectives, assistants, specialists, and a victim's advocate sitting right behind them in the first bench of the galley. Groenweghe's boss, St. Charles County prosecuting attorney Timothy Lohmar, a Republican, was a rising star from a local political dynasty; one day, the trial took a recess for the funeral of his father, a former judge.

Meanwhile, save for an assistant who would come into the courtroom once or twice a day for a few minutes to deliver papers, Public Defender Donovan was alone—except for her client, whom she often did not acknowledge, even neglecting to greet him most times he was led into court.

Weeding out whom he didn't want on his jury, Groenweghe warned that "there will be talk of ejaculation, of men having sex with men, all kinds of explicit discussions," and he wanted to know if such subject matter would offend the sensibilities of would-be jurors. He evoked the Bible and the Pope, citing scripture such as "the wages of sin is death" (Romans 6:23) and repeatedly asking the kinds of questions—and getting the kinds of bigoted answers—about homosexuals one can no longer ask about Black people outright. "I think it's kind of disgusting," one potential juror said in response to a question regarding what he'd heard about the case, before later being dismissed for having a drunk-driving conviction.

Months after the trial, Groenweghe told me he had been trying to weed out anyone who was antigay, but none of the younger potential jurors who explicitly rejected homophobia made it onto his jury. During the actual trial, Groenweghe's balding head and thick neck would turn almost red as he described the "lifestyle" of homosexuals. When talking about HIV and gay sexual acts, he appeared to have visible disgust as he spat out the words *semen*, *blood*, and *mucus membrane*, the parts of our bodies where pathogens are often exchanged. But during the jury selection, he spoke relatively evenly for nearly two hours, using his time to build the central argument he wanted his eventual jurors to buy: whenever people living with HIV don't tell their sexual partners that they're positive, that's a crime, even if their partners don't ask.

Donovan spoke for only about ten minutes during jury selection and brought up prejudice and racism rarely, such as when she asked potential jurors if they would have a problem hearing about interracial gay sex acts. But even before any witnesses were called, the ways in which homophobia is embedded in the law were obvious. At the time, same-sex marriage was still not legal in St. Charles County, and potential jurors felt free to openly express their antigay disgust. And Missouri law backed up how the people most likely to be affected *by* HIV (people who were Black, gay, or both) were the most likely to be blamed for it.

* * *

Once the trial began, it quickly became clear that *State of Missouri v. Michael L. Johnson* was not a case of "he said versus he said," but of "he said versus they said." Each of Johnson's six sex partners called to the stand testified that he had asked Johnson before they hooked up if he was "clean" or disease-free, and that he'd assured him he was.

But their testimony occasionally contradicted what they had initially told police, sometimes on crucial points. The jury never heard about several of these discrepancies, because Donovan sometimes failed to pounce on them during cross-examination, and when she did, she was often overruled. Like many clients relying on public defenders in Missouri (for alleged crimes viral or otherwise), Johnson was set up for failure by the state legislature. In 2018, the American Civil Liberties Union of Missouri would sue the state for underfunding its public defenses so much that Missouri ranked forty-ninth out of the fifty states in what it spent on average for court-appointed attorneys: a paltry $325.31 per case.

Even when an accuser's testimony wasn't contradictory, it revealed the complicated, murky decision-making that happens in sexual hookups, in those intimate spaces where viruses move between us. The sex partners all said the sex was consensual—they willingly engaged in sex that *could* transmit HIV—yet they often used passive language to describe how it was they'd come to have unprotected sex with Johnson, as if they held no responsibility for that decision.

Dylan King-Lemons, a lithe young white man, had been the first person to press charges against Johnson, prompting the prosecution to search for other alleged victims. And his accusation was one of the most serious: Johnson had not merely exposed King-Lemons to HIV, but had actually infected him. King-Lemons testified that he began his sexual relationship with Johnson in January 2013, when they were both students at Lindenwood University. King-Lemons said he was regularly tested for HIV, always asked his partners if they were HIV-positive, and had wanted to use a condom with Johnson.

But, he testified, Johnson had told him that he was HIV-negative, that the condom was "too tight and—too small," and that "they don't make condoms in his size." So, King-Lemons said, he agreed to have unprotected sex in the "traditional female role."

About two weeks later, King-Lemons testified, he went to Mercy Hospital with severe stomach pains. He was hospitalized twice, for a total of fourteen days, according to his testimony and that of his attending physician, Dr. Otha Myles, who is African American. King-Lemons was eventually diagnosed with gonorrhea and HIV.

He also experienced "HIV flu," a condition with symptoms similar to those of influenza, which can sometimes occur shortly after someone has been exposed to HIV, while their immune system is trying to understand what's happening. (Something similar can happen to people when they get a vaccine; your body can have flulike symptoms as it responds to feeling like it has just contracted measles, tetanus, or the novel coronavirus.) The timing of this condition, and the fact that King-Lemons and Johnson both had gonorrhea, formed the circumstantial basis of evidence tying King-Lemons's diagnoses to Johnson's.

But no scientific tests, such as genetic fingerprinting of the virus, were performed to determine if King-Lemons's strain of HIV was the same as Johnson's. This was significant because Johnson was facing the possibility of life in prison, a sentence similar to one for murder, a crime for which genetic fingerprinting is routinely performed. Genetic fingerprinting has been used in other HIV cases, and sequencing is routinely used to study clusters and outbreaks of various infectious diseases. Such sequencing has been very useful for understanding patterns of transmission with the novel coronavirus.

In his opening statement, Groenweghe said King-Lemons knew Johnson had to be the one who infected him because he was the only person King-Lemons had had sex with in the prior eleven months. On the stand, King-Lemons testified that he hadn't had sex with anyone else in nearly a year. But he'd given another story when he first went to police. King-Lemons declined to comment on this (or any matter) to me. His claim is a familiar one, and a dynamic I have found in years of reporting on viruses: from the common cold to COVID-19, people have an uncanny ability to know with certainty who they believe infected them. Even if they've had hundreds or thousands of encounters, any of which could have exposed them to a virus, they will often, with great precision, narrow it down to one encounter, even when such specificity is at odds with other things they report. To me, this facilitates a desire for punishment that, no matter how inaccurate, disease laws reinforce.

In her cross-examination, Donovan did not press King-Lemons on the discrepancies between his testimony in court and what he initially told the police—a point that called into question King-Lemons's credibility and cut to the very heart of the allegation that Johnson was the person who'd infected him. In court, Donovan did not point out that the prosecution had offered no scientific evidence that King-Lemons's and Johnson's viral strains matched.

There is a passage in the police report in which King-Lemons seems afraid that the tables will be turned and that he, the accuser, might become the accused. At trial, King-Lemons testified that he was then engaged to marry a man who was HIV-negative and that they had never had sex, not even with condoms, out of fear of transmission. King-Lemons also testified that without health insurance, his hospitalization had plunged him one hundred thousand dollars in debt and that he had had to declare bankruptcy. Bankruptcy records are public, and an extensive search I performed of online court databases turned up no record of King-Lemons's having filed for it. (When I asked Groenweghe about it later, he said he "didn't check bankruptcy records" and had merely taken King-Lemons at his word.)

King-Lemons's testimony perpetuated one myth and one sad reality about American health care. First, it affirmed the idea that people living with HIV can't have healthy sex lives, which is not true; the antiretroviral medication (ARV) that has been used for decades makes the virus in people living with HIV *undetectable and untransmittable* ("U = U"). Since the mid-1990s, HIV drugs have been able to suppress viral loads so much that they can make it impossible for someone living with HIV to transmit it to anyone else. Second, however truthful it was, King-Lemons's claim about facing bankruptcy reveals how the prosecution of sickness is intertwined with a for-profit health care system. If people did not fear crushing bills, they might not be so likely to try to seek revenge litigiously.

After King-Lemons, there was a parade of witnesses, all of whom condemned Johnson in some way, but many contradicted themselves from earlier statements they'd given, and all revealed how difficult it is to prove viral exposure. One was Andrew Tryon, a tall, thin, blond Lindenwood University cheerleader who consensually filmed a sexual encounter with Johnson (stills of which were printed and handed out to the jury). On the stand, Tryon testified that the sexual encounter he'd had with Johnson matched what the tape showed, but in his initial police report, Tryon described having sex with Johnson on three different occasions, and none matched what the video showed.

But the credibility of Johnson's partners was not on trial—not as to whether they may have exposed themselves to HIV through other sexual encounters, nor if what they were saying about Johnson was to be believed, and least of all if they bore any responsibility for the sex they'd willingly had. Groenweghe kept the focus on whether Johnson had told them he was HIV-positive.

Many doctors and medical experts who took the stand provided evidence that clearly hurt Johnson's case, testifying that he'd tested positive for HIV before he had sex with the six partners accusing him, that he had been treated for gonorrhea at least three times, and that he had received counseling that failing to disclose his HIV infection was a felony. But when two experts tried to testify that HIV is a manageable disease—that with current therapies, a person with the virus can expect to live almost as long as someone without it—Groenweghe objected vociferously. By doing so, he managed to conceal a key truth: HIV in 2015 is nothing like the death sentence it was when Missouri passed the 1988 AIDS law that Johnson was on trial for breaking.

* * *

Dr. Otha Myles, the doctor at Mercy Hospital who treated King-Lemons and testified for the prosecution, called HIV a "terminal" disease. But the defense's medical witnesses, Dr. David Hardy of UCLA Medical

School and Dr. Rupa Patel of Washington University in St. Louis and Barnes-Jewish Hospital, strongly disagreed that HIV is a "terminal" disease when treated properly.

The hospital where Patel worked was the very one where Robert Rayford, the Black teenager who presented with a mysterious cancer in the 1960s, was treated before dying of what is now believed to be AIDS. Patel testified that most people are afraid of HIV because of stigma and what they learned in the 1980s. But when they are treated properly, she said—those infected take as little as one pill a day—their life expectancy should be normal. She added that some patients need to see a doctor only every six to twelve months.

Among HIV experts, Patel's and Hardy's views were anything but controversial. A 2013 study estimated that a person in the United States or Canada who contracts HIV at age twenty and gets treatment "is expected to live into their early 70s, a life expectancy approaching that of the general population." Even if Johnson had transmitted HIV to King-Lemons, Hardy's and Patel's expert opinions were that it was the transmission of a treatable disease and not a death sentence.

Why, given this very uncontroversial medical reality, was the 1988 Missouri law still on the books? It is because laws embody our society's values, and our society values not only consigning certain people to the viral underclass, but also punishing them there, needlessly and viciously. If critical race theory can help us understand how racial disparities are produced by the law, a theory of the viral underclass can help us see how the law itself produces perverse inequalities because of pathogens. The 1988 Missouri AIDS law might have been outdated and unscientific. Still, it was valuable in letting prosecutors like Groenweghe (and his elected boss, Timothy Lohmar) come across as tough on crime. It allows the criminal justice system to crudely, and ineffectively, do the work of disease management, for no other reason than for prisons to gobble up as many surplus resources (and people) as they can. And it produces health disparities in the process.

When Patel attempted to compare HIV to other chronic medical conditions, arguing, for example, that HIV can be easier to treat than diabetes, Groenweghe successfully interrupted her arguments by objecting that she was trying to add unsolicited information to a yes-or-no question. Then, during cross-examination, Groenweghe attacked Patel, yelling at her that, "as a scientist and medical doctor," she was not doing her job properly. Whom, he demanded, did she work for: the public defender paying her or objective science? Groenweghe pointed out that Dr. Patel had not examined Johnson personally, and he accused her of not having reviewed all of the defendant's medical records.

Ultimately, he turned his ire on the public defender herself, accusing Donovan of withholding information from her witness. Donovan objected loudly, saying she "resent[ed]" Groenweghe's accusations. Judge Cunningham called the lawyers to the bench. From about twenty feet away, I could hear Donovan crying, telling the judge she was doing the best she could and working with what she had and that she was being personally attacked by Groenweghe. Her crying got louder as she said, "You are going to need to have a new trial in a few minutes, because I am going to be disqualified." Donovan then stormed out of the courtroom, abandoning an incredulous-looking Dr. Patel on the stand and leaving Johnson looking bewildered and alone.

When Donovan came back in briefly, her eyes still puffy, the bailiff brought her tissues. The judge called a recess for fifteen minutes, which stretched to nearly an hour until Donovan finally returned.

* * *

On the last day of testimony, Johnson took the stand in his own defense. He had learning disabilities and, by his own account, did not read or write very well. When Donovan asked him how he'd gotten to college, intending for him to explain his athletic scholarship, he answered that he'd gotten to Lindenwood University by taking a bus. (Over the years, I have found this detail to be a Rorschach test of sorts: some snicker that he answered literally; some have a classist attitude that he didn't own a car; others believe it reveals how he was so unaware of the situation that he never should have been permitted to testify.)

Calmly, deliberately, and slowly, Johnson testified that he had disclosed his HIV status to each of his six partners prior to having sex and that he remembered doing so with each one. Groenweghe then played an audiotape of Johnson talking in jail with Meredith Rowan, who had befriended him when he played soccer with her stepson and who had remained close to him. Unknown to the jurors or to me, and out of earshot, Donovan had objected to the inclusion of these calls as evidence. Breaking rules dictating the disclosure of evidence, the prosecution had given her more than twenty-four hours of audio recordings on the first day of the trial, preventing her from adequately preparing a defense for her client with full knowledge of the evidence against him. But Judge Cunningham had ruled against her.

On the tape, Johnson said it was difficult to tell Rowan something. The clip was very short and the context unclear, but Groenweghe said the exchange was about how hard it was to come out as HIV-positive. (Rowan and Johnson later told me that he was speaking about coming out as gay, but Johnson didn't challenge Groenweghe on the stand on this point.)

Groenweghe also surprised Johnson with a tape of him talking to his high school wrestling coach, in which he admitted that he was only "pretty sure" he had disclosed his HIV status to his partners.

Groenweghe smiled throughout the last jury day of *Missouri v. Johnson*, including in front of his adult children, who came to watch his closing arguments. His eyes twinkled as he recapped one piece of evidence after another undermining Johnson's credibility, and he warned the jurors that they needed to keep the public safe from Johnson, who roamed the world with a "calling card" of "HIV with a tint of gonorrhea mixed in," by convicting him and locking him up forever. It was the kind of move that stoked a fear not only of Johnson individually, but of people living with sexually transmitted infections broadly.

In her closing statement, Donovan repeated that her client had testified that he had told his partners that he was HIV-positive, and she made points she had been unable to get in during her cross-examinations. For the most serious charges of HIV transmission, she highlighted King-Lemons's contradictory stories on the stand and in previous statements, pointing out that he had altered the date for when he'd had an HIV test—all of which, she said, "bring reasonable doubt into when Mr. King-Lemons contracted HIV and from whom." Regarding one accuser, she said he didn't even talk to the police until more than a year after he'd told authorities his sole sex partner was someone other than Johnson.

That evening, just about two hours after closing arguments were finished, the jurors signaled that they had reached a conclusion: they found Johnson guilty of recklessly transmitting HIV to King-Lemons and of exposing or attempting to expose HIV to four of the other five men who'd pressed charges.

The following morning, the jury convened to hear evidence and arguments on what sentence they should give Johnson. For the transmission conviction alone, the minimum was ten years, while the maximum, according to the statute, was "30 years to life."

Christine King-Lemons, the mother of Dylan King-Lemons, testified for the prosecution at sentencing, telling the jury to send Johnson away for life. "Dylan's diagnosis is a life sentence without parole," she said through tears, even though, with medication, her son could go on to live a very normal life. "So I ask each of you: Why does Michael Johnson deserve any less?"

Eventually, Groenweghe turned on his own witnesses. He called Johnson's accusers "promiscuous." (Even some of *them* were in the viral underclass, for while King-Lemons had come forward to press charges against Johnson, some of the others later told me they had not wanted to press charges at all, and did so only when pressured by the state prosecutor, who ultimately threw *them* under the bus, too.) Hands in his pockets, eyes downcast, Groenweghe told the members of the jury that these young gay men "have a lifestyle I don't understand, that many of us don't understand." But, he said, HIV criminalization laws weren't put on the books by legislators just to protect these young men, but to protect the *public* health, including the health of the jurors.

Compared with the murder cases he'd tried in his career, Groenweghe said, this one was worse: a murder ended when a gun or knife killed someone, but the virus for AIDS that passed through Johnson could still be killing people for years. The HIV virus "may not have a mind," he said, "but it has an agenda. It's a very simple agenda: Make as many copies of itself as it possibly can and, toward that end, infect as many people as it possibly can." Michael Johnson could not have been a "more accommodating host" in this regard, he said, because he helped the virus spread by having sex "with one young man after another." HIV could wind up killing someone who had "never heard of Tiger Mandingo and who might not even be gay"—like, he said, a man who didn't want to press charges because he didn't want his wife to find out he'd had sex with Johnson. To me, this implied that while people who are gay *might* deserve sickness and early death, the good, straight people of the jury standing in for society did not. But this legal approach does not help public health. Facilitating the well-being of the viral underclass would keep rates of communicable disease in the wider society much lower than simply hoping those most likely to become infected will be locked up (or will just die out).

While the jury retreated to deliberate the sentence, spectators filled the courtroom close to capacity for the only time during the trial. Groenweghe's boss, Timothy Lohmar, came and watched, sipping a Diet Coke. In the gallery, I sensed the macabre but festive sensation of a lynching picnic. Not present was Meredith Rowan, who had to return to Indianapolis to care for her children, or even Michael's mother, who had hitched a ride back to her home in Indiana with Rowan. Other than his lawyer and me, Kimber Mallett, the professor of the class in which Johnson had been arrested almost two years before, was the only person who knew him at all and who would witness what would happen to him in person.

It took the jury about an hour to return with a sentence. As the people in the gallery rose and as the jurors filed in for the last time, I could hear several people crying and sniffling in the warm room, including the forewoman of the jury. When Judge Cunningham read that the jury was condemning Johnson to thirty years in prison for HIV transmission, there was an audible gasp in the chamber. There was absolute silence as he announced an additional 30.5 years of sentencing for three counts of exposure and one count for an attempt to expose someone to HIV. Johnson could serve 60.5 years in prison if the judge ordered the sentences to be served consecutively and if he did all that time, he would be more than eighty years old when he was released.

In a posttrial interview, Groenweghe said that the jury's verdict (not guilty on one count but guilty on all the others) "showed that they were fair.

"I think it shows how seriously they took the public health problem," he added. To think of HIV as anything other than a terminal disease was "awfully foolish," he said. It could be "managed," he conceded, but "has no cure."

Groenweghe also dismissed any suggestion of racial bias. His office had reviewed HIV prosecutions in St. Charles County, he explained, and found that only two of the six defendants, or 33 percent, were African Americans—clear evidence, he said, that there was no racial bias. But in Missouri, Black people make up less than 12 percent of the population, and in St. Charles County, just about 5 percent. Years later, research from the Williams Institute would show that, statewide, Black men were 5.5 percent of Missourians, but a majority of its HIV prosecutions. Race and class have always been linked in the United States, and laws that punish disease create a racialized caste system that punishes the people most likely to be living with viruses for having them.

* * *

To me, everything about *Missouri v. Johnson* was a way of seeing in action a concept called fundamental cause, which sociologist Victor Ray explains is when "a lack of resources (material, social, education) means that health outcomes are always likely to differentially impact those at the bottom of various social hierarchies. This is because resources allow people to develop protections (access to medicine or vaccines) that are harder to get if one lacks those resources." This was illustrated for me when, a few days after the trial ended, Johnson spoke to me from behind a glass wall in the St. Charles County jail.

Handcuffed, he had difficulty holding the black intercom receiver to his ear as he told me about the faith he'd had, and continued to have, in the U.S. justice system. Johnson said he'd expected nothing worse than a hung jury. But, he said, the jurors didn't believe him when he testified that he had told his sexual partners he was infected, because "the jury didn't believe a person would ever be with a person" sexually "who was HIV-positive."

An email I obtained showed Johnson's lawyer had been negotiating a plea deal of ten years, which Johnson had nixed. But he had "no regrets," he told me. "I was never going to take a plea," because "it would have been morally wrong," he said.

Johnson said he was still being held in solitary confinement up to twenty-three hours a day, as he had been on and off for several months. In jail, there is a torturous but common experience awaiting the viral underclass: folks living with HIV are often put in "administrative segregation," especially after they've been in a fight. The excuse given by wardens for this cruelty is that the prisoners could infect others—an irony, considering jails often take months to get HIV medications that would stop any cases of onward transmission among the people in their care.

Asked about facing sixty years in prison, Johnson said, "I've thought a lot about how this is something that could happen to other HIV-positive people. If I didn't stand up, who would? I learned from this trial how wrong it is to criminalize people with HIV. Once you have it, you have it for the rest of your life. You will be looking over your shoulder forever, fearing someone could say, 'This person didn't tell me. Lock him up!'"

On July 13, Judge Cunningham ruled that Johnson could serve his sentences concurrently and sentenced him to 30.5 years in prison.

His attorney filed for appeal a few days later, and Johnson was moved to the Fulton Reception and Diagnostic Center, a Missouri state prison about a two-hour drive west of St. Louis. If he served his full sentence, he would be set free when he was fifty-two years old, in the year 2045. The punishment was grotesquely out of proportion to the crime, and his sentence was longer than the average sentence for almost every other crime in the state. According to the Missouri Department of Corrections, Johnson's sentence exceeded the average for physical assault (19.9 years), forcible rape with a weapon (28.2 years), and even second-degree murder (25.2 years).

After the trial, Filip Cukovic, one of Johnson's sex partners, told me that while he thought HIV transmission laws should stay on the books, "Getting thirty years for exposing someone to HIV is just silly." He added, "It would be better for him if he'd killed someone instead."

At the time of Johnson's trial, U.S. prosecutions of HIV outside Missouri resulted in far less severe punishments, with some mandating counseling or a few months of probation. But in Missouri, two months after Johnson was sentenced, David Lee Mangum, a white man from the city of Dexter, was sentenced to thirty years for exposing others to HIV. The state's severe sentences cut against a national trend in medicine, which had begun moving away from dealing with HIV as a criminal matter. A wide swath of medical authorities (including the American Medical Association, the Association of Nurses of AIDS Care, and even the medical director for corrections medicine for the St. Louis County Department of Health) had recently gone on the record with their belief that prosecuting people for not disclosing their HIV status could facilitate an *increase* in the virus's transmission and harm the public health.

Even Charles Pfoutz, an accuser whose testimony did not lead to a conviction, said he didn't think Johnson "deserved thirty years" and should instead have gotten, "like in California, six months to a year." In a phone interview after the trial, Pfoutz told me he'd initially told the prosecuting attorney, "It's fifty-fifty. I'm responsible, he's responsible" for his HIV transmission.

Which raises a question: Who transmitted HIV to Johnson?

Johnson told me he "can't say who. . . . There's always an idea, but I wouldn't want to say if I don't know for sure."

If he did, would he want that person prosecuted?

"No, I wouldn't wish harm on anyone," Johnson said, shaking his head slowly behind the thick jail glass. "I wouldn't want this to happen to anyone."

* * *

Early in the COVID-19 pandemic, nations around the world began criminalizing coronavirus transmission in various ways. Some laws prosecuted people with positive diagnoses if they exposed others, some prosecuted those with unknown diagnoses for failing to wear masks. In New York City, the NYPD was briefly dispatched in May 2020 to enforce the state's social distancing rules, once knocking someone unconscious to do so. (A year later, when vaccines were widely available to them, only 43 percent of the NYPD had elected to take them, and the largest union of this violent force tasked with maintaining public safety eventually sued to try to stop its members from having to get vaccinated.) From California to Maryland, COVID-19 orders turned being out after curfew, breaking quarantine, or gathering in groups into criminal matters punishable by arrest. Predictably, these laws (like all U.S. laws) disproportionately impacted people of color, especially those going to essential jobs at night and denied the privilege of working from home.

South Korea made harsh examples of people who failed to disclose any information to contact tracers. Arresting anyone for COVID-19 was dangerous for the public health, as jails and prisons themselves became enormous engines of transmission. COVID-19 laws had the power to make the very act of breathing illegal. And once they did, such laws would make people less likely, not more, to openly communicate and work together to slow down the spread of the virus.

Research has repeatedly shown that laws governing the criminalization of HIV have no effect on its transmission. And just as *Missouri v. Johnson* made it even harder to get people to embrace prevention and testing, as HIV prevention workers told me, COVID-19 laws can provide an incentive not to know one's status.

There is also an absurdity in thinking of prosecution as a tool for pandemic prevention at a level of scale. When Johnson was sentenced, about thirty million people globally were currently infected with HIV. When the novel coronavirus pandemic began a few years later, nearly one hundred million people had been infected by HIV worldwide over four decades—and just a year later, one hundred million people were infected by SARS-CoV-2. All these hundreds of millions of people were infected by *someone*; will *they* all be locked up?

Punishment can feel good to those who mete it out. And so, when I first saw viral videos of police beating Black people for failing to wear masks in 2020, I thought of Michael's trial. To some, it might feel good to witness someone like Michael get sent to prison for life—to blame him personally for a virus living inside tens of millions of people. To some, it might feel good to see someone who is walking too close to someone else or not wearing a mask have the shit beaten out of them by a cop. But it won't make anyone *safer*. All it will do is ensure that viruses will be used as an excuse to further harm people already predetermined to be hurt by the viruses. Legal punishment condemns the most vulnerable to the viral underclass, so the legal system could consider the ongoing AIDS crisis (affecting millions of people worldwide) and blame an individual like Michael Johnson—without helping anyone.

But punishment is not the only way the state manages and distributes risk. Especially during times of austerity, laws in spots ranging from Athens to Appalachia serve as a tool for cementing people in their place, directing resources to the upper class and viruses to the lower.

5

FROM ATHENS TO APPALACHIA

(Austerity)

On September 11, 2018—not a date when New Yorkers particularly love to fly—I woke up disoriented on a Boeing 767 somewhere over the Ionian Sea. As I came to from a brief and fitful sleep, the jet crossed over the soft dawn hues of the Peloponnesian peninsula and began descending toward Athens International Eleftherios Venizelos Airport.

I was moving to Greece for three months on a writing fellowship. My project was not about Greece in any explicit way; the award merely required that I spend time in residence at a university research center in Athens. I was planning to use the time and distance to write about Michael Johnson, who was stuck in a prison some 5,600 miles away. Still, I expected there to be some overlap between what I was writing about playing out in St. Louis and what I would discover in Athens.

Ever since the Greek economic crisis of 2009 and 2010, when the country's exploding debt burden resulted in a loan from the International Monetary Fund that forced severe austerity policies upon the country, I'd interviewed many activists in American social movements who'd spent time in Athens, especially in its anarchist quarter, the neighborhood of Exarcheia. The Greek crash had affected viruses in depressing ways that would have echoes in the United States. In what economist Roberto Perotti called the "most severe" economic crisis in Europe since World War II, Greece slashed its health spending by a third. Suicides increased. Under pressure from the European Union, public health budget cuts triggered the proliferation of mosquito-borne West Nile virus and elevated influenza deaths among the aging population. Over the same period, Western-backed wars in Iraq, Afghanistan, and Syria, and the corresponding land border closures in Europe, increased mass sea migration to Greece's islands.

"In 2009–10, the first year of austerity," a 2014 study published in the *Lancet* found that one-third of street outreach programs in Greece to distribute sterile syringes "were cut because of scarcity of funding, despite a documented rise in the prevalence of heroin use." As outreach declined, "the number of new HIV infections among injecting drug users rose from 15 in 2009 to 484 in 2012"—an increase of more than 3,000 percent in four years. Another study, published in the journal *Addiction*, found "a 16-fold increase in the number of reported HIV cases in people who inject drugs" in Greece from 2010 to 2011.

This wasn't a uniquely Greek problem. Severe cuts to public health funding in the United States had led to similarly disastrous outbreaks in this country. When he was governor of Indiana, Mike Pence's administration decimated HIV prevention and surveillance efforts, and his budget cuts triggered the closure of the only HIV-testing clinic in Southern Indiana. Then, in 2014 and 2015, Pence governed over the fastest-growing HIV outbreak in U.S. history. (As vice president, Pence would later head up the White House Coronavirus Task Force.)

The outbreak in rural Scott County during Pence's tenure also included some 140 cases of hepatitis C, a 400 percent increase from the 28 cases in 2010. (Prior to approving a limited syringe-exchange program to deal with it, Pence infamously said he needed to "pray on it" first.) This trend wasn't limited to Indiana. In 2015, the Centers for Disease Control and Prevention "declared 220 counties across the United States at risk for outbreaks of HIV and HCV associated with injecting drug use," because they'd similarly been stripped of their public health surveillance efforts as Greece and Indiana had been.

St. Charles, Missouri, was this kind of county. In 2017, it closed its sole sexually transmitted infection (STI) clinic. And yet, incongruously at the same time, the county fought to keep Michael Johnson in prison for decades because he had transmitted HIV to others—as if it were actually interested in identifying every STI case and stopping onward transmission.

Greece, I realized, could be a harbinger for what I was writing about in America. But I was also excited to write there simply because it was far from America. "The years I lived in Paris did one thing for me," the writer James Baldwin once opined. "They released me from that particular social terror, which was not the terror of my own mind, but a real social danger visible in the face of every cop, every boss, everybody." Having reported so much on police—and having been repeatedly teargassed and threatened with arrest—I was frightened and tired. I wanted to slip into a country where I wasn't a citizen and where I'd get a break from police violence.

And so, as I began to wander around the acropolis, work in my office in the posh Kolonaki neighborhood, and pore over court transcripts, I felt a sense of calm I'd never felt before, the calm that one feels when away from America's particular kind of racism. As one of my journalism mentors, Ward Harkavy, had advised me to do (because he knew I was a workaholic), I spent my evenings drinking ouzo and eating all the feta cheese I could stuff into my mouth.

But my reprieve from police violence didn't last long. Ten days after I arrived, a thirty-three-year-old Athenian was kicked to death in broad daylight in Omonia Square, not a mile from where I was writing. I wouldn't have known about the murder—few would have—if it hadn't been surreptitiously recorded on video without the knowledge of the brutal lynch mob, which included at least eight cops. Before the video, the story circulating was that a man mortally wounded himself as he tried to rob a jewelry shop while the owner defended it. A colleague of mine overheard neighborhood gossip that "heroin addicts" tried this all the time and that "this one got what he deserved." The shop owner had cleaned up without his shop ever being declared a crime scene, and the police had filed no charges.

But not unlike how a secret video recorded by George Holliday of members of the Los Angeles Police Department beating Rodney King in 1991 flipped the LAPD's narrative on its head, a video that emerged of the Athens lynching showed a very different story. A small person was seen not breaking into a jewelry store but somehow mysteriously locked *inside* it. He used some kind of blunt object to break out of the front window to escape. As he tried to crawl out over the broken glass, another person and then a mob began to kick him. (The shop owner was later identified by the *Guardian* as a "far-right sympathiser.") The image was grainy, but a second video more clearly showed police officers (who looked to be two or three times the weight of the small, disoriented person lying on broken glass with blood visibly gushing from his head) joining in the lynching. They handcuffed the man, even though he was listless and immobile on the ground. When paramedics finally arrived, the man was reportedly kept in handcuffs for the ride to the hospital, where he was pronounced dead on arrival.

My colleague in the research center quickly told me about the incident because he knew that I was writing about the connections among police violence, gay people, and HIV in the United States. It turned out that the person killed that day in Athens, Zak Kostopoulos (Ζακ Κωστόπουλος), was an outspoken gay activist. Not only that, he was also well known within Athens's LGBTQ community as the drag queen Zackie Oh—and widely believed to be the first Greek to willingly come out as HIV-positive on social media.

Unlike in the United States, where this kind of thing can happen several times a day, Kostopoulos was the first person killed by Greek police in a decade. That Monday night, I went to a protest march, where thousands of Greek leftists, immigrants, sex workers, queers, and drag queens turned out to march for Zackie from Omonia Square, where he was murdered, toward the Hellenic Parliament building on Syntagma Square.

Zak was white—or as white as being Greek can be in the context of European racial politics. Otherwise, everything else about his murder reminded me of the killing of a Black person by the cops in the States. The narrative of Zak as a thief who brought it on himself, how no one would have known about his murder if there hadn't been a secretly recorded video, the fact that he was affected by a stigmatized virus, the justification that life could be destroyed if it meant protecting property, the protest march—it all reminded me of how Black people are executed by American police.

Even the cursed dual function of such "snuff film" videos applied here, too. As with the lynching postcards documenting the public execution of Black Americans that were available at the turn of the twentieth century, videos of police killing people like Oscar Grant in 2009, Eric Garner in 2014, Zak Kostopoulos in 2018, and George Floyd in 2020 serve both as proof of murder and, as they circulate online, a warning to marginalized folks of what could happen to them if they ever step out of line.

Before I arrived in Greece, I understood how governmental debt can lead to austerity, ruthless policing, and disease. Anthropologist David Graeber, in writing about the uprisings in St. Louis County, gave a simple, definitive example of austerity in 2015: "Increasingly, cities find themselves in the business of arresting citizens in order to pay creditors," fining arrestees because "local governments have become deeply indebted to large, private financial institutions—many of the same ones that brought us the crash of 2008. (In Ferguson, for instance, the amount of revenue collected in fines corresponds almost exactly to that shelled out to service municipal debt.)" But debt does not need to lead to austerity, necessarily. Investments in schools, hospitals, or other forms of public welfare can reduce short-term suffering and bolster long-term economic recovery.

But as we saw in chapter 3, neoliberal capitalism, especially during times of enforced austerity, does not do this. With the goal of maximizing the concentration of capital within the ruling class, neoliberal governments shift risks away from society at large and onto individuals, choosing to cut public funding and instead fund tax cuts to benefit the wealthy. This is achieved through austerity budgets that defund public education and social programs. As a bonus to the likes of Ronald Reagan and Margaret Thatcher, who in the 1980s slashed welfare spending on their respective sides of the Atlantic, austerity also allows the poor to be blamed for their perceived moral failures, even when such retribution might cost society more money. For instance, it would actually be cheaper for governments to provide permanent housing to people without homes or to keep the underclass from acquiring pathogens in the first place, but austerity hawks would rather pay more to punish the poor. Under austerity, the main function of the state decreasingly becomes the public welfare; increasingly, the state's central function becomes using the police to protect those hoarding resources from those without them.

In my own experience, I had seen mostly how this had affected Black people in America. The killing of Zak Kostopoulos illustrated for me that the same dynamics were at work in Europe.

As I had many times on the street in Ferguson where Michael Brown was shot, at the Fruitvale BART Station in Oakland where Oscar Grant was shot, and in front of the bodega on Staten Island where Eric Garner was choked to death, I paid my respects to where the mob had kicked Zak to death that fall. When I flew back to New York City as winter approached, I vowed I'd come back to Greece one day to write about him.

* * *

I returned to Athens a little over a year later. By then, Zak had become something of a gay martyr in Europe—so much so that when I walked into the Exarcheia neighborhood one day at the end of February 2020, I passed beneath a five-story-high mural with "#JusticeForZackie" created by the graffiti crew Political Stencil.

Painted across the building's second and third floors were Zak Kostopoulos's head and shoulders; he was dressed in a red shirt dripping toward the ground like blood, his naked baby face looking out sweetly beneath a crown of neatly cut black hair. Towering above Zak across floors four and five was his other form: the drag queen Zackie Oh; she was clad in a black dress and green sweater. Fidgeting with a flourescent pink wig, she looked out with bright red lipstick and an inscrutable expression.

Zak was looking out at Exarcheia, a truly heterogeneous, diverse living community. It's a place where you can lose yourself for hours while wandering its zigzag maze, surrounded by squats, anticapitalist graffiti, and antifascist political organizing. Exarcheia is also a space of mutual aid. As the lawyer and trans activist Dean Spade wrote, mutual aid "gives people a way to plug into movements based on their immediate concerns, and it produces spaces where people grow new solidarities" when "government policies actively produce and exacerbate the harm, inadequately respond to crises, and ensure that certain populations bear the brunt of pollution, poverty, disease and violence." In my years reporting on many social movements in the United States, I have met many activists who traveled to Exarcheia and learned about anarchist organizing.

Zak was not the only martyr depicted in the neighborhood. I also passed murals of Pavlos Fyssas, a Greek rapper who was stabbed to death by a member of Greece's far-right Golden Dawn Party in 2013, and of Alexandros Grigoropoulos, a fifteen-year-old kid killed by police in 2008. The deaths of all three coincided with the global recession of the late aughts, the subsequent Greek debt disaster, and the fallout in the form of health crises, inequality, social divisions, and the rise of the far right.

In Greece, austerity meant few prospects for young people as they finished their studies at a moment when public-sector jobs became scarcer. The private sector increasingly relied on tourism as its main economic engine—which meant more short-term rentals in Athens, more low-paying service jobs, less access to long-term housing for Athenians, and rising rents. In a country of just ten million, hundreds of thousands of young people went to work at sea or abroad. Those who stayed faced the possibility of cutthroat competition for fewer jobs, increased violence from strangers, domestic violence, self-harm, addiction, and homelessness. Indirect harms came from a politics of scarcity. This led to a rise in vigilantism and nativist groups, plus an increased "othering" and blaming of those on the margins—much as migrants and queers have been scapegoated for reduced job prospects in the United States.

In Greece, scarcity was triggered by the country's exploding debt burden, caused by loan payments to the International Monetary Fund that Greece could not repay. In retribution, the IMF and the European Union had imposed austerity measures upon the country. Many countries around the world were primed to feel such scarcity after the coronavirus pandemic began, as Oxfam International warned in 2020, because most IMF COVID "loans recommend poor countries hit hard by the economic fallout from the pandemic adopt tough new austerity measures." Indeed, as Oxfam's research showed, "76 out of 91 IMF loans"—some 84 percent—"negotiated with 81 countries push for belt-tightening that could result in deep cuts to public healthcare systems and social protection."

When I'd first lived in Greece, the police infamously treated Exarcheia as a "no-go" zone, but in the year since then, police had begun to push inside, bust squats, and deport migrants. This created rising clashes between protesters and police, with the former using Molotov cocktails and the latter tear gas. Immigrants were rounded up in raids and sent to squalid camps on islands like Chios.

From Seoul to Ferguson to New York to Athens—poison gas and pepper spray have become common tools of social control used against protesters. Since I'd started getting gassed myself, in Missouri in 2014 and Baltimore in 2015, I'd taken to keeping goggles and a face mask in my backpack wherever I went. (At the urging of the American writer Cara Hoffman, whom I befriended in Exarcheia, I'd started keeping a tube of the drug Riopan on me, too, which can mitigate the effects of tear gas.)

The day of my walk into Exarcheia was cold for a city where the Mediterranean buildings are not constructed for low temperatures and where the damp winter air settles into your bones with a chill. I was on my way to Locomotiva Cafe Bar, a collective space where I met Zak's younger brother, Nikos, and two of his friends and collaborators, writer

Maria Louka and photographer Alexandros Katsis. We talked over coffee, then beers, about the story of Zak's death and Christ-length life.

"If I had a puzzle to make my own society, one of the personalities that I would pick up was him," Alexandros told me he'd told Zak. They loved Zak because he was "a very open-minded, radical person," Maria added.

Alexandros and Maria had begun collaborating on a book with Zak in 2017. It was composed of an interview Maria did with him, photos Alexandros took of him (and Zackie Oh), and Zak's own words from social media. The book is aptly titled *Society Doesn't Fit Me but My Little Black Dress Does*. They released it the year after his murder, adding only one posthumous photo.

Zak was born in the United States, into a life forever intertwined with migration. "My parents emigrated in the 80s, like about half of Greece back then," he wrote—just as many of his peers had to go abroad due to the 2009–10 financial crash. "I can't tell you precisely when I became aware of my sexuality, because I remember myself as always having been different," he wrote. "I never felt like a boy, but I also never wanted to transition. All these things I sensed but couldn't give shape or words to," until he discovered the term *genderqueer* from reading Judith Butler. (Late in life, able to "shake off all kinds of labels," Zak would say, "I no longer self-identify as a man or a woman.")

When Zak was eight, the Kostopoulos family moved to Itea, a tiny Greek village of just a few thousand people, near Delphi. Zak didn't speak Greek at first, was dismayed that there was no McDonald's, and didn't make friends with the other boys. "Once, my father even asked why I didn't have friends who were boys, and I told him boys were stupid." Whenever boys taunted him for not playing sports, he was grateful for "four or five really good girlfriends who really protected me."

Zak also became friends with other migrants. "Ever since I was a kid I worked alongside immigrants, helping in my father's store. When I read about parents threating to occupy their kids' schools in order to keep them from accepting refugee children, I think, among other things, about when I was in school, and since parents couldn't force the school to kick out the queer kid, they threatened their *own* children instead, trying to keep them from hanging out with me."

As a teenager, Zak returned to the United States to live with his uncles, where he planned to finish high school in New Jersey. But as his brother, Nikos, told me, their "uncles were homophobic."

"Instead of finding more freedom, I found oppression," Zak wrote. "They were deeply conservative people, they read my diary, they figured out what was going on and tried to make me change. I packed my bag and came back" to Greece. "When I knocked on my parents' door, I told them everything. It was a totally different story, they didn't try to change my mind or make me ashamed of who I was. After that I was completely out in the village, signed, sealed and delivered."

He moved to Athens after high school, where he realized he'd "experienced homophobia" but had "thought of it as a personal problem rather than a social one." (This is a common response to discrimination while living under neoliberalism.) He became more active in politics around homophobia and racism. For me, as a gay American raised within Christian theocracy, there was something very freeing about Greece, its history of polytheism, and its *extremely* homoerotic iconography. But this sense was not the same for queers raised within the state-sanctioned Greek Orthodox Church—especially not for those as femme as Zak.

Zak was twenty-four years old and doing his obligatory Greek Army service when he was diagnosed with HIV. This would have been around the time of the Greek economic crash. "Before they even told me," he told Maria for their book, "I saw doctors coming towards me with gloves and masks. That was terrifying, and proof of the massive amount of ignorance and fear that exists even among doctors." Stigma was rampant. I interviewed Greek filmmaker and artist Menelas, who worked with Zak on videos and had directed him in a short film. Menelas told me that Zak once explained on video that after he was diagnosed, the army quarantined him, gave him disposable plastic utensils to eat, wore masks when dealing with him—and then discharged him.

Zak used a sense of play to subvert the stigma he faced. "'Zackie' is like a play word on *Prezaki*," Menelas explained to me. "*Prezai* is like a slang word for heroin. So *Prezakias* is a word we use for somebody who is a junkie." If his stage name dissuaded anyone from thinking he was embarrassed about his drug use, two of Zak's tattoos told everyone he was gay and HIV-positive. One, above his left pectoral, read, "Rebel Heart" (in the same font as the Madonna album of the same name), and another, on his upper right bicep, was a symbol for hazardous waste. "You could sense no shame in Zak," Menelas said. "And that was very good for Greece, because Greece is a very conservative country."

While Zak said his parents "took the news" about his diagnosis "calmly and caringly," their neighbors did not. At the time, some Greek people living with HIV had been outed publicly, but Zak voluntarily talked about his status online and in the press.

After this, he said, his "mother told me that people in the village came to her with the newspaper in their hands, demanding explanations, and my father, who owned a taverna, heard a friend of his saying that she wasn't going to bring her family back because she didn't want them to get sick. Can you imagine? I was living 200 kilometers away and they were afraid of catching what I had."

Zak knew that there were "drugs that suppress the virus, that keep you healthy and give you a good quality of life." And yet, even though "we like to say you don't die of HIV anymore," he presciently added, "people are still dying," including drug "users, homeless trans folk, immigrants and refugees without papers, marginalized people, people who don't have access to the test, or to health care, or who don't seek out care because they don't see the point, who've been crushed by the stigma, the rejection, the shame, the social isolation, and have given up."

He didn't ever give up on *them*. "Zak was an active activist," Alexandros said, and not the kind to "just hide behind the keyboards and write things and then sit on his sofa, safe and alone, let's say. He was a guy that was outside all the time," showing up for others. If only a few queer people would show up to protests over conditions in the migrant camps on Lesbos or police harassment of transgender sex workers, he'd be one of them. "If you support equality and freedom, you can't help but be concerned about other issues, too," Zak once said.

In his twenties, Zak developed his drag alter ego, Zackie Oh. To me, the name conjured First Lady Jacqueline Kennedy Onassis, who married Greek shipping magnate Aristotle Onassis and earned the nick-name "Jackie O." Her face is all over Athens's wealthier areas, a throw-back to a different perception of the United States in the world. But for Zak, Zackie Oh was "a fallen society lady who's hit rock bottom and risen again as a whore." His tragicomic drag shows, he said, were "based on some bad experience I've had."

Zak said he "experienced my first really bad physical homophobic at-tack in 2012." He was in a carful of queer friends, laughing gaily at a stoplight—"from the way we were talking, laughing, having fun, it was clear we were gay"—when a gang of men pulled them from the vehicle and broke the driver's jaw. The group ran to a gay bar in the Gazi neigh-borhood, and when they tried to "explain what happened and we wanted to come inside and take shelter, they asked us to pay the entrance fee."

Zak knew the limits of the law to help vulnerable people. "It doesn't matter how many laws are passed or how many texts are written, or how texts are written or how loudly we shout our condemnation of violence, if we don't learn to react when we see it happening in front of us, I'm afraid we're not going to get very far."

Zak was thirty-three years old when he suffered his final attack. De-spite its documentation and finality, it is perhaps the biggest puzzle of his too-short life. His brother, Nikos, has been understandably unable to watch the video of his brother's murder. Unfortunately, I've had to watch it, many times, including a multimedia investigation by Forensic Architecture. The latter includes the original viral video—Nikos said it had surfaced because it was sold to a newspaper for five hundred euros—security camera footage, another cell phone video, and 3-D computer modeling. There are gaps in the time sequence, but they flatly sketch out Zak's final moments.

In the videos of the afternoon of September 21, 2018, Zak steps from Omonia Square onto Gladstonos Street. He clearly looks spooked about something and seems to be running from someone. (His family told me that a bystander later testified that Zak had asked for help.) Zak attempts to enter a bakery on a corner, but a man—often referred to as the "man in the yellow shirt"—blocks him from entering. Moments later, he enters a seedy jewelry store. He had no relationship to it, and the owner inexplicably was not inside at the time. Somehow, the owner locks Zak in. Zak looks agitated; he can't get out. A crowd forms, including the man with the yellow shirt. Zak breaks into a display case and then uses a fire extinguisher to break out.

He looks like someone who could have been having a psychotic break or a drug trip, but toxicology reports later showed he had no drugs in his system. In the video, the man in the yellow shirt has followed him and talks to police; he seems to have a police baton on him.

As I watch his last moments, I always think of the words Zak prophetically wrote: "It's true, you don't die of HIV anymore. It's other people who kill you."

In the video, the law arrives in the form of cops, but they do not help him; they join in the kicking. They handcuff Zak, and he bleeds on the ground—like Michael Brown.

Though Zackie Oh was a drag queen who served up beauty very consciously, the last images of Zak Kostopoulos on this earth are of him writhing on shattered glass like a broken bird. He would die moments after the videos were shot.

Without excusing the violence, Zak's friends and family pensively talked to me about trying to understand both Zak and his killers in terms of the Greek economic crash. "You know, the people are just depressed after ten years in austerity," Alexandros said. They are ready for a fight. They are ready to beat someone up. They may not have known who exactly Zak was, but anyone could have seen he was femme.

"Austerity hits everybody," he continued. "First of all, let's say about Zak, he could not find a proper full-time job. So this can cause domino problems in your life," which plagued so many young people of his generation. "Let's say he had his problems," which Zak dramatized in his drag. "I think a lot of people feel a rage toward other people," Nikos added, saying austerity had been used to turn Greeks against one another and to whip up hysteria of "the other."

Our conversation then turned to the world's biggest concern in February 2020, and how austerity thinking was shaping Greece's response to it. While it was already wreaking havoc nearby in Italy, the first reported case of the novel coronavirus in Athens had just been confirmed a couple of days before we met. "Many Greeks feel like refugees are the problem of the unemployment. Or," Nikos added, "it's China's fault because of coronavirus. So many people use that mentality. And austerity, when it comes to money, unemployment," the rage turns xenophobic, he said, looking sad and noting that immigrants were now being blamed for COVID-19 coming to Greece. The rage turns on people deemed the other: people who are gay and HIV-positive like Zak.

While who all did it and why may never be known, this kind of bigoted rage exploded on the twenty-first of September, killing this person beloved by Nikos, Alex, Maria, and so many others. Meanwhile, Greek and EU lawmakers, and the bankers who own them, didn't seem to feel much responsibility for catalyzing fear of the other, for setting such violence in motion. There has been little justice for the uptick in viruses, suffering, and misery in Greece. The election of the Syriza Party in the Hellenic Parliament and the brief rise of the economist Yanis Varoufakis were promising turns, but were ultimately disappointing for the Greek left. While fifty thousand protesters greeted German chancellor Angela Merkel when she visited Athens—she was widely blamed for pushing the European Union to enact austerity in Greece—her reign as the face of the international liberal order continued unabated.

And the bankers themselves, who preyed on the weak position of the marginalized, never had to pay a price, of course. But the wick they lit exploded all the same—including at a place where Zak worked over the years. The week before I met with his friends, I visited Positive Voice and Checkpoint, two HIV testing and prevention organizations in Athens's Monastiraki neighborhood. When I arrived at Checkpoint, staff were finishing renovations after a firebombing the year before. An arsonist had climbed the building's façade, removed its rainbow flag, and thrown gasoline-soaked crude bombs inside, trying to destroy it. I had mistakenly thought such homophobic attacks were primarily an American phenomenon. But, of course, they are global, and every time such violence erupts, the viral underclass gets hit directly or becomes collateral damage.

I asked the filmmaker Menelas what he thought had happened to Zak. "To me it's a mystery, equivalent to *Twin Peaks*," he said, referring to the 1990s David Lynch TV show that had recently been revived. "We will never find out what happened, really. We know that the death came from people kicking him and then the police kicking him. But what brought him to that point the night before is going to be a mystery, the same as Laura Palmer."

Zak is now dead, and criminal courts cannot change that or restore wholeness to his community. Besides, coming out of the most severe phase of a decade of austerity, the Greek state seemed to have no shortage of money for cops, but it didn't move quickly on interrogating the cops involved in Zak's death in a court of law. Athens may be the birthplace of the jury trial, the first one happening in the sixth century BCE. And the Greek government was supposed to have a trial in November 2020 to charge two shopkeepers and four police officers for "inflicting fatal bodily harm," according to the *Guardian*. But another virus postponed that trial from even starting until late 2021, and as of this writing it has not been resolved.

In the meantime, with every passing day over three years, Zak's friends fear that the law is protecting the police, letting the clock run out until the story of the murdered Greek American becomes a myth as ethereal as the myths told about Dionysus or Laura Palmer.

* * *

Eight months later and five thousand miles to the west, I found myself reporting on the effects of austerity politics not in Athens, but in the coalfields of Appalachia.

In October 2020, the Department of Health for Cabell County and the city of Huntington, West Virginia, was struggling to contend with not one viral epidemic, but four—HIV, hepatitis C, influenza, and the novel coronavirus.

My interest in the region had been piqued by a Black lesbian HIV activist named A. Toni Young. In Washington, D.C., Young had observed AIDS develop among urban African Americans in the 1980s and '90s, just as deindustrialization and AIDS were plaguing cities across the nation. When she relocated to West Virginia mining country, she began seeing HIV and hepatitis C unspooling in the bodies of rural white people, too.

One can often see a clear "before" and "after" line when it comes to the impact that austerity has on cities. You can see it in relatively poor U.S. cities like Detroit, where disinvestment in roads or streetlights leads to housing prices falling, a smaller population, and a declining tax base. But you can also see it in wealthy cities like San Francisco, where disinvestments in public housing and public health care have created a crisis of people who live outdoors while suffering from mental illness.

Austerity is already taking its toll on rural America with the mining industry, but it's so gradual and commonplace that it's not always noticed. Nearly two centuries ago, mining companies came into states like West Virginia, bored into the earth, and blasted the tops of mountains off with dynamite. By 1880, they needed so many workers that the laborers had a critical mass to unionize. But as the unsustainable resources ripped from the land dwindled, the layoffs began, the unions were broken, and the tax base declined. As social support was cut for unemployed workers, addiction to drugs and alcohol increased. And having already stripped the ground of its geological resources, austerity began stripping the immune systems and livers of the folks left behind of their most basic functions.

Cabell County was one of the 220 counties the CDC warned of being "at risk for outbreaks of HIV and HCV associated with injecting drug use" after the Scott County, Indiana, outbreak in 2015—but it was also facing a related crisis. For years, the CDC had identified West Virginia as the state with the highest rate of overdose deaths in the country. Between 2006 and 2016, nearly 21 million opioid pills were shipped to Williamson, West Virginia, alone—a town of just 2,900 people. By 2019, the state had settled with thirteen different drug companies for a total of $84 million. But these lawsuits and Big Pharma payouts have so far done little to stem the tide of overdose deaths. After the "pill mills" flooding the state with opioid pain relievers were shut down, a toxic mix of heroin and illicitly manufactured fentanyl was there to meet demand and drive up the overdose death rate to new highs.

When I look at the lucrative opioid pharmaceutical industry, it seems to me that people overdosing on their products might just be a cost of doing business. In a 2017 presentation reported by the *New York Times*, the consulting firm McKinsey suggested that Purdue Pharmaceuticals actually pay *rebates* to pharmacies for every prescription that led to an overdose. And yet, even amid all this organized death for corporate profit, Cabell County stood out. As Cabell-Huntington Health Department medical director Michael Kilkenny, MD, told me, his was "the county with the most overdose deaths in the state with the most overdose deaths."

When I spent time talking to them over two days via video calls in the fall of 2020—a spike in COVID-19 cases the week before prevented my physical visit—Kilkenny and his colleagues had their hands full. A surge of HIV and HCV cases in the county at the beginning of 2019, followed by SARS-CoV-2 a year later, had added to their customary work mitigating overdoses and engaging in their annual influenza vaccine campaign. Outside their headquarters as we spoke, large tents were being used to administer COVID-19 tests and flu shots on alternating days of the week.

Cabell's twin crises of viruses and overdoses are both tied to austerity and exploitative labor in West Virginia (which is sometimes ranked as the poorest state in the nation), but not in the overly simplistic way I'd imagined. I thought addiction in Appalachia typically began when workers were prescribed opioid painkillers while injured on the job in the region's diminishing coal mines. But the number of actual mining jobs in West Virginia had peaked decades prior. Many of the newer jobs are in the health care industry. Those *could* make for well-paying careers *if* so much of the profits weren't being funneled toward upper management and corporate earnings. And in 2016, the West Virginia legislature overrode their governor's veto to pass HB 2643, a bill that prohibits labor unions from mandating dues from every employee in a unionized shop. This guaranteed that the care work sites of the present would be much harder to unionize than the mine shafts of the past.

West Virginia laborers who did physical work did get pain prescriptions for work-related injuries. But by the twenty-first century, that work was more likely in informal construction jobs or as day laborers. Sometimes injured workers found that OxyContin, the brand name for an opioid called oxycodone, or more powerful opioids like fentanyl kept their pain at bay.

But more than that, economic precarity coupled with depression and other mental distress created fertile ground for addiction to flourish. Many workers found that the opioids didn't relieve only physical pain; the comforting euphoria also helped them cope with the emotional conditions that austerity had created: alienation and depression. And the drugs themselves created new baselines, which drove people to use new techniques to experience the drugs' intended effects. According to the *New York Times* in 2018, officials at Purdue Pharma "had received reports that the pills were being crushed and snorted; stolen from pharmacies; and that some doctors were being charged with selling prescriptions, according to dozens of previously undisclosed documents that offer a detailed look inside Purdue Pharma. But the drugmaker continued 'in the face of this knowledge' to market OxyContin as less prone to abuse and addiction than other prescription opioids, prosecutors wrote in 2006."

Because addiction *itself* is viral, and often develops during adolescence, young people living in a region flooded with opioids found their own reprieve. Many pills prescribed for legitimate pain worked their way into a lucrative illicit market where OxyContin could be sold for a dollar per milligram—a single eighty-milligram pill could sell for upward of eighty dollars, creating an informal cash economy in towns where the only work available was minimum-wage jobs with few benefits or off-the-books day laboring.

"I've been asked multiple times 'what's the best OD prevention policy,'" the journalist Zachary Siegel has written, "and my answer typically has nothing directly to do with drugs or drug use. It's about how we live our lives: Do people feel valued? Jobs, unions, communities—decent life conditions can go a long way." Such conditions are too often casualties of austerity measures.

When the pills eventually became scarce or too expensive, addiction did not magically disappear. Without easy access to public rehabilitation programs or other community-based harm reduction options, people switched to ever-more-potent and dangerous drugs like heroin and illicitly manufactured fentanyl to stave off dope sickness, in addition to mixing opioids with alcohol or stimulants like methamphetamine, which increases the risk of a fatal overdose. The supply of illicit drugs grew increasingly more dangerous over time, especially when carfentanil, a drug used to tranquilize elephants, hit the scene.

The overdose epidemic prompted the creation of Cabell County's Harm Reduction Program in 2015. "When I was first approached with the concept of providing sterile injection equipment to people who were injecting heroin illegally, I felt like that was probably an exceptionally bad idea," Kilkenny told me. "So, I had many of the biases that we now refer to as stigma," he admitted.

People often erroneously think "harm reduction" means only preventing overdoses, stopping HIV or HCV transmission, creating supervised injection sites, or distributing sterile syringes. But "harm reduction" really means "meeting people where they are in regard to their lifestyle and health rather than making judgments about where we think they should be," Michelle Perdue, director of the Cabell-Huntington Harm Reduction Program, explained to me.

Like many people who perform this work, Perdue (no relation to the drug manufacturer) has personally lost relatives to overdoses. As she explained, and as with sex and sex education, drug abstinence rarely works with any population, especially one in the throes of austerity. But if you give people a chance to make healthier choices, they'll often choose the option that does less harm to themselves and others. It can be as simple as "any positive change," as several people put it to me, evoking a phrase used by Dan Bigg, the "godfather of harm reduction." Perdue and her colleagues *do* distribute sterile syringes and provide people with naloxone, an opioid antagonist that can be administered to save a person's life if they begin to overdose. But their important work also connects people to housing assistance and drug treatment programs, reflecting how research has long shown that harm reduction programs put people, as Kilkenny phrased it, "on a pathway that ends the root problem of addiction."

Though Cabell and Huntington Counties have a compound population of fewer than one hundred fifty thousand residents, when it opened its Harm Reduction Program it quickly went from seeing fifteen people a week to more than two thousand. As it had in Athens before the debt crash, harm reduction worked in Cabell County. At one point, in 2016, carfentanil caused an outbreak of more than twenty overdoses in just a two-day span across Huntington County. But from 2017 to 2018, thanks in large part to the Harm Reduction Program, Kilkenny saw a 25 percent decrease in overdose deaths.

Still, "there's a lot of stigma toward people who struggle with substance use, as well as people with any kind of virus," Hayley Brown, a recovery coach in the Cabell-Huntington Health Department, told me. "You know, that *you're dirty . . .* Just *degenerate*." Not *clean*. Whether a person is queer, experiencing homelessness, struggling with addiction, or moving across borders to avoid war or starvation, the same few words are used to disparage the members of viral underclass around the world.

But the stigma doesn't come only from people—it comes from the law, even when people who inject drugs are trying to use in a way that reduces their risk of overdose and infection. To access harm reduction services in Cabell County, people need an ID or utility bill—which means that those without documents or without stable housing, those who might need the services most, are weeded out. Other would-be clients get spooked, believing that a record of their participation means the moment they walk out the door with drug paraphernalia, they'll be arrested.

But as pharmacist C. K. Babcock explained to me, police make this dynamic even worse when they take a person's ID from them. "They'll take a homeless person in and take their ID because it's expired," he said. "Well, in order to get a picture ID, if you have an expired one, you can go get a new one for ten bucks. But if somebody *takes* your expired ID, in order to get another one, it costs you about a hundred dollars to get a birth certificate. Then you have to wait to get that, and then you have to follow a whole process in order to get a new ID. And it is insane, the amount of work that it takes and the amount of effort that it takes." It's another way, he said, that people who are already outcast "are brutalized." While Michelle Perdue says she can get "very creative" in helping such people, they might just give up. They might inject alone, or inject with unsterilized syringes—placing themselves and their social circle at higher risk for both viruses and overdose death.

The coronavirus pandemic made all this worse. Perdue told me that in the six months after the COVID-19 lockdowns of 2020, the Cabell-Huntington Harm Reduction Program started seeing about half as many people as it had before the pandemic, and not because rates of addiction and drug use were decreasing—which likely means more risk of HIV and HCV transmission and overdose deaths. And by April 2021, West Virginia governor Jim Justice signed an onerous law making it harder to distribute and obtain sterile syringes, against the advice of public health professionals in the state and around the nation.

But if COVID-19's economic ruination hit everyone hard, it hit the members of the viral underclass served by these kinds of programs the worst. "We have people set up encampments" in "different places, or abandoned houses," Hayley Brown, the recovery coach, told me. From refugee camps on the Greek island of Lesbos to a makeshift shantytown in West Virginia—even in the best of times, living tightly in tent cities without adequate sanitation makes people more vulnerable to all sorts of viruses, bacteria, and harm. That is to say nothing of the kind of risk that staying in cramped temporary housing poses during a global pandemic. In the United States, people without housing are more likely to become positive with hepatitis A or HIV. It also makes them more likely to be arrested and less likely to adhere to HIV medication protocols—meaning their viral load will not become or stay undetectable.

According to a 2019 paper published in *Social Science and Medicine*, people who are unhoused also "had disproportionately higher adjusted risk of opioid-related" overdose deaths "compared to low-income housed individuals treated at the same hospital." And research has also shown that incarceration, the primary state response to opioid addiction, more than doubles the risk of overdose death.

In Huntington County, it is illegal to camp on public property, which means that those living in tent cities are at an even higher risk of being arrested and of having their possessions and IDs taken, which will make it harder for them to get sterile syringes. As I learned all this, it made me think of a conversation I had had with a colleague eight months prior, in Athens, right before I left Greece. My colleague had known Zak Kostopoulos and also had a relative who'd overdosed and died on the streets of Athens—but the relative *could* have died in any number of ways. Maybe someone killed him and left his body to look like he had overdosed. Maybe the police roughed him up. My colleague would never know for sure. Since the economic crash, people without homes (especially immigrants) have likely been killed like this in Greece and elsewhere. But it's hard to prove, and the law doesn't usually even try.

If not for the viral video that captured his murder, the same could have happened to Zak—or to any of the people in tent camps in Cabell County, Lesbos, Los Angeles, or Chicago. Any of them might be killed, and the law would never investigate—just as the law could kill them explicitly through police violence or implicitly by denying them care.

"I hope this doesn't sound strange," I said when I spoke to Dr. Kilkenny, "but I am thinking of your region in terms of an HIV outbreak in Athens, Greece."

He paused for a moment. I figured he thought that I was insultingly misguided. Then he told me that in all his interviews, no one had ever brought up Greece before—and yet, the Cabell-Huntington Health Department had modeled its HIV response on the Athens outbreak after the Greek economic crash. "We'd been worried about it being the next Scott County," he told me, referring to the HIV outbreak that happened on Indiana governor Mike Pence's watch. But when the CDC came in to help, they said, *No, you're not Indiana*. They pointed Kilkenny to a "program that was used in Athens, Greece, to stop that outbreak, to stop our outbreak here in 2019."

I got chills as he told me this; how connected our struggles are! Like homophobia and stigma, austerity is a plague around the world. Debt shapes our options in life, making it hard to build community and shelter. When this happens, viruses and addiction flourish freely.

While Athens and Appalachia were both made vulnerable by austerity, their people were resilient in using community-based interventions when possible to mitigate austerity's impact upon the viral underclass. Their examples illustrate how anarchy does *not* mean chaos, as it is often mischaracterized in the United States. Rather, anarchy means a horizontal politics of mutual aid and communal responsibility without the threat of violence from the state; it means a community where people share their abundance and care for and prioritize one another in a way that governments, time and time again, have failed to do.

The answer in pandemics, then, from Appalachia to Athens to the Big Apple, isn't austerity. The answer is a community-based response of mutual care and responsibility—anarchy and abundance—an ethos enacted bravely by transgressive gender-bending angels like Zackie Oh and like Queens, New York, activist Lorena Borjas.

6

BORDERLANDS

(Borders)

It was a Saturday night in 2004 or 2005, and Cecilia Gentili found herself in a club in Jackson Heights, Queens, meeting someone who would change her life—and the lives of so many other transgender immigrant women.

Jackson Heights is among the most diverse neighborhoods on the face of our planet. A short train ride from Manhattan, its low-rise buildings feel a world away from Manhattan's skyscrapers. Located in one of New York City's outer boroughs, Jackson Heights is home to 100,000 residents speaking some 167 languages, expressing gender in all sorts of ways, and hailing from all over earth. Doctors from India, cab drivers from Pakistan, waiters from China, nurses from Haiti, builders from Mexico, sex workers from Argentina—you can find them all living in the unusually racially and economically integrated neighborhood.

Beneath the elevated 7 Train, which hovers over Roosevelt Avenue, a cacophony of sights and sounds dominates the senses on any given night. The neighborhood's main thoroughfare is filled with the roar of the overhead train, the vision of bright Indian saris, the beats of Reggaeton spilling out of bars, the aroma of Mexican tortas and Nepalese momos being sold from carts, the sight of young men sporting fresh fades so tight they threaten to cut off your circulation just by looking at them, and the rhythm of queer and trans Latinx folks ducking in and out of Latin dance clubs.

"I was an internet escort," Gentili told me in the summer of 2020, referring to how she earned her living about a decade and a half earlier. A beautiful trans woman from Argentina with blond hair and a mischievous but open smile, Gentili was new to New York City in the mid-aughts. "I was doing very well for myself, and I was making an impressive amount of money" by finding clients over the internet from the comfort of her apartment in Manhattan.

One weekend, she went to a Latin club in Jackson Heights "to hang out on a Saturday night, and there she was." *She* was Lorena Borjas, a shorter, demure transgender woman from Mexico who was no less than an icon in Jackson Heights. In cold weather, Lorena would dress in an understated black puffer coat and bright red lipstick, often sporting a necklace covered in writing pens. She had high eyebrows and the kind of smile that made you want to smile back, even through photographs.

And that evening in Jackson Heights, Lorena was doing what she often did on Saturday nights: handing out condoms and trying to protect people from HIV.

Scrunching her nose in disdain as she recalled their original meeting, Cecilia admits that her first impression of Lorena and the women she was serving was not positive. "I kind of looked down at them. I was like, *Oh, these girls are like, just street whores*." Cecilia saw what Lorena was doing and thought, *I don't need your condoms, you know. I buy my own condoms!* "So, I was kind of like a bougie bitch at the time."

It came back to haunt her. "My mom used to say, '*No escupas para el cielo que te va a caer encima*,'" which Cecilia translates into English roughly as "If you spit at heaven, it will drop back on your forehead." Well, "it really came back on my forehead really hard because, you know, my situation changed very rapidly." Within two years after first seeing Lorena, Cecilia began "using heroin and crack cocaine and crystal meth and basically anything that would get me high. And then, because of that, I lost a lot of clientele, and I lost my apartment, and I lost everything. And then I was homeless, and I ended up on Roosevelt Avenue, being one of those cheap street whores that I talked shit about years ago.

"And there she was again": Lorena Borjas. Another transgender

Latina, not there to gloat over Cecilia's plight, but to help. "And at that time, I really *needed* those condoms. So. You know, she saw me, and she spoke with me."

To Cecilia, Lorena was "judgment free." By meeting people where they were and offering whatever help they might need, Lorena was practicing harm reduction. "If you get high, if you use condoms or not, she would just give you the condoms, and she would tell you why you should use them," Cecilia said. "But she wasn't, like, pressing you."

Around the time the two women reconnected, Cecilia was arrested multiple times, accused of drug use or sex work. This would happen often after she was "stopped and frisked" on the streets by the NYPD under a 1976 antiloitering statute that, technically, was supposed to criminalize sex work, but in practice allowed police to arrest women based on their clothing or if they found condoms on their person. For this reason, it's often known as the "walking while trans" law. This put Cecilia, who was then undocumented, in danger of deportation. But through it all, Lorena was there for her. She helped Cecilia get a job working for a community health center, where she was supposed to "get these trans Latinas who do sex work on the corner of Roosevelt Avenue to be able to see doctors."

Transgender Latin women are susceptible to viruses for all sorts of reasons. Some risks are more direct, such as when the syringes used to inject hormones during the gender-affirmation process can become vectors for HIV and hepatitis C (especially for those transitioning without doctors and getting their hormones on the contraband market). Being at disproportionate danger for arrest also boosts transgender women's peril of being raped by cops or in jail, each of which increases their odds of becoming infected by a number of sexually transmitted pathogens. But undocumented trans women are even more vulnerable to viruses, as their undocumented status can make it legally risky or prohibitively expensive for them to get medical attention.

More indirectly, viral vulnerability is manufactured in the many ways that being trans, undocumented, or both locks people out of the formal economy and keeps them from accessing safe housing and work. For much of U.S. history, and in many ways still, it has been legal to discriminate against transgender people. As a result, transgender people are more likely to face job, food, and housing insecurity. They sometimes have few options for survival *but* drug, sex, domestic, or manual work in the informal economy.

Though she eventually became a permanent U.S. resident, Jennicet Gutiérrez was a longtime undocumented transgender activist who, like Lorena, was born in Mexico, misgendered throughout her youth, and traveled to the United States as a young person. As she once told me, "Surviving in this country as an undocumented person puts people at a higher risk" for viruses and poor health in ways many LGBTQ political brokers ignore. This happens because undocumented people do very important work, yet do not get "full access to health care that can help people sustain themselves." Gutiérrez worked for ten years in radiology as an X-ray assistant, intimately tending to the health of *other* people, but she had to quit her job when her employer said they were going to closely inspect everyone's documentation.

"People are in so much fear, but also desperate for survival," Gutiérrez told me, "that they will go to whatever extremes to be able to seek employment" when safe work is unavailable. Unsafe work risks undocumented people's lives and limbs, taxes their immune systems, denies them insurance coverage, and makes their mucus membranes, lungs, veins, and genitals more likely to encounter viruses—making the workers less likely to survive such exposure. This is the kind of work Cecilia and Lorena did. And it's the kind of precarious labor the people working Roosevelt Avenue as sex workers, food mongers, and day laborers performed.

In serving their fellow workers, Lorena and Cecilia would hit the streets together around 10 p.m., staying out until the sun threatened to rise on them. Lorena would have lots of condoms in shiny wrappers, and she'd always be pulling "her cart," Cecilia recalled with a smirk. "God knows what she had in that cart!"

(Everyone who loved Lorena has a story about her cart.)

"*Everything* was in there," Cecilia said. "Anything that you may need, you would ask, and it would come out of" Lorena's rolling cart: legal paperwork, pens, alcohol rubbing pads, sterile syringes, food.

When she first started to do outreach, Cecilia was nervous about getting "the girls" to trust her, a total stranger, to take her referral and "go to a clinic and get their body checked out." But "because I was with Lorena, I kind of skipped that—because everyone knew her."

And that was how a beautiful friendship between the two women began. It was a friendship born of trying to help their girls stave off HIV, HCV, illicit-market hormones, and the police—and a friendship that would last for fifteen years, until another virus no one had yet heard of intervened.

* * *

The United States has long viewed itself as a nation defined by its lack of pathogens and has required people to be "clean" to lay claim to its lands. This is ableist, revisionist, and ironic, considering that white settlers consciously and unconsciously brought with them pathogens that killed tens of millions of Native Americans; that white enslavers facilitated the widespread movement of pathogens across the Atlantic via slavery; and that, in 2020, the Sioux tribe had to sue the U.S. government to maintain its coronavirus checkpoints.

In the policing of its borders, the United States has created a long association of immigrants as "unclean." At the same time, the immigration system, via the creation of "criminal aliens," has delineated a vast underclass useful for American capitalism (in the form of cheaply paid labor), but to which the state claims no responsibility. The state will relax its boundaries to welcome various immigrants into this underclass at certain times and then will demonize those same groups when capital has lost its need for them. The justification for later quarantining these groups, curbing the migration of their families, or expelling them is often viruses.

For instance, Chinese workers were welcomed to help with the California gold rush of the mid-nineteenth century and then, during the

U.S. Civil War, to help build the Transcontinental Railroad. It was dangerous work and, as the *Guardian* put it, Chinese workers "were paid less than American workers and lived in tents, while white workers were given accommodation in train cars." By the 1880s, the gold rush was long over, the railroads were built, and the Chinese workers were considered no longer useful by U.S. industry. It was then that, as we saw in chapter 4, the Chinese were unfairly blamed for the presence of the bubonic plague in San Francisco—an unjust accusation used to justify the Chinese Exclusion Act of 1882.

This pattern has continued. From the 1980s until 2010, for example, people living with HIV were formally barred from entering the United States, which triggered international boycotts of scientific AIDS conferences happening inside the States and ignored the rapid spread of the disease within the country's borders. Early in his presidency, Donald Trump was reported to have said that Africans and Haitians "all have AIDS" as an excuse for his xenophobic immigration policies. As the COVID-19 pandemic raged, Trump and various politicians tried to blame the novel coronavirus on China, Mexico, and Hispanic and Asian people in the United States, even as the policies of those politicians—not to mention Trump himself running around the country holding huge rallies—were responsible for transmitting the virus within the country.

The United States doesn't just use viruses to create national borders; in conflating viruses with nonwhite people, it also tries to create borders of whiteness, where healthy white people are on one side of national belonging and people living with viruses are kept outside it.

For those living undocumented in the United States, just trying to survive can put them at risk of deportation. The criminal justice system and the immigration system overlap for them when the work they do in the informal economy might get them arrested. It was an Obama administration policy embodying this dynamic that made life even more precarious for Lorena's "girls" and that first brought her into Chase Strangio's life.

Long before he was known as an attorney who helped free transgender whistleblower army lieutenant Chelsea Manning from prison and worked on the landmark trans Supreme Court case *R. G. and G. R. Harris Funeral Homes Inc. v. EEOC and Aimee Stephens*, Chase was a "baby lawyer" working at the Sylvia Rivera Law Project (SRLP). After finishing law school in 2010, Chase worked there on a fellowship focused on "carceral systems and disability." Named for the groundbreaking activist Sylvia Rivera, the legal aid clinic had been formed in 2002 to serve low-income transgender, nonbinary, and gender-nonconforming people.

On a Friday in 2010, when SRLP did open intakes, a woman walked in with a rolling cart, yelling, "There's a crisis in Jackson Heights—these girls are getting arrested!"

"It was at the escalation of the Secure Communities program," Chase explained to me, referring to an Obama administration attempt to force cooperation between local law enforcement and Immigration and Customs Enforcement (ICE). This meant two dangerous things for the most marginalized, like Lorena's girls. First, if someone was picked up by the NYPD for drug use or soliciting sex, they could be deported. Second, it scared *any* undocumented person who was a victim of *anything* from ever seeking governmental help of *any* kind—opening them up to wage theft, domestic violence, rape, enslavement, viral exposure, and even murder.

Lorena came to the law office named after a radical Latin activist with a message for the trans lawyers of Manhattan: "My community is completely under siege here. Why aren't you guys paying attention?"

Put on notice by Lorena, Chase thought, *She really has a point, you know?* Thereafter, many a Friday, Lorena would show up at SRLP and yell, "CHAAAASE!"

"I don't give a shit what's gonna happen," she'd tell the people in the office. "I'm gonna make sure Chase is here. If I have to wait three hours, I'll wait three hours."

And with her, Chase recalled, Lorena would always have her cart. "I have five girls today," Lorena would say, before pulling legal paperwork about all five of the girls out of her cart.

Lorena turned Chase onto a case involving two trans women ensnared in the legal system in a common way: assaulted by a man, they had fought back and were now themselves being charged with felony assault. Over the next year and a half, Lorena made sure Chase or attorney Lynly Egyes "were at every single court date" for the women. If they ever tried to get out of it, Lorena would say, "Nope, we have to go." The women facing charges were both undocumented, and Lorena pushed the lawyers to engage in a "combination of working on their criminal cases, showing up in court, and then figuring out their immigration cases." The three of them "started a very consistent process anytime someone was arrested in Jackson Heights that Lorena knew about, which was almost *every* trans Latina that was arrested."

"Okay, who's writing advocacy letters and who's showing up at arraignments and who is getting cash in case bail is set?" Lorena would ask as they delegated the tasks. When undocumented trans people were arrested in a city jail, the goal was to get them out not just before they were sexually assaulted (a frequent event when transgender women are kept in jails for men), but also before local officials turned them over to ICE. One of the biggest challenges was convincing judges that the defendants would show up in court, because, on paper, they were considered flight risks.

The questions the judges would pose were: Are you in school? Do you have a job? Do you have family?

"All of those things are things that trans people are way less likely to have," Chase told me. "Particularly Black and Latina trans women. So, we set up a system where we're like, we'll show the judges that they *do* have a community."

And that's where Lorena would work her magic. She'd show up herself and hustle other trans Latina women to show up in arraignment court—even if she didn't know them personally—so that the judge would always see they had people.

A huge number of people are kept in jail, become infected with viruses in jail, and even *die* in jail every year not because they are guilty—jails are used mostly for holding people *before* they have faced arraignment or a trial and while they are still legally innocent—but simply because they are too poor to post bail. Cases of tuberculosis, HIV, HCV, and influenza are high in jails, affecting not only those who are arrested but also their families and social networks upon their release. While even those who have been convicted don't deserve this kind of death penalty, in November 2020, 80 percent of the 230 people who died of COVID-19 in Texas correctional facilities had never been convicted of any crime.

Long before the Black Lives Matter movement made famous the use of community bail funds to get people out of jail who might not have family who could afford to bail them out, Chase and Lorena started the Lorena Borjas Community Fund to spring Lorena's girls as quickly as possible. Often, they succeeded. According to the *New York Times*, their fund raised more than forty-five thousand dollars, helping more than fifty people get out of jail. But sometimes, they felt frustrated they couldn't save everyone—such as when an Afro-Latin transgender woman named Layleen Polanco died in solitary confinement in New York City's Rikers Island jail of an epileptic seizure in 2019. Polanco had been moved into "the hole" for allegedly hitting a guard. But her original arrest had been due to a 2017 charge of sex work, and her bail was only five hundred dollars. If someone had paid it, Polanco wouldn't have lost two years of her life in jail awaiting trial, and she likely would not have lost her life. But Chase and Lorena didn't know about her case. They couldn't possibly know about every case when Rikers, just one of New York City's jails, processed some one hundred thousand admissions a year.

Lorena cared about people in jail not just because she herself was a transgender migrant who'd been arrested: Lorena, Chase told me, had also been "living with HIV for decades." People losing access to HIV medication in jail and being abused by law enforcement is terribly common. For instance, though Michael Johnson had been arrested for alleged HIV transmission, he was not given HIV medication during his first seven months in jail—something that is not unusual. The year before he was arrested, an article published in the journal *Current Opinion in Infectious Disease* found that "a national survey of prison and jail systems suggested" that only "39% of prisons do mandatory or routine HIV testing and only 36% of jails offer any HIV testing," while a scant "33% of HIV-infected inmates were receiving" medication to treat it. This is to say nothing of gender-affirming hormones. Making sure people got their hormones *and* their HIV medications in jail was paramount to Lorena.

Lorena became such a fixture at bail hearings that, according to Lynly Egyes, the attorney who would often be with her in court, bailiffs would "stop Lorena or any of the other women from leaving to go to the bathroom" if the bailiff knew the person the women were there to support was about to be called up on the docket.

Like Chase, Egyes met Lorena while she was a young attorney, and she credited her with teaching her "how to be a community lawyer and not be a lawyer who claims to work with community, but doesn't actually work with community." Egyes had once "agreed to take on a case of a young transgender girl" charged with allegedly assaulting someone with a shoe. While *another* young trans girl was also allegedly involved in the same attack, Egyes had the capacity to represent the pending criminal and immigration cases involving only one of them.

"I needed the young person's birth certificate for part of her immigration case," Egyes told me, and though she "didn't know Lorena at the time, somehow it got back to her that I needed this. And one day, she just kind of appeared in my office with her—I used to call it her Mary Poppins bag. You just never knew what was going to be in there." Then she reached into it and pulled out the original birth certificate of Egyes's client.

"How did you get this girl's original birth certificate?" she asked Lorena.

"Well, I'm Lorena," she told her, before talking the lawyer into taking on *both* women's cases.

"You just couldn't say no to Lorena."

Egyes was touched that every time there was a court date for these girls, Lorena would show up with a crew of other trans women. "She just really needed the court to know that these young girls were supported and loved and cared for."

But if no one could say no to Lorena Borjas, Lorena couldn't really say no to helping others, either. When doing outreach in the early 2000s, trying to get women in Queens to go to Manhattan to get tested, the organization she worked for thought it would be easier to test them in Queens instead. So, they set up a testing site in Lorena's Jackson Heights studio apartment. The organization didn't pay her rent, Egyes said; they just gave her some gift cards.

Smiling, Egyes said Lorena would even "go to food pantries and take a whole bunch of food and just hand it out at night. And she wasn't getting paid for this. It was just what she did because it was who she was.

"It was, as she told me, the right thing to do."

* * *

Lorena Borjas was born in Mexico City in 1960. Misgendered as male as a child, she did not grow up knowing what being transgender meant. "The reason I came to this country," Lorena told Queens Public Television in 2018, was because she "didn't have a future in Mexico at the time.

"I considered myself a gay man," she explained. When she immigrated in 1981 at age twenty, her "main goal was to find a hormones specialist, so I could do my transition supervised by a physician" and live her life as a woman. While she was ultimately successful in her gender transition, she "did not have legal documents," and her life was extremely difficult in her first few years in the United States.

Lorena wound up in coercive situations, trafficked as a sex worker against her will. When she moved to Jackson Heights, according to *El Diario*, she was living with twenty other transgender women who were also trafficked. She began to use crack cocaine.

By 1986, Lorena said, she was "able to obtain my documents by President Ronald Reagan," eventually obtaining a green card under the amnesty program. In the subsequent years, she decided to get sober, and when she did, she became relentless about helping other people. She eventually worked for the Community Health Network. But much of her work was on a volunteer basis.

"Sometimes, our transgender folks don't even have the self-esteem to think that they're worth organizing for and fighting for their own rights," Daniel Dromm, an openly gay member of the New York City Council and its representative for Jackson Heights from 2010 to 2021, also told Queens Public TV. "But Lorena gave them dignity. She went out and said to them, 'No, you are valuable. You're worth something. We're going to fight for our rights together.'"

And once she got her own modest studio apartment, Lorena "would give people places to sleep," Egyes told me—even if that meant putting them up in her one-room home. "Her goal wasn't to get people out of sex work," Egyes said. "That was never it. Her goal was to get people out of situations that they didn't want to be in anymore. So, if they were doing sex work because there was someone who was abusing them or was exploiting them or coercing them to do it, she just wanted people to know there was another way, there was a way to get away from that person, if that's what they wanted.

"And she would start, just with a cup of coffee, bringing people a cup of coffee, building relationships."

AIDS has claimed the lives of many transgender and Latin people in New York City, and Lorena eventually ran a support group at the AIDS Center of Queens County. There, Cecilia Gentili attended Lorena's group, where people could get sterile syringes to safely inject recreational drugs or hormones. As Lorena's colleagues doing similar work in Greece and West Virginia explained to me, syringe exchanges have long been known as a pathway for getting people other medical and social support. When Lorena facilitated them for transgender people in Queens, the service didn't help protect her girls only from viruses. It gave them "an opportunity to have a group and talk about their issues," Cecilia said.

"Lorena was like really visionary," Cecilia said of how welcome her friend made people feel, particularly those who didn't outwardly embody traditional gender roles. "The case with most of the girls in Queens," Cecilia told me, was "very binary. You know, you're a girl if you have boobs. And you are looking to get a vagina and like men. And have long hair and a big ass. You know? That's the definition of, like, what most of us understood as a trans person—and some girls still are there."

But Lorena Borjas knew better. "You're a woman because you're a woman," she would say to her girls—and that's where it ended. She accepted herself, her friend Cecilia (who is a lesbian), and the butch and femme girls at the clubs on Roosevelt Avenue alike as women.

While Lorena would always hammer Lynly Egyes to help others, "it took a long time for her to ask me for help" for herself, Egyes said. While she'd gotten her green card in the 1986 amnesty, by 1990, as Lorena told Queens Public TV, she had some convictions that did not allow her to renew her permanent residence or become a U.S. citizen: "I was arrested for prostitution and human trafficking issues, when in fact I was the victim."

By then, Egyes was working at the Transgender Law Center and was able to get some of Lorena's convictions cleared under New York's human trafficking laws—but not all of them. In general, human trafficking laws actually harm sex workers more than they help them. They encourage racial profiling, criminalize the people they purport to protect, and further distance marginalized people from the kinds of public health and community support they need. And in preventing sex workers from conducting their work in open settings with less risk, they do the opposite of harm reduction, as they drive sex work into the shadows and onto the dark web.

So Egyes decided to ask New York governor Andrew Cuomo for a pardon for her client. By the time she submitted the application, Egyes had amassed several hundred pages of testimony on Lorena's behalf, including recommendations and proclamations from former mayor David Dinkins, the Queens Borough president, the New York City Council, the New York State Senate, and future New York State attorney general Letitia James.

On December 26, 2017, Lorena said that Governor Cuomo gave her a slightly late Christmas gift: "He called me . . . he says, 'Congratulations, I reviewed your case and I've noticed the honorable community work that you've done for twenty-five years. Your arrest and convictions were in the past. You don't have an arrest since 1998, and your life has been dedicated to serving the trans community, and as of now, I will pardon you.'

"I started crying, and I still couldn't believe what was happening in my life," she told Queens Public TV.

Lorena became a citizen of the United States in 2019 and visited Mexico that same year, seeing her homeland for the first time in nearly four decades—and just months before the emergence of COVID-19.

* * *

After Chase Strangio moved to Jackson Heights himself, he learned firsthand something all of Lorena's friends knew: despite all her work in the streets, Lorena loved to party.

"When my kid's mom was like eight months pregnant," Chase said, Lorena "threw this incredible baby shower with, like, all the trans Latinas in all of New York. And once, she threw me this party to just, like, say thank you," Chase recalled, his eyes glimmering and his spritely smile dancing beneath his pencil-thin moustache. "We spent so much time, like, eating together and celebrating, like she was *so good at celebrating*—you'd just celebrate that you're there, you're celebrating because people need joy and space to congregate."

Cecilia Gentili would party with Lorena most Saturday nights. Lorena would come over, and they'd cook Argentine steaks and chicken together—sometimes alone, sometimes with Lorena's partner, a man named Chaparro. Sometimes they'd organize for grants and think about community building, and sometimes they'd just hang and be silly.

One Saturday in early March 2020, Cecilia missed their standing Saturday night date because she was in Miami for work. "I was in a CVS, and this woman had like forty Purells in her cart. And I thought that was very weird. I was like, *What? What's this about?* And I went on Twitter, and I searched for Purell, and I learned that people were, like, getting all the Purell because COVID was really exploding."

Cecilia immediately tried to buy some Purell herself, but it was all sold out in Miami. She returned to New York and expected to see her friend the next Saturday. But instead, Lorena called her.

"Cecilia, I don't think I can go this Saturday."

"Okay, no problem. Are you okay?"

"I have fever and I have a cough."

"Lorena, that's what they said COVID-19 is."

"Yeah, but I don't think I have it."

"What do you mean you don't think you have it? You have all the symptoms."

"Yeah, but I'm fine. Maybe it's just a cold."

"Well, I think you should go to a doctor—how long have you had this?"

"Like a week."

"That's a long time to have that for a cold. That's a long time even for the *flu*. I think you should go to the doctor."

"No, I'm sure it's a cold or the flu."

"Lorena, if this is a cold or a flu, you really need to see a doctor anyways."

"No, I don't want to go to the doctor."

"Why, Lorena?"

"I just don't want to go to the doctor, don't ask me why."

"Okay, Lorena. I understand, but this is not a choice for me. You know, you need to see a professional."

"No, no, no, no!"

"Let me see if I can get you to an urgent care. Would you go to an urgent care?"

"Yes, for an urgent care, maybe I could go. I'm just not gonna go to a hospital."

Cecilia called an urgent care, but they told her they weren't accepting patients with COVID-19 symptoms. She needed to call 911, and she needed to go to the hospital. "If I would have asked her, she would say no. So, I did something that I usually regret, which I don't at this time: I called the ambulance first and then I told her. And she was a little bit upset at me."

"Why did you do that?"

"Sometimes, you just have to let others do what's right for you."

"No, I don't want to go to the hospital—I don't know what's going to happen there!"

Cecilia said she knew Lorena was "talking about being trans, and I knew she was talking about the fact that, you know, her English was not the best."

As I listened to Cecilia talk about her frightened friend not wanting to go to the hospital—even with the symptoms of the deadly and mysterious virus that was rapidly becoming the most quickly killing organism known to New Yorkers—I thought of a less dramatic experience I'd had seeking medical care myself in multicultural New York City.

A couple years before, I had found a lump on one of my testicles. Concerned, I went to my doctor, a kind man at my university health center. Examining me, he thought the lump was likely a benign cyst, but he wanted me to have a sonogram as soon as possible to be sure, and he scheduled me to get a scan from a testicular sonogram specialist the very next day.

When I arrived at the facility, the receptionist eyed me warily. She asked me the doctor's name, and I told her. She asked me my name and date of birth, and I told her. She asked me if I was sure I was in the right place, and I said yes (though I was getting uncomfortable). Then, noting that I had been referred from a student health center, she laughed and said, "You just don't look like what I was expecting. I was expecting someone younger."

I was forty-one years old at the time, and she thought I was too old to be a college student. I laughed nervously and tried deflecting her doubt, saying, "I *am* a graduate student, but I've taught undergrads who are older than me." Still, it was an absurd and nasty thing for her to say, especially considering she'd had my date of birth before I came in.

Blood rushed to my face as I was overcome with a wave of shame and humiliation. It is hard enough to walk into an office and say, "Excuse me, can I pull down my pants and have you examine my balls, and then can you tell me if I have something that is going to kill me?" without being made to feel you don't look the right way.

At a moment of great vulnerability, I was made to feel unwelcome. I remember thinking, *What if a trans woman who was femme presenting and had testicles came in, vulnerable and needing help? What if the receptionist said, "You don't look like what I was expecting"?* The person might walk away and leave, maybe with an undiagnosed case of cancer.

This is part of why lethal health disparities plague queer and trans people at such high rates, and why viruses circulate more often in our bodies.

When I heard about Lorena Borjas coughing but not wanting to go to the hospital because she feared what would happen to her there, I thought about that receptionist. My heart hurt for Lorena.

* * *

By the time Lorena got in the ambulance, the true center of the global pandemic was not just in the United States or in New York City, but in the Jackson Heights neighborhood of Queens. You could even argue that the epicenter of the epicenter had moved inside Elmhurst Hospital, where the ambulance took Lorena. Her neighbors, the so-called "essential" workers—day laborers, nursing home orderlies, fast-food workers, and sex workers—had not been able to protect themselves by working from home. The climb toward the peak of New York's first wave was rapidly accelerating, and more than a hundred people were dying of COVID-19 every day.

By the time Lorena got to that hospital, a refrigerated tractor trailer had already been backed up to it to handle the flow of death. Corpses were piling up faster than they could be taken away. Soon, the city would turn to temp workers to move the deluge of bodies and to people locked up at Rikers Island to dig mass graves for them.

The medical staff treating Lorena did not speak Spanish, and Cecilia had to translate by phone for her. Lorena seemed confused, according to her friend. Still, while she was in the hospital, she was also working her phone trying to arrange bail for people locked up at Rikers Island. The jail was already becoming one of the most potent COVID-19 vectors in the nation, and Lorena was desperately trying to free people from it before they, too, got sick.

The Elmhurst staff eventually sent her home. Cecilia kept in touch with Lorena by phone, and for a day, her symptoms seemed to have subsided. But the next day, she started coughing again. The day after that, Cecilia said, Lorena "started having a fever before she didn't answer the phone anymore. And that's how I heard that Chaparro had to call the ambulance again." But this time, Lorena couldn't be admitted to the nearest hospital, Elmhurst, which "told me that they had to send her to Coney Island, because she needed to be on a respirator, and they didn't have one." (Though he'd been repeatedly warned of their shortage, President Trump had yet to invoke the Defense Production Act to order the manufacture of respiratory equipment and had recently told states to "try getting it yourselves"—which made states bid against one another, driving up prices paid like ransoms to unconscionable medical tech companies.)

"When I called Coney Island," Cecilia said, "they told me that she was sedated and in an induced coma with the respirator. And they also told me that they needed someone to make decisions for her." Cecilia had to track down who Lorena's health proxies were. When she found them, neither spoke English, and Cecilia spent the night on the "phone with the doctors translating to them" and "helping them make decisions based on a couple of words" Lorena left saying what she wanted.

There was a sad irony at the end of her life. Lorena always showed up with people. When she hit the streets, she'd do it with friends. When she showed up at Egyes's or Chase's offices demanding legal support, she'd bring friends with her. When she went to court for a stranger, she'd have a gaggle of friends along.

But at the end of it all, except perhaps for the respiratory technician and nurses on duty as she drew her final breaths, Lorena Borjas was physically alone. Chaparro, Cecilia, Chase, Egyes, all the thousands of people she'd given condoms and syringes and food to on Roosevelt Avenue—none of them could be with her to hold her hand in the final transitional moments of her earthly journey.

"At five twenty-two in the morning, I got a call from the hospital, and they told me that she had died," Cecilia told me quietly.

The day she died, Lorena was one of about 330 people known to have died of COVID-19 in New York City. It was March 30, the eve of a kind of trans holiday. On March 31, the U.S. representative for Jackson Heights, Congresswoman Alexandria Ocasio-Cortez, wrote on Facebook, "On International Transgender Day of Visibility, we honor our transgender siblings and celebrate our heroes. Yesterday we lost the mother of the trans Latinx community of Queens, Lorena Borjas. Lorena immigrated to the United States from Mexico and became one of the greatest activists in Jackson Heights. Our community will sorely miss Lorena and her tireless advocacy for the rights, visibility and safety of the transgender community."

* * *

When I'm giving lectures about the criminalization of HIV, I often ask the audience, "When did the United States Naval Base at Guantánamo Bay become a site of indefinite detention?" Nearly everyone who raises their hand and ventures a guess says the same thing: that this happened in the weeks following September 11, 2001, in the early days of the U.S. War on Terror.

This is incorrect. The War on Terror *was* begun by George W. Bush, and that failed two-decade war *has* involved confining alleged perpetrators under the dubious label "enemy combatants" to forty-five square miles the United States has occupied on the southeastern coast of Cuba since the Spanish American War in 1898. But Guantánamo Bay's use as a site of prolonged, hellish incarceration on land the United States *controls* (but on which the federal government argues U.S. law doesn't necessarily *apply*) was in fact started by George *H.* W. Bush, the forty-third president's *father*.

In 1991, when the elder Bush was the forty-first president, thousands of Haitians who had supported Jean-Bertrand Aristide fled their country after their democratically elected president was ousted in a coup. Intercepted by the U.S. Coast Guard en route to Florida, the refuge-seeking Haitians were kept from getting to the U.S. mainland, which, under international treaties, would have forced the United States to accept them as political asylum seekers.

But the United States couldn't send them back to almost-certain death in Haiti. So, the first Bush administration sent them to Guantánamo Bay, where they'd be under U.S. authority but wouldn't necessarily have access to civil rights under U.S. law.

Once there—as the Haitians waited to see if their petitions for refugee status would be granted or not—they were screened for HIV. As the scholar Cathy Hannabach has written, "While all Haitian refugees incarcerated at" Guantánamo "had their blood forcibly drawn and tested, it was only HIV-positive women who were subjected to technologies of reproductive intervention. Without their consent and often even without their knowledge, HIV-positive women refugees were either sterilized or forcibly injected with Depo-Provera, a semipermanent form of birth control." Not all women can birth children, and not all people who can birth children are women; still, the ability to do so is often (if unfairly) used as a defining characteristic of legitimate womanhood. And at Guantánamo Bay, the United States used this definition to draw a harsh border around what it meant to be a woman, and used eugenics to place the Haitians outside it.

The Haitian refugee crisis of 1991, not the attacks of 9/11, was the inciting event that converted Guantánamo Bay into a space for indefinite detention. Much as the Los Alamos National Laboratory has been home to both the Manhattan Project and the Pathogen Research Database, the history of HIV in America is intertwined with U.S. militarism. A fear of immigrants bolstered by surgical eugenics formed the legal architecture for how the base would later be used for accused terrorists. The forced sterilizations weren't happening in Nazi Germany; they were perpetrated by the U.S. government at the same time as *Twin Peaks* and *The Oprah Winfrey Show* were on the air. And when news broke in the summer of 2020 that women in ICE custody had had hysterectomies performed on them without their consent, it was clear that the centuries-long American practice of sterilizing Black, brown, and native women had still not ended.

At Guantánamo Bay, the ostensible justification for this forced sterilization was imagined viral purity. The mere possibility that any Haitians might win their legal appeals and be allowed into the United States was reason enough, the eugenicists seemed to have believed, to sterilize all the detained refugees they thought could carry and birth children with HIV.

Almost three decades later, in 2020, while most international borders were closed due to the COVID-19 pandemic, ICE deported people with coronavirus from its U.S. prisons to Haiti, threatening to overwhelm the impoverished nation. And in a single week the following year, when the Haitian president was assassinated in his own home, the United States was contemplating giving its own people a third booster COVID-19 shot, while no one in Haiti had yet been vaccinated at all; Haiti was the only country in the Western Hemisphere with no vaccines in mid-2021. That fall, the Biden administration continued to exile Haitian refugees under Rule 42, a provision of the 1944 Public Health Service Act that allows federal authorities to expedite deportations during a pandemic (and which the Trump administration controversially invoked to expel migrants seeking asylum). In fact, as the *Guardian* reported, the Biden administration "deported more Haitians in a few weeks than the Trump administration did in a whole year," and the administration sought contractors who spoke Spanish and Creole to prepare detention facilities at Guantánamo Bay for an expected influx, once again, of Haitian refugees seeking asylum.

Viruses are used to determine who is deserving of being allowed to cross various borders—of geography, of gender, of Americanness, of worthiness. By challenging the gender norms people are assigned at birth, drag performers transgress such borders onstage, and transgender people transgress them throughout their lives. And while Zak Kostopoulos performed gender as a "personal construction that highlights and mocks other social constructions," militarized nationalism often tries to reinforce gender borders around social constructions in ways that can be lethal.

As a transnational traveler and transgender activist, Lorena Borjas transgressed many borders herself—borders of gender, of nation, and of belonging. As a woman who lived with HIV and died of SARS-CoV-2, she also experienced how viruses transgressed the boundaries of her own body. But in her rich life and her needlessly premature death, Lorena exposed the entire fiction of borders.

Think about the body you live in: with every breath you breathe in and out, the idea that your body has permanent borders between what's inside and outside it is revealed to be a fiction. Or, think about the borders of what it means to be *American*. "American" could refer to being of the United States of America, *or* it could refer to any space between Canada's Arctic Circle, at the top of North America, and Chile's Cape Horn, at the bottom of South America. That harsh border the United States tried to create at Guantánamo Bay between the worthy and the unworthy, and the wall Trump tried to build to create a finite U.S.-Mexico border, and the notion that the novel coronavirus lived neatly outside the U.S. border? These are all fictions. There are no stark borders between races, between those living with viruses and without, between those in the United States and outside it, between being American and non-American (or un-American), between men and women. Borders are myths, and while viruses are used to justify their necessity and marginalize those who don't fit neatly on one side of them, viruses ironically disprove them.

Truer than the fiction of borders is the messy reality of how life operates in the zone in between binary markers—in the spaces Zak, Cecilia, Gutiérrez, and Lorena have dared or dare to dwell. Borderlands are spaces populated by migrants drawn across fake national borders, by citizens living inside fake national borders, by nonconforming people who have the courage to live in between gender norms, and by people from all over the world speaking 167 different languages in Jackson Heights.

And those borderlands are where Lorena Borjas, mother to the viral underclass she tended to so lovingly, tried to free others from cages in her final days.

7

CAGES

(The Liberal Carceral State)

In March 1992, Arkansas governor Bill Clinton was in New York City hauling in cash as he sought the Democratic Party's nomination for the presidency. He was running as a tough-on-crime "New Democrat," the kind who wasn't afraid to lock people up in cages—forever, if necessary. He'd recently left the campaign trail to return to his home state, so that he could personally oversee the execution of Ricky Ray Rector, a convicted murderer so cognitively unaware of his own impending death that he left the pecan pie dessert from his final meal uneaten because he was "saving it for later."

While speaking at a fundraiser at Laura Belle, a movie house turned nightclub in Midtown Manhattan, Clinton was interrupted by Bob Rafsky, a pesky protester with the AIDS Coalition to Unleash Power, or ACT UP. "This is the center of the AIDS epidemic!" Rafsky yelled off-screen at Clinton, on video captured by the recently formed Cable News Network. The two men were almost the same age, born just a year apart; both were wearing suits that night, though the cut of Rafsky's was much tighter than the candidate's.

"What are you going to do?" Rafsky pressed the Democratic hopeful. "Are you going to start a war on AIDS? Are you going to just go on and ignore it? Are you going to do more than you did as Governor of Arkansas?"

Clinton looked momentarily rattled. The former head of the centrist Democratic Leadership Coalition, he was being called out for campaigning on his "third way" of doing politics, which prioritized balanced budgets and public-private partnerships over the kind of robust state aid that was needed to address the root causes of the current viral pandemic.

Sarcastically, he said, "Can we talk now?"

"Go ahead and talk," Rafsky retorted.

"I'm listening. You can talk. I know how it hurts. I've got friends who've died of AIDS."

"Bill, we're not dying of AIDS as much as we are from eleven years of government neglect."

"And that's why I'm running for president, to do something about it," Clinton said, before rattling off a litany of actions, including that he'd broaden the definition of AIDS to include people who injected drugs and women who, until then, had been mostly ignored.

But Rafsky wasn't having it, and he tried to interrupt him again.

"Now, would you just calm down?" Clinton said condescendingly, drawing applause from the audience.

"I can't calm down. I'm dying of AIDS while you're dying of ambition."

"Let me tell you something," Clinton exploded, moving his microphone a few inches closer toward the sound of Rafsky's voice. "If I were dying of ambition, I wouldn't have stood up here and put up with all this crap I've put up with for the last six months. I'm fighting to change this country!

"And let me tell you something else." Clinton's voice rose over the approving cheers of the crowd; he removed the mic from its stand. "You do not have the right to treat any human being, including me, with no respect because of what *you're* worried about." He wagged his finger angrily, his eyes narrowing with visible rage. "I did not cause it. I'm trying to do something about it. I have treated you and all the people who've interrupted my rallies with a hell of a lot more respect than you've treated me, and it's time you started thinking about *that*."

Then he dropped four words that would define Clinton for years: "I feel your pain." He punctuated each word with a finger jab toward Rafsky, making the declaration of empathy look more like a threat.

The phrase would become shorthand for Bill Clinton's bullshit, a mocking example of how breezily he would identify with people in an insincere manner. But whether the phrase was evoked in a skit on *Saturday Night Live* in the 1990s or as a GIF on the internet in the 2010s, the context would mostly be forgotten: in that moment, "I feel your pain" was a way for Clinton to put a man dying of AIDS in his place for biting the hand that could feed him.

"If you don't agree with me, go support somebody else for president, but quit talking to me like that," Clinton yelled. "You can be for George Bush, you can be for somebody else, but do not stand up here at *my* rally, where other people paid to come."

Despite Clinton's suggestion that Rafsky might be for his opponent, the heckler was hardly a Republican supporter. On the following November 2, the eve of the 1992 presidential election, Rafsky helped lead an ACT UP contingent carrying the body of deceased activist Mark Fisher in a casket to Bush's New York City reelection headquarters. By then, AIDS was the second-biggest killer of people in the United States ages twenty-two to forty-four, and it would take more than 33,000 American lives that year overall.

By then, Rafsky was gaunt. Clad in a black leather jacket and jeans, he bore purple Kaposi sarcoma lesions on his face. Speaking into a microphone, he yelled, "This isn't a political funeral for Mark. It's a political funeral for the man who killed him. George Bush, we believe you will be defeated tomorrow, because we believe there's still some justice left in the universe and some compassion left in the American people." As he hexed the forty-first president, he seemed to want Clinton to win. "We put this curse on you: Mark's spirit will haunt you until the end of your days, so that in a moment of your defeat, you will remember our defeats. And in the moment of your death, you'll remember our deaths."

Rafsky's desperation to curse the outgoing president and influence the future president was prescient and urgent. Just nine months after

Rafsky crashed the governor of Arkansas's fundraiser and two months after he taunted President Bush, William Jefferson Clinton was inaugurated as the forty-second president of the United States.

But a mere month after that, Rafsky died of AIDS. He was only forty-seven years old.

In the early days of the American novel coronavirus epidemic, I heard Rafsky's haunting, prophetically angry voice in my head often, particularly as equally desperate activists yelled at Democratic political leaders. I heard it when protesters gathered outside the mansion of California governor Gavin Newsom to demand that people in prison be freed before more died at San Quentin, and when they staged a die-in outside San Francisco mayor London Breed's home to demand hotel rooms for the unhoused. I heard it when they protested New York State governor Andrew Cuomo's budget, which slashed Medicaid spending even as the state's hospital system teetered on the verge of collapse, and I heard it when they begged New York City mayor Bill de Blasio to release people from COVID-19 hot spot Rikers Island jail. While it appeared easy for Americans on the left to express anger at the obvious malfeasance of Republican president Donald Trump's failure to enact a national coronavirus pandemic response throughout 2020, it looked much more painful for activists who tried to hold Democratic mayors and governors in "blue" jurisdictions accountable for *their* virus-inducing actions. Those activists were often ignored in the mainstream press and widely mocked on social media.

At this frightening time, people in the United States could have looked to ACT UP for one kind of blueprint. But even when Americans know anything about ACT UP's history, they often know only how hard the group had gone against Republicans: how they'd shamed President Reagan for his silence on AIDS, covered Senator Jesse Helms's home with a gigantic condom, and taken the cremated remains of their lovers who'd died of AIDS to the White House, where they tossed them onto the lawn. But if activists found ACT UP's legacy useful for confronting the novel coronavirus pandemic, they also needed to understand how ACT UP had challenged Democrats.

Specifically, they needed to know how Democrats have made the conditions of viral transmission horrifically worse by undermining social programs, consistently turning to markets to solve nonmarket problems (especially regarding health care), and, most of all, perpetuating a carceral state.

In enacting the New Deal, Franklin Delano Roosevelt led the Democrats as the party of the liberal welfare state. But since World War II, many Democratic presidents, including Harry Truman, Lyndon Johnson, Bill Clinton, Barack Obama, and Joe Biden, have expanded the scope of policing and the carceral state. This includes not just an increase in prisons and jails and immigration detention centers, but a sprawl of *where* these things exist and a logic of punishment that permeates increasing facets of American life. (Think of the rise of police officers in schools and of drug tests to get jobs; or of how letters mailed through the U.S. Postal Service were once considered private, but their envelopes are now scanned so the government can see who is mailing whom; or of how telephone calls were once largely protected as confidential, but now electronic communications can easily be analyzed by corporations.)

Of course, Republican presidents do this, too. But whereas Republican presidents (especially Ronald Reagan, George W. Bush, and Donald Trump) have ignited significant protests against their investments in the carceral state, Democratic presidents largely have not, slipping under the radar. Democratic legislators, mayors, and governors receive relatively little pushback against creating a police state, allowing it to grow almost unchecked. This is because, in the interest of gaining and maintaining power, Democratic candidates have too often followed a pattern of embracing marginalized people during election years, co-opting their identities to gin up votes, and then, once elected, enacting carceral policies that will harm their most ardent, but vulnerable, supporters.

Being told by Democrats that you have nowhere else to go, many (though not all) activists who might oppose carceral politics under Republicans do not protest Democrats who are just as prone to lock people up in cages. And once the Democratic Party embraced the carceral state, it hid from view its most violent effects, mitigated a lot of opposition, and stymied efforts to build a politics of care.

When Rafsky was booed in 1992 in the Laura Belle nightclub as he challenged the future president, he was booed not by Republicans, but by Democrats. They should have been his allies. But the donors didn't want the gadfly challenging and embarrassing their guy on an unacceptable viral response. However, ACT UP, formed in 1987, was created as "a diverse, non-partisan group of individuals united in anger and committed to direct action to end the AIDS crisis." It was not aligned with any party or government agency. The group had vociferously challenged Democratic mayor Ed Koch for his bungling inaction on AIDS. Rafsky called out Bush *and* Clinton in the 1992 election. And in the early 1990s, ACT UP routinely challenged the nonpartisan head of the National Institute of Allergy and Infectious Diseases, Dr. Anthony Fauci, a man who would still be running NIAID as SARS, Zika, Ebola, avian flu, swine flu, and SARS-CoV-2 broke out over the next four decades.

Clinton's first "AIDS czar," Kristine M. Gebbie, resigned after less than a year on the job, after activists complained about the "ill-defined nature of her job" and that she was not the kind of high-profile figure Clinton had promised, according to the *New York Times*. Still, except for Rafsky, it is odd that President Clinton did not receive the kinds of protests from AIDS advocates that his two predecessors received, given that the year with the most U.S. AIDS deaths happened during his presidency (about fifty thousand in 1995).

Perhaps Clinton got some slack because of gay exhaustion after the Reagan/Bush years; perhaps it was partially because of the political opportunism of some well-connected gay operatives and organizations that make up "Gay Inc.," who benefit from their association with Democrats; perhaps it was because the drugs to fight AIDS mercifully arrived in 1996, during his tenure.

Perhaps it was because people like Rafsky died shortly into Clinton's term, and Clinton didn't have to deal with them anymore. Or maybe it was because, as one ACT UP member told me, many activists became addicted to crystal methamphetamine in the mid-90s and wanted to slip away from activist life.

But even though AIDS death rates declined dramatically in his second term, Clinton's desire to project himself as an anticrime budget hawk had a deleterious effect on the HIV crisis. Clinton passed two important pieces of domestic legislation, the 1994 crime bill and the 1996 welfare reform bill, that made the factors that led to increased levels of HIV horrifically worse.

What Clinton's two signature domestic achievements have in common is that they increased Black incarceration, homelessness, and precarity, which has had the alarming effect of increasing pathogenic transmission among Black people in the subsequent decades.

For instance, racial disparities around HIV/AIDS didn't just *increase* during the Clinton years; the policies Clinton put in motion are why the rate of AIDS among Black Americans eventually became *more* prevalent per capita after medications were created to treat it than it ever was for white America when there were no medications available at all.

If we look at these two Clinton legislative victories, we can understand how, in the twentieth century, the liberal carceral state snuffed out the liberal welfare state, which in turn created the conditions through which many viruses and other pathogens have flourished over the last few decades, especially among Black people.

Conservative order is maintained by policing, but so is liberal order; yet only the latter reality is obscured. If we look back at these moments in the Clinton administration and at the policy blueprint they created, we can understand how the Democratic mayor of Minneapolis, Jacob Frey, could preside over a city where, in 2020, a third of the budget went to policing while minimal funding went to housing or health; these budget priorities connected why George Floyd contracted the novel coronavirus *and* why he was killed by police. Minneapolis is in Minnesota, where the governorship and both houses of the legislature were also controlled by Democrats when Floyd was killed. The state's budget priorities, then, reflect the values of the Democratic Party, which frequently prioritizes policies that help the party's wealthy donors. For this reason, Democrats will enact housing policies that position cities as playgrounds for tech millionaires (displacing poor people), health care policies that concentrate wealth in the hands of their donors from the insurance industry (leaving many uninsured), and financial policies that treat housing as a commodity (and not as a right), to appease their Wall Street backers. All these policies turn marginalized people into a surplus population. When people are cut off from work and housing in liberal economics, they are of little use to capital within liberal economics. Just as Republicans do, Democrats control this surplus population with violent policing, and when needed, they warehouse this population in prisons.

The carceral state is one of the most potent vectors of an underclass deemed disposable and unworthy of care or health. For, while Democrats are generally much better at cleaning up viral outbreaks than their Republicans counterparts, Democrats also expand the power of the carceral vector of disease in the first place, while hypocritically condemning to imprisonment, homelessness, and viruses the very people they claim to represent.

* * *

It would be unfair to blame the racial HIV/AIDS disparities of Black people entirely on Bill Clinton. Antiretroviral drugs developed during his administration have saved millions of lives globally. But they were developed in what ACT UP member Avram Finkelstein calls a "deregulation-mad political landscape," when the goals of certain activists, Big Pharma, and Clintonian centrism aligned. While some members of ACT UP wanted broad societal changes to deal with the root causes of AIDS, others broke off to form the more targeted Treatment Action Group. TAG wanted to get drugs into bodies quickly by working with pharmaceutical companies, which were *very* happy to cut government red tape and speed up protocols to start manufacturing medicine with haste.

Still, a lot of this was the doing of the forty-second president, who was all about deregulating medicine, telecommunications, and banks. As legal scholar Michelle Alexander wrote in a 2016 essay for the *Nation*, Clinton "was the standard-bearer for the New Democrats," a group that promoted not only neoliberal economics but also conservative social policies and that "firmly believed the only way to win back the millions of white voters in the South who had defected to the Republican Party was to adopt the right-wing narrative that black communities ought to be disciplined with severe punishment rather than coddled with welfare."

And punish, he did. The Violent Crime Control and Law Enforcement Act of 1994 (guided through the Senate by Judiciary Committee chairman and future president Joe Biden) and the Personal Responsibility and Work Opportunity Reconciliation Act of 1996 showed how punitive Clinton's vision of government was. The former bill added one hundred thousand police to America's streets—police who would disproportionately patrol, harm, and kill Black people and, in ways direct and indirect, make Black people homeless. In an attempt to woo back "Reagan Democrats," the latter act fulfilled Clinton's campaign promise to "end welfare as we know it." And in signing the welfare bill, he paved the way for states to limit access to food stamps. (People ever convicted of a felony for drugs could be banned from food assistance for *life*.)

The bill also limited housing assistance, which might have been intended to show upper-middle-class voters that Clinton wouldn't give *handouts* to people they might think of as lazy or who were unwilling to take "personal responsibility." New Democrats were as eager to reject welfare as New Deal Democrats had been proud to create it. As a result, more children went hungry, more people became incarcerated, and more families experienced homelessness. And because being incarcerated or without a home makes it harder, if not impossible, to vote, these bills resulted in a loss not only of freedom but also of political power.

As Alexander put it, Clinton rode the support of Black voters into office, only to "preside over the largest increase in federal and state prison inmates of any president in American history," which included "supporting the 100-to-1 sentencing disparity for crack versus powder cocaine." Black people were not more likely to use drugs than white people, but if they used cocaine, they were more likely to use the hard crystal version than the powder form, which resulted in wildly harsher sentences. The crime bill also "created dozens of new federal capital crimes, mandated life sentences for some three-time offenders, and authorized more than $16 billion for state prison grants and the expansion of police forces," Alexander noted. This meant that by the time Clinton left office, the United States had "the highest rate of incarceration in the world" and "prison admissions for drug offense reached a level in 2000 for African Americans more than 26 times the level they had been in 1983," just around the time Ronald Reagan was ramping up the war on drugs. If you included those behind bars when Clinton left office, Black unemployment for young, non-college-educated men was a staggering 42 percent.

Cruelly and expensively, as part of the crime bill, Clinton ended federal funding for prison education programs, even though research has repeatedly shown that such programs sharply reduce recidivism, help people to lead meaningful lives after release, and save governments money.

But despite Clinton's being an ostensibly budget-minded Democrat who hated deficits as much as Republicans, even crudely saving money wasn't his game when it came to locking people up in cages. All those new prisons and one hundred thousand cops he proudly put on the streets in the mid-1990s were expensive. As Alexander wrote, "the Clinton administration didn't reduce the amount of money devoted to the management of the urban poor; it changed what the funds would be used for. Billions of dollars were slashed from public-housing and child-welfare budgets and transferred to the mass-incarceration machine. By 1996, the penal budget was twice the amount that had been allocated to food stamps."

Prioritizing penal and policing budgets while simultaneously reducing welfare created, in ways implicit and explicit, a population ever more vulnerable not just to hunger, but also to viruses and pandemics.

When densely locked in cages, humans (just like chickens or pigs) predictably get sick. A national survey of jails and prisons completed in 1997, the year after treatment for HIV was first available, found that "compared to the general population, rates of human immunodeficiency virus . . . among incarcerated individuals are 8 to 10 times higher." By 2013, other research found that "a generalized epidemic of HIV persists among the incarcerated US population," with an overall incarceration HIV rate "approximately 3 times greater than among the general US population" and with "HIV prevalence in the state prisons of Florida, Maryland and New York . . . higher than the national prevalence of any country outside of sub-Saharan Africa." People who are incarcerated are under the complete control of the state, which is responsible for their health. There is no reason that, with existing HIV treatments, they should be sick, or that the disease should be spreading. (Unless, of course, they are deemed unworthy of the cost of care under capitalism and a privatized, profit-driven health system. Which they are.)

Similarly, with tuberculosis, the World Health Organization has reported that, globally, the "level of TB in prisons has been reported to be up to 100 times higher than that of the civilian population." TB is not a major problem in the United States. But with the United States turning into the most incarceration-heavy nation in the world, the Clinton administration needlessly helped the relatively rare *Mycobacterium tuberculosis* flourish under certain conditions.

At the same time as he was expanding the carceral state, Clinton did oversee an effort at reforming the health care system and appointed his wife, Hillary Rodham Clinton, to head the task force creating the Health Security Bill. But despite having majorities in both houses of Congress, the Clintons' plan collapsed by the fall of 1994. The result of this policy failure was a massive consolidation of GOP power, which undermined President Clinton's legislative agenda.

During the Clinton years, jails and prisons didn't just concentrate people already at high risk for HIV and TB where they were likely to become infected. Because of all those cops Clinton put on the streets with federal money, greater numbers of people were churned in and out of local jails, where they'd contract pathogens and then carry them back into their communities. In order to be seen as tough on crime, Clinton had built up the United States' carceral architecture—just as Obama built up and Trump augmented the deportation machine in order to be seen as tough on immigrants. In 2020, these county jails, state prisons, and federal ICE detention centers would become powerful vectors of the novel coronavirus.

But Clinton's carcerality also created two additional indirect conditions in which viruses are prone to reproducing: homelessness and unemployment. Epidemiologically, being unhoused or without employment creates configurations in which increased risk for viruses is produced. And, not coincidentally, the exploding rates of homelessness and unemployment caused by imprisonment disproportionately affect Black people.

As its name suggests, the Personal Responsibility and Work Opportunity Reconciliation Act that Clinton signed in 1996 was meant to shift risk from the state onto individuals. It was a signature part of the Republican Party's Contract with America, which sought to deal a blow to the mythical "welfare queen" whom the party had been complaining about since Ronald Reagan was president. It limited aid and allowed, but did not require, states to tie drug testing to receiving benefits. Together with the crime bill, the welfare bill created an assault on the viral underclass that could, at times, be outright eugenic. As Cathy Hannabach wrote in 2013, the long-term, injectable birth control drugs "Depo-Provera and Norplant began to be required as a condition of release for women arrested for certain crimes and were forced on women receiving welfare—policies that continue today in various forms." (Drugs like these needn't lead to permanent sterilization, but when given under coercion on the U.S. mainland as well as at Guantánamo Bay, as we saw with Haitians diagnosed with HIV in chapter 6, the drugs can stop women, especially when given during their final childbearing years, from reproducing for the rest of their lives.)

One element of the act that made Black people particularly at risk for homelessness was that it banned people with records of criminal arrest—not even with criminal convictions but with mere criminal *arrests*—from living in public housing. This meant that if the family of someone who was arrested or got out of jail lived in public housing, that person's moving back home could place the entire family at risk for eviction. Saddled with a record that made it impossible to rent a home in their own name and unable to live with family, record numbers of Black people were rendered homeless upon making contact with the criminal justice system after the 1996 bill passed. And homelessness inevitably led to their committing more "crimes" associated with being unhoused, such as panhandling, lying down outside, working in the informal economy, or urinating in public (the latter of which could lead to being labeled a "sex offender," which would make securing employment or housing effectively impossible for the rest of their lives). This led to *more* incarceration, which created *more* homelessness, in an inescapable whirlpool of catastrophe.

Incarceration and homelessness are linked in that people experiencing both are often perceived by those experiencing neither to be disposable. Homelessness isn't caused only by incarceration; gentrification (itself sustained by policing) is a major driver as well. But the carceral crisis caused by Clinton's crime and welfare bills is a major reason the unhoused population of the United States has not only grown in recent decades but has become Blacker. According to the U.S. Interagency Council on Homelessness, by 2013, about two-thirds of the unhoused in America were Black, though Black people accounted for only about 12 percent of the population. White people, by comparison, were three-quarters of the population but only about a quarter of the U.S. homeless population. This means that, proportionately, Black people were about *fourteen times* more likely to be homeless than white people.

At the same time, research has long found that up to half of people with AIDS are in danger of becoming homeless, that AIDS is three times higher among people who are already unhoused compared to people who are housed, and that there are strong connections between AIDS, homelessness, incarceration, and Blackness.

The racial health disparities that emerged from the era of the New Democrats are grim, and the story can be told in viruses. If we look at per capita cases, Black people were about three times more likely than their white counterparts to have AIDS when the CDC began compiling AIDS statistics by race during the Reagan administration. By 1995, the CDC's annual Surveillance Report declared that the "AIDS incidence rate per 100,000 among blacks (92.6) was 6 times higher than that among whites (15.4)." And by the printing of the CDC's 2015–2016 Surveillance Report, the rate of AIDS per 100,000 white people was just 2.4, while it was 21.8 for Black Americans. This isn't just a 9-to-1 racial disparity; with the Black rate per 100,000 being 21.8 in 2015 after the white rate peaked at 15.4 in 1995, there was a *higher* per capita rate of AIDS for Black people some *two decades after* medicine was available than there ever was for white people when there were no effective drugs.

A similar kind of viral disparity happened with COVID-19. Through much of 2020, there was no vaccine and there was little effective treatment for COVID-19's worst symptoms for anyone of any race. Yet, in September of that year, sociologist Elizabeth Wrigley-Field modeled that for white Americans, "life expectancy in 2020 will remain higher than Black life expectancy has ever been." Even *with* COVID-19, white Americans did not experience as much premature death as Black Americans did pre-COVID-19.

These kinds of disparities have persisted and increased across both Republican and Democratic administrations. However, the populations most affected by them are reliable voting constituents for the Democratic Party, which sometimes *says* it feels viral pain while causing so much of it to proliferate.

When Hillary Rodham Clinton unsuccessfully ran for president in

2016, a young Black activist named Ashley Williams challenged her about her past use of the term *superpredators* at a fundraiser. But by then, missing from Democratic cash hauls were any white gay men with the anger of Bob Rafsky in 1992—and all that remains of his exchange with Bill Clinton is a viral GIF stripped of context, a floating signifier.

* * *

One day in August 2020, I logged on to the *New York Times*'s coronavirus tracker, which, among other factors, displayed how many COVID-19 cases could be traced to institutions. Besides a pork-processing plant in South Dakota and a chicken plant in Iowa, fifteen of the seventeen institutions on that date with a thousand or more coronavirus cases traced to them were jails or prisons. Six of them were located in California, three in Florida, two each in Ohio and Arkansas, and one each in Tennessee and Illinois, including Chicago's Cook County jail. The governors who could have reduced these incarcerated populations with pardons to stop the largest clusters of COVID-19 in the nation were Republicans and Democrats alike. The viral danger had nothing to do with whether a state was "red" or "blue." And if one were to trace the responsibility for the deadliest institution of them all on that day—San Quentin State Prison in California, where about twenty-five hundred people had tested positive for coronavirus and twenty-five had died of it—it would lead to the door of Democratic governor Gavin Newsom.

That very same month, more than 350 fires raged out of control across the state Newsom governed. While ash fell on Oakland, nonprofit organizations and mutual aid networks struggled to get N95 masks to vulnerable people before the smoke triggered asthma attacks or other lethal breathing problems. But the masks were already in short supply due to COVID-19. The same day, Cal Fire told the press it had no way to treat all the flames burning throughout the state, because for years it had been relying upon incarcerated firefighters to smother such blazes. These workers earned as little as a dollar per hour, and their criminal records kept them from becoming firefighters once they were released. And because California's prisons were among the most powerful COVID-19 hot spots in the nation, so many firefighters were sick or under quarantine that there weren't enough available to fight the hundreds of fires. It was a moment in which America's twin epidemics of incarceration and COVID-19 entered into a three-way race with the global pandemic of the climate crisis.

This was a disaster of the Democrats' making. Governor Gavin Newsom, a darling of Gay Inc. since he'd supported same-sex marriages as mayor of San Francisco in 2004, slowly began releasing some incarcerated firefighters in the summer of 2020. But he could have done so months or years earlier. Many of them were eligible to be firefighters for the same reasons their release dates had been moved forward: their model behavior. If Newsom had released them *before* COVID-19 spread in prisons, when activists had first begged him to, they could have gone home to their families, where they would have been far less at risk than in prison. If he had then pardoned them, they could have been called to duty not as enslaved workers—people convicted of crimes are legally enslaved under the Thirteenth Amendment of the U.S. Constitution—but as crisis ready firefighters.

But Democratic policy in the Golden State had long been to incarcerate people needlessly. In 2011, the U.S. Supreme Court ruled that California had to reduce its dangerously overcrowded prisons by granting early release to people convicted of nonviolent offenses. Then–California attorney general Kamala Harris sued in 2014 to stop these court-mandated releases. By using cheaply paid, enslaved firefighters, California was saving one hundred million dollars a year, and Harris's office argued that it would be too "dangerous" to let these firefighters go—not because they would pose a danger to their communities, but because it would be "a difficult fire season" without enslaved labor.

California wasn't the only state using enslaved labor during the coronavirus pandemic. During a shortage of hand sanitizer, New York governor

Andrew Cuomo bragged about bottling it in Empire State prisons, and Texas paid incarcerated workers just two dollars an hour to move the corpses of people killed by COVID-19.

When Harris accepted her nomination for the vice presidency the same week her home state burned, she said there was "no vaccine for racism." This made me think about how, as attorney general, she *could* have released the kinds of prisoners who made excellent firefighters years before. If Newsom then pardoned them and taxed Silicon Valley, they could have been paid fairly as *free* firefighters as they rebuilt their lives during the pandemic. This would have granted some protection to the families of incarcerated people (and to all Californians facing wildfires).

It also would have protected them from viral transmission in prisons. Instead, in the legacy of Bill Clinton, the policies enacted by Harris and Newsom effectively kept them locked up. As a result, many of the firefighters were infected by coronavirus and kept from duty—which fanned the flames of climate change outside the prison walls as wildly as the virus burned inside its walls.

These Democrats' reliance on enslaved labor in a way that increases and harms the viral underclass is just a symptom of the wider disease of neoliberalism. During the first year of the coronavirus pandemic, Newsom and Cuomo were governors of states that were home to Hollywood, Wall Street, and Silicon Valley, some of the wealthiest tax bases in the nation. Both governors enjoyed majorities or supermajorities in their legislatures and could have significantly raised taxes on their wealthiest citizens, who only got richer from the pandemic. Instead, they largely condemned their poorest residents to viral immiseration, poverty, and even death—especially those behind bars.

* * *

In a fiery 1988 speech called "Why We Fight"—a reference to the U.S. propaganda war movie of the same title, directed by Frank Capra—cinephile and ACT UP activist Vito Russo said of AIDS, "We're so busy putting out fires right now, that we don't have the time to talk to each other and strategize and plan for the next wave, and the next day, and next month and the next week and the next year." He added that, after things calmed down, "we have to commit ourselves to doing that. And then, after we kick the shit out of this disease, we're all going to be alive to kick the shit out of this system, so that this never happens again."

Russo died less than two years after giving that charge.

In the decades since Rafsky and Russo spoke up and died, it has become no easier for liberals to hear about their role in the carceral state that reproduces a viral underclass. This reckoning has been especially painful in a queer context, where it should be better considered. Yet, a quarter century after Rafsky confronted Bill Clinton, a trans Latina activist interrupted the first Black president—and her critique was unwelcome in a room of Democratic queer and trans folx.

In June 2015, Jennicet Gutiérrez, the undocumented transgender activist we met in chapter 6, was invited by the group GetEQUAL to be their guest at a White House LGBTQ Pride Month reception—but with a caveat: they wanted someone willing to interrupt President Obama about his immigration policies. Sometimes called the "deporter in chief," Obama had expelled more immigrants from the nation than any president in U.S. history.

Gutiérrez had mixed feelings. She'd been excited when Senator Obama "ran on a platform that was going to give immigrants within the first year of office some path to legalization or reform" and was enthusiastic when he'd been elected in 2008. "But obviously," she said, the promised immigration relief "didn't happen." Well into Obama's second term, queer and trans Latinx people were still losing their lives in his deportation machine. People Gutiérrez knew would disappear, be locked in cages, and then be shipped across the border.

Gutiérrez accepted GetEQUAL's invitation, and on June 24, 2015, she entered the East Room of the White House. As the president was saying he was "hopeful about what we can accomplish" for the civil rights of LGBTQ Americans, Gutiérrez yelled, "President Obama!"

Heads turned away from President Obama, at the front of the East Room, and toward the woman shouting at him.

"Release all LGBTQ detention centers! President Obama, stop the torture and abuse of trans women in detention centers! President Obama, I am a trans woman. I'm tired of the abuse."

"Listen, you're in *my* house," Obama said (even though the White House is the people's house, not any president's), as many in the crowd cheered loudly. "As a general rule, I am just fine with a few hecklers," he said, to much laughter, "but not when I'm up in the house!" Vice President Biden grabbed Obama's shoulder and laughed.

(At this moment, Gutiérrez was thinking, *Am I going to get in trouble? Am I going to get arrested? Will that give the government a reason for me to be deported?* Especially since she had an arrest record, I find the courage of what she did almost unfathomable. In my one and only day reporting at the White House, I stood in the Rose Garden while a white immigrant blogger from Ireland yelled at Obama for being too soft on immigrants, and he was *not* led away by guards—and I found just reporting next to him almost unbearably anxiety inducing.)

It looked like everyone—apart from the codirector of GetEQUAL who'd accompanied and invited her, a Black woman named Angela Peoples—was laughing at Gutiérrez as she was escorted out. No one offered her any support. She sensed that there was a "disconnection of priorities" in the crowd, as if the things happening to her and her community weren't important to LGBTQ politicos.

As long as I'm doing okay, she imagined the gay revelers were thinking as they laughed, *we can wait for this undocumented trans woman not to be so rude.*

But the reason Gutiérrez was interrupting the festivities was no laughing matter. When she spoke up to the Black president who was very popular with the gays, she was thinking of people like Victoria Arellano, who had died of AIDS in immigration custody in 2007. And she was thinking of people like Roxanna Hernandez from Honduras and Johana Medina from El Salvador, two trans women who would later die from complications from HIV in ICE custody in 2019.

She was speaking in the spirit of ACT UPers like Bob Rafsky. But she spoke long after Gay Inc. politics had mostly moved away from taking an interest in the viral underclass. In 2003, one of my close mentors, historian Lisa Duggan, coined the term *homonormativity.* It describes a gay "politics that does not contest dominant heteronormative assumptions and institutions but upholds and sustains them while promising the possibility of a demobilized gay culture anchored in domesticity and consumption." Homonormativity is a politics in which well-to-do gays ignore the carceral reality of how, according to research from the Williams Institute published in the *American Journal of Public Health* in 2017, the "incarceration rate of self-identified lesbian, gay, or bisexual persons" is "more than 3 times that of the US adult population." Under homonormativity, queer sexuality isn't discriminatory—as long as you have the bank balance to be a Democratic donor and the skin color to avoid being housed in a cage or on the street, that is.

Although HIV had once threatened many of the older gay men in the room, the politics cheered at the White House that day were homonormative and unconcerned with how HIV/AIDS and incarceration were harming the broader community in terms of viral risk and violence. Unlike some members of ACT UP from back in the day, the gay politicos in that room in 2015 had given up the dream of universal health care, settling for the crumbs of health coverage for a lucky few through same-sex marriage. Most at that reception probably had access to medication to treat or even prevent HIV if they needed it, and they didn't want to be associated with people at risk for viruses.

To them, viruses may have meant *dirty people* who used drugs, had sex for money, or were locked up behind bars, perhaps awaiting deportation. But there was at least one powerful trans leader who very much appreciated what Gutiérrez did that day.

"Oh, you're the trans woman who interrupted the president! That was so brave!" Lorena Borjas told Gutiérrez when they met at a conference for the first time, just a few months later.

"She was just so full of love and admiration and respect," Gutiérrez recalled, "and totally agreed with what had to be done at that moment."

The most effective organizers around viruses and the conditions that fuel them understand, as Frederick Douglass put it, that "Power concedes nothing without a demand. It never has and it never will." Being friendly with the powerful isn't an effective strategy for liberation.

Bob Rafsky understood this with Clinton.

Jennicet Gutiérrez understood this with Obama.

Zak Kostopoulos understood this when he marched against cops.

And Lorena Borjas knew this every time she walked into a lawyer's office with her cart, trying to get a human out of a cage.

Liberalism has built into the law many of the vectors that drive viral transmission, especially via the carceral state. This must be undone if we are to reduce the trauma of our current and future plagues, expand access to prophylaxis, and mitigate the trauma of social death.

III

SOCIAL DEATH

Engendered by corporate capital and the neoliberal state, ineligibility to personhood refers to the state of being legally recognized as rightless, located in the space of social death where demands for humanity are ultimately disempowering because they can be interpreted only by asking to be given something sacred in return for nothing at all.

Lisa Marie Cacho,
Social Death: Racialized Rightlessness and the Criminalization of the Unprotected

8

ONE IN TWO

(Unequal Prophylaxis)

After Michael Johnson was sentenced in the summer of 2015 to three decades in prison for exposing and transmitting HIV to other men, his few friends tried to get help to mount a legal appeal. These included Meredith Rowan, the white stepmother of his friend, who'd testified at his trial, and Akil Patterson, the Black wrestling coach and advocate for LGBTQ athletes who'd never met Michael before he flew from Baltimore to St. Louis to visit him in jail. They were part of a multiracial, multistate effort to overturn his sentence.

Armed with transcripts and the account I'd written, Michael's supporters organized dozens of amicus briefs from groups like the ACLU of Missouri Foundation and the American Academy of HIV Medicine. In an appeal to Missouri's Eastern District Court of Appeals, a new appellate public attorney, Samuel Buffaloe, argued that the trial had been improper because Michael's lawyer had been denied proper access to evidence under rules of discovery and that his long sentence was so disproportionate to the crime that it violated the constitutional ban on cruel and unusual punishment.

As a journalist, you always hope the story you are writing will lead to material change, though it rarely does. But in December 2016, a year and a half after his conviction, the appeals court finally ruled that Johnson's trial had been "fundamentally unfair" because the prosecutor had engaged in "a trial-by-ambush strategy." The trial had turned on whether Johnson had told his partners that he was HIV-positive. They all said he hadn't, but he insisted that he had. In one prison phone recording, however, Michael had said that he was only "pretty sure" he had let all his partners know he had HIV. That statement was crucial, the appeals court noted, because it was "the only evidence in the record of Johnson stating to anyone that he was not certain about whether he disclosed his HIV status to his sexual partners."

Shortly after he was arrested in 2013, Johnson's previous public defender, Heather Donovan, requested that the prosecution hand over any "written or recorded statement" Johnson had made. Prosecutors are required to comply with such requests under Missouri law, and failing to do this would be a serious violation of prosecutorial ethics. But, the appeals court wrote, the prosecution delivered "tapes at defense counsel's office on the Friday before the trial while the office was closed for a state holiday" in 2015, about a year and a half after she'd requested all such material. So, Michael's attorneys received the voluminous recordings totaling twenty-four hours of taped calls the morning of the trial's opening day, denying them "a decent opportunity to prepare his case in advance of trial."

This was no accident, the court ruled; prosecutors had "intentionally withheld the recordings from the defense to gain a strategic advantage." The court quoted prosecuting attorney Philip Groenweghe saying in a conference in Judge Jon Cunningham's chambers, "If we disclose them to the defense, they'll tell their client. And I'm not impugning anyone's integrity, I'd do the same thing: Hey, they're listening to your conversation, shut up. So we don't disclose them until towards the end."

Ironically, Groenweghe had prosecuted Johnson for failing to disclose his HIV status, as required by law, and Groenweghe's win was overturned because of his own failure to disclose evidence as required by law.

With his sentence vacated and conviction overturned, Michael was legally innocent again. But he remained in prison while the prosecution decided if it wanted to pursue a new trial, appeal to the Missouri

Supreme Court, or let him go free. (This wasn't "double jeopardy." When someone's sentence is overturned, the prosecutor is free to begin the whole process again, as was seen in the absurd case of Curtis Flowers, a Black man in Mississippi prosecuted by the same white district attorney for a quadruple homicide in six trials over twenty-three years, before finally being released in the summer of 2020—right into a pandemic world that looked nothing like life in the 1990s, when he'd last been free.)

The appeals court had made no ruling on the wider matter of whether sentencing someone to more time in prison for failing to disclose a virus than for murder constituted cruel and unusual punishment.

The court also made no mention of news that broke earlier that year about race and HIV. In February 2016, the Centers for Disease Control and Prevention predicted that, if current trends did not change, one in every two Black men who had sex with men in the United States—and one out of every four Latino men who had sex with men—would become HIV-positive in his lifetime.

When I first read this, I was shocked: half of all Black queer men like me were likely to become HIV-positive in our lifetimes.

The writer Linda Villarosa, who is a mentor of mine, put it in stunning relief when she wrote in the *New York Times Magazine* that "Swaziland, a tiny African nation, has the world's highest rate of H.I.V., at 28.8 percent of the population." Meanwhile, if "gay and bisexual African-American men made up a country," *that country's* "rate would surpass that of this impoverished African nation—and all other nations" on planet earth.

By comparison, about one in eleven white gay men were projected to become HIV-positive in their lifetime, and only one in *twenty-five hundred* straight white men. (While rates are much lower for American women than men, Black women are 13 percent of the population of women in the United States—and 60 percent of its new HIV diagnoses.)

Black queer men's behavior doesn't account for our heightened viral risk; we actually have been shown to have fewer sexual partners and engage in less recreational drug use than our white peers. What we have is more exposure to racism and less protection from prophylaxis.

* * *

To public health experts, prophylaxis refers to practices and physical objects that can prevent the transmission of communicable diseases. Condoms, which provide good protection against a wide variety of viruses, are sometimes clinically referred to as prophylactics. Face shields and masks similarly offer physical prophylaxis against influenza and SARS-CoV-2.

Prophylaxis can also be pharmaceutical—for example, in the form of antiretroviral medications (ARVs). Often known by the brand name Truvada, PrEP stands for "pre-exposure prophylaxis." People living without HIV and taking PrEP always have a medication in their body that will stop HIV from taking hold in them if they encounter it. (While it's often associated with gay men in the United States, PrEP can be very helpful for heterosexual populations around the world, as well as for communities affected by incarceration and addiction.) Regular ARVs do the same thing, but in reverse: for a person living with HIV, antiretroviral medications can make their viral loads so low that, if the HIV in them moves into another person, the load will be so small that it won't be able to transmit. Both are powerful forms of pharmacological prophylaxis. So are birth control pills, which offer hormonal prophylaxis against pregnancy (as condoms do physically).

Medications and vaccinations can also offer community prophylaxis. Vaccines not only train the immune system of the person receiving them to very successfully keep viruses out or at manageable levels, but they can also lower the risk of onward transmission for everyone around them—especially sterilizing vaccines, which eliminated smallpox. And when more people in a community get vaccines (or ARVs), the risk to everyone is lowered, particularly when herd immunity is reached and the viruses, with nowhere to jump, cycle out of the community.

The same principles apply with COVID-19 vaccines. They not only protect those who receive them, but they lower community risk around the recipient in two ways: by making the recipient personally less likely to expose those around them to SARS-CoV-2 (or, in the case that they do, to do so with a lower viral load, so that exposure is less likely to result in onward transmission) and by lowering the viral level of the community overall, so the chances that anyone in the community even encounters the virus diminish.

Access to regular, free, and culturally welcoming health care is also a form of prophylaxis. The reason poor Black patients will turn up in the U.S. South with full-blown AIDS, which can take up to a decade to develop after HIV infection, is because they haven't seen a doctor in more than a decade. If people can't afford regular medical checkups, or if they feel unwelcome to do so because of transphobia or racism, they are unable to benefit from the prophylaxis of routine health care.

Health insurance *can* be a potent form of prophylaxis, especially when it has no cost at the point of service. But in a for-profit system, health insurance can be a deceptive burden, too, for it is a financial product meant to enrich shareholders. In November 2019, just a couple of months before cases of the novel coronavirus showed up in the United States, a study published in the *Journal of General Internal Medicine* found that 137 million Americans were struggling with medical debt—more than 1 out of every 3 people in the country. An inability to pay medical bills is often cited as the leading cause of personal bankruptcies in the United States. Many of the people who file for bankruptcy *do* have health insurance; it's just that when they go to use the thing they've been paying for, the insurance doesn't cover their bills enough to keep them from economic ruin. And when people have bankruptcies on their credit reports, they have a hard time getting housing or jobs—which pushes them further into the margins.

It needn't be this way. The United States spends more money per person on health care than any other nation on the planet. It *could* offer the kind of prophylaxis the United Kingdom's National Health Service offers without any risk of bankruptcy or the disastrous health outcomes it causes. Yet much of the money spent on health care in the United States goes to top-heavy hospital management, usurious insurers, and obscene profits for the makers of pharmaceuticals (and their Wall Street backers) instead of toward actual care.

There's also what I call conceptual prophylaxis. Access to education and freedom from being incarcerated are powerful forms of prophylaxis, too, for they protect people in invisible ways that greatly reduce their likelihood of ever encountering viruses (or increase their likelihood of surviving if they do). Safe housing offers physical protection, but its full prophylaxis is harder to perceive. For instance, as Yale School of Public Health epidemiologist Gregg Gonsalves has researched, having an indoor toilet in South Africa is a form of prophylaxis against the epidemic of sexual assault of women, because when women don't have to go out in the night to use the bathroom, they're much less likely to be raped. The ability to work from home was a profoundly powerful form of prophylaxis for a certain class of professionals during the COVID-19 pandemic. Whiteness also offers a form of conceptual prophylaxis (though, as we'll see in chapter 11, it has its limits).

But we cannot always live with physical prophylaxis. We *need* to touch and exchange air molecules and cells with one another, at least periodically. Reproduction literally depends upon it.

And for people living with different levels of pharmacological and conceptual prophylaxis who interact, this is where things get interesting. Someone living with one level of prophylaxis (which may be invisible to the naked eye) can engage in the very same activities as someone else with a different level of such prophylaxis, yet their levels of risk will be totally different.

Consider that if everyone in one house has been vaccinated against SARS-CoV-2 and is working from home, they can eat, pray, or have sex with one another, and there's relatively little risk they'll get that virus. But if no one in the house across the street from them has been vaccinated against COVID-19, and the members of that household work as fast-food workers and clerks in a grocery store, then their engagement in the *very same normal life activities* results in a much higher level of risk for COVID-19.

It's the same with HIV. If a white gay man is having sex without condoms with a lot of other white gay men, their level of risk of contracting HIV is far lower than if a Black gay man does the same with other Black gay men. This is due not just to the pharmacological prophylaxis that more commonly protects white people, but (as we saw in the previous chapter) because Black people are much less likely to enjoy the conceptual prophylactic protections afforded by equitable education, stable housing, and freedom from incarceration.

Thus, while Michael Johnson and Dylan King-Lemons walked into their encounter consensually and both now have HIV, they engaged in the same activities with *very* different levels of risk, both in terms of viral susceptibility *and* risk of legal repercussion. The court overturning *Missouri v. Johnson* did not take this into account in its ruling. But I think about this a lot.

I think about how unfair it is that so many people prosecuted for HIV are Black gay men, when one in two of us may become HIV-positive despite our activities; we simply lack the prophylactic power of whiteness or heterosexuality.

And I think that, if one in two straight white women were going to become HIV-positive, not only would they *not* be prosecuted for exposing others to such a common virus, but the ongoing crisis of AIDS might dominate the news as COVID-19 has.

While it would have been difficult to pull off, the United States *could* have taken an approach to HIV like it did with polio, when it worked in global solidarity to suppress the poliovirus. In the 1950s, Jonas Salk and Albert Sabin separately developed different vaccines for polio, and neither man pursued a patent. When CBS's Edward R. Murrow asked,

"Who owns the patent on this vaccine?" Salk famously said, "The people, I would say. There is no patent." Smiling, Salk turned the question back on Murrow, asking, "Could you patent the sun?" Salk framed his decision to forgo what might have been billions in profits as an ethical matter, and while he may have believed this, as the writer Jane Smith has noted, his lab and university had already researched patenting the vaccine but didn't even try because they didn't believe it would be eligible.

The polio vaccine was first manufactured when pharmacological research in the United States was developed more in federally funded university laboratories and less by private drug companies. Later, those drug companies (whose research was still subsidized by federally funded labs and whose employees were educated in federally funded graduate programs) began to aggressively protect the drugs they made as privately held intellectual property. Drugmakers began to see what they made not so much as drugs to *help* people, but as biochemical financial products that just happened to pass *through* people. And these products needed not only to earn profits at the point of sale, but also to fund Wall Street speculation and to generate abstract value. While U.S. drugmakers have often said they need to earn big profits to invest in research and development for new drugs, a 2021 congressional investigation found that pharma companies have spent more in recent years on buying back their own stock and paying big dividends to their shareholders than they have on research and development. Unsurprisingly, they have also fought especially hard to patent drugs that treat chronic conditions, since the people using those drugs will need to purchase them for life—as corporations like Gilead have tried to do with HIV medications.

Salk developed his polio vaccine before all this, and the United States successfully used his research to administer the vaccine to everyone for free. International campaigns led to the elimination of the poliovirus in so many people globally that two of the three wild viral strains have been eradicated from the human race.

A similar approach could have been taken to tackling AIDS: The

United States *could* have aggressively made sure everyone with HIV had medication freely and easily, as it did with the COVID-19 vaccine. Equally important, the United States *could* have given people living with HIV the housing and economic support they needed to keep that virus tamped down. It *could* have used robust state support to intervene in the cycle of that virus so aggressively that in a generation, AIDS, too, could have been mostly eradicated from the population.

But by the time HIV broke out, medical drug corporations had learned to game the system so effectively that they could get the government to pay for their research, farm out development to universities, and *still* get patents they could privately control—even on a product almost as necessary to some human lives for survival as the sun. With America's HIV approach, the priority became protecting private pharma profits and intellectual property over providing public prophylaxis. Those who controlled the means of pharmacological production controlled access to life itself, and the ongoing AIDS crisis has continued to kill up to an estimated one million people a year globally.

When the novel coronavirus hit the United States, the populations it was initially considered likely to kill were loudly dismissed as expendable—such as elderly people in nursing homes who had already been disappeared from public view. Still, as this communicable virus could, in theory, harm anyone, measures of care were employed, including the closure of most "nonessential" businesses. States even mandated that testing and treatment for COVID-19 (and later vaccines) be free at the point of service, a rare break within the profit-driven health system. This was about public health, but not entirely because the government had finally decided to prioritize the well-being of marginalized populations. Because the ruling class would have no way to extract profit from laborers if the laborers couldn't go to work, the government paid for everyone's vaccines.

It's a very different story when a laborer gets a cancer diagnosis. After all, cancer in a working poor person doesn't put any rich people's lives in danger, and it doesn't infect fellow workers. But during the COVID-19 pandemic, poor people suddenly could get screened and sometimes even treated for COVID-19 for free in a way they never could for cancer. And as the ruling class understood that there were powerful forms of prophylaxis (such as working from home) at their disposal that could keep danger at a safe distance, a sense of emergency about the pandemic by politicians and the press waxed and waned relative to the risk posed to the wealthy.

By the summer of 2021, the United States faced a very different problem with vaccines: it had more of them available than people willing or able to take them. Why wouldn't people get vaccinated who seemingly could? Some never will, and they were ill served by their conservative leaders in politics and the media. But many people who hadn't gotten jabbed were interested but unable to do so, because they were low-income workers who were afraid to lose a shift, food insecure, had responsibilities as the caregivers of family members, didn't have a car to get to a vaccine site, or some combination of all these. The many vectors in this book that create a viral underclass can also impede access to a mass vaccination campaign and can predict where pandemics will rage hardest. Indeed, some of the states with the lowest rates of vaccination in mid-2021 (like Alabama, Mississippi, Louisiana, and Arkansas) were also among those the Chamber of Commerce deemed the poorest states in the nation, and which the Census Bureau reports have the highest rates of poverty. Of *course* economic precariousness and the warping mentality of poverty affect the infrastructure of who can access the prophylaxis of vaccination.

Also, the for-profit system that had plagued the viral underclass with mistrust for years made it difficult to get vaccines to some of those who needed them most. If people are rightly suspicious that any interaction with the U.S. medical system might have hidden costs that could ruin them financially—for example, patients going to a hospital and surgeon for an operation believing both are covered by their insurance, only to find out afterward that the anesthesiologist was out of network and not covered—they might be suspicious when they hear about a "free vaccine."

When the COVID-19 vaccines began their uneven rollout, I was sad but not surprised to see ads on U.S. dating apps of young people bragging that they'd already been vaccinated and were now seeking "vax for vax"—vaccinated people who wanted to hook up with or date other vaccinated people. This approach to mating is known as *serosorting*, and it recreates the kind of viral divide HIV drugs created in the mid-1990s, when some people got them while others did not.

"Getting the vaccine is the hottest thing you could be doing on a dating app right now," a spokesperson for OKCupid told the *New York Times* in early 2021, speaking of it as if it were a luxury commodity. The article was titled "The Vaccinated Class," and it reflected what epidemiological maps were also showing: that those getting the vaccine first were *not* members of the viral underclass most likely to be harmed by SARS-CoV-2, but those who were already blessed with class status that granted access to *other* kinds of prophylaxis.

If certain "clean" people with the right economic standing and ability to master communications technology can get access to medical technology, and if that medication allows them to find sexual pleasure and build lives with other "clean" people, then they may stop caring about what happens to the "dirty" people who are still affected by a communicable disease. If the idea that the whole world was affected by COVID-19 dissipates, then those with the political clout who drove the initial global response to it may stop caring. The right to health and pleasure as exclusive domains of those above the viral divide may be justified by vaccination.

When people vaccinated against any contagious virus socialize with other vaccinated people and stop caring about unvaccinated people (who, increasingly, are socializing only with *other* unvaccinated people), a self-fulfilling prophecy develops. The virus winds down among those with access to the prophylaxis of vaccination while moving freely among those without it. The stakes of this are the concentration of health above the viral divide and sickness below it.

* * *

My friend and colleague the LGBTQ sexual health scholar Brian Mustanski often tells a horrifying story from his research. Once, when conducting a focus group with sexually active queer teenage boys, he asked them how often they used condoms. Never, they answered. Why not? When they were pressed, the reason came down to: We don't have sex with girls, so we can't get them pregnant. What would we need condoms for?

The boys had been taught that condoms were to be used only for birth control; the boys were never provided with a robust sexual health education, and so they didn't know that condoms also could be used to protect against gonorrhea, chlamydia, or HIV—information that is necessary for young people of all sexual orientations and identities to know. This was unconscionable. Their school district and political leaders had failed them, abandoning their responsibility toward the very children they were charged with protecting. The United States hates nonprocreative sexuality in general, but it disdains queer sex specifically. Many states have abstinence-only education laws, which result in higher rates of sexually transmitted infections among young people and are, one could argue, a form of child abuse. The majority of states offer no LGBTQ sexual education of any kind. As a result, the bodies of queer and trans kids are made vulnerable to viral transmission by the state. Not only were those boys denied access to the physical prophylaxis of condoms and the prophylactic knowledge of how to protect themselves broadly, but the pathways of their bodies were, in a sense, opened up by the state so that pathogens could more effectively enter into them.

Growing up in the 1980s, I learned about HIV in my public school's sexual education curriculum, and I learned that condoms could prevent it. This was nominally better than what my friend and once-boyfriend André didn't learn; he simply assumed he was going to die of AIDS someday because he was gay and therefore deserved to die by this disease. Still, what I received was a fear-based sexual health education, which isn't a very effective approach; I grew up so terrified of the virus that I didn't want to have sex with others for years into my twenties. I never learned anything in school or from my parents about how to practice (let alone *enjoy*) gay sex; because of this, I failed in my thirties to reassure Olivier, my French friend whom we met in chapter 2, as I should have when he talked to me about HIV. And until I started a PhD at age thirty-seven, I didn't learn *anything* in college or public school about gayness, queer history, the gay rights movement, or LGBTQ health.

But while my own education harmed me psychologically (and in terms of experiencing connection and pleasure), because of other forms of prophylaxis in my life, it didn't manifest itself in viral risk the way it did for the boys in Brian Mustanski's group, for Michael Johnson, or for the homeless queer teens I began interviewing around 2010. When many of these kids came out to their families, they were kicked out of their homes. They survived on the streets by engaging in informal sex work, occasionally having sex with people for money, but more often doing so for a place to sleep. And because the street value of unprotected sex was so much higher, they often had sex without condoms.

Viruses are not evil. They don't practice ethics or morals. They *do* try to get inside living hosts and hack into their cells to reproduce, but there is no ethical or political impetus here. But even if viruses themselves can't act politically, the distribution (or withholding) of prophylaxis is extremely political. Who does and doesn't get access to such protection is wildly inequitable. This power over prophylaxis, then, performs like a traffic cop, directing viruses toward some people and away from others so that pandemics pool in particular populations.

The school board member who votes to withhold the prophylactic power of a responsible health education to students of *all* sexual and gender identities is like a cop directing viruses into their bodies. And like the force wielded by a cop, this power can determine who lives and who dies.

Media stories love to blame viral transmission on tropes of lazy irresponsibility committed by individual members of the viral underclass—like those boys with their improper sex education; or like a butcher who isn't wearing a mask on the cold, crowded kill floor of a slaughterhouse; or like dear Olivier. But these people have terrible chances of avoiding viruses because *other* people have decided to deny them proven tools of protection.

Queer and trans people are not more vulnerable to a host of viruses simply because of our sexual practices or how education systems directly withhold the knowledge we need to keep safe from pathogens. When Lorena Borjas entered that hospital for the last time, she wasn't just contending with SARS-CoV-2 and HIV; she was contending with the lack of protection afforded to her transgender, migrant body for decades—and with how that dearth of prophylaxis had accumulated in her body.

Queer and trans people suffer from a wide variety of health disparities due to the discrimination we face more broadly. In U.S. history, it has been widely legal for the government and private businesses to discriminate against people because of their sexuality or gender identity. As a result, LGBTQ people have been more likely to be poor, unemployed, homeless, and uninsured. And if queer people do have health care but feel unwelcome, or if the care doesn't meet their needs, they don't actually have access to it. This leads to worse health outcomes for queer hearts and lungs and grants pathogens more entry points through pathways of poverty.

I think of my friend Henry Bradley, a rail-thin Black gay singer and composer whom I met in the late 1990s when we both sang in the Jerriese Johnson Gospel Choir in the East Village. Henry had contracted HIV in its earliest days, and even when he was at his sickest, he had to fight to hold on to his most potent prophylaxis: housing. Under Mayor Rudy Giuliani, the City of New York had begun demanding that people who needed social services like food and housing assistance would have to physically come in person to city offices to get them, something many of them could not do. Henry joined the lawsuit *Henrietta D. v. Giuliani*, which successfully argued that people with "unique physical barriers" needed reasonable accommodation. By 2003, under the protections of the Americans with Disability Act, Henry helped win the right for people like him to continue to receive such lifesaving services without having to risk their lives to travel for them.

When the novel coronavirus pandemic hit in the United States, some forms of prophylaxis were more obvious than others. People in medical jobs who had proper face shields, masks, gloves, and gowns had more protection than those who did not. People who lost their formal jobs were often pushed into the informal economy, doing labor in intimate settings that were even more precarious. People who could work from home without losing income enjoyed the most prophylaxis of all. This is why Black and Latinx workers, already more likely to be working on-site in the more physically dangerous service industry, were so much more likely to contract coronavirus. Black people and immigrants already had an increased likelihood of living in denser households, which limited their ability to practice social distancing; when they were incarcerated, social distancing was impossible. And when they were evicted, they often wound up in even *more* densely packed, intergenerational households, which put them even more acutely at risk for COVID-19.

At the same time, people who were elderly, disabled, or experiencing homelessness often lacked the prophylactic possibilities of literacy and computer literacy. And yet, even as the pandemic unduly slaughtered people like them, U.S. governmental agencies often required them to use internet sign-ups, QR codes, or even two-factor cell phone authentication to access the prophylactic possibility of vaccination.

The postcolonial scholar Achille Mbembe described *necropolitics* as revealing how "the ultimate expression of sovereignty resides, to a large degree, in the power and the capacity to dictate who may live and who must die." The necropolitical conditions existing long before COVID-19 showed up revealed who had prophylaxis and who did not, and dictated the odds of who would perish in the viral underclass and who would escape its grip.

Such odds are often framed as a matter of personal choice, but they have been set prior to any one person making a decision. Michael Johnson, who could not read well, was punished by a prosecutor with illegal tactics for a virus he had fifty-fifty odds of acquiring. Prophylaxis is often kept from people in the United States if they are already considered disposable. Then, when they become infected by a virus, their diagnosis makes them even more marginalized, if not untouchable.

And if a virus, aging, or disability leaves them weak, too often they are left on their own and blamed for being considered disposable.

9

DISABILITY AS DISPOSABILITY

(Ableism)

In late March 2020, former *Village Voice* editor Ward Harkavy mysteriously and abruptly stopped using Facebook and Twitter.

It was something that worried his friends, including me. Ward had been my most frequent editor when I was a staff writer at the *Voice* years before, and he was one of the editors who influenced my reporting the most. He taught me when to pack a punch, when to write with a light touch, and when to trust my readers. He was an avuncular, argumentative, old-school editor of alt-weekly newspapers who later became a prolific user of social media.

Since the 1990s, long before most other journalists, Ward had been writing about the wicked ways of Donald Trump, and he'd been documenting the economic cruelty of New York governor Andrew Cuomo for a decade. He was the rare white male cynic who was angry not out of a sense of nihilism, but because he cared deeply about the world—a smart-ass who wasn't also an asshole. A self-described "former hot-metal printer and former newspaperman" who'd "destroyed both industries," Ward wrote in his Twitter profile that "Every day I try to write part of Trump's obit."

In early 2020, he posted critically and daily about his nation's president, his state's governor, and the unfolding coronavirus crisis. His penultimate post was a retweet of Senator Bernie Sanders: "When Jonas Salk developed the polio vaccine 65 years ago, he understood its tremendous benefit to all of humanity and he refused to patent it. . . . Any coronavirus treatment must be made free for everyone."

An Oklahoma native, Ward lived just outside New York City's outer boroughs, on Long Island, not far from where COVID-19 had recently taken the life of Lorena Borjas. Despite having given up smoking and taken up running in recent years, at seventy-two with long-challenged lungs, he was a prime target for COVID-19. When he did not post online for a few days, it was, for his friends, like someone not showing up at the office. (Indeed, it was especially scary for some of them because, when Ward was at the *Voice*, one of his writers didn't show up to work for days, only to be found dead later at home.)

Ward had no family nearby, but many of his friends were nosy investigative reporters, and one eventually sleuthed that he was in a hospital on Long Island. Mercifully, he did *not* have the dreaded novel coronavirus. But he'd had a tooth extracted prior to the pandemic, and it had become so badly infected that when he sought medical attention, he was admitted to the hospital's intensive care unit.

"Leave it to Ward to wind up in the ICU during the pandemic and not have COVID!" my friend, the writer Camille Dodero, texted me.

"Can't make this shit up," I responded, using Ward's favorite phrase (always delivered with a light western twang) to express incredulousness at the world.

Relieved that he wasn't going to die from the coronavirus, Ward's friends faced a conundrum: What to do when he got out of the hospital? The options felt limited. Hundreds of people were dying of COVID-19 in New York State every day, meaning none of us could stay with Ward upon his release, for fear of infecting him. We weren't allowed to visit him, and we couldn't even talk to him on the phone.

The very nature of COVID-19 was so crushingly alienating, I thought, that it made getting care to any vulnerable people at this time damn near impossible.

Ward was released from the ICU after a few weeks but was too fragile to return home alone. It's dangerous to be single and unable to take care of oneself in a country that loathes dependence. Together, his friends decided to pool resources to get him a home nurse. But when it didn't seem possible to hire one in the pandemic, Ward was discharged from the hospital and sent to a nursing home to convalesce while he healed.

And *that's* where he contracted the novel coronavirus, which sent him back into the hospital and back into the ICU—and which took his life on May 17, 2020.

A *tooth infection* that led to death. *Can't make this shit up, Thrasher*, I could almost hear him saying to me when I found out he was gone and the tears came. Ward's death was spectacularly unnecessary and deeply ironic. He'd criticized Donald Trump for decades, but rather than getting to write Trump's obit, Trump's cruelty wrote his instead.

But while Republican disdain had helped kill him, a Democratic governor had helped, too. The administration of Andrew Cuomo, New York State's governor, had controversially decided to send some 4,500 patients recovering from SARS-CoV-2 to nursing homes, like the one where Ward was sent to recuperate, which played a role in New York State's initial reporting of 6,200 deaths in long-term-care facilities from COVID-19 by that summer. Like influenza, another contagious respiratory virus that has cast a deadly spell over nursing homes for years, the novel coronavirus was merciless in acting the part of the Grim Reaper in long-term-care facilities across the nation and around the world.

There are many reasons for this that transcend a Democratic-versus-Republican political paradigm. In part, it's because caregivers come and go in nursing homes, transferring pathogens from the outside world to residents. In part, it's because old people's immune systems are tired after decades of living. And in part, it's because those in nursing homes live with sores and tubes and needles, which puncture the protective membrane of the skin, blurring the distinction between the inside and the outside of the body and allowing viruses to enter more easily.

But in some states, increased vulnerability to the novel coronavirus in nursing home populations was also manufactured. As ProPublica reported, states like New York, New Jersey, and Michigan that sent people recovering from COVID-19 *into* already vulnerable nursing homes suffered, predictably, far more deaths in those homes than states that did not. And this created a kind of needless geriatric genocide. "The Most Important Coronavirus Statistic," a headline in *Forbes* read the month Ward died, was that "42% of US Deaths Are from 0.6% of the Population." Those in long-term-care facilities were bearing the brunt of the pandemic in the United States. Almost a year later, the COVID Tracking Project would show that about one in every ten nursing home residents had died of COVID-19.

This policy is part of why, nearly a year into the pandemic, New York and New Jersey still topped the list of states with the most COVID-19 deaths per one hundred thousand people, the culmination of a pattern of public health negligence that had been occurring for many years. Since 2000, the *New York Post* reported, New York state had cut some 20,000 hospital beds—more than a quarter of the nearly 74,000 beds it once had.

Cuomo was governor for half this time. Just a few years before the pandemic, his administration had overseen the closure of a five-hundred-bed hospital in Brooklyn. During the pandemic, he tried to cut nearly a half-billion dollars in Medicaid funding from the state budget. He also fought raising taxes on the state's wealthiest inhabitants, something even Republican governors had done in times of past crises.

I often found myself wondering: If Andrew Cuomo hadn't spent so many years stripping the New York hospital system to the bone, would people with COVID-19 have been sent into nursing homes to recover? Would my dear friend and former editor have needlessly died of a viral infection while recovering from a *tooth extraction*?

This is why Trump and Cuomo *both* have the blood of older Americans on their hands. In early 2021, New York State attorney general Letitia James accused the Cuomo administration of undercounting the number of people who had died in the state's nursing homes by thousands, and the administration itself subsequently admitted that at least 12,743 people died of COVID-19 in New York's nursing homes by the end of 2020—more than double the number that had originally been reported. When Cuomo received an enormous five-million-dollar advance to publish a book on his pandemic response and was awarded an Emmy for his pandemic press conferences, I could hear Ward again: *Can't make this shit up.*

* * *

During the COVID-19 pandemic, it has been easiest to see how viruses affected disabled populations by seeing how people living in congregated settings, especially elderly people, were affected.

But in the United States and the United Kingdom, one of the biggest drivers creating an unvaccinated underclass has been the ableist myth that vaccines increase autism in children. The origin of this myth lies largely with an unusual press conference organized by a British medical doctor named Andrew Wakefield, who convened media outside the Royal Free Hospital in 1998 to promote a paper he had coauthored in the *Lancet*. The paper was a small study of twelve children, and it called for further research to see if the combination of receiving three vaccines together at one time was a cause of colitis and autism in the children.

But at the press conference, as Brian Deer wrote in the *Sunday Times*, Wakefield dramatically "called for a boycott of the triple MMR" combination vaccine "in favour of breaking it up into single measles, mumps and rubella shots, to be given at yearly intervals. 'I can't support the continued use of these three vaccines, given in combination, until this issue has been resolved,'" Wakefield said, claiming that an MMR shot could trigger irritable bowels or autism within a matter of days. Rates of vaccination in the United Kingdom dropped. They plummeted in the United States as well—especially after Wakefield published a book called *Callous Disregard: Autism and Vaccines—The Truth Behind a Tragedy*, whose foreword was written by *Baywatch* actress Jenny McCarthy.

Wakefield's research was incorrect. He was eventually charged by the U.K.'s General Medical Council with hiding conflicts of interest and manipulating data. The 1998 paper was so discredited that the *Lancet* partially retracted it in 2004 and fully retracted it in 2010 (largely based on Deer's journalism in the *Sunday Times*). Also, in 2010, Britain's General Medical Council investigated Wakefield, and he was barred from practicing medicine in the United Kingdom.

But the damage had been done: Wakefield's false claim that MMR shots caused autism created an international wave of parents refusing to vaccinate their children—and not just against measles, mumps, and rubella, but against *many* diseases. Wakefield's fiction revealed a grotesque, ableist truth: many parents would rather increase the likelihood that their children *died* from a preventable disease like measles (and that others in their social networks also died) than face the possibility of parenting a child with autism. Again, vaccines do *not* cause or increase the chances of autism. Yet, even if Wakefield's misunderstanding were true and they did, it is revealing about U.S. and U.K. societies that disability is justified as a reason for disposability; so many parents would rather have a *dead* child than a neurodivergent child.

At the other end of the age spectrum, viruses exposed a related dynamic of disposability in nursing homes. This tragedy was also the result of ableism, another vector for death by viruses and neglect. The death of someone like my friend Ward was more likely to happen because he had become too old to produce value in a profit-obsessed society. He had been trying to survive in a country that *hates* aging and that sees those who are no longer in the workforce as lacking value. When Ward was laid off from the *Village Voice* nine years earlier, he knew he was too old to get another journalism job, even though he wasn't ready for retirement. He bleakly joked that he would spend his old age as a greeter at Walmart, homeless, or both. As with the other one hundred thousand people who would die in U.S. nursing homes by Thanksgiving of that year, Ward's personhood was no longer useful to capitalism.

As I helped plan Ward's memorial service, I thought about how breezily politicians and major scientists wrote off old age as not worth living. In 2014, Ezekiel Emanuel, MD, wrote a controversial essay in the *Atlantic* titled "Why I Hope to Die at 75." In the essay, he unapologetically wrote that "living too long . . . renders many of us, if not disabled, then faltering and declining, a state that may not be worse than death but is nonetheless deprived. It robs us of our creativity and ability to contribute to work, society, the world. It transforms how people experience us, relate to us, and, most important, remember us. We are no longer remembered as vibrant and engaged but as feeble, ineffectual, even pathetic." For this, Emanuel wanted to be dead by seventy-five.

Emanuel is no fringe crank; he is a professor at the University of Pennsylvania's medical school and an architect of President Obama's Affordable Care Act. And despite this clearly ableist stance—and even though he reaffirmed it in 2019—Emanuel was appointed to then-President-elect Joe Biden's COVID-19 transition task force in 2020.

Similarly to how racism privileges whiteness and punishes people of color, ableism privileges able-bodied people and punishes people who are disabled in law, culture, and the built environment, among other arenas. And it is a defining, structural force in U.S. society.

America is designed to accommodate a mythical person who is a certain size and whose body has certain idealized, profit-generating abilities. Decisions are made all the time that affect this. For instance, a building with stairs in front of its entry and no ramp privileges people who can climb those stairs and disadvantages people in wheelchairs (young and old), people using crutches, and babies in strollers. In New York City, only about a quarter of subway stations are considered accessible under the Americans with Disability Act—meaning riders who can't climb stairs might have to travel a mile or more out of their way to get to an elevator (which are often not working). Stairs not only signal that people without certain abilities are unwelcome; they can literally keep those people out of spaces entirely or force them to use a back entrance, as other groups have been humiliatingly forced to do in U.S. history.

Meanwhile, pop culture is full of tropes of people who are praised for "overcoming" their disabilities, which marks disability as undesirable and creates a neoliberal sense that if people just had enough grit, they could change their physical bodies and be more productive. Such narratives also reinforce the idea that being disabled means people have failed at John Wayne–style independence, when the truth is we are *all* interdependent. We all *need* one another. And as much as disabled people are often depicted only as needing help from others, able-bodied people need help as well, from disabled and able-bodied people alike. I disagree with Emanuel that being elderly or disabled robs anyone of their creativity or ability to contribute to society; such states often foster great learning, unlearning, and wisdom.

Viruses disable people all the time and leave them with debilitating diseases; think of how long-haul COVID affects various organs, poliovirus affects mobility, or cytomegalovirus (CMV) affects vision. But in an ableist world, all kinds of disabilities needlessly make people more at risk for viruses, too. Disability causes poverty in the United States, which leads to homelessness and incarceration, two other major viral vectors. The Department of Justice has admitted that "Prisoners were nearly 3 times more likely and jail inmates were more than 4 times more likely than the general population to report having at least one disability." Meanwhile, research has estimated that a quarter of people experiencing homelessness are affected by a physical, intellectual, or developmental disability.

Disability as a precursor to increased viral risk need not be preordained. People who have trouble breathing or need immune system treatment could have their health protected with the ability to work from home, accessible mental health care, guaranteed housing to keep them off the street, freedom from mass incarceration, and the right to live near friends and family (with the help of home aides, if needed) in small settings, instead of being hidden away in a care center.

COVID-19 removed so much touch from our lives that, after learning Ward had died, I found myself thinking about how transgressively queer people had maintained intimacy with people who could not care for themselves in the early years of AIDS. I've long been moved by a video of a 1988 ACT UP action in which hundreds of gays and lesbians made out in the lobby of St. Vincent's Hospital in a "Kiss-In." I'm also touched by a scene in the film *BPM* (about ACT UP Paris), in which a healthy gay man masturbates his friend who is dying of AIDS in a French hospital. The friend had gone blind from the ocular cytomegalovirus, but the moment he achieves climax reveals ecstasy in his cloudy eyes and is among the most honest depictions of sexual intimacy I have ever seen in a feature film. The scene is powerful not because it is depicted graphically—all the viewer sees is movement rapidly happening under a sheet while one man holds another—but because it captures how diligently gay people worked to make sure their sick and despised friends still experienced intimacy and care, even in the midst of a crisis.

No such physical intimacy was possible with the respiratory coronavirus, which was harming patients who might have benefited from that kind of care. Already denied sufficient touch, COVID-19 robbed people in nursing homes not just of years of life, but of hugs, caresses, and social presence in their final days.

But for people who are disabled earlier in life than during their geriatric years, this is already a familiar problem. Exacerbated by the emphasis on large long-term care institutions in our society, instead of community ones or home care, ableism has denied many people who are disabled touch and fellowship. Neoliberal capitalism wants to place the economic costs of being disabled in a world designed not to include them *on* the people with disabilities themselves—for example, the cost of traveling an extra mile to exit a subway system is on them—rather than sharing the costs broadly across the society that created the ableist barriers. While this takes a large toll on their mental and emotional health, it takes a large biological toll, too—as COVID-19 made lethally obvious. The COVID Tracking Project estimated that about 8 percent of people in long-term-care facilities, which are often home to disabled people, died of COVID-19. This means that, once again, people who are disabled are punished with the higher pathogenic risks of congregate living.

And for elderly and disabled people *not* living in group settings, bars to health can be absurdly high. For instance, while local and state governments in the United States did prioritize vaccinating people in nursing homes in early 2021, elderly and disabled people who were not living in such institutions were largely left to figure out how to get vaccinated themselves, even if they were not mobile. Unlike in some other countries, where the government went to its citizens to vaccinate them from the start, the United States initially created a survival-of-the-fittest free-for-all, challenging people to compete online to get a slot. The sign-up mechanisms were often confusing and did not have accessible computer interfaces.

Asking the people most affected by a pandemic to navigate complicated technology they might not understand or be able to use because they are elderly, physically disabled, or neurodivergent was cruel. But that's how ableism operates.

* * *

In August 2020, about a month after Ward's online memorial, I had a wide-ranging conversation with disability activist and author Alice Wong, which helped me better understand why so many people were dying of COVID-19 in nursing homes. We talked on a video call, she from her home in San Francisco.

Alice was born with spinal muscular atrophy, a neuromuscular disability that has progressively deteriorated her strength. Because of this, she has used a wheelchair since childhood, and for the past few years, she has breathed full-time with the assistance of a BiPAP machine, a ventilator that helps force air in and out of her lungs. She wears a translucent plastic mask over her nose that has a single tube extending away from her face and straps that wrap around the back of her head. Her mask sits just above her playful, often laughing mouth and just beneath her expressive, friendly eyes.

"Knowing what I know about the symptoms, knowing about the inflammatory effects" of the coronavirus, she told me, "my reserve is not enough—I'm gonna die if I get it."

At the time of our call, Alice had not gone outside her home at all since March 2020, when she and her parents left it to fill out advanced directives for their care in the event that things got bad. And she wouldn't leave it again for another three more months, until managing another virus forced her outside that October, when she carefully ventured out under a face shield to get a flu shot.

Ward and Alice were two of my most frequent online interlocutors, and though they'd never met, they reminded me of each other in a couple of ways. Ward had been a stutterer and an early and influential member of the online stuttering community since it first developed in the 1990s. He was the first editor who talked to me about depictions of disability in the media, from news reporting on HIV to the cartoon character Timmy Burch, who uses an animated wheelchair on *South Park.* Alice is an influential member of online disabled activism communities, including the Disability Visibility Project and the hashtag #CripTheVote, both developed by and amplifying the voices of communities of disabled people that mainstream media often ignore.

Alice was following the dance that SARS-CoV-2 was doing with humans in Asia long before most Americans were taking the virus seriously. Her parents are from China, and she was watching carefully what was unfolding in Wuhan and Hong Kong. Then the novel coronavirus showed up in the kind of all-American place Alice studies very closely.

"The first major outbreak was at a nursing home in Washington State," she recalled, referring to the Life Care Center of Kirkland, where thirty-five people died. "This is another disability thing where these congregate settings such as prisons, such as nursing homes, are really traps. Right? People are trapped. Talk about your viral underclass!" Most people in long-term-care facilities, whether because of age or a disability, don't have other options. Unlike people in cities with professional jobs, who chose to flee to the countryside and work remotely, people in care homes don't have anywhere else to go. As Alice explained, "We live in a system that supports institutions more than community-based living."

In her forties, Alice lives with her parents, but that is somewhat unusual. People who are disabled *could* broadly be given the resources they need to live in their community. This might look like people living in small group homes with friends, or the government subsidizing fairly paid professional home aides, instead of big nursing homes, so that people with disabilities could have easier access to friends, family, pets, sex, fellowship, and intergenerational relationships. But this is less possible when government resources are gobbled up by the nursing home industrial complex.

Long-term-care facilities squeeze profits out of the bodies of the vulnerable people who live in them *and* from the poorly paid workforce that staffs them, the latter made up largely of women of color. And while "nursing home operators have long complained that Medicaid doesn't pay them enough to provide adequate care," as E. Tammy Kim reported in the *New York Times* near the end of 2020, "the business is not, apparently, a bad one to be in. Two thirds of nursing homes are for-profits, and the sector has been swallowed up by corporate chains and investment firms whose involvement correlates to lower staffing and worse care."

But ableism is about more than the particular direct and indirect harms disabled and elderly people face from American institutions and culture; it is a matter of the necropolitics we began to explore in the previous chapter: "the power and the capacity to dictate who may live and who must die." That America began its COVID-19 tragedy in a nursing home, Alice told me, is "part of this larger, more complex conversation about freedom, right? About who gets to be seen, who gets to be in public, who gets to participate, who counts." Who gets to live.

"It should be everybody. I mean, that's the party line about America. *Everybody counts*," she said, giving me a cheeky look. But, she continued, "There's a lot of people who don't count in America."

The language used in U.S. news reports about coronavirus worried Alice immediately, especially when those reports claimed that the only people who would be affected by COVID-19 were "high risk."

"As you know, with the history of HIV," she told me, "high risk—that's kind of a dog whistle, right?" It's a shorthand for "certain populations that are just considered expendable." *Queers. Crips.* People who are *too promiscuous* or *too fat*. People who have let themselves get *too sick* or become *too elderly*.

In March 2020, the lieutenant governor of Texas, Dan Patrick, said he thought "lots of grandparents" agreed with him when he'd said that "No one reached out to me and said, as a senior citizen, are you willing to take a chance on your survival in exchange for keeping the America that all America loves for your children and grandchildren? And if that's the exchange, I'm all in." He was essentially saying that elders ought to risk their own survival for the sake of the economy.

I asked Alice about how casually eugenics was being used by politicians to justify rationed care, as hospital systems were repeatedly and predictably stretched to their breaking points in Texas and elsewhere. (Even the United Kingdom's National Health Service had resorted to imposing "do not resuscitate" orders for people with learning disabilities.)

"'People who are sick, their lives are better off dead'—that's a very real sentiment," Alice said, explaining it as "genocide by other names."

Hiding from view certain people who don't count is a part of why so many people are kept in congregate settings in the United States in the first place. In her 2009 book, *The Ugly Laws: Disability in Public*, University of California, Berkeley, professor Sue Schweik wrote that for more than a century, cities had laws like San Francisco's 1867 ordinance that forbade "any person, who is diseased, maimed, mutilated or deformed in any way, so as to be an unsightly or disgusting object" from exposing "himself or herself to public view."

"So many people are just in denial about the realities that we're all going to die," Alice said. "That it can happen to any of us." As she explains, able-bodied people have demanded that we keep up this fantasy, and if you're not part of the fantasy, you're going to be made the nightmare. It's a similar sentiment that HIV activist Sean Strub, who first conjured the phrase *viral underclass*, refers to as "the tyranny of the well." The idea that people who are sick are unworthy of care hurts people who are disabled, of course. But it also hurts able-bodied people, whose bodies, if they live long enough, will eventually become sore or break down or become infirm. There isn't necessarily a harsh binary between abled and disabled through life; I have gone through periods of being unable to walk, due to medical issues, and then being able to walk again. And because of this, I believe that if able-bodied people prioritized the experiences of people who were disabled, it would be a great opportunity for learning and solidarity over the actual material conditions of our human lives.

When reading Andrew Cuomo's 2020 book, *American Crisis: Leadership Lessons from the COVID-19 Pandemic*, the reader is left to conclude that the governor found the thousands of people in nursing homes who died on his watch, like Ward, unremarkable, given that he doesn't even mention how many of them perished. In March 2021, when New York State attorney general Letitia James released her report showing that the Cuomo administration had undercounted the deaths of about sixty-five hundred elderly people in nursing homes, while also offering limited legal immunity to the nursing homes, I called in the pages of *Scientific American* for the governor to resign or be impeached. But I was one of few people calling for him to do so. It wasn't until James released a *second* report, in August 2021, detailing how Cuomo had reportedly sexually harassed eleven women, that a critical mass of people called for his resignation, the state legislature began impeachment proceedings, and Cuomo stepped down.

The very next day, the International Academy of Television Arts and Sciences took away his Emmy. A few days after that, the new governor, Kathy Hochul, announced that New York State's COVID-19 death toll actually included *twelve thousand* more souls than the Cuomo administration had misled the public to believe.

Harassing women is certainly an impeachable offense. But why didn't causing, and then covering up, the deaths of people in nursing homes on such a scale drive Cuomo from office with the first attorney general's report in March 2021?

"It's because they're undesirables" that some people are erased from public space and memory, Alice told me. "People don't want them in their neighborhoods. Right? They're scared. They don't want to see homeless people. They don't want to see mentally ill people. They don't want to see scary older disabled people." And when the viral underclass has already been erased from public view, it's hard to get the public to care about what happens to them.

"Reform is not the answer," Alice said of the system, noting how the Black Lives Matter movement exploding across the country from where she was in San Francisco to where I was in New York had been demanding *abolition* of prisons. "Abolition applies not just to prisons but to nursing homes, detention centers, youth juvenile facilities—ICE facilities," she says. "*Every* type of congregate setting."

I agree. Clearly, the system that created our present cannot be "reformed"; it must be abolished so that something better can be born in its wake. We cannot continue with a world that warehouses people who are disabled or elderly, hiding them from view; that allows them to fester physically and emotionally and leaves them for dead when viruses circulate. We cannot merely chip away at the way things are; we must imagine something beautiful anew.

* * *

On a warm day near the end of the strange summer of 2020, I rented a car in Manhattan and drove to Brooklyn to pick up my friend Camille Dodero. We had become close while serving on our union bargaining committee at the *Village Voice* about a decade earlier. We'd also bonded over being kicked to the curb by the *Voice* a year later, in a mass layoff. (I learned I had been laid off by reading about it publicly on Twitter, before meeting Camille and *Voice*rs past and present at the Scratcher, a favorite bar, to toast our performing a rite of passage with a long history for New York journalists: getting shit-canned.)

We had fallen out of regular touch in the years since—that is, until we teamed up with our fellow *Voice* alum, novelist Jen Doll, to plan Ward's Zoom memorial and, a few months after that, the spreading of his ashes.

Nine of us gathered on a boardwalk in Long Beach, then crossed over a large sand dune covered in seagrass and moved closer to the Atlantic Ocean our friend had loved. Despite the overhead sun, there was a hint of fall in the sea breeze, which felt nice on my masked face.

Journalist Cynthia Cotts asked us to sit in a circle on the sand, placing a black urn containing Ward's ashes gently on the beach and spacing Ward equidistant among us, as if he were just another one of us sitting there. She read words from people who couldn't come in person, then asked me to read "Footnote to 'Howl,'" by the Beat poet Allen Ginsberg.

As I read aloud—beginning with Ginsberg's fifteen cries of the word *Holy* and followed by "The world is holy! The soul is holy! The skin is holy! The nose is holy! The tongue and cock and hand and asshole holy!"—I felt the poem as much as I've ever felt any poem I ever read aloud. I felt in my bones that my friend was holy, and his friends were holy, and even viruses were holy, and that "forgiveness! mercy! charity! faith!" are ours, even when we've fallen out with folks.

Are ours, even in death.

Then, passing out gloves, Cynthia invited us all to take handfuls of Ward and to return him to the sea.

When my turn came, Cynthia held the box for me, and I dipped my hand into my friend. I felt scared, nervous, honored, flummoxed, and in awe to be so intimate with one of my former coworkers, a man who'd once nixed most of my story ideas, telling me, "You're a personable guy, just talk to people and listen to them! Everyone likes to be listened to! And stop trying so hard!"

Ward's remains felt grainy, like ground seashells. I scooped up a handful of my friend's ashes, savoring the texture of what remained of him—the ground remnants of seventy-two trips around our nearest star, after decades that included moments of laughter; of jokes; of surviving anti-Semitism; of enduring stuttering stigma; of Trump; of Cuomo; of the humiliation of being laid off near the end of his career; of decades of smoking; of years of life after smoking; of running; of cuddles with his cat, Cooter; of a tooth that could kill you; of a final encounter with a virus—a virus that could reduce the teeth and bones and blood of someone I hadn't realized I loved so much to mere dust.

At that moment, I also remembered how Ward had edited my very first cover story, in 2009. Because I was a *Voice* virgin, he'd asked me to sit by his side as he did the final hand proofing, to show me how things were done. My story was about the pet death business. After my landlady's cat died and I'd been forced to dispose of the kitty corpse, I had decided to write about how apartment-dwelling New Yorkers couldn't bury their dead pets in backyards, as I had done as a child in suburbia. Ward was the son of a vet and an animal lover himself. He edited the piece carefully, balancing the gallows humor and the pathos of my subjects, showing me how to do edits by hand as he put the *Voice* to bed on a Monday evening. I remember him showing me what *stet* meant (a note to retain the original text) as he read through the mock-up of my story through the lower half of his glasses. There was a beat about a virus in my copy, showing a human turned pet cremator bemoaning how slow business had gotten because not enough humans were dying anymore: "'Remember the AIDS virus?' says funeral director Ralph Francisco, 66, almost regretfully. 'That was supposed to wipe out everybody. But people are living with it for years!'"

Capitalism pushes us to wish for absurd things. When he came to that line, Ward marked it to be a pull quote (copy that is usually featured in larger print), looked up from the copy, chuckled, and said, "Can't make this shit up, Thrasher!"

The story had a cover illustration of a pug looking scared, and Ward gave it its subhead: "All dogs go to heaven. Yours is probably getting there in an urn." Remembering this as I removed *him* from an urn made me laugh amid the tears. Indeed, as Ward blew into our faces, several of us were letting our friend tickle us into bawdy laughter once more—as he'd done so many times in the *Voice* offices or over beers at the Scratcher.

Clenching him hard one last time, I tried to throw my friend into the sea. But, freed from the weight of the world, he flew mostly upward into a small cloud, which seemed to still itself for a moment before blowing westward and disappearing into thin air.

Released from his suffering, Ward was at one with the world. A neglectful government let a virus kill him. But the virus had also paradoxically made him *so* light that all that was left of him was sunshine, and wind, and laughter—and people by the sea talking about how much they'd loved him.

That disabled people are disposable is a lie. But what Ward shared with his friends? What Alice Wong shares with her friends and readers around the world?

That's the *true* shit you just can't make up.

10

RIDE-ALONG

(Speciesism)

In 2015, as I was flying all over the country reporting on how police had been using guns, gas, and even dogs to terrorize the Black Lives Matter movement, I got a surprising email from a reader. It was from a police officer named Suzanne Kessler, who also happens to be my cousin, from the white side of my family. I hadn't been in touch with her since I was a teenager. Something we had in common was that my father was Black and hers was Palestinian, placing us both a bit on the outside at family functions. Suzanne had been a big fan of my dad, "Uncle Bill," who intervened loudly when an elderly white relative mocked her for being Arab and then took her aside and told her to hold her head high because she came from a people with a proud history.

A vegetarian who also ran a small organic farm, Suzanne worked as a police officer in Bellevue, Nebraska, a modest Midwest city of about fifty thousand people just south of Omaha. Her husband, a white man, was an officer in the same department. Their son also worked in law enforcement, and their son-in-law was a military veteran. All of them had been reading my dispatches from St. Louis, New York, Baltimore, and Oakland describing the racist horrors of policing. They wanted to talk to me about them, and even invited me to visit. I was nervous but intrigued.

It took me two years, but in September 2017, I embarked on a long road trip to take my Nebraska cousins up on their offer. To my surprise, my cop relatives were *not* angry at me for depicting policing from the point of view of those harmed by it, nor for having spent years reporting on Michael Johnson, the young Black wrestler accused of breaking the law. Rather, they were generally curious about what I had to say, and they trusted my analysis. They spoke candidly about the racism in their own department and shared with me how they'd been taking stock of their own participation in a structurally racist institution. (I shared that I, too, was examining the institutional racism of journalism.)

Suzanne offered to take me on a ride-along with her in her police car. So, one day, I accompanied her in her cruiser, on foot, and at her police station for a twelve-hour shift. At one point, she drove the cruiser into a trailer park. The children I saw playing in its streets had brown skin and eyed the car warily. I felt guilty, like I was some kind of native informant riding on a colonial patrol. The park's streets were lined with dumpy, dilapidated mobile homes, and many of them had several cars in front of them. Some of these "homes," Suzanne told me, were the very same Federal Emergency Management Agency trailers used after Hurricanes Katrina and Rita displaced tens of thousands of people from New Orleans and the Mississippi Gulf in 2005. Even though these FEMA units had long been known to leak toxic chemicals and make their inhabitants sick with respiratory problems and headaches, they were still turning up all over the country—including in this trailer park more than a decade later, where they were renting for $1,800 to $2,500 a month, cash, plus $100 a month or more for the lot rental.

I was shocked. How could a mobile home in a small midwestern city be renting for more than what I was paying at the time for an apartment in Manhattan?

Suzanne explained what was going on. Often, the people who lived in these mobile homes were undocumented workers. Many of them were from Mexico or other Latin American countries, and they worked in nearby slaughterhouses and "CAFOs" (for "concentrated animal feeding operation" facilities, buildings where overcrowded farmed animals are literally made to defecate where they eat, often without ever seeing daylight). As often happens with work done in violation of immigration law, most of the risk of the work is shifted onto the low-paid laborers and away from the corporation employing them. If caught, the workers might be arrested and detained in immigration camps, where they'd be at high risk for contracting influenza, mumps, and chicken pox. Then they might be deported—even if that meant separating them from their children who were U.S. citizens. Meanwhile, the employers who'd brought them to town and profited from their labor would risk only a slap on the wrist, if that.

Most landlords in town would not rent to workers without papers or to people with bad credit, but the trailer park would. With an absurd price set by a limited supply *and* by a tacit ransom agreement not to call immigration authorities, the landlords shook down these poorly paid rural workers for big-city real estate prices. And to be able to afford these extortionate payments, far too many of these workers (and sometimes their multigenerational families) piled into these FEMA hellholes.

"Who are they going to tell?" Suzanne later told me. "There's no one to report it to, because they don't want to come forward" for fear of deportation.

"It's total exploitation of people's fears."

But the exploitation, Suzanne told me, didn't stop there. Because they are frightened that talking to government authorities for *any* reason could lead to their deportation, these workers and their families are vulnerable to all kinds of atrocities they can never report—like wage theft, unsafe housing, and domestic violence. Suzanne recalled that once, she stopped a truck with improper license plates. When the young driver showed her an ID that was probably fake, saying that he was nineteen, she noticed that "he only had, like, two fingers on each hand. And I asked him, 'What happened to your hands?'"

"Oh, they got cut off. They were caught in a machine, down at the meatpacking house."

"That looks like a workman's comp situation. Did you get workman's comp?"

"No, they fired me."

"Fired you? Why?"

"I couldn't do the work anymore, without my other fingers."

"Did you see a doctor at all? Did they get you any medical care?"

"They have a clinic, they gave me some stitches, then they fired me."

"Stitches?" she described her incredulity to me. "Most of his fingers were missing!"

Suzanne didn't ticket the man. Instead, she gave him a card with the phone number for his nation's consulate, where she said people from his government could help him.

While the horrors of American meatpacking in cities like Chicago have been widely available to readers at least since Upton Sinclair published *The Jungle* at the start of the twentieth century, the dangers have mutated over time. A desire to stymie unionization efforts, reduce the possibility of ethnic community building, and utilize cheaper commercial real estate has driven such work out of cities. The meat overlords have made the work they profit from even *more* dangerous and alienating by moving slaughterhouses far from urban life and into low-density regions. And while white supremacists have tried to depict immigrants moving into "the heartland" as viruses, it's really industrialized farming that is blighting rural America with increased violence, union busting, lower wages, and ecological destruction.

And this is only what happens in the United States. Meat production is a transcontinental affair. It is possible for an animal to be raised on one continent and killed, flown to another to be ground up, and flown to a *third* to be cooked and eaten. And at every step, that carcass is creating vectors of viral transmission among countless drivers, pilots, seamen, and butchers. (At the same time, it increases global warming with an enormous carbon footprint, creating conditions that are the most likely to dangerously affect people who can't even afford to eat meat.)

This is a cycle that implicates all of us, including those of us who buy meat from grocery stores or burgers from McDonald's (or even vegetarians who eat crops fertilized with manure from industrial animals). But our relationship with the world is too often one of extraction and exploitation, with no regard for the costs. In fact, the costs are myriad, from increasing the likelihood of zoonotic jumps (when viruses transmit from nonhuman animals to humans or vice versa) to creating lethal conditions for people working in factories. For many, it took the novel coronavirus pandemic to consider the ways that speciesism (defined as the presumption that human beings are superior to nonhuman animals and can treat or kill those nonhuman animals however we like) unleashes viruses on the human world and condemns to sickness or death the members of the viral underclass who are forced onto the front lines.

* * *

While he didn't use it to fulfill the massive shortage of protective gear for workers, President Donald Trump did invoke the Defense Production Act (DPA) in April 2020 to make ventilators and keep slaughterhouses open. Yet, while ventilators clearly helped save the lives of people affected by SARS-CoV-2, meat production did the opposite. On the day I logged on to the *New York Times* during the summer of 2020 to check its coronavirus maps (which I wrote about in chapter 7), fifteen of the top seventeen locations with a thousand or more coronavirus cases were jails or prisons; the lone two exceptions were a Smithfield Foods pork plant in South Dakota and a Tyson chicken plant in Iowa. Because of their cold temperatures, which better allow viruses to thrive; their conveyor belts, which quickly shuttle hundreds or thousands of carcasses an hour; and their workers standing shoulder to shoulder with knives that purposely cut the carcasses and unintentionally cut the workers, slaughterhouses were the most potent vectors of viral transmission for people who weren't incarcerated—even more so than the kind of nursing homes where my friend Ward Harkavy died.

As Axel Fuentes, the executive director of the Rural Community Workers Alliance, told me, workers he helped organize at the Smithfield Foods plant in Milan, Missouri, told him while crying that they "feel like they are treated like animals." Sometimes, he said, "workers have to wear diapers" and even "defecate on themselves, urinate on themselves" because "the speed of the line" moving pigs cannot stop, for any reason. Ever since I first read Eric Schlosser's book *Fast Food Nation: The Dark Side of the All-American Meal* in 2002, one line has stayed with me: when it comes to U.S. beef, Schlosser reported, "There is shit in the meat," a disaster of one kind. Two decades later, I realized that meat workers having to shit on *themselves* was a disaster of another magnitude altogether.

Defecation is used not only to make workers vulnerable, but over a certain age (say, three years old), it is used to determine who is valuable and who is disposable. We rarely look at infants who need Pampers and think, *You're disgusting and worthy of death.* But an adult who depends on Depends? When Alice Wong described people in congregate settings as "trapped," a justification for locking them up is often their incontinence, which betrays the dream of American independence with the "nightmare" of interdependence.

Even as millions of Americans were food insecure during the COVID-19 pandemic, Trump's enforcement of the DPA did little to get food to those who actually needed it. The reopened meat processing plants could not keep up with the supply of hogs in the United States; the National Pork Producers Council predicted that farmers and plant workers would have to kill as many as ten million pigs by even more brutal means than usual, only to throw them away. Meanwhile, the workers who continued to supply America with its meat were set up to be infected at work and then to have pathogens ride along with them home to crowded FEMA trailers.

As a lawsuit against Smithfield Foods alleged, its Milan plant failed to offer personal protective gear, stagger breaks, or develop a plan to test and trace the SARS-CoV-2 virus. According to the suit, this was *after* "hundreds of employees of Smithfield's plant in South Dakota contracted COVID-19," two of them died, "and Smithfield was forced to close that plant after it became the country's leading hot spot" for COVID. Indeed, as one worker on the "cut floor" in Milan who sued Smithfield as "Jane Doe" wrote in the *Washington Post*, "maintaining distance is almost impossible in our plant." Smithfield was "disciplining workers who missed a scheduled shift" even if they had COVID-19 symptoms, and the company was even offering "a $500 'responsibility' bonus to anyone who manages not to miss a single shift from April 1 through May 1," to incentivize working while sick.

Already dangerous before the pandemic, pork production became even more lethal during COVID-19. In another lawsuit, Oscar Fernandez alleged that his father, Isidro, was one of 1,000 employees at Tyson Foods' pork plant in Waterloo, Iowa, to become infected with the novel coronavirus—more than one-third of the 2,800 workers who processed "approximately 19,500 hogs per day." While refusing the local sheriff's pressure to close the plant, the suit charged, "most managers at the Waterloo Facility started avoiding the plant floor because they were afraid of contracting the virus." And yet, according to the suit, "Defendant Tom Hart, the Plant Manager of the Waterloo Facility, organized a cash buy-in, winner-take-all betting pool for supervisors and managers to wager how many employees would test positive for COVID-19."

Remember in chapter 2 how ABC News, CNN, and the AP perpetuated the myth of "COVID parties" without any direct evidence? Alleging that young people should be ashamed for gambling on who got the virus first? Turns out it was corporate supervisors doing the gambling with workers' lives. A month after Oscar Fernandez filed suit, Tyson fired seven managers for the betting ring at the Waterloo facility.

It's true that workers in low-wage jobs of all kinds face increased viral risk in a pandemic. But people who work with animals face some of the severest risks. Because of how speciesism devalues nonhuman animals, companies squeeze together too many species into tight spaces and deny them room to live in relation to one another with any sense of equilibrium. This, in turn, places the humans who work with these animals in some of the most dangerous working conditions possible.

The viral danger faced by people working or living in close proximity to nonhuman animals can't be blamed entirely on Trump or cartoonishly evil factory managers. It's not new, and it's not random. Such proximity is an example of what geographer Ruth Wilson Gilmore calls *organized abandonment*. People who work with animals don't just wind up moving thousands of miles from their homeland, traveling across dangerous borders, killing mammals in frigid temperatures, living in crowded FEMA trailers on the outskirts of a minor U.S. city, being patrolled by my vegetarian cop cousin (and observed by me), and/or having managers bet on their lives *by accident*. It's systemic, and its drivers are deeply entrenched in our legal, business, policing, and social systems.

For instance, the Occupational Safety and Health Administration, or OSHA, is set up to protect workers from the very kinds of risks these meat production workers were facing. But when Reuters identified 106 U.S. workplaces "where employees complained of slipshod pandemic safety practices around the time of" COVID-19 outbreaks in 2020, a mere 12 resulted in discipline by OSHA by the end of the year. "The agency," Reuters reported, "never inspected 70 of those workplaces, where at least 4,500 workers were infected by the coronavirus and 26 died after contracting COVID-19." Of the work sites Reuters identified, the government largely deserted the workers it deemed the most essential in a majority of the cases—at a time when those workers needed protections the most.

As with so many other members of the viral underclass, the vulnerability of people who work killing (nonhuman) animals is as manufactured as a box of Smithfield's Fully Cooked Maple Sausage Patties. And the justification for consigning people to such damnation? Their proximity to animalness.

* * *

If we think of ourselves as animals at all, we humans tend to imagine ourselves as the *best* animal. We draw pyramids of hierarchy and imagine ourselves on top of them, at the pinnacle, as royalty ruling over the animal kingdom. We conjure zoonotic threats where they don't exist, being told in childhood that we will get warts from frogs (when, in fact, warts are caused by the human papillomavirus and move only from human to human). We downplay how 99 percent of the DNA of humans and bonobo chimpanzees is the same. And even though nature has literally coded us almost the same way as certain monkeys, we regularly divide the world into the "man-made" and "natural," which smacks not just of sexism but of speciesism—as if *Homo sapiens* were separate from and above all other living beings in nature.

Who is considered a human animal or a nonhuman animal is also highly gendered, racialized, and ableist, with those closest to white, straight maleness being categorized as human, while the rest of us have historically been considered nonhuman to varying degrees.

Taxonomy is the scientific classification of organisms, and the eighteenth-century "father of modern taxonomy," Carl Linnaeus, classified *Mammalia* as organisms with breasts. As the historian of science Londa Schiebinger has noted, one of the reasons Linnaeus did this was because, at the time, men were defined by their brainy reason while women were defined by their beastly bodies.

When nineteenth-century taxonomists Josiah Clark Nott (who owned enslaved humans) and George R. Gliddon organized biological beings, they created nasty hierarchies of race and species. They were informed by phrenology, a pseudoscience that argued that measuring the dimensions of skulls proved how races were intellectually inferior or superior. In 1854—just five years before Charles Darwin's 1859 landmark *On the Origin of Species* would argue that humans of different races were of one species—Nott and Gliddon published *Types of Mankind*, a book that "documented what they saw as objective racial hierarchies with illustrations comparing blacks to chimpanzees, gorillas, and orangutans," as Wulf D. Hund and Charles W. Mills wrote in the *Conversation*. In 1857, Nott and Gliddon followed up *Types of Mankind* with *Indigenous Races of the Earth*, which argued that Black people fell somewhere between Greek people and chimps.

Under a twisted logic, if women and Black people are closer to animals, then they *deserve* the kinds of lives and deaths of farmed animals. If Michael Johnson is an animal, he should be allowed to die in prison or of AIDS; if Isidro Fernandez is an animal, his life should be mere gambling fodder, as expendable as the hogs in America's hot dogs. If an elder (or a factory worker, or someone gay like Zak Kostopoulos, who once lost control of his bowels while running from attackers) defecates without a toilet, they deserve anything else that happens to them. If any child crossing the border into the United States is an animal, then they deserve to possibly die of influenza in an ICE detention camp.

The hubris with which some humans have sought to master the so-called natural world, through colonialism and capitalism, has led directly to the spread of viruses from animals to humans. But this risk is not shared by all humans equally. The viral underclass bears the most risk of infection, and once afflicted by viruses, these humans are needlessly marked as *un*human, perpetuating a vicious circle.

But viruses could be a guide to a different kind of taxonomy—to a transgressive taxonomy in which humans aren't on top of or master of anything, but live *in relation to* every other species on earth. This approach might help alleviate the suffering of the viral underclass and help us address current and future pandemics.

While its exact origins are as yet unknown, the novel coronavirus is close to viruses found in bats and pangolins. Some bats have been flying around with certain viruses for millions of years, and bats have evolved to live symbiotically with all kinds of pathogens that might harm other mammals. But while SARS-CoV-2 brought humanity to a halt in 2020, it didn't seem to be harming these flying nocturnal mammals.

As various empires have shown, even some members of the same species who live on different parts of the globe have adapted to life with pathogens while others have not—but if they are brought into close contact too quickly, a virus living harmoniously with one group might kill off the other. For instance, when Europeans arrived in the Americas between the sixteenth and eighteenth centuries, they had some level of immunity to smallpox; but Native Americans had never encountered the smallpox virus and had no immunity, and it wiped out millions of them.

Like certain seabirds, bats defecate near one another in caves in large quantities that accumulate to make guano. Many species in cave ecosystems rely upon guano, and humans use it for fertilizer. In fact, it is so valuable that, as my colleague Daniel Immerwahr wrote in *How to Hide an Empire*, the United States vastly expanded its geographical footprint in the nineteenth century to gain more access to it. Many life-sustaining nutrients are bountiful in guano, but guano is also rich in pathogens. And so, the quest to harvest it has made humans vulnerable to the viruses it carries.

It is possible that SARS-CoV-2 jumped from bats to some poor person whose livelihood depended on scooping up guano in a remote region of central Asia. People may have died from it over many years without the virus moving broadly between groups of humans before it made its way, in 2019, to the Wuhan Huanan Seafood Wholesale Market that is its suspected source. There, it may have spread *not* through exotic animals for sale, but between human workers and shoppers.

People outside the United States who live or work near "exotic" animals—like people farming guano or selling pangolins in China—are highly stigmatized and othered by Americans. It is precisely the sort of work the United States (and other empires) demands, but from which those in power distance themselves. This process constitutes a kind of organized abandonment, where interests in the United States depend upon such work, even if those in the country pretend not to benefit from it. When Donald Trump repeatedly called SARS-CoV-2 the "China virus," the remark was meant not only to make the novel coronavirus seem un-American, but to mark those people originally infected by it as subhuman *others*, in part because of their proximity to the animals from which the virus may have derived.

A decade prior, the 2009 H1N1 "swine flu" pandemic originated in North America. A "nasty mash-up of swine, avian, and human viruses," Tim Philpot wrote at the time in *Grist*, the swine flu outbreak was associated with a subsidiary of Smithfield Farms in Mexico. Still, many of the pork workers who were infected by H1N1 were othered by the United States—not coincidentally because they were either working in Mexico or were immigrant workers from Latin America in the United States. And rather than being given respect and support for providing humans with food, these members of the viral underclass have been widely despised by those they feed. They became hated not merely for being considered animallike, but because the viruses in their bodies connected all of us human animals to other animals. When they became exposed to a virus, the essentialist boundary between the species was exposed, too, and the boundary itself began to look as batshit as guano. Yet, because this zoonotic outbreak originated in North America with the beloved pig—and because the U.S. pork industry was at fault for its initial transmission—swine flu has never been othered *nationally* as a virus as the coronavirus has been.

Since humans first became aware of HIV in the 1980s, the virus has been associated with monkeys. Like bats with SARS-CoV-2 or any cousin virus, simians have likely been living with a close relative of HIV called SIV (simian immunodeficiency virus) without harm for a very long time. Though HIV and SIV are both a kind of lentivirus, which attacks the immune system, primates have lived with SIV for so long that they've adapted to it. It doesn't affect them as HIV affects humans.

Incorrectly, rumors have swirled for decades that HIV jumped from simians to humans when people on the African continent had sex with monkeys. Researchers have long believed that HIV likely jumped when hunters with machetes killed chimpanzees for bushmeat in the early twentieth century—probably in the 1920s, in what is now the Democratic Republic of the Congo. It likely entered the hunters' blood through cuts in their skin—a fairly common way slaughterhouse workers still become plagued by infections. The virus may have traveled with African "porters," who were coerced laborers forced to cut deep into forests by Belgian colonizers. HIV then likely hitched rides along routes of colonialism, as the European "Scramble for Africa" robbed the continent of its resources—which means that neocolonialism moved HIV in the twentieth century around the globe much as European classical colonialism moved pathogens to the Americas during the Atlantic slave trade.

So much of why and how people come into contact with animals is economic; thus, the risk of humans encountering zoonotic viruses is very classed. It is *not* wealthy meat eaters who are in immediate danger, but the lower classes. Whether they are butchering meat in the bush or in a factory, those on a lower rung of the social ladder are the ones wielding machetes and factory saws.

Also, factory-farmed animals are bred to have weakened immune systems and are given high quantities of antibiotics and then crowded together in toxic environments. This is the perfect breeding ground for antibiotic-resistant mutations of pathogens. The poor are also the most likely to live near animal kill sites and their inherent dangers—such as in 2018, when a town near a meat processing plant in North Carolina flooded and was overwhelmed by waters teeming with pig feces, hog ash, and viruses.

Months into the COVID-19 era, poor people were *still* collecting guano from seabirds in Thailand, despite its known dangers and despite the growing pandemic. Not doing so might have resulted in their starvation. As the COVID-19 pandemic was unfolding in February 2020, the World Bank South Asia Twitter account wrote that 71 percent of Bhutan's "territory is covered in forest, but with a contribution of only about 2% to GDP per year, the forest sector remains underutilized. How can the country sustainably invest in its forests?" Perhaps the most valuable investment Bhutan could make on behalf of humanity would be to just leave its forests, which are full of bats, alone. As climate change destroys diverse biohabitats for both animals and humans, the ruling class wants to push an increasingly desperate viral underclass to harvest the forests that sustain them, much as European colonizers pushed African porters into the territory of chimpanzees living with SIV. The climate crisis is only going to make the encounters between nonhuman animals and human animals more common, as all animals amass upon a decreasingly hospitable portion of the globe.

Proximity to mosquitoes is also a marker of the viral underclass, and a result of the forces that create it: capitalism, racism, environmental destruction, and speciesism. While neither COVID-19 nor HIV can move between humans by mosquitoes, many pathogens *do* move through mosquitoes, like the parasite *Plasmodium malariae* (malaria) and the Zika, West Nile (WNV), and dengue fever viruses. Outside the United States, class determines who has prophylaxis against mosquitoes, and even though protection can be as complex as a dengue vaccine or as simple as mosquito netting, the results of a lack of protection can be equally deadly.

Inside the United States, proximity to mosquitoes is driven by economics and class as well. For instance, the mortgage crash of 2008 began a foreclosure crisis of some ten million U.S. homes. Many of those homes had pools, and when the families living in them were evicted, the pool maintenance stopped, turning the standing water into dank, fetid mosquito breeding grounds. At the same time, neighbors who could keep paying their mortgages not only were left with "underwater" homes whose debts exceeded their value but became targets for the mosquitoes breeding in those unchlorinated pools and the West Nile virus they carried. As the *New York Times* reported, a 300 percent increase in mortgage delinquencies in 2008 led to a 200 percent increase in cases of West Nile virus.

The predation of the subprime lending crisis literally led to the breeding of mosquitoes who could bite, infect, and condemn people living in zip codes of foreclosure to West Nile virus *and* to the viral underclass. Even socializing with or just living *near* those who could not pay back their debt ensnared people in viral vulnerability and premature death—not unlike how the Greek debt crisis led to increased cases of West Nile virus, too.

And much like when the Defense Production Act was invoked with meat processing workers, when the United States does try to counter the spread of viruses and diseases like West Nile virus or malaria, the policies often further dehumanize the very people most at risk. In the

1940s, the United States and Mexico created a program for *braceros*, or farmworkers, that allowed citizens of Mexico to travel to the States to harvest crops. But upon legally crossing the border, the *braceros* were sprayed down with dichlorodiphenyltrichloroethane. DDT, while effective at killing mosquitoes, has also been shown to be extremely toxic to humans. (In 1972, the U.S. Environmental Protection Agency banned its use entirely.) And although DDT had been used to kill mosquitoes mostly with aerial spraying, the United States willingly used it directly on people as if they were ridden with insects—or as if they themselves were insects—without any concern for the toxic effects of the chemical.

When the United States washes humans down with chemicals at the border like they're bugs, or forces migrants onto cold kill floors during a pandemic when viruses are flowing freely, it is not only policing a manufactured human/nonhuman animal species divide. It is policing the boundaries of who should have access to life itself.

* * *

The day I spent riding along with my police officer cousin Suzanne in Nebraska ended at her police station. There, as she filled out paperwork, I talked to one of her fellow officers, who trained their police dogs. And I met the dog he was currently training, which he took home at night to live with his family, a menacing Belgian Malinois/German shepherd mix with several titanium teeth, to help the dog take a harsher "bite out of crime." In front of several other people, the officer casually referred to the female canines as "bitches" and joked that he used his "bitches" not just to keep the public in line, but to establish his own animallike pecking order. *He* was the alpha leader of his pack, the K9 dogs were below him, and *then* came his "bitches": my cousin Suzanne (the only woman police officer on the force) at work and his wife at home.

I had been obsessed with police dogs ever since reading the 2015 Department of Justice *Investigation of the Ferguson Police Department* after the shooting of Michael Brown. In addition to finding that "Nearly

90% of documented force used by FPD officers was used against African Americans," the DOJ found that "in every canine bite incident for which racial information is available, the person bitten was African American."

Even though K9s tend to be vaccinated, dog bites represent a moment in which a pathogen like the *Rabies lyssavirus*, which is zoonotic, can jump from a dog to a human. Once their skin is broken, a human's epidermal prophylaxis becomes open to any pathogens in the dog's mouth as the K9 tries to eat them alive. Whether or not rabies or other microbes are riding along in any given cop dog's mouth, moments of actual viral transmission are just the last event in a chain of social predeterminants of health. From Selma to Ferguson, any police dog's teeth are likely to slice the human flesh of people *already* plagued by pathogens.

My interest in this subject only grew when I read an essay by a scholar of police dogs, Tyler Wall, on how "German police dogs" had been imported as a biotechnology in the United States after World War II. This was expressly *because* they'd been so good at causing racial terror in Nazi Germany. German shepherds were first systematically used as "canine cops" in the 1950s, in St. Louis and Baltimore, two heavily Black cities where I'd been reporting. Two K9s were used to suppress a sit-in of Black college students fighting for civil rights in Mississippi in 1961. Eventually, K9s became a staple in American police departments, even in small towns in the rural Midwest.

Anthropomorphism is the process of assigning (nonhuman) animals human qualities, and zoomorphism is the process of turning human (animals) into nonhuman beasts. When police dogs and emotional support dogs are depicted in certain media, prosecutors play a role in assigning sympathetic, human qualities to them for the benefit of white people. The dogs are meant to bolster white people's sense of comfort and humanity. But as Wall has shown (and my own reporting has revealed to me), those very same dogs are used by police and local media to scare Black people and relegate them to the domain of the nonhuman—potentially exposing them to viruses.

This brings me back to my cousin. When we reconnected online, I was fascinated to learn that while she was a police officer—a violent job in which she was trained to potentially kill people—she was also an animal activist, an organic farmer, and a vegetarian. As a journalist who has covered police torture and murders, I was not surprised to learn that many cops are carnivorous hunters who enjoy killing animals. Similarly, it didn't surprise me when I heard a streak of sadism in the voice of Suzanne's colleague, who bragged about how he trains his "bitches."

When not on duty, Suzanne does not train dogs at home to kill or go hunting; she spends much of her time tending to a small farm with horses and egg-laying chickens. Officer Kessler's life as a vegetarian cop is a stark portrait in contradiction.

When I think of Suzanne's life as a vegetarian, I think about the violence-plagued lives of the people who work on a factory's kill floor and who live in the trailers she showed me on the ride-along. I think about how vegetarianism can lead us away from the hierarchy of speciesism, which could lead not only to less cruelty experienced by nonhuman animals but to less vulnerability for the most marginalized human animals, too. And I think about how, if we didn't eat meat, maybe the young man Suzanne pulled over wouldn't have lost his fingers, and maybe the migrants in those trailers wouldn't have had to dangerously travel so far from home in the first place.

In other words, vegetarianism, veganism, and organic, humane farming are good forms of harm reduction. But if we're going to abolish the other isms and hierarchies that produce a viral underclass, speciesism, and the hierarchies it imposes on our understanding of the world, needs to be abolished, too.

We are all, as Alice Wong says, "in the same soup—the very same soup." What if humans didn't believe that viruses and bacteria were at the bottom of the food pyramid, but at the top of it? Or between every step? What if we didn't imagine a species *pyramid* at all, but a species *cycle*—a round map without beginning or end, which we all share? We humans need other animals. Even vegans do. We depend on bat feces for guano and horse manure to grow vegetables. Plant agriculture would collapse without animals. But what if we humans respected other animals more and didn't condemn them to living in their own feces in "animallike conditions"? If we didn't believe that certain humans are not human *and* if we didn't think nonhuman animals should be condemned to hellish circumstances, perhaps it would be harder to condemn those certain humans to wallowing in their waste, not having ventilation, and not having time or space to enjoy their lives "like animals."

And what if we stopped thinking of nonhuman animals as not just the *cause* of human illness but also the *solution*? After all, healthy animal ecosystems have provided a healthier planet for all of us animals, and they offer a model for how to live sustainably without capitalism.

If we human animals want to avoid the next viral pandemic, we can't rely upon meat eating, even under the force of the Defense Production Act. Such a world could free the viral underclass considerably not just from infection, but from the many ways social death predicts and compounds it.

IV

RECKONING

Amid all these difficulties, we managed to live, dance, laugh, cry, love and be loved, let new people into our lives and remember those who left. So we should say our thank yous, forgive mes, good jobs, and I'm sorrys where they're due.

—Zak Kostopoulos (Ζακ Κωστόπουλος)

11

RELEASE

(The Myth of White Immunity)

When I got into a rental car in Chicago in July 2019, it had been more than five years since I first heard the name "Tiger Mandingo." Sentenced to thirty years, Michael Johnson was scheduled to get out of prison in 2045. I had spent the years since his trial wondering if I would even live to the age of sixty-eight (my father's age when he died) to see Michael free. But as I drove toward Indiana on that mercilessly hot day, I knew that in less than twenty-four hours, Michael was supposed to be released from prison.

Because of my reporting and the activism of his supporters, Michael's thirty-year sentence was overturned in 2016. Then, following a no-contest "Alford" plea deal he'd taken in 2017, in which he did not admit to guilt, Michael accepted a ten-year sentence that included time already served, knowing he could get out in a few years if he didn't get in trouble. And so, by July 2019, he was finally scheduled to be released.

As I drove, it occurred to me that much of what had transpired in his life over the past half decade had flowed from the myth of white immunity: the misconception that white people are totally exempt from health risks, particularly viral risk. This myth tricks white people not only into making themselves needlessly susceptible to viruses, but also into refusing to see how at risk they are from all the harms and violence of society, which can grind one into the viral underclass. For instance, while police disproportionately kill people of color, they in fact kill more white people annually. And as we've seen, austerity budgets harm poor white people in Europe and North America as well, pitting poor people of different races and ethnicities against one another while the rich gobble up all the resources. Everyone should be enraged about police killings, but because the myth of white immunity is so overpowering, many white people support a system that imperfectly protects them and mostly harms the underclass—and leaves the myth of whiteness in place.

When Michael's first accuser, Dylan King-Lemons, had sex with him without a condom, he exposed himself to the viral risks of unprotected sex. (Although HIV does affect mostly people of color in the United States, the CDC still predicts that one out of every eleven white men who have sex with men will become HIV-positive in his lifetime—a not-insignificant number.) The narrative of Michael Johnson's trial reinforced this line of thinking, placing the blame solely on Michael's shoulders instead of narrating how he *and* Dylan King-Lemons, the white sex partner who it was assumed should never have had to come in contact with HIV, needed to negotiate risk *together*.

On my way to the prison, I picked up Akil Patterson, one of Michael's few and staunchest supporters, at the Indianapolis Airport. A Black gay man who had been a high school and college wrestler himself, Akil became a wrestling coach and an advocate for racial and LGBTQ civil rights. He had seen "Tiger" wrestle in a tournament once, in 2012, and when he heard about the arrest in 2013, Akil flew from his home in Baltimore to St. Louis to visit Michael in jail. Over the years, Akil had visited Michael many times, called him weekly, and regularly put money on his "book," the account people in prison are required to have in order to buy food, pay for nonemergency doctor's visits, get a haircut, make phone calls, or even purchase shampoo and deodorant.

Akil helped organize a letter from a hundred Black gay men in support of Michael before his trial and helped raise money to hire a lawyer for his appeal. When I asked why he'd decided in 2013 to buy that plane ticket and visit a young man he'd never spoken to before—not to mention a demonized college student living with HIV who called himself "Tiger Mandingo"—Akil told me it was because Michael reminded him of himself.

In some ways, I can see how Akil and Michael have much in common. They are both personable Black men who are gay, extremely handsome, have struggled with dyslexia, and share a deep, abiding faith in God. But in other ways, they seem quite different to me. Though they are both wrestlers, Akil has a commanding, Herculean presence, and he's as overtly confrontational in his bombastic demeanor as Michael is demure. A college graduate, entrepreneur, activist, and politician, Akil also has a close relationship with both his parents. Michael never knew his father, and neither his mother nor any of his five brothers visited him in prison even once. Akil's life has seemed to me over the years to be as stable as Michael's is chaotic. Akil is also HIV-negative—though, like me, he recognizes that HIV is still always an intimate part of his life as a Black gay man, regardless of his status. But as Akil has told me many times, he attributes much of his good fortune to luck (as do I).

"I could have wound up just like Michael," he told me. And because of this, he treats Michael like a kid brother in need of a steady, guiding hand. Akil seemed to have heard the biblical question God poses to Cain in the Book of Genesis, "Am I my brother's keeper?" and answered with a resounding *yes*. He's lived a life dedicated to the love of "Brother to Brother," as the poet Joseph Beam put it—much as Lorena Borjas lived a life dedicated to her "girls" in Jackson Heights. Akil and Lorena both model an approach we, as a world, need to embrace if we want to get a handle on viruses and other social plagues. They cared for the health of their communities by personally attending to the welfare of people who were not only unknown to them, but widely despised by the rest of society. They did not assume any myth of immunity, nor of American exceptionalism or individualism. They seemed to understand that immunity wasn't innate to anyone's identity but was achieved through access to tactile (sterile syringes, condoms, medications) and societal (the right to housing, freedom from incarceration) prophylaxis. And in their example, they showed something that the white immunity myth obscures, and which can harm anyone: that we can't look out just for ourselves but must protect one another and our interactions. Such tender human-to-human care is necessary if humans want to live on a planet where we're vastly outnumbered by viruses and bacteria.

This made me think about something surprising I had learned about smallpox, the only virus ever to be eradicated. One of the reasons its elimination from humans was possible was because, incredibly, during the height of the Cold War, the United States and the Soviet Union worked together to achieve this goal. In a rare act of self-preservation that, miraculously, benefited all the people of the earth, the world's communist and capitalist superpowers collaborated, despite being ideological enemies.

After I picked up Akil, we met up with Meredith Rowan, the white stepmother of one of Michael's friends, who had stepped into a maternal role when Michael was arrested and she saw that his family wasn't able to effectively support him. The three of us then began the three-hundred-mile drive to the Boonville Correctional Facility, two states to the west, where we hoped Michael would be released into Meredith's care the following morning.

At no point on that drive could we *not* think about incarceration. Certainly not when we passed through a town in Illinois with a sign posted directly in front of a prison that read, "If You Lived Here, You'd Be Home Now!" Not when Michael called us by phone and we heard the computerized Securus operator tell us we were being recorded and that the phone call would cut off soon. And certainly not as we all reflected on our five-year journey of meeting because of Michael, and of learning together about HIV criminalization and medication and viral loads, and of enduring the endless ways one is made to feel unfairly humiliated by even *knowing* someone in prison. We had all undergone background checks and answered endless invasive questions and had been frisked and felt up entering jails and prisons to see him—as if *we* were being punished, too.

At a certain point on that drive, it occurred to me that there are two kinds of people in the United States: those who understand the imposed shame of knowing someone who's incarcerated, and those who don't. Knowing people who are behind bars isn't an unusual experience for Americans of any race, but it is a very stigmatized one. Half of Black men and 40 percent of white men in the United States have been arrested by age twenty-three, and as the Prison Policy Initiative reported in 2019, "Women's incarceration has grown at twice the pace of men's incarceration in recent decades," which "has disproportionately been located in local jails."

So, much of the populace of the nation is likely to be related in some way to *someone* who has been arrested. But because this fact is so shameful, it is rarely discussed openly—and the myth of immunity makes it even harder for white people to disclose their experiences with the criminal justice system, let alone to form solidarity with people even more disproportionately impacted by it than they are. This myth allows white people to look at COVID-19 or HIV or prison or addiction and say, *This isn't happening to us. We don't need to be concerned with those affected*, when it is, in fact, happening to them. The shame helps expand the boundaries of the viral underclass by keeping people unused to having to protect their communities from taking precautions that could save their very lives.

* * *

Meredith, Akil, and I spent the night in a cheap motel and drove to Boonville, a sleepy town of just about eight thousand mostly white people, the next morning. As for too many American small towns, the prison is the main economic engine of this community and cages a population of disproportionately nonwhite people compared to the majority-white demographics of the surrounding region and state. The effect of this is a hardening of a perceived border between citizen and prisoner, between disposable and valuable, between white and nonwhite. But these distinctions belie who is behind bars. Mirroring a national dynamic, while

Black people are overrepresented in Missouri's prisons, white people are still a majority of the state's incarcerated population.

We had been told to arrive at the prison after 8 a.m. with Michael's street clothes. After the wardens searched them for contraband, it would then take about an hour to process his release. We had been warned emphatically to wait in the visitors' parking lot, adjacent to the prison's barbed wire fencing, about a quarter mile from the actual gate. On the free side of the fence, a picnic table with an overhead awning sat next to the parking spaces. But if it was intended to make the difficult circumstances of being related to someone in prison a little more bearable, the bench nearby did not. Carved into it were large letters reading, "In Memory of the Victims of Crime." It was a pointed message, and one that would never be seen by the actual victims of crime. The prison wanted visiting family members and friends to think about what their friend or relative had been convicted of and whom they had hurt, in order to assign guilt by association upon the visitors.

Meredith turned in Michael's street clothes, and then we waited. During the next hour—when I *still* didn't think Michael would actually be set free—I got to see three other parties greet a released person. This was a fascinating blessing. While reporting over the years, I'd seen lots of folks get out of arraignment holding and had once greeted a cousin coming out of a short-term stint in a county jail, but I'd never personally witnessed people who had spent years or decades inside emerging from their cage. The process was particularly suspenseful for all those waiting, because, peering at the prison from a quarter mile away, the greeters couldn't really tell when someone was being released or who it was when each human speck began moving in our direction.

Among those waiting to greet their people were an elderly white couple, one Black woman, two white men, and two miniature poodles. Every party greeted their person with hugs and kisses (especially the dogs).

Finally, Meredith screamed, "*Michael!*" As soon as she saw him emerging in the distance, and though she'd been warned not to, she tore off into the employee parking lot to greet him. Akil and I followed, with me shooting video on my phone.

The sun was shining brightly, and a warm breeze blew over us. As Meredith ran, whatever burdens she carried in her middle-aged body seemed to dissipate as she sprinted with the carefree zeal of a young girl. Michael flashed his characteristic smile as he embraced her. He tried to comfort her and tell her not to cry as she wept in his arms.

"I don't ever want to let you go!" she wailed.

Michael had filled out around his middle since we first met, and Akil told him he had gotten fat before embracing him. Michael hugged them both, and then, as I handed off my phone, he hugged me, too. It was brief but so nice to actually embrace the person I had written and thought about more than any other for the better part of a decade. It was also strange to have a haptic connection, because our communication up until then had been verbal or, during court appearances, nonverbally visual. I thought of the months Michael had spent in solitary confinement (separated by jail officials who had incorrectly decided his HIV status made him dangerous to others), and of how long he'd had to go without a hug or a pat on the back or touch of any kind.

Later, I'd think many times about how strange and wonderful that moment was. It was very unlike my encounters writing about Michael Brown in Ferguson, Zak Kostopoulos in Athens, Olivier Le Borgne in Paris, or the ghosts of so many others I had been chasing.

The first thing we did before we left the prison parking lot was to go through Michael's HIV medications. I was amazed at how much each of us had come to know about antiretroviral drugs and T-cell counts over the years, including Michael himself. We'd been told that he would be getting thirty days' worth of pills upon his release, but he only had eleven days' worth, and we made a note to immediately let the team of people waiting to help Michael navigate his HIV care know that he was short on meds.

While unsettling, this wasn't at all unusual. Not only do prisons concentrate large groups of Black people at risk for HIV into one place, but most prisons don't test people who are imprisoned for HIV. These prisons ultimately *then* release people living with HIV (or even AIDS) back into their communities with a highly contagious viral load. Even the prisons that *do* test for HIV and that provide drugs that make viral loads untransmittable may release people living with the virus back into their communities with as little as three days' worth of medication.

Especially considering how a prison stint or being on parole can make housing and working impossible, Michael was lucky to have people help him navigate this.

After the pill count, we called Michael's parole officer, got in the car, and got the hell out of Dodge. Meredith had gassed up the car so that we wouldn't have to stop until we had left the state of Missouri.

As we drove off, Michael told us that the guards had said to him, "Don't come back too soon," while some of his incarcerated acquaintances had told him, "You come on vacation, you leave on probation." (After nearly six years in various facilities, Michael did not feel he had any friends there to bid farewell to.)

It was fascinating and wondrous seeing Michael under the sun, to see his strong right arm neither handcuffed nor clutching a black phone receiver behind jailhouse glass, but leisurely hanging out the window of Meredith's car. And it was delightful to spend the whole day together, even if seven hours of it was while driving. It felt relaxing not to be on the Securus clock, or to have an armed guard staring us down with unspoken threats.

As we quickly drove through St. Charles on Interstate 70, Michael said, "Coming here for school was the worst mistake I ever made." Perhaps the most absurd thing he told us was that he'd heard that his public defender was now teaching law at his alma mater, Lindenwood University. A quick Google search on my phone showed that this was true: Heather Donovan, who had left the courtroom with a witness on the stand, was now teaching law to a new generation of Missouri attorneys.

We drove past the exit for West Florissant Boulevard in Ferguson. Had we taken it, it would have led us right to the Canfield Green Apartments, where that *other* young Black man named Michael had also been caught up in the criminal justice system and captured the attention of the world. As we drove near where I had spent so many tear gas–filled nights reporting—where I had first begun to notice the overlapping maps of racism and policing and viruses—I recalled a walk I had taken around the Canfield Green Apartments just a few weeks earlier. It had been a muggy day, and I had gone to pay my respects to Michael Brown, as I did every time I visited St. Louis.

Trying to find the exact spot where he spent his last moments, I stumbled upon a new bronze plaque embedded in the sidewalk, parallel to the place in the street where Brown had been killed. It was a modest plaque, adorned with a simple poem. If you weren't looking, you'd walk right over it—and it drove home how small Canfield Drive is. It all felt so *small*—the buildings, the street, the distance between where Darren Wilson's car and Michael Brown's bleeding body had been.

How could such an intimate, close interaction in such a small place unleash such a big movement in this state, this country, this world? The tragic incident revealed a lot about how Black people live in America, but its fallout affected white people, too.

The same is true of viruses. They are so small, occupying the most intimate domains of our lives. Yet they have the power to infect political consciousness and disrupt the world so thoroughly, they can upend the entire way of life for billions of people around the planet.

* * *

And yet, despite the ways viruses can inspire radical political possibilities, they can also ignite very powerful resistance to their revolutionary potential—resistance born because of the fiction of white superiority.

This is where the antivaccination and antimask movements come in.

Even though vaccine hesitancy spans racial lines, the loudly proud antivaccination ideology in the United States was spawned in the myth of white immunity. It can be traced in this country to when some parents in California decided to stop vaccinating their children with safe, long-used, and well-established vaccines in the early 2000s. These parents are more likely to be economically affluent, college-educated, and white; their unvaccinated children are now at risk for viruses like measles. (The children of working-class parents, for their part, are more likely to be vaccinated.) As a result, the percentage of unvaccinated children in the United States has quadrupled in the first two decades of the twenty-first century—and in some wealthy schools in Southern California, the vaccination rate is lower than that of a poor country like South Sudan.

Of course, vaccination protects populations, not just individuals, and so, whenever parents in California's upper class decide not to vaccinate their kids, they are putting children in the viral underclass at increased risk. (The kids in the viral underclass may not have access to good medical care if they contract measles, and their families certainly don't have access to any fiction of immunity.) Not unlike how race scientists believed skull measurement showed intellectual superiority, white parents who believe their offspring's "natural immunity" means they don't need vaccines are practicing a belief in a kind of biological white supremacy.

But that so-called supremacy is a lie. By the summer of 2021, many white politicians, media figures, and religious leaders were proudly against vaccines and masks. Yet, by the end of that summer, three prominent white radio hosts had died of COVID-19, including one known as "Mr. Anti-Vax" and another known as "Mr. Anti-Mask." Their whiteness alone did not protect them.

This is not to say that whiteness is not a powerful prophylaxis. Being white *does* provide structural protections from viruses and other harms in society; on average, it confers more years of life. Still, like all forms of immunity, the safeguards afforded by whiteness are not absolute and can lead white people down a mortal path of self-delusion that the author Jonathan M. Metzl describes in his 2019 book, *Dying of Whiteness: How the Politics of Racial Resentment Is Killing America's Heartland.*

When I think about why some of Michael's sexual partners may have thought they were safe from HIV even while having unprotected sexual intercourse, and when I think about why white Evangelicals think they'll be protected from the novel coronavirus without using masks or getting a vaccine, I am reminded of something my mentor and friend, the critical race theorist and law professor Kendall Thomas, once said. In 2003, he told the ACT UP Oral History Project about witnessing AIDS ravage New York City in the 1980s and '90s. As a Black gay man, he'd marveled at seeing white men experience "the shock of being marked as queer and of being subjected to a politics of abjection. . . . And that sense of not being willing to acknowledge their investment in the structures of social and economic and gender and racial power—even though that very same structure was killing them—was one of the most painful things in the world for me to watch, because these were smart people."

Much of the time, the viral underclass is composed of people who are economically and racially already in the underclass, but not always, and believing in the myth of white immunity can push even rich white people into its clutches. As Kendall observed, their "willful refusal to recognize that their investment in this world was also killing them, because it was occluding a vision of the only kind of politics that would be adequate to the crisis we were facing. That willful refusal, to this day, is, for me, one of the most powerful examples of the strength of white supremacy as an ideology and as an institution—the way it can make white people, effectively, commit suicide, in its name, and not even see it as such."

The myth of white immunity can deceive white people, keeping them from seeing that they are plagued by the same harms as people of other races—and from seeing that their challenges and destinies are shared.

* * *

After we crossed the Mississippi River, we stopped at a burger chain. We'd told Michael we'd treat him to lunch, but he appeared overwhelmed when he approached the counter and looked at the moving images on the video wall menu. He was unused to getting to make any choices about what he ate in prison, and none of this technology existed when he'd last been to a fast-food restaurant six years earlier.

As with the characters on *The Golden Girls* in their kitchen eating cheesecake, the conversation among the four of us inevitably turned to sex. How was Michael going to navigate a sex life after his time in prison due to a virus?

It was a difficult question. While the myth of immunity doesn't fully protect white people, it gives them more latitude to make mistakes without punishment as severe. On parole, Michael had little latitude; the majority of people who leave prison become incarcerated again within five years. Sex is a necessary part of life, but one that is legally stigmatized among people in the viral underclass. Did he need to be able to prove he'd disclosed his status to any future partners? And if so, how? In our own ways, we all advised him to be careful whom he shared intimacy with and to make sure they were interested in the whole Michael Johnson, not just the cartoon "Tiger Mandingo" they knew from the news.

When, a few hours later, we arrived at Meredith's house, we were greeted by an enormous banner welcoming Michael home. After years in shared cells, he was shown to his own bedroom. Within an hour, two Black men from the Indianapolis-based HIV group Brothers United came to greet him and help him navigate his HIV care. As I left, I got to thank Michael, and he thanked me. The relationship between a journalist and a source is complicated and delicate, and it requires nuanced trust. The relationship between a journalist and source who share a minoritized racial identity, but who have different HIV statuses, is also tricky. I was, and continue to be, proud of how we negotiated and built this relationship together over the years.

That night, Akil and I stayed in an efficiency motel by the Indianapolis International Airport, before catching early flights to different cities the next morning. From the time I'd first flown into St. Louis Lambert International Airport in the spring of 2014, it had felt like I'd been living in dive motels at the end of runways ever since. Sometimes, the planes were far louder in my room than they were in the airport terminal. The bad carpeting, the garish fluorescent lights, the front desk staff who seemed desperate to escape (and who were often doing homework at the desk with plans to do just that)—all of these dumps had felt interchangeable.

This awful motel in Indiana was no different from the others in another respect: it was full of people who seemed to be struggling with addiction to meth, and most of them were white. Lost souls, many of whom appeared to be long-term tenants, aimlessly wandered the halls as if looking for their next high and barely conscious of reality. And who could blame them for wanting to check out? Life had led them to "living" in an efficiency motel so close to an airport runway that, every few minutes, it felt like a plane would crash through the windows. Their whiteness did not render them immune to the effects of being in the viral underclass. Unlike me, they didn't get to check out and catch one of those loud-ass planes to a big city. Drugs may have been the only way they could temporarily escape. Some had yellow eyes, looking as if HCV had taken hold of their livers and given them jaundice.

These people had no neighbors or schools or parks nearby; the views out their windows were of barbed wire and office buildings and runways. There were few comforts of home here.

On a night I wanted to feel celebratory about Michael's release—a night that, for years, I had literally dreamed would happen—I was reminded of how near to sadness and decay we always are in this country. As I tried unsuccessfully to sleep amid the motel's raucous noise, I felt how these United States are as endlessly heartbreaking as they are endlessly fascinating.

Michael was free (or on parole, at least). But he was just one person who'd gotten out. Millions of people were still imprisoned unfairly in America, and millions more were stuck in prisons of other sorts—like the people trapped in nursing homes who'd be sitting targets for SARS-CoV-2 in just a few months or those wandering souls plagued by addiction in this awful motel. And most lost folks didn't have people like Akil or Meredith to catch them when they fell.

Michael's story shows us how the state will punish someone who has forced us to confront the limitations of white immunity. It has implications, too, for how this society will respond to white people whose lives are similarly marked by precarity. It teaches us that white supremacy (or so-called white supremacy) doesn't offer immunity to white people trapped in Missouri's prisons, nor to those who are warehoused in Indiana's runway motels, nor to the people of Scott County (97 percent of whom are white) in the face of austere public health cuts and rising addiction.

* * *

I wonder what would have happened if Michael had still been in jail in 2020. I would have been very worried that his severe punishment for transmitting one treatable virus had put him at risk for an untreatable one. By April 2020, the first person to have tested positive for the novel coronavirus in Missouri's prison system had died from it. By July, forty people at Boonville, where Michael had last been kept, tested positive for COVID-19. At the same time, Missouri was among the only states in the region that did not mandate that prison workers use masks, even though enslaved prison labor was making masks for use by the public outside the prison and even as hundreds inside the Missouri prison system had tested positive.

What if Michael had been in jail another year, only to die of COVID-19?

But that didn't happen. Michael got a chance to restart his life. As the global HIV pandemic groaned on, churning through Black, brown, and white bodies in prisons across the United States, Michael got out. His story was an auspicious one. It is rare for a journalist to get to write the end of a story, and rarer still when the end leads to a new beginning of hopeful possibility.

Michael was *not* stuck in a halfway house or a seedy motel; he was released into the care of a loving family. He benefited from a strong and long-standing community health group to get him onto medication. He had housing assistance and, within just a few months, was able to get his very own apartment. He got jobs working at a coffee shop and in a warehouse, waiting out his time on parole, during which he wasn't allowed to attend school.

When he'd entered prison, he'd been vilified by random blogs around the world as "Tiger Mandingo," an HIV-spreading monster. When he got out, the *New York Times* calmly wrote that he'd "Emerged from Prison a Potent Symbol of H.I.V. Criminalization."

Perhaps the most dramatic sign of how the world had changed since Michael was first pursued by the office of St. Charles County prosecuting attorney Timothy Lohmar was how Lohmar himself had changed. By the time Michael got out, Lohmar was the president of the Missouri Association of Prosecuting Attorneys. And just a few months before Michael's release, Lohmar testified before a committee of the Missouri legislature to lobby them to *repeal* the Missouri AIDS law and replace it with one based on current science.

Saying he'd been "hamstrung in a sense because I was forced to operate under the current laws that we now have," Lohmar said he'd "had a case a few years ago that got a lot of national attention, and it wasn't in a good way," alluding to *Missouri v. Johnson*. "It was quite embarrassing, to be honest," he admitted. Lohmar said after the case was over that he'd been "presented with some of the science" and realized he "just was ignorant." This seemed to me to be a bit disingenuous; his office had been presented with the science before and at trial. An op-ed he authored shortly after the trial was nonetheless silent on this issue. Still, it was heartening to see he'd finally learned his lesson and to watch him on video tell the Missouri legislature that, "on behalf of prosecutors statewide, we don't want to have to use the statute to charge someone with a crime" for HIV anymore.

Lohmar played a role in why, in 2021, Missouri's Republican governor and legislature modernized the state's HIV laws for the first time in thirty years. The updates included prosecuting only people who had "knowingly" exposed others to HIV, not just those who did it "recklessly," and lowering the mandatory minimum of any sentence from ten years to three. The update does not go far enough, and abolishing such laws entirely would be the best way to mitigate harm to the viral underclass. Still, this modernization creates the likelihood of less time in prison for Missourians prosecuted for transmitting HIV and creates a higher burden of proof for prosecutors. And it is part of an encouraging national trend of states decriminalizing HIV partially or, in rare instances like Illinois in 2021, entirely.

Lohmar, a white man, was not immune to having his consciousness raised. Nor were the white legislators who reassessed a law and a virus that disproportionately affected nonwhite people in a majority-white state.

Occasionally, someone escapes bondage, like Michael Johnson, if only partially. They escape, and the people who caged them even see the light. But for every person like Michael who gets a second chance, there are unknown thousands whose lives remain in some form of bondage or end in premature death—people like Lorena Borjas, who continue to be ensnared in the vicissitudes of viral confinement in America until it takes their very lives.

12

COMPOUND LOSS

(Collective Punishment)

While the early days of the coronavirus pandemic in New York City were all terrible, March 30, 2020, was particularly difficult. As all days did around then, it began for me with the sound of sirens in the distance waking me up from another night of restless slumber. Then, on social media, I learned that Lorena Borjas had died of COVID-19.

If Michael Johnson's getting out of prison a few months earlier had given a boost to a circle of gay and Black people I cared about in the viral underclass, I could tell that Lorena's death had dealt a blow to another circle of transgender and immigrant folx.

My heart hurt for them.

Lorena had died between five and six that morning. By seven that evening, Chase Strangio and Cecilia Gentili had organized an online memorial. It was the first-ever "Zoom funeral" I attended, the first of many I'd watch and organize in the year that followed.

As with a number of memorials for transgender women of color and Black queer people in New York City over the years, I attended this one not because I knew the deceased well. Rather, I went because I wanted to be in community with and support others who were mourning.

With just a few hours' notice, more than two hundred people joined that Zoom call to celebrate Lorena's life. And while it was touching to hear stories (delivered in English and Spanish), it was still wretched to see friends I couldn't hug or console. At least we could see who was there, so we could follow up with one another with a phone call later.

But as the Zoom screen shifted awkwardly, highlighting the wailing sobs of people in the visible agony of grief, my sense of estrangement selfishly turned to one of resentment.

I hated juggling these multiple streams of compounded abstraction, as each and every one of us was reduced to being a bunch of little digital cubes—flat, like we were in the opening of *The Brady Bunch* or on an episode of *Hollywood Squares*. Each alone, discrete.

The levels upon levels upon levels of alienation that viruses can force humans to endure, I thought. Absent to me in that moment was any consideration of how viruses might connect us. Instead, even at a digital funeral, I felt reminded that, like those facing the bubonic plague in Michel Foucault's description of a seventeenth-century lockdown in Europe, "Each individual is fixed in his place. And, if he moves, he does so at the risk of his life, contagion or punishment."

During the memorial, people spoke for hours about Lorena's kindness, how she showed up in court for others, and about her infamous rolling cart. I found myself wondering where her cart was that night. When people die, there is something so lonely about the mundane objects they leave behind that wait in vain for their human to return: the toothbrush that will never scrub molars again, the glasses that will never help eyes to see once more, the book that will never finish being read.

Listening to dozens of people bear witness to Lorena's life on Zoom, I felt self-conscious about crying while on camera in a way I had never felt at an in-person funeral. I thought about how I'd taken for granted hugging others at funerals. And I thought about how, when gay men got AIDS in the 1980s and their families of origin abandoned them, lesbians and other gay men took care of them and creatively gave them intimacy and community. Or their funerals were treated as political protests, giving the bereaved a chance to grieve communally and to vent their anger and fight the conditions that had taken their friend prematurely. But with this new plague, none of these modes of queer comfort or haptic care were possible without facilitating the further transmission of the virus, more sickness, and more death.

There would be so *many* online memorials in the next year for so *many* people, including queer friends who died young and not from COVID. The least we should have done to honor them was to hold a wake in a piano bar like Marie's Crisis, followed by a dance party in someone's loft that turned into an orgy in their memory. And now, not only were the trans people in mourning bereft of physical comfort from one another, they had lost the leadership of one of the strongest pillars of their community—Lorena herself.

What gets lost when a leader of the viral underclass is erased from their flock?

When SARS-CoV-2 silenced Lorena, what effect did that have on *other* viruses? How free were they to circulate even *more*? Without Lorena to give out condoms and sterile syringes, how many more people would become infected with HIV and hepatitis C? Without her hustling up support in court for young women in trouble, how many of them would wind up in jail for long periods of time—where they'd be more likely to contract influenza or COVID-19?

When Zak Kostopoulos was killed in Omonia Square and Zackie Oh disappeared from the drag stages of Athens, how did that loss compound the precariousness of the viral underclass of Greece? Without Zak's beautiful face smiling openly when he spoke about living with HIV, what harm befell queer, trans, and gender-nonconforming Athenians? With the video circulating of his slight body being kicked to death by a shop owner with the aid of police (and with few consequences), how was the far-right Golden Dawn empowered to enact vigilante violence against queers, migrants, sex workers, and people without homes?

For the people who killed Zak didn't just mortally wound him. Like cops in the United States who commit murder on video in a way that haunts the dreams of Black Americans, Zak's killers plagued the slumber of Greece's queer underclass with nightmares. "There are people who shouldn't be able to sleep at night," Zak himself wrote, and yet, "they've made people who deserve better lose their sleep."

When film archivist Vito Russo died of AIDS in 1990, what role did that have in allowing gay male politics in the United States to mutate conservatively—and to abandon the viral underclass without ever kicking "the shit out of this system," as Vito had charged us to do? When the formerly incarcerated Black feminist Katrina Haslip died in 1992 from AIDS at age thirty-three, what did her death do, not just to other people living with AIDS, but also to imprisoned Black women already so vulnerable to so many pathogens (while being ignored by so much of the world)?

When Bob Rafsky died of AIDS in 1993, shortly after Bill Clinton became president, how did the loss of this agitator affect Democratic carceral policies in a way such that HIV, influenza, and the coronavirus could more freely flourish in cages?

In the fall of 2020, what immeasurable losses occurred when eighty-one members of the Mississippi band of the Choctaw died of COVID-19—more than 10 percent of the tribe? How did the loss of elders' stories and leadership wound not just the hearts of the Choctaw, but their ability to form community and resistance within the U.S. empire?

When COVID-19 took the life of Asian American writer Kimarlee Nguyen at the age of thirty-three, how did that cut down the Cambodian immigrant community she came from? Her former writing professor, author Kiese Laymon, once described Nguyen to me as a teacher who was "really good at loving people." How did losing Nguyen's love hamper the Asian American students who relied on her to understand their own health, culture, art, and selves in the world—and how did those losses leave them more exposed to health disparities?

And when my friend, *Village Voice* editor Ward Harkavy, died of COVID at the age of seventy-two, what did his loss do to marginalized people who were disabled and who stuttered—for whom, as a journalist and fellow stutterer, he'd always advocated? What effect would his inability to mentor young journalists have on the coverage and fate of the viral underclass?

Akin to how plants growing around the Chernobyl Nuclear Power Plant are affected by the half-life of radioactive waste, the unnecessary deaths of these beautiful people created fallouts beyond mere absences. Their deaths went viral, the effects of their vacancies growing exponentially to harm more of the underclass. Like infections that couldn't be contained, their deaths created collateral damage—such as the community spread of grief itself. This resulted in decreased prophylaxis and increased vulnerability for already marginalized people.

In this way, when a virus takes the life of one of the viral underclass's leaders, the impact radiates outward and death becomes a form of collective punishment meted out on an entire community already hurt by marginalization.

It's hard to predict how severe the fallout will eventually be from a death like Lorena's, because when it comes to understanding the importance of a leader in their circle, death often reveals how their importance has long been unspoken or unacknowledged. And Lorena's death was a reminder that the full measure of what she'd been enduring, and what she'd meant to her *familia*, had been obscured for some time.

* * *

In the first few months of the coronavirus pandemic, many writers understood that it was going to exacerbate the dangers that members of the underclass already faced with other pathogens. Even before any COVID-19 vaccine was in production, strains on the supply chain for medical resources like syringes were already affecting millions of people around the world living with tuberculosis, HIV, and malaria. Researchers estimated that the interruptions to HIV care caused by COVID-19 would result in an additional four hundred thousand AIDS deaths worldwide in 2020. Meanwhile in the United States, as Zachary Siegel reported for the *New Republic*, the coronavirus pandemic became an excuse to defund the best efforts for dealing with the opioid addiction crisis. While dentists and physical therapists were supported in having the necessary resources to see patients in person, addiction health experts often were not. This led to *more* isolation, HIV, HCV, and overdose deaths.

In April 2020, not long after Lorena Borjas died, the National Institute of Allergy and Infectious Diseases director, Dr. Anthony Fauci, talked about various metrics of the coronavirus. When measuring the number of people diagnosed, infected, sick, and hospitalized, the one metric "that's the furthest out is the deaths, that lags behind the others." Fauci sounded slightly optimistic at that moment, explaining that someday we might "continue to see deaths at a time when you have actually very good control of the new infections and the outbreak itself."

Death is out of precise synchronization with the other symptoms of a pandemic; it arrives later than other worrying signs and lingers longer than signs of improvement. In the United States, COVID-19 skeptics failed to comprehend this, or even how hospitalizations lag behind new cases. Why weren't hospital rates rising *precisely* with infections? they wanted to know, not understanding how the incubation period impacted time lines. Sure enough, a week after diagnoses spiked, hospitalization rates correspondingly rose, and a couple weeks after that, so did deaths—just as the CDC had predicted. (This happened again with the Delta and Omicron variants.) And so, just as death is an imperfect metric for understanding a pandemic, it is also an incomplete metric for understanding the marginalization and vulnerability of a community.

"I always say yes to everything, and end up spreading myself pretty thin," Zak Kostopoulos once said, without regret. "I was visible, and that struggle for visibility mattered a lot to me." Zak's visibility mattered a lot to others in Athens, too, as did Lorena's in Jackson Heights. But prior to their deaths, both had been in danger for some time, as much of the viral underclass had been.

Yet that danger didn't come into stark relief for all to see until they died. For them, death was the final act in a series of traumas they had faced over the course of a life of struggle, of so much more than a virus. They had been vibrant lights within their respective communities. But an understanding of just *how* important their light was in guiding their people didn't fully materialize until it was snuffed out.

When California rolled out its COVID-19 vaccination program in 2021, it prioritized people by age, placing relatively healthy older people ahead of severely immunocompromised younger people. After treating old people as disposable in 2020, the state got vaccines to them first, but in a way that was still ableist. It made little distinction between people of any age and offered little accommodation to people who were younger, severely disabled, or unable to travel to a vaccination site. As activist Alice Wong told news media early that year, she was scared for the "very young, disabled, critically ill and immunocompromised people who could die before it's their turn to be vaccinated."

Alice is such a pillar within disabled communities, and to me personally. Her loss would have been incalculable if SARS-CoV-2 had gotten to her before a vaccine did. Other disabled activists did perish before they got vaccinated.

The potential and actual loss of leaders in minoritized communities has the power to create a compound loss. For every person like Michael Johnson who gets out of prison early, there are so many more like Lorena and Zackie Oh—people living with one virus whose lives are ended too soon by another, or by police, or by addiction. That Lorena's death was recognized by the *New York Times*, the *New Yorker*, and the *Washington Post* is a testament to how powerfully her loss was felt, even to a news media that had largely ignored her activism while she was alive. But for every Lorena, there are dozens of activists and organizers who never get this kind of public recognition, but whose losses are nonetheless felt deeply by their communities. And if someone's plight isn't recognized until they are *dead*, what can be done to help them in life?

How will her *comunidad* cope without Lorena? A community already so exposed to HIV, ICE raids, and transphobia *before* the novel coronavirus came along? Her loss will be felt in the liver of a transgender person injecting contraband hormones with unsterilized syringes. Her loss will be felt in the soul of an immigrant showing up for arraignment in the Queens County Courthouse who looks out to see that no one has shown up for her—before she is taken back to holding for months or years to await trial, while being repeatedly exposed to the flu and other pathogens.

The loss of Lorena will take a long time to comprehend *if* it can be fully mapped and understood at all.

* * *

As I finished writing this book, I accidentally stumbled upon a video that Zak Kostopoulos had made many years before, in 2013. By the time I saw it, I had seen a nonverbal short film starring Zak called *U* (for "undetectable equals untransmissible"), a lot of videos of Zackie Oh lip-synching to pop songs (like "Sweet Transvestite," from *The Rocky Horror Picture Show*), and of Zak speaking in Greek, which I don't understand at all. Yet I'd never really heard his voice in a way I could fully comprehend.

This YouTube video was different, for Zak was speaking in his first language, from his childhood in the United States: American English. In years of trying to know him, I had no idea such a video existed.

"Hi there, my name is Zak Kostopoulos, and I'm sending you this message from Greece," he said, looking directly into the camera.

Sending this from the other side of the Great Divide, I thought.

Addressing people who are newly diagnosed with HIV, Zak smiles gently in the video. Unlike in the film *U* or in his book, *Society Doesn't Fit Me but My Little Black Dress Does*, Zak seems lighthearted and open about his viral status. He tells people he's been living with HIV for some time, "and it's been quite a journey, but not an unpleasant one, all the way."

Calmly, he speaks to people who may have just been diagnosed with HIV as well. And while he is sympathetic that it's new information that can be frightening and might feel overwhelming at first, he wants these kinfolk to know that they can handle it and "can live a full and happy life living with HIV, as long as you don't let it get the best of you and you don't give up." Friends can offer support, because no one should go through it alone.

"Also, I know being diagnosed with HIV comes with a lot of stigma and discrimination and stereotypes you'll have to face," he continues. "But it's nothing to be ashamed about, and no matter what anybody says, the fact that you have HIV does *not* make you unworthy, or dirty, or anything like that.

"It just makes you human," he says, succinctly conveying in just five words a sentiment I wish *every* human could believe about themselves—*and* about every other human affected by every virus.

We each need relationships with other people to understand who we are; there is nothing like looking into the face of another human or tracing it with your fingers to understand who you are as a person. And maybe—maybe that is the most valuable aspect of humankind's relationship with viruses: they remind us that in our breathing, and in our kissing, and in our hugging, and in our dancing, and in our fucking, we are human.

These are the things that *make* us human! I pray Olivier knew this at the end of his life.

We will never eradicate all viruses; there are more of them on our planet than there are stars in the universe. But if we accept our vulnerable humanity, and if we learn as a species to live in *relationship* with viruses, we will not need to let their harshest consequences pool within a viral underclass. Indeed, if we learned what it meant to cohabitate with them responsibly, viruses could teach us to create a world without class or other hierarchies.

In his YouTube message, Zak assures the newly diagnosed that they will, indeed, find people who will "love and support you for who you are, because you're basically the same person." He also tells people without HIV that if they know someone who is recently diagnosed with the virus, there's no need "to change the way you act around them. You don't have to change the way you treat them—there is nothing to be afraid of." The video is so gentle, so human. Unlike his howls in his own writing and his primal prancing in his drag sets, here Zak gently calls people in.

"So, basically, I think that's about it. Just don't give up, keep on smiling, fight the stigma, fight the stereotypes, be yourself, and—love."

His eyebrows rise in a smile.

When those men kicked Zak to death, flaying him alive on a carpet of broken glass, they not only stole his life from him and from the people who loved him. They removed the guardian who stood ready to welcome any immigrant newly arrived in Athens. And they kept any newly diagnosed member of the viral underclass who could have found him online from connecting with him in real life.

Watching him on video, I wondered: *How can the loss of such an immeasurable gift be measured?*

"That's all," he says, kissing the air. "Thank you, bye."

we are all already polluted by each other, our bodies
connected and permeable, energised and endangered
by the life (vitality, livingness, flourishing, decay, dehiscence)
that that connection engenders.

THOMAS STRONG

EPILOGUE

Why Am I "Me" and You Are "You"?

In April 2020, a photograph by Sergio Flores depicting a young protester attending a rally in Austin, Texas, went viral. The protester sported a nose ring and tinted glasses and carried a large sign reading, "My Body, My Choice," a staple slogan of liberal reproductive justice politics.

But the protester was not at a rally for abortion rights. Their sign featured an image of a face mask inside a red circle with a line through it, above the words "TRUMP 2020." The protester was one of hundreds of people (many armed) at an antimask rally at the Texas State Capitol. They were loudly telling their state politicians how much they did *not* approve of any possible mask mandate due to the novel coronavirus pandemic—even though the Lone Star State had a long history of its citizens wearing bandannas.

The sign trolled liberals using their own words, but it neither distorted what liberals meant when they used it nor misappropriated their intent. It was actually using the very same political logic liberals use to think about bodies, in the same way liberals apply it. About a year later, many conservatives would begin to use the phrase in their proud refusal to become vaccinated—even if it eventually meant losing their jobs. "My body, my choice" is a bipartisan tenet in U.S. politics, scripture considered by many to be as sacrosanct as the right to stand your ground and defend your property with a gun.

In the 1970s, when liberals wanted to enshrine reproductive justice in U.S. law, they did not frame their arguments in terms of wanting free abortions as part of universal health care for the entire society. They rarely articulated it as a desire for abortion at all—nor have they named abortion access much in the decades since. Instead, they framed abortion in the context of privacy and choice, encouraging society to consider intimate health matters with the same neoliberal logic that was marketizing so many areas of contemporary life.

If I own my body, such logic asserts, I should be able to do anything I want with it. With an ownership mentality, if one *owns* one's body, one is also freed from all social obligations to and from others. So, if it's "my body, my choice," then anyone can think, *Yes, I* can *have an abortion*, which is a health necessity.

But this same logic can also lead to thinking, *I don't have to join a union; my destiny is mine, and mine alone.*

It can also lead one down the path of believing, *I also don't want to be taxed and forced to pay for schools for someone else's kids.*

Or toward feeling that *If I am buying bottled water—or if I am brave and I* choose *to drink tap water knowing its risks—why do I need to be forced to pay for treating the water in Flint, Michigan?*

And it can mean, *If I don't want to wear a mask or get a vaccine, that is my right, and repercussions of this on those around me don't concern me.*

Across the political spectrum, "my body, my choice" can be used to conjure America's sense of how individual ownership should supersede all else. But this notion of individuality, despite being a core element of American society, is a myth. It is a myth that we are each the master of our own distinct destiny. It is a myth that the risks inherent in experiencing child-rearing, pandemics, and climate change should never be experienced collectively. And it is a belief that results in behavior with regard to one's health, and its consequences, being seen as entirely the choice and burden (financial and otherwise) of the lone person experiencing it.

The logic of this myth works only if we pointedly ignore the hierarchies of power, class, and American history. Pay no mind to the fact that the myth often comes from people who want to bust unions or who own bottled water companies. Forget that an ownership mentality about individual bodies has been dangerous on the North American continent from before the birth of the United States. After all, if a body can be owned, ownership of that body can be *transferred*—by force of enslavement, for example.

But *do* consider how often we are encouraged to frame our internal thinking, in some form, along the lines of *I should be able to do what I want, when I want, because it's my body and my choice!* Thinking *I have a body* is very different from thinking *I am a body*. This schism can make it difficult for us not only to feel in alignment with our full selves, but also to understand just how deeply we are connected to other humans—how inextricably all our fates are bound together.

Viruses challenge the concept that any one of us "has" one body. As they move freely between the lungs, bloodstream, and genitals of one of us to another, they show how *we* is a more relevant concept than *you* or *me*.

How can any of us "own" a part of this body we all share?

We can't. And yet, so much of our thinking is wedded to this concept of *my* body, as if it existed discretely.

I believe people who are pregnant should be able to end pregnancies. I also believe that if someone has an abortion, they should not have to deal with it or pay for it alone. It should be free and supported, as part of universal health care. And I believe that if someone has a child, it is not up to them alone to provide *everything* that child will need for the next couple of decades.

Similarly, I believe every transgender person should get the health care they need, including gender-affirming surgery. But the burden should *not* be on them alone; they exist in relationship with others, and it is up to the cisgender people around them to offer them gender-affirming care.

Letting go of this ownership framing wouldn't necessarily mean letting go of agency for anyone to get what they desired. Still, it could mean letting go of the burden that everything must be shouldered alone. It certainly would require relinquishing the illusion that we are all floating specks bobbing through the universe without ties to one another. Unlike so many economic and political forces in the United States that pressure us to see ourselves as siloed and alienated, viruses offer us a deeper understanding of how to think ethically in relation to one another—and a sense of how much more power that gives us.

For any person to enjoy the benefits of lower community viral loads, breathable air, and the kind of equitable vaccination that leads to herd immunity, communal thinking is required. But true communal thinking is not nationalist thinking. By the middle of 2021, more vaccines were freely available in the United States than there were people who readily wanted them; by the end of the year, many Americans could even get a third booster shot, if they wanted. Yet even as thousands were dying in countries where people desperate for vaccines couldn't even get one shot, many proud U.S. citizens loudly bragged about refusing to take any that were available to them. By 2022, the United States was behind dozens of other countries in its vaccination rate.

Most of us in the United States are socialized to think as consumers, not as citizens of a society with collective health responsibilities—even me. For instance, before COVID-19, I could get on planes easily and fly anywhere I could afford in the world, with little thought to how that choice affected the asthmatic Black and brown children living near the airports I departed from and arrived at, whose lungs inhaled exhaust from the jets ferrying me around. Or how the carbon footprint of my travel would affect wildfires in California or Greece.

Why did I need to think of *their* bodies when I thought about flying? I was free to do whatever I chose with *my* body, as long as I could afford the price of the ticket.

But remember way back in the introduction to this book, when I asked you to go on a journey focusing on the viral underclass, so that their stories could help you rethink your most deeply held assumptions? The most fundamental, largely unexamined premise we have in the United States is the belief that I am me and you are you and that each of us is the master of our own hero's journey.

What if viruses teach us that there is no "me" and no "you" at all and that we all share one collective body? And that such individualistic thinking creates not only an underclass, but alienation across lines of class?

Think back to how viruses literally take a part of one person's code and transfer it to another, which transforms that person individually and forever alters their offspring. As the poet and medical doctor Seema Yasmin puts it, "Eight percent of your genome / is viral—we are literal cousins of ancient pathogens / wretched offspring of pandemics."

What if we all share just *one* body—a body that stretches across not just our egos and political philosophies and national borders, but even species?

When I asked disability activist Alice Wong about protests against wearing simple face coverings, she told me (through the BiPAP mask she's worn twenty-four hours a day for years) that she just had to "wrap my head around why people don't realize it's not just for you. It's for others. It just gets back to this very fucked-up individualist culture" in the United States.

"Because, if you look at Asia," she reminded me, people there had been wearing masks long before COVID-19, to deal with the first SARS outbreak of 2003, and for seasonal flu, and even just for smog. "It is not seen as an infringement upon freedom."

If we humans are going to survive pandemics from *any* virus—let alone if we are going to survive the existential climate crisis—we *cannot* do so while behaving as if each of our destinies were disconnected.

"It's not a bad thing to say we're interdependent," Alice continued, raising a concept foreign to many Americans. It requires courage and an acceptance of vulnerability to admit how SARS-CoV-2 has shown, as Alice put it, that "we're in the same soup. Exactly in the same soup and open to the exact same things." Our connection is not merely biophysical but cultural: "This is about the invisible conditions that are swirling around us. In our air. In our atmosphere. Through our words."

* * *

After antiretroviral medications were developed in the 1990s to treat AIDS, many white gay men in New York who had so far survived that plague used the new drugs as a ticket out of the viral underclass in which they'd recently dwelled.

While HIV concentrated among people who were poor, Black, and who didn't get those drugs, a lot of the newly medicated survivors stopped caring much about AIDS. Some of these surviving gay men bought weekend homes within a couple of hours of New York City. Still alive because of loud gay activists, they started spending their weekends in sleepy hamlets, quietly turning the word *antique* into a gerund.

In September 2020, I took my first post-lockdown reporting trip to one of those towns, or so I assumed—Milford, Pennsylvania, population 1,172. When I arrived and put on my KN95 mask and face shield before exiting my rental car, I realized I'd parked near an SUV with a rear window completely covered in crudely painted letters that screamed, "Wearing a Mask & Rubber Gloves While You Are Alone in Your Car Is Like Wearing a Condom to Bed While You Are Alone!!!" Milford was the kind of place where painstakingly restored country houses owned by some of the town's gay male couples had "TRUMP-PENCE 2020" signs on their perfectly manicured lawns. Meanwhile, seemingly straight white men openly brandished guns at the local diner.

I had traveled to interview Milford's most famous homosexual, Sean Strub. But even though he was the town's Democratic mayor, Sean had *not* become one of those white gays who had abandoned the viral underclass. Far from it. He had not only named the idea into being back in 2011, but he had also committed much of his life to the people who lived in it ever since.

Sean was the executive director of the Sero Project, a nonprofit dedicated to helping people harmed by the criminalization of HIV. Sero had organized the 2018 conference where I first heard the term *viral underclass* used (though, there, it had mutated a bit into a strain different from Sean's original usage). Recently, Sero had joined organizing efforts to flatten the rising curve of COVID-19 criminalization happening around the world.

I had connected with Sean six years earlier, when I was commissioned to write about Michael Johnson. Over the years, I had noticed how Sero was unlike many civil rights organizations I had covered in my career, in one respect: it did not demand "respectability" from the people it supported publicly. From legal advocacy to organizing letter-writing campaigns to people in prison, Sero supported anyone who had been incarcerated due to HIV and asked for its help—the kinds of people ignored by almost all advocacy groups and journalists.

After I arrived, Sean and I went for a hike in the Pocono Mountains. The pandemic had kept me cooped up for months in the city by then, and I was grateful for the chance to interview someone not on Zoom, but safely outside while walking together among trees in a glorious forest.

In COVID-19 times, some people knew a bit about ACT UP, which had directed its power externally. Its targets were organizations like the Food and Drug Administration, and its success with that agency was a reason that drug trials were already happening that summer for potential COVID-19 vaccines.

But Sean had been an activist even before that—since a time when "there was no distinction between AIDS activism and a gay activism," as he put it. "What I think of as *real* AIDS activism," he told me, "really began when people with AIDS started finding each other and organizing and came out in support groups and out of anger at the gay organizations for not listening to us." That work was internal, and could also be called a kind of mutual aid, a concept new to many in 2020.

Sean was a part of the gays who did this decades ago. When governments around the world left us to fend for ourselves in the COVID-19 pandemic, many people looked to the example of activists like Sean as they set up Google Docs to schedule regular check-ins on their elderly neighbors, shopped for groceries for immunocompromised friends, pooled resources in their communities, and learned together about viruses in teach-ins.

Why, I asked Sean, did he keep doing this work after he got the good drugs, when so many people of his standing had stopped slumming in the viral underclass?

Saying he didn't "begrudge people who got better and went on with their lives and other things," he told me, "It never felt like an option for me. For one, I was so wrapped up in it." He ran a magazine about people living with HIV, and he was close to so many people harmed not just by the AIDS virus, but by the conditions that caused it. (After Lorena Borjas died of COVID-19 in the spring, the next two people I read about online in my social circle who died were both African American HIV activist friends of Sean's—Deloris Dockrey and Ed Shaw.)

Sean wouldn't say it about himself, but I will say it about him: Unlike many people, he didn't allow a viral divide to develop in his life, where he saw himself as deserving and those afflicted by the social vectors that cause HIV/AIDS as suddenly undeserving. He is the rare person with privilege who leverages that privilege on behalf of people with the least—and I mean the *least*—social standing. He doesn't even let prison bars keep him from trying to create an intact sense of community with other people living with HIV. When the Human Rights Campaign, ACLU, and NAACP wouldn't even take my calls about Michael Johnson in 2014, Sean had been actively building up support for him for months. And unlike many who got the drugs and ran, Sean saw that people with viruses should *not* be carted off to jail; they are still part of the body politic and deserve care.

When we discussed this, it was a spectacularly sunny day, and our hike took us up a bluff high above the expanse of the Delaware Valley, to look down upon a bend in the mighty, muddy Delaware River. It's the same river George Washington crossed on Christmas night in 1776, mythologized by Emanuel Leutze's 1851 oil painting *Washington Crossing the Delaware* (which includes an enslaved Black man, Prince Whipple, whom Washington owned). But on that day, it reminded me of the mighty, muddy Missouri River, which snaked downhill from the jail in St. Charles where I would visit Michael Johnson. Unlike when I'd interview Michael, though, Sean and I were free to talk under the sun and enjoy the bounty of natural beauty around us.

Though his work had begun around viruses, his journey, Sean told me, had led him "deeper into understanding the systemic flaws in our society and our system. And the most satisfying work that we do is the prison work. That is, in some ways, where I feel we are being least effective at changing anything systemically, but most effective at influencing individual lives."

Some of the people the Sero Project corresponds with (imprisoned for failing to disclose that they have a virus thirty million people live with) may never get out of prison, and there's nothing they can do about it. While the one person I covered who was imprisoned for transmitting HIV got out—albeit, after Herculean efforts over six years—I, too, write about and work with people who will likely *never* escape being in the underclass, viral or otherwise.

How did Sean cope with this?

You start, he told me, by "simply acknowledging it, letting them know somebody heard them and sympathized. That's all you can do. You *need* to do that. You can't just ignore it."

Even if it feels like there is no way to solve their crisis, "If all you can do is witness, you need to be doing that. And not to diminish the value of that."

* * *

The novel coronavirus has made millions, if not billions, of humans consider for the first time how living with a common virus can make a person feel like a pariah.

I did not acquire SARS-CoV-2 prior to being vaccinated. And yet, before I got jabbed, even though I would never lob such a stigmatizing label at others, I deeply feared being a vector myself—even though I preach that it is societal structures and not people that are vectors. I so feared infecting others that I even had suicidal ideation, under the warped logic of thinking that *if someone has to die, it might as well be me before I am a vector and accidentally kill others.*

Some of this was a familiar sensation for me. As a single, gay Black man, I've long internalized a fear of being an undiagnosed "one in two" who could unwittingly transmit HIV to someone else; I fear this more than becoming HIV-positive myself. And as I began to overhear straight white people discussing community positivity rates, trying to understand viral testing windows, and even asking each other questions like "So, when did you last get tested?"—things gay men have talked about for decades—I could tell that many people in the pandemic were suddenly struggling to process the kinds of fears that have long plagued queer folks like me.

There is tremendous power in how, for the first time in human history, all humans on the planet have been going through some version of the same thing, at nearly the same time, with the ability to communicate globally about it. "Some of us have lived here for years: that place to which others confine you when you are a 'disease vector.' (Even when you are not.) It's a place where people don't touch you or talk to you," anthropologist and HIV activist Thomas Strong has observed. Now that billions may be having this sensation, Thomas has asked, "Will the 'general public' now experience this form of abjection, and therefore reject it? How will we come to terms with this? A fantasy of immunity? More walls? Or careful, reflexive dialogue about the fact that we are all already polluted by each other, our bodies connected and permeable, energised and endangered by the life (vitality, livingness, flourishing, decay, dehiscence) that that connection engenders?"

What if SARS-CoV-2 finally allows us to drop "patient zero" scapegoat narratives? To release the morality plays of "Tiger Mandingo" and "COVID parties" that the extractive news media has foisted upon us? To let go of the language of "superspreaders," "personal responsibility," and declaring "war" on everything? And to finally embrace notions of communal responsibility and collective care?

COVID-19 demanded that we pause and reconsider why we saw ourselves as different beings in the first place, and to ask ourselves different questions without that assumption.

Perhaps then, the most fundamental question viruses probe us to ask ourselves is: Why am I "me" and you are "you"? If we believe that "you" and "I" are *not* separate, but that *we* face common challenges, then our hierarchies might melt away.

Racism would be gone.

Ableism would cease to exist.

Sexism, homophobia, and cisgender superiority would all perish.

American exceptionalism wouldn't need to exist, either, in its modern, jingoistic sense, nor as the insult Joseph Stalin originally meant it to mean—because the U.S. empire would be irrelevant.

The hoarding of resources through capitalism? Totally unnecessary; austerity would be replaced by anarchy and abundance.

If we accepted, as Alice Wong put it, that the world is "one big petri dish," even speciesism would disappear, granting us perhaps our greatest chance of success at addressing the climate crisis.

In encouraging me to learn and unlearn these lessons, despite all the trauma they have caused, viruses have been among my greatest teachers. Or, rather, they have the possibility to be *our* greatest teachers. And they offer us perhaps the best possibility of a new ethic of care—one not steeped in me getting mine first, but in us taking care of one another and of our very planet.

In this way, viruses have the potential to help us make a world predicated upon love and mutual respect for all living things, not just in the here and now, but across time and space.

AFTERWORD

The End?

> But anger expressed and translated into action in the service of our vision and our future is a liberating and strengthening act of clarification, for it is in the painful process of this translation that we identify who are our allies with whom we have grave differences, and who are our genuine enemies. Anger is loaded with information and energy.
>
> —Audre Lorde

June 2023

The Summer of 2023: Anger

On May 11, 2023, the United States federal government joined the World Health Organization in declaring the end of the COVID-19 Public Health Emergency. In the same week, at least one thousand people died of COVID-19 in the United States, though it's hard to say how many for sure because state governments, the *New York Times*, and the exhaustive COVID-19 project at Johns Hopkins University had stopped counting. But over the previous twelve months, far more people had died of COVID than the fifty thousand who died of AIDS in 1995, its deadliest American year, when the United States was ramping up its efforts to contain HIV and conducting trials on the antiretroviral medications that would soon begin saving lives.

The official COVID emergency had been sputtering toward its end for some time in the United States, despite the official death toll climbing above 1.1 million. The gaps in the social safety net triggered by COVID had long since vanished. People who'd been protected from eviction were back on the streets. The roughly 50 percent of children who'd been lifted out of poverty by federal COVID tax policy were tossed back into it. And millions who'd received Medicaid coverage under COVID spending were uninsured once more. Given that global research clearly showed that people without insurance were more likely to get COVID, get seriously sick from COVID, and die from COVID, those millions were actively consigned to the viral underclass, set up for early death.

When the public health emergency began on January 31, 2020, Donald J. Trump was in office. No one should have been shocked to see that he presided over the unfurling pandemic as he presided over so much else, from the real estate he owned to the set of *The Apprentice*, his campaign, the White House, the January 6 insurrection, and beyond: with a combination of egotistical cruelty, terror, racism, crude ableism, and feckless indifference.

But when the formal emergency ended three years later, everything was happening under a Democratic president.

In his final debate against Trump in October 2020, then-candidate Joe Biden famously noted that COVID had taken some 220,000 American lives: "Anyone who's responsible for that many deaths should not remain as president." He railed against a death toll of one thousand Americans a day and promised that, if elected, his administration would instead "follow the science."

By the time Trump left office on January 20, 2021—against his will, though he'd lost—the first vaccines were newly approved for emergency use, mass vaccination had just begun, and about four hundred thousand Americans had died of COVID. The Biden administration *did* throw almost everything it could at getting Americans vaccinated in its first few months in office. But it did *not* redress many of the root vectors producing a viral underclass as outlined in this book. Hell, it made matters worse in many ways by expanding the liberal carceral state through policing, deportation efforts, and the eventual enactment of austerity measures. Far from addressing the viral underclass, the democratic majority *expanded* it. More people were sucked under. More people died. By the end of Biden's first year in office, the American COVID death toll was nearing about 150 percent of what Trump's had been *without* vaccines.

February 2022, fueled by the Omicron variant of SARS-CoV-2, was the deadliest month of the pandemic yet, with four thousand people dying every *day* in the United States. The country was approaching a million dead. Those numbers were *four times* the daily and cumulative casualties Biden had thundered should be disqualifying for any president.

And while every nation's life expectancy dropped and mortality increased around the world in 2020, most countries reversed in 2021 and 2022 and returned to normal. But in the United States, under a Democratic president and Congress, our life expectancy continued to *plummet.* As I write in the summer of 2023, it continues its downward slide.

A lot has happened since I turned in the final manuscript of this book's first edition, in the first days of the Biden administration. It has reinforced the way I theorize the viral underclass as a cross-party phenomena in the United States. And it has challenged my hope that the United States can learn from, evolve with, adapt to, and grow from what viruses have to teach us.

Throughout spring 2022, the Democrats tried to pass further COVID relief money. But in an ill-conceived spending resolution, they bundled about $10 billion of COVID relief with $33 billion to send to Ukraine for that country's (NATO proxy) war with Russia. Unable to win over their own caucus, let alone any Republicans, the Democrats eventually jettisoned the COVID money from the bill. They succeeded in securing the war money, though, and have since sent between $75 and $100 billion in money and equipment to Ukraine. No additional major COVID spending bills were ever passed or are on the horizon.

Like most wars before it, the war in Ukraine, predictably, has been its own epidemiological catastrophe, with major implications for tuberculosis, HIV, hepatitis, and COVID transmission. In the region of

Europe where these pathogens have been hardest to contain or mitigate, the war quickly erased hard-won gains. For his part, when he ran out of soldiers as cannon fodder, Russian president Vladimir Putin took to withholding medication from people living with hepatitis and HIV in Russian prisons. Cruelly, they were told that if they wanted lifesaving medications, they'd better "volunteer" for the front lines. In April 2021, the *New York Times* reported that an estimated 20 percent of Russian recruits captured as prisoners of war are HIV-positive, meaning they'd been incarcerated and forced to choose between a "slow death" or what was looking ever more likely to be a "quick death" at war.

The United States continues to choose war and militarism. Had, for instance, the nation continued to push for diplomacy in the lead-up to Putin's invasion, rather than doubling down on the expansion of NATO so close to Russia's border, it could have, perhaps, helped to avert the war. That would have staunched the free flourishing of HIV and hepatitis in Russia and Ukraine *and* left tens of billions of dollars *more* to spend on the COVID, HIV, and hepatitis crises at home. Garnering fewer headlines, but following the same bellicose logic, in September 2022, in the same week Biden told *60 Minutes* that "the pandemic is over," the president also signed a continuation of the National Emergency with Respect to Certain Terrorist Attacks. *What's that?* you may be wondering. A declaration that the United States is *still*, more than two decades later, in a state of emergency from the September 11 attacks on the Pentagon and the World Trade Center.

Meanwhile, where candidates Biden and Kamala Harris had promised to hire a corps of one hundred thousand federal health care workers, in office they instead planned to hire one hundred thousand additional domestic cops—just as Bill Clinton did in the 1990s. (Return to chapter 7 to review how this worked out for the viral underclass the first time around.) Biden would have hit the road to gin up support for this plan, but was stymied by his own COVID infection (likely contracted by hosting, as his predecessor had, large, maskless events during a pandemic of an airborne virus). Still, Biden managed to work toward his policing goal by encouraging cities to spend their money from the federal Coronavirus Aid, Relief, and Economic Security (CARES) Act *not* on ventilation or housing relief, but on *hiring more cops.*

And they did. In Chicago, where I live and where we were already spending about 40 cents of every city dollar on police, our then mayor Lori Lightfoot earmarked a whopping $281 million of CARES money for the already-flush police force rather than for schools, medical infrastructure, ventilation upgrades, housing, or other pressing public health needs. (Nationally, within six months, any serious political debate about COVID was done, and even many labor unions and leftist political organizations stopped caring about the virus; by the fall election season, the pandemic simply wasn't a midterm issue in any significant way—even though 2,482 people officially died of COVID election week.)

In late April 2022, Biden attended a maskless White House Correspondents' Dinner, the first in person since before the pandemic. Predictably, it was a mass-infection event. Less than a week later, the United States officially surpassed *one million* COVID deaths (the actual milestone was likely reached sometime before that date). It struck me that it felt like an unmarked nonevent, particularly compared to the uncountable public ceremonies and works of art that mourned seven hundred thousand U.S. HIV/AIDS deaths over four decades. Biden promised better, yet even with a vaccine, more than seven hundred thousand people have already died of COVID on his watch.

The million-death mark cemented for me that Trump was *not* the deadliest president of my lifetime—far from it. The most lethal president for people outside of the United States during my lifetime was certainly George W. Bush, who presided over perhaps a million deaths in Iraq and Afghanistan during the so-called War on Terror.

But *inside* the United States? The most lethal president of my lifetime has clearly been Joe Biden. Had Trump stayed in office (and he certainly *tried* to) that dubious honor would likely have gone to him; his administration oversaw the development of COVID vaccines under Operation Warp Speed, but had an inadequate plan to deliver them. Still, kicking and screaming, Trump *was* pushed out, and Biden *did* take the oath of office and pledged to protect the United States. Had his laudable effort to vaccinate people quickly in 2020 snuffed out SARS-CoV-2, Biden would have taken credit. Had the United States gone twelve months without any COVID deaths—as Cuba recently has—Biden would have taken credit for that, too.

Instead, as the novel coronavirus evolved, the Biden administration's plan to mitigate its harms failed to evolve. Biden didn't change tactics. Instead, Biden and his administration largely gave up and turned their attention elsewhere—leaving hundreds of thousands more people to suffer or die.

And that's as much his responsibility as achieving no COVID deaths would have been.

If you feel angry at Biden for letting so many die, or feel angry at *me* for pointing this out, *good*. More than a million people dying *should* make you angry at *someone* and spur you to not just passively accept it. "Anger is loaded with information and energy," as the writer Audre Lorde said, and that's a blessing: "Anger expressed and translated into action in the service of our vision and our future is a liberating and strengthening act of clarification, for it is in the painful process of this translation that we identify who are our allies with whom we have grave differences, and who are our genuine enemies."

Viruses don't differentiate between allies and enemies; they just seek out bodies to replicate inside. But to humans, allyship demands accountability, anger, and action. And in recent years, I've gotten great clarification that trying to avoid the painful process of identifying grave differences with liberal so-called allies will only lead to *more* mass COVID graves, which is unacceptable.

* * *

On June 24, 2022, the Supreme Court effectively overturned a half decade of federal abortion protections provided by *Roe v. Wade* with its ruling in *Dobbs v. Jackson Women's Health Organization*. Within one hundred days of the ruling, the Guttmacher Institute found, sixty-six clinics that performed abortions had closed in fifteen states, and, as of this writing, about twenty states have restricted or effectively banned abortion outright. The ruling has affected the viral underclass in several significant ways. First, it is well known that forcing patients to give birth against their will creates deleterious economic, mental, and physical health outcomes that will lead to more viral harm. Second, the fastest HIV outbreak in United States history happened in 2014 and 2015 in Scott County, Indiana. As explained in chapter 5, the reason this happened was because all the places that tested for HIV had been run out of the lower half of Indiana *prior* to the outbreak—so, when the virus came to the region, there was no surveillance apparatus to see that HIV (and hepatitis) was moving. Understanding that the same clinics and organizations that provide abortions—think Planned Parenthood—*also* do testing, treatment, and prevention for sexually transmitted infections, the loss of sixty-six clinics and counting all but guarantees Scott County–style STI outbreaks in many states.

But there is a *third* way in which *Dobbs* is a disaster for the viral underclass: it has emboldened judges to invoke the anti-vice Comstock Act of 1873 to criminalize medications because they are "obscene." The law was named for Anthony Comstock, a former U.S. Postal Service inspector and a moralist who used the mail to try to stop contraception, pornography, sex work, and even masturbation. Since *Dobbs*, federal judge Reed O'Conner, an ideological descendant of Comstock, has used judicial rulings to try to ban the medical-abortion drug mifepristone and to allow employers to *not* cover HIV-prevention medications. Restricting access to pre-exposure prophylaxis will allow HIV to infect more members of the viral underclass and will open their bodies up to all of HIV's coinfections. (As of this writing, neither of O'Conner's rulings has been legally implemented, though some states and medical providers are already restricting access as the decisions wind their way through the federal judiciary.)

All this means that as access to abortion disappeared, so, too, did access to many other matters of sexual health and infectious disease. COVID testing sites evaporated almost as quickly as they'd popped up. Temporary ventilation systems seemed to go extinct without being replaced by robust, permanent ones. The ten-day COVID isolation window was cut in half during the Omicron surge *not* because clinical research suggested it should be, but because too many people were sick to keep the more-or-less open economy going. The new five-day isolation window coincided with the deadliest period of the pandemic in the United States.

After years of wrangling to make COVID vaccines mandatory for various kinds of employment, the mandates were also abandoned, even by the U.S. military, which has, for centuries, enforced inoculations of various kinds for its troops. Excused and paid time off to recover from illness evaporated from workplaces. And mask mandates fell, too.

Seeing masks go away was, perhaps, the most perplexing of these ill-advised changes. It wasn't just from planes, buses, and offices, but *everywhere.* Masks were suddenly off in nursing homes, in cancer treatment wards, even in children's hospitals—health care settings where everyone should know better. Consider that doctors and dentists did not routinely use gloves prior to the AIDS pandemic; if you're old enough, you may recall a dentist rooting around in your mouth with bare fingers before the mid-1980s. Much like germ theory led to handwashing in medical settings, HIV transmission led to gloves as a universal precaution. And both these measures had all kinds of positive benefits beyond just preventing one pathogen! From this view, the end of masking struck me as if, when HIV medications became available in 1996, the medical establishment had said, *All right, stop using gloves everyone! Go back to raw-dogging in people's orifices! Don't worry—if you or your patients get HIV, there are pills for that. And while you're at it, boys, stop using condoms, too!*

In the first years of the COVID pandemic, a few supervised injection sites, places where people can consume drugs with sterile materials under supervision, began to open in the United States. As they have everywhere else they've been used in the world, these sites saved lives in ways both fast (by reviving people who have overdosed) and more slowly—by helping people connect to social, economic, and addiction support, as well as by preventing them (and their social networks) from becoming infected with HIV and hepatitis. But even in liberal cities like New York and San Francisco, real estate interests have tried to close them as soon as they've opened.

And as *all* these viral-mitigating forces were disappearing, a potent vector was spreading itself across the country, like the fungal Cordyceps infection on the apocalyptic 2023 TV show *The Last of Us*: hundreds of anti-LGBTQ bills. More specifically, anti-trans bills were introduced in forty-five states (90 percent of the United States, for those who are counting). The most draconian laws that passed banned medical care for trans youth (Tennessee, Kentucky) and, effectively, for all youth *and adults* (Missouri, Florida). Robbing trans people of the care they need pushes them further into the viral underclass. Rather than letting trans people get their medicine in sterile environments under a physician's care, these states are pushing vulnerable patients needlessly into the contraband market for hormone replacement therapy and opening up their veins to the HIV and hepatitis infections that come with using unsterilized syringes. But even when a state is "only" passing "Don't Say Gay" bills, where schools or libraries are forbidden from teaching about LGBTQ sexuality or life, the state is denying LGBTQ people the information they need to protect themselves and their communities—and producing or reproducing a viral underclass.

Now, let's turn back to July 2022, when Biden wanted to hit the road to sell the nation on his plan to hire one hundred thousand cops, but instead got COVID—remaining infected for at least seventeen days, or nearly two *weeks* longer than the new CDC quarantine period. The setback was embarrassing, but in some ways he had a bigger, more pressing problem on his hands.

There was an outbreak of monkeypox raging among men who have sex with men.

The Summer of 2022: The Monkeypox Chronicles

In May 2022, epidemiologists and queer men understood a biological reality: there was about to be an outbreak of what was commonly called monkeypox (also known as MPV, hMPVx, or mpox) in the United States. The virus had been observed for decades in about a dozen countries in western Central Africa, where it was endemic *not* among monkeys but rodents. When it very rarely spilled over into the human population, it was transmitted through generic contact and it was highly deadly—up to one in every ten people infected could die.

But, as Dr. Dimie Ogoina first noted seemed to be happening during an outbreak in Nigeria, sometime around 2017, the mpox virus mutated. It started transmitting through sexual contact between men, primarily through unprotected anal intercourse. This strain of monkeypox was, mercifully, not as fatal, but it still could kill. Globally, 99 percent of the people contracting it were men, almost all of whom identified as men who had sex with other men (MSM). Turning up in gay saunas in Europe and Canada, it was only a matter of time before it emerged in the United States.

Whether they were gay MDs or sex-party operators, people in queer communities in the United States knew what had to be done, and done quickly: We needed to use a "ring strategy" to vaccinate MSM, ideally by using the Strategic National Stockpile, which, since 9/11, the federal government had said included hundreds of millions of smallpox vaccines (which would work for monkeypox, too), enough to vaccinate everyone in the nation in months in the event of biological warfare. We needed to use the COVID vaccine delivery infrastructure, which recently had the capacity to deliver up to four million shots a day. And, with gay pride coming, we needed to take advantage of the historic anomaly that the American people had recently been socialized to get vaccines as adults—and to deliver shots at mass LGBTQ pride events throughout the summer.

This did not happen.

Despite two decades of living under the 9/11 emergency order, the United States is lucky there hasn't been a biological attack, because most of the smallpox vaccines in our stockpile had been allowed to expire (if so many doses had ever existed in the first place). By mid-2022, the COVID vaccine infrastructure had largely been dismantled, meaning it couldn't be used to distribute mpox vaccines. (Nor could it be used to deliver COVID boosters for that matter; while the United States initially vaccinated most people over sixty-five, just a fraction have been boosted. Our elders hadn't become vaccine skeptics; the system to deliver shots simply vanished.)

The Biden administration *did* have a purchase order on three hundred thousand doses of a monkeypox vaccine called Jynneos made in Europe, which it could have rapidly gotten into the arms of willing queer men to nip the outbreak in the bud. But the administration got cheap and took a "wait-and-see" approach, as the *New York Times* reported, leaving most of those shots in Denmark for too long. As predicted, monkeypox spread in the U.S. among men who have sex with men. So many people wanted vaccines that the few shots available were rationed—as the COVID vaccine had been the year before, and with all of the *same* racial disparities, as if nothing had been learned. With mpox in more than one hundred countries, the United States and the European Union began a controversial intradermal "dose-stretching" campaign, in which each vaccine dose was stretched into five by injecting a one-fifth amount directly into patients' veins. A side effect was that this would leave a visible scar on patients' forearms for weeks or even months, creating a kind of visible stigma that harkened back to the word's original Greek meaning, *to mark*—a brand of being queer that drove away some potential patients for whom it wasn't safe to be outed.

By spring 2023, some 32,235 mpox cases had been recorded in the United States—an astounding 37 percent of the world's recorded cases, condensed into just 4 percent of the world's population.

The mpox outbreak did seem to have an end in the United States. By May 2023, the average weekly case rate fell, briefly, to zero. Fortunately, this strain wasn't *as* lethal as previous strains of MPX, but people *did* die. As of this writing, there have been 112 confirmed deaths globally, with 38 of them—one out of every three—occurring in the United States.

Of those 38, many of those who died were homeless, 33 (87 percent) were HIV-positive, and 33 (again, 87 percent) were Black. The lifespan of this MPV wave illustrated two epidemiological theories I've developed: the *inverse risk paradox*, or IRP, and the *postcolonial paradox*, or PCP.

The IRP is an epidemiological condition in which the people at the least risk within an affected population get the *most* prophylactic care, and those at the most risk get the least. Within weeks of mpox's arrival in the States, it was apparent most cases were not merely happening among MSM, but among Black and Latino MSM. Anecdotally, it was easy enough to hear stories about white men—desperate from the fear of *breathing* around men during COVID, and now afraid of *touching* men due to mpox—flying around the United States, or even to Canada, to get the elusive Jynneos vaccine. Data soon backed up how they were getting the most shots, nationally and in individual states like Georgia and North Carolina.

Overall, Black and Latino men made up about two-thirds monkeypox cases, and white men made up less than one-third—and yet white men consistently got the majority of vaccines.

These related realities are not accidental. When New York and Chicago began giving out MPX shots, they first did so in the middle of weekdays, in white-majority gayborhoods, when—just like with COVID vaccines—shift workers couldn't easily get them. Even when New York, the epicenter of the North American mpox outbreak, began offering shots around the city, its digital infrastructure was plagued by the same built-in structural racism as its COVID websites had inflicted. For instance, sign-up was mostly first come, first served, and *anyone* could sign up *anywhere* in the city. Functionally, this meant that white men with well-paying remote office jobs could (and *did*) hit refresh all day long, jockeying for appointments, and they had the flexibility to travel to majority-Black neighborhoods in Brooklyn or the Bronx on a Tuesday at 3 p.m. if they wanted. A Black person who lived in those same neighborhoods but who drove a bus all day could not get the shot. (Chicago, for its part, was a bit better about doing pop-up vaccination sites in the city's majority-Black wards, no appointment needed.) As more white men got vaccinated, hMPXv concentrated more among Black and Latin men; the inverse risk paradox was and is manufactured.

Then there's PCP, the postcolonial paradox. In my research, I've long seen that formerly *colonized* countries have much higher rates of infectious pathogens than former *colonizer* nations. Sometimes geography and climate play a role; for instance, mosquitoes are more plentiful in Africa and Asia than in Europe, and so Zika, malaria, and West Nile are more likely to transmit there. But, because colonizer nations hoard resources and outsource risk, this has also been true of infections largely unaffected by climate, such as HIV, tuberculosis, and pretty much every disease I've studied—that is, until 2019.

Since SARS-CoV-2 spilled over into humans in Western China, it has been the former *colonizer* countries in Europe and North America that have seen the most COVID infections and deaths, while the formerly colonized have fared relatively well. The same is true of monkeypox: it has been an outbreak with an outsize impact on wealthy nations—despite the fact that, as with COVID, the Global North gobbled up all the mpox vaccines and left the Global South relatively unvaccinated.

Does a theory of a postcolonial paradox disprove a theory of a viral underclass?

Not exactly.

Both the SARS-CoV-2 and MPX viruses initially moved between nations *not* inside desperate migrants traveling by land or by boat, but inside business and leisure air travelers (and, sometimes, inside cruise-ship travelers). Put differently, most often viruses now move between nations by hitching a ride inside people who have an easy time crossing borders quickly. And so, while a virus like mpox might travel to the

United States in a wealthier gay traveler, because of the IRP, the class standing of such a traveler means their social network will have some existing structural prophylaxis (housing, health insurance, employment, race) *and* they will be the most likely to get vaccinated. So, when a virus like mpox arrives in the States with frequent fliers, it will soon get blocked in their circles and pool in the queer viral underclass: Black and Latino men (and trans and nonbinary folks), who are more likely to be uninsured, poor, incarcerated, and unvaccinated.

Indeed, rather than disprove a theory of the viral underclass, the PCP illustrates how one of its vectors works: that borders bolster a viral underclass and, as we saw in chapter 6, that borders are *fictions*. It's not that the United States *per se* has the world's highest rates of mpox: it's that thinking of national borders in terms of viruses is a fiction with real limits. Consider again, as I quoted Linda Villarosa in chapter 8, how if "gay and bisexual African-American men made up a country," that country's rate of HIV "would surpass that of . . . all other nations." With HIV or mpox, it's not that straight white America has a high rate of either virus, or even gay white America—it's queer Black America, the viral underclass of the viral underclasses. While queer Black men like me may share a sexuality with gay white men, when it comes to imagined national risk, we are *not* living in the same country—and like viruses before it, monkeypox, once again, has exposed the fallacy of borders.

Returning to COVID: When the novel coronavirus first arrived in the United States, it, too, may have come with air travelers, but it quickly pooled among people who were elderly and/or disabled in congregate care settings, as well as in the poorly paid staff who worked there. When COVID was out of sight, it was out of the mind for the ruling class—*until* it threatened to take down workers and limit profits, at which point the United States belatedly kicked into gear.

And now, three years later, this virus is *again* mostly lodged in the same group of people who originally bore its worst effects. Now that the threat to young workers is perceived to be over (it's *not* over, especially regarding long COVID, but the ruling class does not *perceive* it to be a sufficient threat to a critical mass of able-bodied workers to remain vigilant), well, our leaders don't really give a shit anymore. As we explored throughout this book, when it comes to viruses, we functionally share one collective body—and it's on all of us to make sure SARS-CoV-2 doesn't transmit to the elderly, the disabled, and those who care for the most vulnerable among us.

And yet, our society is largely shrugging off this shared ethical responsibility.

Monkeypox and the summer of 2022 have shown us a case study of how the U.S. approached a pandemic of a relatively hard-to-transmit virus moving almost entirely in one specific part of the population: poorly, tardily, and with needless suffering and death. It showed how little we preserved infrastructure (or even lessons) from COVID.

That outbreak is probably the best indicator of how badly we might face the next wave of COVID or the next pandemic—*especially* if we are unlucky and get a more transmissible virus than hMPXV.

My *head* tells me this is true.

And yet.

The most common question I got on my initial tour for this book was "What gives you hope?" Eventually, I had a variety of ready answers (including, if I was having a bad day, "Nothing"). Most often, I'd quote the writer Mariame Kaba, who learned from a nun that "Hope is a discipline." It's something we work at, that we practice. Cynicism and optimism are too easy, because they assume outcomes without putting in the effort to make the world we want.

And so, when I want—when I *need*—to do the work to feel hopeful, I draw upon the dreamlike summer of 2020 and the wonder that it held. Even though I experienced so *much* death and mourning that year, even though we had no vaccine yet (and didn't know if we ever would), it's to that summer where my *heart* goes when I need to talk myself into acting hopefully for our future.

Longing for the Summer of 2020

Take me back.

It's almost like a prayer, a plea, a whisper in my mind. It grows increasingly desperate, the further I get from the magical summer of 2020.

People still weren't gathering much indoors, but—in perhaps the largest social protest movement in U.S. history—tens of millions of Americans took to the streets. People of all races joined the Black Lives Matter protest, triggered this time by outrage over the killing of George Floyd. The streets rang with cries for justice.

Take me back.

I know I am not *supposed* to feel it.

And yet.

I have often heard ACT UP activists talk about how the late 1980s and early 1990s were awful in that all their friends were perishing and there were no drugs to stop people with HIV from dying of AIDS.

And yet, in fighting for their lives, they had the time of their lives. They had community. And love. And friendship. Queer theory tells us how, without any expectation of a future, the present becomes *everything*—it glows in stark contrast against an unguaranteed future.

One time, when I was screening the ACT UP documentary *United in Anger* for my students, I snapped a video of a scene on my iPhone of my friend, the novelist and AIDS historian Sarah Schulman. She's at the Stop the Church protest in 1989, where protesters interrupted a Sunday church service at St. Patrick's Cathedral. Sarah is now the wise author of twenty books, an elder stateswoman of American arts and letters. But in the video, despite having the same droll voice, she is a baby-faced kid.

I sent the video to Sarah. She seemed happy to be reminded of that time, but responded, "Nostalgia is the one thing we are not supposed to feel."

I know.

And yet.

Take me back. To that time of a feeling of possibility.

Many ACT UP alumni describe the years right before antiretrovirals started to save lives as chaotic and frightening, but also as a time when they felt angry, joyous, horny, cruisy, connected, and wonderfully, dynamically alive. Their very mortality triggered a collective hunger to wring *everything* out each day. They didn't know how many days they had left.

For me, the era I find myself wanting to go back to is the summer of 2020.

I am *not* nostalgic for the spring of that year, for the sirens we heard at the beginning of this book, nor for the *apex* of hundreds of daily deaths in New York—including Ward's and Lorena's—as the Empire State's first wave crested and receded.

I am *not* nostalgic for April 2020, when *ten thousand people* died of COVID in New York City alone.

Rather, what I long for is the nadir after that first surge, which unfolded over the following summer—for the most magical summer of my life.

It felt like everyone on earth was involved in the same common struggle because, probably much more so than in any other era of our species—certainly more so than during any part of human history since we've been able to communicate with one another instantly across the globe—we *were*.

It felt as if life had slowed down for the human race—because to a degree, it *had*.

Elsewhere in the nation and around the world, surges *were* happening. But compared to the triple-digit daily deaths we had just endured, the deaths were very low in New York that summer, in the single digits across the state many days. The sirens hadn't disappeared, but they were infrequent enough that you *noticed* them again; and, increasingly, their ubiquity was replaced by the pervasive, omnipresent sound of fireworks, bought on the cheap from canceled Fourth of July gatherings and lit across Brooklyn and Queens by bored teenagers.

The fireworks, which sometimes kept me from sleeping (but I didn't mind), were a signal—like so many things that summer—that *something was different.*

It's not that there wasn't danger. The adrenaline the fireworks caused, and the way they made dogs howl, was a reminder of the precarity. But they also sounded an alarm that life had changed, possibly for good—and *maybe, just maybe, we didn't have to go back to how shitty everything had been.*

If, as the poet Rumi wrote the better part of a millennium ago, "the wound is the place where the Light enters you," then a great deal of light entered our collective wounds in those vulnerable days.

COVID was everywhere. But it felt like everyone was doing their part to keep it from transmitting—even governments! Even some businesses! If the default nature of the United States is omnicidal, at least it was challenged that summer by a culture of care.

Denial is also a default American setting. But in the face of so much death, there was a mass American recognition of the sanctity of life—a deep mourning for sociality, and a conscious appreciation for our friends and loved ones. As a species, it felt like we eschewed so many of the distractions of modern life under capitalism; in their absence, we had time and space to appreciate what's important for our humanity.

Take me back.

We got to practice our responsibility to one another. People who were suddenly working from home who'd never heard of mutual aid before were setting up Google docs with their neighbors to determine who needed help with what and who could help them—and finding that they actually took *joy* in performing tasks like picking up groceries for their elderly neighbors.

Take me back.

In sight and sound, signposts of the crisis were everywhere in Brooklyn, including a literal six-foot-wide sign telling us to KEEP THIS FAR APART in Prospect Park, and the banging of pots from balconies to acknowledge health care workers at 7 p.m. every night.

Masks were used *everywhere*—even outside.

There was no real anxiety about vaccines just yet; we knew they were many months, possibly a year, away from coming. The *Hunger Games*–style desperation to get them, and the challenges of delivering them to people who couldn't or wouldn't take them, did not yet exist.

The world was just *waiting*—and New York City, a rather impatient town full of rather impatient people, was doing so somewhat gently.

Take me back.

Though we had differing levels of risk, we thought about risk as a *collective* responsibility. We socialized outside. Our lives were shaped by the weather and the light of the sun—probably more so than during any time since the advent of electricity.

Take me back. Take us *back.*

The problem with nostalgia is that we remember the good and forget the bad. But looking back on that summer, a critical mass of us did *not* want to return to "normal." We knew normal had gotten us into this mess. We wanted something *more.* We wanted something *better.* And in New York that summer, it didn't feel like an individual desire, but a group one.

It's not that the viral underclass was without risk that summer. Many so-called essential workers still worked in precarious conditions. But that summer, much of New York City was doing its part to keep as little virus from getting to them as possible.

Buses were free, to protect drivers and to make life a little less dangerous for workers. *(Might they stay free forever? Were we investing in the commons of a permanent public good?)*

Working in kitchens was still dangerous for line cooks, but less so because suddenly, as if New York had been turned into Paris overnight, there was outdoor dining *everywhere.* (Even just not being indoors with customers made staff safer.) Accompanied by the sound of hammers and drills, little huts cropped up, made with elegant, uncomplicated carpentry and adorned by living plants. When my friend A. J. and I got to meet at our bar, the Scratcher, and enjoy a beer safely outside, and we found our bartenders Natalie and Franscesa alive and well, I cried.

But far more important than public space being used by privately owned restaurants was the way public space was reclaimed for truly public use. The summer of '20 was one of protest, fellowship, and interpersonal discovery—and New York's public infrastructure reflected that and made it possible. Cars were displaced for Open Streets promoting recreation, exercise, and fellowship—and, given how many office workers had been freed from their offices and children sent home from their schools, the streets rivaled the tales told by older New Yorkers. *Back in the day, our streets were safe enough for our kids to play in them!* In this time of amorphous viral danger, the streets were safer again.

The most dangerous people in the streets remained, as usual, the police. In at least one hundred cities, police departments gassed many of the tens of millions of activists. Countering their loopy depiction on the sitcom *Brooklyn Nine-Nine*, the NYPD was especially vicious. And yet, mass protests, teach-ins, and art projects popped up all over the city. Nearly a decade after Occupy Wall Street had taken over Zuccotti Park, a new occupation took over City Hall Park—again offering food, fellowship, and shelter to whoever was in need. Prior to that summer, the only other place I'd seen with so much use of open space in such creative ways was the Nevada desert at the private Burning Man festival; but during that summer, the public reclaimed land in a city where every inch of space is usually monetized to extract maximum profit.

At one point, I remember I'd hop on my bike—an increasingly popular form of travel as people tried to avoid subways—and just fall into a Ride for Black Lives without seeking one out, because so *many* protests were going on all the time. And you'd be entertained by music along the way; with no formal live concerts, Brooklyn musicians played on their stoops, churches held gospel services in front of their sanctuaries, and people listened to (and got to know) their neighbors.

Routinely, people stood in long lines to buy necessities, spaced six feet apart—but the waiting shoppers seemed awfully patient for New Yorkers. Perhaps it was because most didn't have *anywhere else they had to be*. Perhaps they were happy to have some time away from the family members or roommates they'd been quarantining with for months.

Regardless, a beautiful by-product of the lack of games, concerts, movie theaters, commutes to offices, and indoor entertainment was how much *time* we had. Apart from work, care for loved ones, and acquiring the means for survival (and not much else), there were few demands competing for our time. It was a kind of temporal freedom.

Take me back.

For me, the apex of this freedom was four Saturday nights I spent in Grand Army Plaza in July with four of my best friends: A. J., Premo, Tej, and Anthony. All of us were friends with one another in some combination, yet except for one occasion I could recall—the day I defended my dissertation, which was chaotic—the five of us had never all hung out together, certainly not *just* the five of us. But someone suggested we do so. And so, freed from how much money it takes to eat in New York restaurants (and how, in the Before Times, waiters pushed you to eat quickly so they could turn the table over to a new customer for another tip), we met on a Saturday around dusk. Each brought his own beer and sandwiches, and we sat in a circle, six feet apart. We never touched, but I'd never felt closer to my friends than as we talked and laughed and ate—and marveled at the fireflies and the fireworks, which dissolved into our field of vision as night fell around us. We talked for hours. And hours. *And hours.* I couldn't remember a time with such unfettered, undiluted conversation with friends since church summer camps. We were five guys, two single, two or three queer, one a dad, the youngest in his midtwenties, the oldest (me) in his forties, Black, white, Asian, and Latin—but partners, kids, and adulting were somewhere else. It was just us, friends. Even though we have overlapping areas of work, even *work* was somewhere else. Someone (*me?*) started a group text chat, which we used to hold a running conversation between what became weekly meetups. Someone (*Tej?*) dubbed us the Five Heartbeats.

My nostalgia doesn't erase the suffering I felt living alone and never touching anyone that summer. But, with life stripped of so much distraction and bullshit, I had space for my feelings—even the difficult ones—and I looked forward all week long to the thing I cherish above everything else: time with my friends, with people I love. I tried marijuana for the first time with the Five Heartbeats, when we all did edibles on our third Saturday together. (Yes, even though I've backpacked across Thailand, been to Burning Man, had locs for almost a decade, and have worked at both *Saturday Night Live* and the *Village Voice*, it took a pandemic to get me to try pot.) I will never forget my first sensation, at forty-two, of looking around our group and realizing *something* was happening to everyone, of hearing more laughter, and of feeling everything getting funnier. Of fumbling my way home, and looking at the fireworks and fireflies over Brooklyn as if I were on some distant planet, or maybe I was at the bottom of the sea and I was looking up at bioluminescent creatures flying or swimming above me. Nor will I forget how we stumbled upon glowing humans, and I thought I was hallucinating, but no, no, they were real. It wasn't just *me* tripping; we had tripped upon an actual, honest-to-God *rave*, with dozens or hundreds of people decked out in electroluminescent wire lights and socially distanced, dancing in the middle of the night, in the middle of a forest, in the middle of Prospect Park, in the middle of Brooklyn. After *everything* New York had suffered, couldn't life be more like this going forward, forever? Goodbye to Saturday dinners in restaurants or at big concerts; hello to eating sandwiches, having good conversation, and getting high with a few friends in a public park? *If* a vaccine came someday, couldn't life be more like this? With less empty infotainment and more community? If anyone in the country could show up at a hospital or drive-through testing site to get medical help for COVID when they were scared, couldn't we do the same for cancer—or for *any* illness? As the specter of AIDS had imbued ACT UPers with an appreciation for living, so, too, had COVID cranked up our capacity to live life more fully.

Did we have to go back to just "normal"? Everything felt possible in those days. *Anything* felt possible. Abolition. Freedom. Love. Justice. It was there, on our horizon. We could see it. We were so close, we could almost *smell* it. It all felt within our grasp that summer.

It's not that we weren't—that I wasn't—also mourning. That's the summer Jen, Camille, and I organized Ward's memorial and cast his ashes into the Atlantic. But, for once, we didn't have to pretend we weren't grieving—because so many people were in a state of grief that we could openly extend grace to one another. In our tenderness, there was a sweetness. We were real with one another. And while walking through the valley of the shadow of death, we were so aware of *life*, and we valued it with a collective appreciation I'd never experienced in our death-driven society.

Take. Me. Back.

Sometimes you have to look backward through time to find what you need to develop the hope you need to move forward. Looking back to my ancestors fleeing a lynching in the Jim Crow South has helped me. Looking to the civil rights movement of the mid-twentieth century has helped many activists.

But so, too, can looking back to, well, *us*—to *our* experiences from not so long ago. To the spirit of collectivity many of us embraced in 2020, some for the first time. To the way we allowed ourselves to mourn, and to *feel*, and to just *be* in those wild, unpredictable, and most *ab*normal days.

Take us back.

ACKNOWLEDGMENTS

With heartfelt gratitude to everyone listed here (and many others) who made it possible for me to share a glimpse of life in the viral underclass.

Eagle eyes—Thank you for editing me with such care over the years, Mark Schoofs, Ben Smith, Megan Carpentier, Laura Helmuth, Michael Lemonick, Tom Scocca, John Cook, Shani Hinton, Saeed Jones, Steve Kandell, Julia Furlan, Jenée Desmond-Harris, Tyler Coates, Kath Viner, David Taylor, Ashley Clark, Alex Needham, Lanre Bakare, Philip Cohen, and especially my first set of eagle eyes (and two-thirds of our three-headed hydra), Amber Winans and Nancy Lin of *The Buzz*.

Yellowjackets—The 'Nard is strong with us, Reginé Gilbert, Ryan Raffaelli, Kathy Raffaelli, Jory Harfouche, Stacie Thurman, Kimi Walrod, Anderson .Paak, Vincente Torres, Jeri PhilbrickDaniels, Boyd Cothran, Daniele Lasher, Catherine Marie Lewis, Carol Cannon, Janet Lindquist, Stan Beal, Caroline Lee Howard, and Cynthia Bentsen.

Music makers—Thank you for all you have done for my heart and my mind, Philip Glass, Gordon Beeferman, Greg Saunier (plus all of Deerhoof), Riz Ahmed, Enid and Gary Press, and especially Michael R. Jackson.

Violets, Round I—My filmmaking, dancing beauties, thank you for such great years of my life, Peter Frintrup, Ted Kho, Katrina Markel, Lois Spangler, Tatiana Bryan Christensen, Sasha Motalygo, Brian Edward Hill,

Laiza N. Otero Garcia, Mirla Otero, Gabrielle Pietrangelo Brown, Matthew Bosica, Christina Johnson, Imoye Francis, Jason Lee, Jason Pattan, Elena Pinto Simon, David Betances, and Arnie Baskin (Rest in Comedy).

Keepers of the faith—Thanks for holding mine for me when I had little or none, all you good people of St. Paul's United Methodist Church, the Taizé community, GLIDE Memorial Church, and Middle Collegiate Church, for you have all taught me what it means to be gay, to be in community, and "that Christ has no body on earth but yours"—especially Marcia Gordon (Rest in Smiles), Sue Odgers, Reverend Al Gorsline, Gloria Knapstad (Rest in Music), B. J. Boone, Dave Gattey, Paul Murdock, Sarah Gessler, Marta Narlesky, Sigmund Knapstad, Denise Camp, Hope Peale, Rev. Freeman Palmer, Brunilda Pabon, Stu Cohen, Denis Gawley, Ericka Mays, Jan Fisher, Mats Christiansen, Arlene Gottfried (Rest in Hallelujah), Rev. Adriene Thorne, Rev. Mike Hegeman, Lisa Masotta, Rev. Ann Kansfield, Rev. Jennifer Aull, Dana Anthony Belmonte, Wendy Silverthorn, Emily Ballance, Tanya Cothran, Sally "Fish Friday" Rosen, Christine Dick, Belinda Johnson, and Stephan Thimme.

Guardians of the press—What a wonder it was to write alongside you, *innit*, Jeb Lund, Matt Sullivan, Syreeta McFadden, Amana Fontanella-Khan, Erin McCann, Nicky Woolf, Julia Carrie Wong, Lois Beckett, Jessica Reed, Dave Schilling, Roxane Gay, Jessica Valenti, Gary Younge, Hari Ziyad, Sabrina Siddiqui, and Mae Ryan.

Care—For taking care of my body and mind, I am very grateful to Aaron Skinner-Spain, Paul Evora, and Rosey Puloka.

Show me—In Missouri, I am eternally grateful to everyone at Saint Louis Effort for AIDS, especially Carolyn Guild Johnson (who knew that a virus could lead me to monkey bread, *Captain Underpants*, and family I love so much?), and to Johnetta Elzie, Kimber Mallett, Tony Rothert, Diane

Burkholder, Jeffrey Q. McCune, Molly Pearson, Justin Phillip Reed, and Maurice Tracy.

The world's best bartenders and waiters—To the staff of the Scratcher (NYC), the Rooster (Athens), and Spiga (San Juan), my waistline thanks you for feeding and caring for me.

My New York writers—Where would I be without you, Samhita Mukhopadhyay, Michael Arceneaux, Gabriel Arana, Arun Venugopal, Tim Murphy, Steven Valentino, and Meera Nair (not at the Scratcher, that's for sure).

Bay Area folks—Thanks for letting me leave a bit of my heart in San Francisco (and Oakland), Kyoko Sato, Jeff Chang, Eric Talbert, Elizabeth Travelslight, Brooke Oliver, Elba Rivera, John Basile, and Christian L. Frock.

Burners—Oh, how your dusty ways changed my pen, thinking, and life, Alexander Heilner, Amy Scott, Alex Goldmark, Liza Stark, L.T., Nick "Honeyshot" Powers, Comfort & Joy, Que Viva! Camp, Tyra Fennell, Favianna Rodriguez, Michelle Shireen Muri, Megan Wilson, "Crispy," "Tiger" Mike Eros, Kyle DeVries, Thor Young, Cream Puff, Brooke Oliver, and Elba Rivera.

Discourse partners—Jill Blackford and Jonathan Washburn, your deep conversations mean more to me than you know.

HIV doulas—Thanks for thinking through and teaching me about AIDS and HIV (and adjacent parts of life), Sarah Schulman, Matt Brim, Alexander McClelland, Stephen Molldrem, Richard T. D'Aquila, Gregg Gonsalves, Julia Marcus, Greg Millet, Julio Capó Jr., Theodore Kerr, Jason Rosenberg, Linda Villarosa, and Jennifer Brier, and with a shared prism on related topics, thank you to Melissa Gira Grant, Mariame Kaba, Amin Ghaziani, Patrick Blanchfield, Lewis Raven Wallace, Chase Strangio, Laleh Khalili, Lisa Hajjar, George Chauncey, Alicia Schmidt Camacho, and Michael Luongo.

Doylestown—Ann Norris Pattan, "I thought this was about a robot!?"

Voic*ers*—Thank you for developing *my* loud-ass voice and for loudly sharing *your* loud-ass voices, too, Camille Dodero, Jen Doll, Jesus Diaz, Harry Siegel, Albert Samaha, Adam Weinstein, Tom Robbins, Roy Edroso, J. Hoberman, Sam Levin, John Surico, Myles Tanzer, Ruby Cramer, Michael Musto, Nick Pinto, Jessica Lustig, Sharyn Jackson, Weldon Berger, Joan Morgan, and the late, great Greg Tate (Rest in Eternal Funk).

That Black abundance—Your words, deeds, and heart have meant more to me than I can say, Robert Jones Jr., Kiese Laymon, Chanda Prescod-Weinstein, Imani Perry, Brittney Cooper, Ben Carrington, Gene Demby, Jafari Allen, Jean Beaman, A. Michael Vermy, Nicole Fleetwood, Darien Alexander Williams, Kia Penso, and Racquel Gates.

Gorgers—Thank you for always making me feel home among the falls, Mostafa Minawi, Sam Queen, Sam Dwinnel, Sharon Dittman, Ann Palmer Stephenson, Riché Richardson, Ed Baptist, Roz Kenworthy, and Yvette Rubio.

Violets, Round II—Thanks for making life a little easier during my second time at the rodeo as an old-ass grad student, Emma Shaw Crane, Betts Brown, Jackson Smith, Maya Wind, Sam Markwell, Michelle Pfeifer, Daniel Aldana Cohen, Emily Rogers, Alondra Nelson, Andrew Ross, Lisa Duggan, Gayatri Gopinath, Emmaia Gelman, Eman Abdelhadi, Amrit Trewn, Jose Díaz, Kingsley Row, Aman Gabe, Minh-Ha T. Pham, Jen Ayres, Elliott Powell, Justin Leroy, Nikhil Pal Singh, and Kevin Murphy.

Αγάπες μου—Demosthen Kouvidis, John Davis, Cara Hoffman, Stathis Kyrillidis, Δέσποινα Μιχαηλίδου, Sophocles Chanos, Maria Arettines, Grigoris Gkougkousis, and Dimitris Papanikolaou.

Farai Chideya, thank you for inspiring me when you gave a talk on *Don't Believe the Hype: Fighting Cultural Misinformation About African Americans* in 1995. It has been the honor of my life to have you as a friend, and the support you granted me at the Ford Foundation has been invaluable.

StoryCorps—The working conditions were difficult, but the storytellers were great, and I met you, my loves, Daniel Littlewood, Mitra Bonshahi, and Rachel Falcone.

Wildcats—I am grateful for support from my colleagues at Northwestern University, including E. Patrick Johnson, Charles Whitaker, Douglas Foster, Brian Mustanski, Kathryn Macapagal, Francesca Gaiba, Hefize Luttoli, Jagadīśa-devaśrī Dācus, Mei-Ling Hopgood, Patty Loew, Patti Wolter, Mary Weismantel, Steve Epstein, Héctor Carrillo, Greg Ward, Celeste Watkins-Hayes, Malú Machuca Rose, Derrick Clinton, and the faculties and staff of Northwestern University's Institute for Sexual and Gender Minority Health and Wellbeing, the Medill School of Journalism, the Third Coast Center for AIDS Research, and the Buffett Institute.

Urban exploring—J Saxon-Maldanaldo, you have been an amazing friend and guide.

Disability scholars—Thank you for all you've taught me in your work and words, Catherine Kudlick, Sandy Sufian, Krishna Washburn, and Sunaura Taylor.

Readers—I am grateful for readers of this book in progress, especially Zachary Siegel, Jeff Sebo, Monica H. Green, Victor Ray, E. Tammy Kim, Diana Iwanski, Paul David Wadler, dear Brian Goldstone, and wonderful Katy O'Donnell.

Four-fifths of our five heartbeats—Thank you for getting us through the summer of 2020, Anthony Torres, Michael Premo, Tejasvi Nagaraja, and A. J. Bauer. Till next year in Grand Army Plaza.

Gays from the internet—Thank you for sharpening my pen and brightening my days, Chris Geidner, Alex Abad-Santos, Rich Juzwiak, Scott Wooledge, Garth Greenwell, Jonathan Rosa, Mo Torres, Mike McCabe, Michael Galván, and Francisco Duarte Pedro.

My students, my teachers—Thank you to the students who worked through the ideas in this book with me (especially Andrés Rosero) in my courses Before Ferguson: A History of Police Violence (New York University, 2016), Sex and the American Empire (Northwestern University, 2019), Reading and Reporting LGBTQ Health (Northwestern University, 2020), and The Viral Underclass (Northwestern University, 2020).

Mispocha of origin—Thanks for trying to raise me right, as challenging as I was to you, Jinger Dixon, James Schmitz, Sharron Thrasher (Rest in Laughter), Catherine Thrasher-Carroll, James Thrasher, Maria Thrasher, and Karen Thrasher Russell.

Thank you, Anwar Uhuru, André Bideau, and Kyoko Sato for letting me know you *been knew* as I moved through grad school.

My book team—Harrison McQuinn, Alex Chun, Tanya McKinnon, Carol Taylor, Cecily van Buren-Freedman, and Jamie Raab, I cannot thank you enough for your belief in me as guardians of this book.

The griots—Finally, my infinite gratitude to the storytellers (and their chosen next of kin) who trusted me to sketch a part of their story. And the biggest thanks of all go to Michael Johnson and Sean Strub.

SUPPORT STATEMENT

Research for this book was made possible with a 2015 Al Neuharth Grant for Investigative Reporting from the Gannett Foundation, an NYU MacCracken Fellowship (2014–19), a 2018 and 2020 Ford Foundation Grant for Creativity and Free Expression, and a 2018 fellowship at New York University's Global Research Institute in Athens, Greece.

Chapter 1, "Mandingo," and chapter 4, "Guilty Until Proven Innocent," were published in different forms by BuzzFeed News in 2014 and 2015, respectively.

The author is grateful to these institutions for their support of his research over the years.

NOTES

Foreword

xviii **to become structurally competent:** Jonathan M. Metzl, Aletha Maybank, and Fernando De Maio, "Responding to the COVID-19 Pandemic: The Need for a Structurally Competent Heath Care System," *JAMA* 324, no. 3 (2020): 231–32.

An Invitation

2 **automobile, bicycle, and pedestrian collisions:** Dan Kopf, "Traffic Collisions Are Plummeting in Several US Cities," Quartz, March 24, 2020, https://qz.com/1822492/traffic-accidents-are-plummeting-because-of-the-pandemic/.

4 **the influenza pandemic of 1918:** Akshay Syal, "COVID-19's Death Toll in New York City Was Similar to the 1918 Flu," NBC News, August 13, 2020, https://www.nbcnews.com/health/health-news/covid-19-s-death-toll-new-york-city-was-similar-n1236591.

5 **"because they have been to jail":** Chase Strangio (@chasestrangio), tweet, Twitter, March 28, 2020, 5:35 p.m., https://twitter.com/chasestrangio/status/1244060622620426240.

5 **were of Black people:** Chad Davis, "12 People Have Died of COVID-19 in St. Louis—All Were Black," St. Louis Public Radio, April 8, 2020, https://news.stlpublicradio.org/health-science-environment/2020–04–08/12-people-have-died-of-covid-19-in-st-louis-all-were-black.

5 **All over the United States:** Akilah Johnson and Talia Buford, "Early Data Shows African Americans Have Contracted and Died of Coronavirus at an Alarming Rate," ProPublica, April 3, 2020, https://www.propublica.org/article/early-data-shows-african-americans-have-contracted-and-died-of-coronavirus-at-an-alarming-rate.

5 **also showing that Latinx people:** Julian Mark and Lydia Chavez, "Preliminary Results of Mission Covid-19 Tests Show 95 Percent of Positive Cases Were Latinx,"

Mission Local, May 4, 2020, https://missionlocal.org/2020/05/preliminary-results-of-mission-covid-tests-show-95-percent-of-positive-cases-were-latinx/.

5 **disproportionately from the disease, as well:** Rebecca Nagle, "Native Americans Being Left Out of US Coronavirus Data and Labeled as 'Other,'" *Guardian*, April 24, 2020, https://www.theguardian.com/us-news/2020/apr/24/us-native-americans-left-out-coronavirus-data.

6 **more than 40 million people:** Avie Schneider, "40.8 Million Out of Work in the Past 10 Weeks—26% of Labor Force," NPR, May 28, 2020, https://www.npr.org/sections/coronavirus-live-updates/2020/05/28/863120102/40–8-million-out-of-work-in-the-past-10-weeks.

6 **health care workers:** Meg Anderson, "Amid Pandemic, Hospitals Lay Off 1.4M Workers in April," NPR, May 10, 2020, https://www.npr.org/2020/05/10/853524764/amid-pandemic-hospitals-lay-off-1–4m-workers-in-april.

6 **approximately 27 million people:** Bob Herman, "Coronavirus Likely Forced 27 Million off Their Health Insurance," Axios, May 13, 2020, https://www.axios.com/coronavirus-27-million-lost-employer-health-insurance-c77fe46a-691d-49b3–9cd2–3ad6d19df159.html.

6 **coronavirus infection and COVID-19 death:** Emily Benfer et al., "Eviction, Health Inequity, and the Spread of Covid-19: Housing Policy as a Primary Pandemic Mitigation Strategy," *Journal of Urban Health* 98, no. 1 (2021): 1–12.

6 **reform but not abolish HIV laws:** Stephanie Pappas, "HIV Laws That Appear to Do More Harm Than Good," *Monitor on Psychology*, October 2018, https://www.apa.org/education/ce/hiv-laws.pdf.

7 **viral loads are disproportionately Black:** Eugene McCray, "Viral Suppression, Linkage to Care Still Lagging in Blacks with HIV/AIDS," Healio, February 2, 2017, https://www.healio.com/news/primary-care/20170202/viral-suppression-linkage-to-care-still-lagging-in-blacks-with-hiv-aids#.

7 **Black and unhoused:** Kinna Thakarar et al., "Homelessness, HIV, and Incomplete Viral Suppression," *Journal of Health Care for the Poor and Underserved* 27, no. 1 (February 2016): 145–56.

7 **"tested positive for HIV, unremarkable":** Steven Thrasher, "An Uprising Comes from the Viral Underclass," *Slate*, June 12, 2020, https://slate.com/news-and-politics/2020/06/black-lives-matter-viral-underclass.html.

8 **upward of ten trillion dollars:** Rupert Neate, "Billionaires' Wealth Rises to $10.2 Trillion amid Covid Crisis," *Guardian*, October 7, 2020, https://www.theguardian.com/business/2020/oct/07/covid-19-crisis-boosts-the-fortunes-of-worlds-billionaires.

8 **wrote in *Scientific American*:** David Pride, "Viruses Can Help Us as Well as Harm Us," *Scientific American*, December 1, 2020, https://www.scientificamerican.com/article/viruses-can-help-us-as-well-as-harm-us/.

9 **"against moments and spaces of connections":** Adia Benton (@Ethnography 911), "I'm revising my position on viruses living *in* bodies; they live briefly in spaces where bodies interface, making the war against the virus also a war against moments and spaces of connections," tweet, Twitter, March 26, 2020, 10:58 a.m., https://twitter.com/Ethnography911/status/1243235938895093761.

9 **fifteen years into *that* pandemic:** "Update: Trends in AIDS Incidence, Deaths, and Prevalence—United States, 1996," CDC, updated February 28, 1997, https://www.cdc.gov/mmwr/preview/mmwrhtml/00046531.htm#:~:text=The%20 estimated%20number%20of%20deaths,1995%20.

10 **the United States of America:** Morgan Keith, "Over the Last Four Decades, HIV/ AIDS Has Killed at Least 700,000 Americans: COVID-19 Has Killed More in Two Years," *Business Insider*, October 30, 2021, https://www.businessinsider.com /covid-19-deaths-americans-hiv-aids-united-states-2021–10.

10 **"the ninety-nine percent":** Sam Roberts, "David Graeber, Caustic Critic of Inequality, Is Dead at 59," *New York Times*, September 4, 2020, https://www.nytimes .com/2020/09/04/books/david-graeber-dead.html.

11 **"long-term psychological impoverishment":** The School of Life, "SARTRE ON: Bad Faith," YouTube video, 3:37, October 30, 2015, https://www.youtube.com /watch?v=xxrmOHJQRSs&feature=emb_logo&ab_channel=TheSchoolofLife.

16 **"all the systems of oppression":** Combahee River Collective, *The Combahee River Collective Statement*, 1977, https://www.blackpast.org/african-american-history /combahee-river-collective-statement-1977/.

16 **"toward the promised land":** Dr. Martin Luther King Jr., "I've Been to the Mountaintop," transcript, AFSCME, https://www.afscme.org/about/history/mlk/mountaintop.

18 **"we are all terminal cases":** John Irving, *The World According to Garp* (New York: Ballantine Books; reissue edition, 1990), 609.

1: Mandingo

21 **to pay for the counterfeit bill:** "Clerk Who Took Counterfeit $20 Bill from George Floyd Says He Feels Guilty," CBS News, March 31, 2021, https://www .cbs17.com/news/national-news/clerk-who-took-counterfeit-20-bill-from-george -floyd-says-he-feels-guilty/.

21 **every two thousand police killings:** David Leonhardt, "A Very Rare Conviction," *New York Times*, April 21, 2021, https://www.nytimes.com/2021/04/21/briefing /chauvin-verdict-super-league-dementia.html.

21 **SARS-CoV-2 antibodies in his system:** "George Floyd Was Infected with COVID-19, Autopsy Reveals," Reuters, June 4, 2020, https://www.reuters.com /article/us-minneapolis-police-autopsy/george-floyd-was-infected-with-covid-19 -autopsy-reveals-idUSKBN23B1HX.

22 **with falsifying evidence and murder:** Aaron Barker, "Harris County DA Requests Posthumous Pardon for George Floyd in 2004 Drug Conviction," Click-2Houston, April 29, 2021, https://www.click2houston.com/news/local/2021/04/29/harris-county-da-requests-posthumous-pardon-for-george-floyd-of-2004-drug-conviction/.

22 **closed by the COVID-19 pandemic:** Maya Rao, "George Floyd's Search for Salvation," *Star Tribune*, December 27, 2020, https://www.startribune.com/george-floyd-hoped-moving-to-minnesota-would-save-him-what-he-faced-here-killed-him/573417181/.

23 **the world's incarcerated people:** Steven Thrasher, "An Uprising Comes from America's Viral Underclass," *Slate*, June 10, 2020, https://slate.com/news-and-politics/2020/06/black-lives-matter-viral-underclass.html.

23 **condition he calls *John Henryism*:** Sherman James, "John Henryism and the Health of African Americans," *Culture, Medicine and Psychiatry* 18 (June 1994): 163–82.

24 **With its 91 percent white:** "Race and Ethnicity," graph, Data USA, January 2013, https://datausa.io/profile/geo/st-charles-county-mo#category_race-and-ethnicity.

25 **told me over the phone:** Anonymous, telephone interview with Steven Thrasher, May 5, 2014.

27 **lit up local broadcasts:** Reba Chenoweth, "Indianapolis Native Accused of Failing to Disclose HIV Status," WXIN, October 11, 2013, https://fox59.com/news/indianapolis-native-accused-of-failing-to-disclose-hiv-status/#axzz34AupYs21.

27 **made international headlines:** News Corp Australia Network, "HIV-Positive Student Michael Johnson aka Tiger Mandingo 'Filmed Sex Victims' at Lindenwood University," News.com.au, January 21, 2014, https://www.news.com.au/world/hiv-positive-student-michael-johnson-aka-tiger-mandingo-filmed-sex-victims-at-lindenwood-university/news-story/f56614ebae4ca1307aad7f875e5bb489.

27 **had "intimate contact":** Lindenwood University, "Campus Announcement Important," email message to Lindenwood University students and faculty, October 10, 2014, https://www.documentcloud.org/documents/1201562-lindenwood-campus-announcement.html.

27 **With few exceptions:** Nick Delmacy, "The Curious Case of Michael Johnson and the Unhealthy Fear of HIV Shaming," Cypher Avenue, January 2014, https://cypheravenue.com/the-curious-case-of-michael-johnson-and-the-unhealthy-fear-of-hiv-shaming/.

27 **was intentionally "spreading HIV/AIDS":** Armani Valentino, "Men Intentionally Spreading HIV/AIDS," ArmaniValentino.com, January 24, 2014, https://armanivalentino.webs.com/apps/blog/show/41021484-men-intentionally-spreading-hiv-aids.

27 **blogs, like Chimpmania.com:** "Down Low AIDS Wrestler Sharing the Love," Chimpmania, October 11, 2013, forums, http://chimpmania.com/forum/showthread.php?39410-Down-low-AIDS-wrestler-sharing-the-love.

27 **replicating inside their bodies:** "More Than Half of Young HIV-Infected Americans Are Not Aware of Their Status," CDC, November 17, 2012, https://www.cdc.gov/nchhstp/newsroom/2012/vital-signs-pressrelease.html.

28 **to as little as 42 percent:** R. J. Wolitski et al., "HIV Serostatus Disclosure Among Gay and Bisexual Men in Four American Cities: General Patterns and Relation to Sexual Practices," *AIDS Care: Psychological and Socio-medical Aspects of AIDS/HIV* 10, no. 5 (October 1998): 599–610.

28 **having open conversations about it:** Michael Evangeli and Abigail L. Woe, "HIV Disclosure Anxiety: A Systematic Review and Theoretical Synthesis," *AIDS and Behavior* 21 (July 12, 2016): 1–11.

28 **to avoid contracting any virus:** Scott Burris and Matthew Weait, "Criminalisation and Moral Responsibility for the Sexual Transmission of HIV," Global Commission on HIV and the Law, August 9, 2012, http://www.hivlawcommission.org/index.php/working-papers?task=document.viewdoc&id=89.

28 **hepatitis (B and C), tuberculosis:** CDC, "Health Disparities in HIV/AIDS, Viral Hepatitis, STDs, and TB," National Center for HIV/AIDS, Viral Hepatitis, STD, and TB Prevention, February 7, 2019, https://www.cdc.gov/nchhstp/healthdisparities/africanamericans.html.

29 **tuberculosis, and the novel coronavirus:** CDC, "Health Equity Considerations and Racial and Ethnic Minority Groups," National Center for Immunization and Respiratory Diseases, August 3, 2020, https://www.cdc.gov/coronavirus/2019-ncov/community/health-equity/race-ethnicity.html.

29 **"the political category of race":** Dorothy Roberts, *Fatal Invention: How Science, Politics, and Big Business Re-create Race in the Twenty-First Century* (New York: New Press, 2011), 82.

29 **calls "medical apartheid":** Harriet Washington, *Medical Apartheid: The Dark History of Medical Experimentation on Black Americans from Colonial Times to the Present* (New York: Doubleday, 2006).

30 **defecation, vomiting, and even death:** BBC World Service Online, s.v. "The Story of Africa," last modified 2014, https://www.bbc.co.uk/worldservice/specials/1624_story_of_africa/page53.shtml.

30 **"parasites, and dysentery to spread":** Elise Mitchell, "The Shortages May Be Worse Than the Disease," *Atlantic*, March 11, 2020, https://www.theatlantic.com/ideas/archive/2020/03/humanitys-long-history-of-making-epidemics-worse/607780/.

31 **improved birthing for white people:** Brynn Holland, "The 'Father of Modern Gynecology' Performed Shocking Experiments on Enslaved Women," History.com,

updated December 4, 2018, https://www.history.com/news/the-father-of-modern-gynecology-performed-shocking-experiments-on-slaves.

31 **mortality persist to this day:** Linda Villarosa, "Why America's Black Mothers and Babies Are in a Life-or-Death Crisis," *New York Times Magazine*, April 11, 2018, https://www.nytimes.com/2018/04/11/magazine/black-mothers-babies-death-maternal-mortality.html.

31 **"people's immunity became white people's capital":** Kathryn Olivarius, "The Dangerous History of Immunoprivilege," *New York Times*, April 12, 2020, https://www.nytimes.com/2020/04/12/opinion/coronavirus-immunity-passports.html.

31 **"Syphilis in the Negro Male":** CDC, "The U.S. Public Health Service Syphilis Study at Tuskegee," National Center for HIV/AIDS, Viral Hepatitis, STD, and TB Prevention, April 22, 2021, https://www.cdc.gov/tuskegee/timeline.htm.

31 **getting medical treatment "for free":** Jeneen Interlandi, "Why Doesn't the United States Have Universal Health Care? The Answer Has Everything to Do with Race," *New York Times Magazine*, August 14, 2019, https://www.nytimes.com/interactive/2019/08/14/magazine/universal-health-care-racism.html.

32 **cooked into a soup:** Roger Ebert, "Mandingo," *Chicago Sun-Times*, July 25, 1975, https://www.rogerebert.com/reviews/mandingo-1975.

32 **"mandingoism":** Ann duCille, "The Unbearable Darkness of Being," in *Birth of a Nation'hood: Gaze, Script, and Spectacle in the O.J. Simpson Case*, ed. Toni Morrison and Claudia Brodsky (New York: Pantheon, 1999).

33 **shown that the law punishes:** Carol Galletly and Zita Lazzarini, "Charges for Criminal Exposure to HIV and Aggravated Prostitution Filed in the Nashville, Tennessee Prosecutorial Region 2000–2010," *AIDS and Behavior* 17 (January 22, 2013): 2624–36, https://www.ncbi.nlm.nih.gov/pmc/articles/PMC4060526/.

33 **combination thereof are disproportionately punished:** Matthew Weait, "Criminalisation of HIV Exposure and Transmission: A Global Review," United Nations Global Commission on HIV and the Law, July 2011, https://hivlawcommission.org/wp-content/uploads/2017/06/Criminalisation-of-HIV-Exposure-and-Transmission.pdf; Sarah Schulman, *Conflict Is Not Abuse: Overstating Harm, Community Responsibility, and the Duty of Repair* (Vancouver: Arsenal Pulp Press, 2016); and Amira Hasenbush et al., "HIV Criminalization in California: Penal Implications for People Living with HIV/AIDS (2015)," The Williams Institute, School of Law, University of California, Los Angeles, June 2016, https://williamsinstitute.law.ucla.edu/publications/hiv-criminalization-ca-penal/.

34 **"very shocked and scared":** Michael Johnson, interview with Steven Thrasher, St. Louis, May 7, 2014.

35 **"lucky tiger shirt":** Michael Johnson, "Championship's-state, nationals," post, Facebook, May 27, 2013, https://www.facebook.com/photo.php?fbid=523788437658949&set=a.144359628935167&type=1&theater.

35 **drag balls in Indianapolis:** In the early 2010s, ballroom drag was very much a subculture in the Midwest. When Johnson began walking balls, the FX show *Pose* was still many years away, and if people in the Midwest outside the scene knew much about it, it would have been from the 1990 film *Paris Is Burning*.

35 **BQ ("Butch Queen") Body:** Ballroom Throwbacks Television—Brtbtv, "BQ BODY @ ST LOUIS AWARDS BALL 2013," YouTube video, 0:40, September 24, 2013, https://www.youtube.com/watch?v=ylg5uUfOCGo.

36 **see its members' status:** Azeen Ghorayshi and Sri Ray, "Grindr Is Letting Other Companies See User HIV Status and Location Data," BuzzFeed News, April 2, 2018, https://www.buzzfeednews.com/article/azeenghorayshi/grindr-hiv-status-privacy.

36 **its own particular challenges:** Catherine Kramarczuk Voulgarides, Edward Fergus, and Kathleen A. King Thorius, "Pursuing Equity: Disproportionality in Special Education and the Reframing of Technical Solutions to Address Systemic Inequities," *American Journal of Health Promotion* 41, no. 1 (March 2017): 200–204.

37 **came in first place:** Andrew Hipps, "Labette Runs Away with NJCAA Team Title," InterMat, February 26, 2012, https://intermatwrestle.com/articles/9852?.

37 **"'big, and he can't read'":** Citing federal privacy issues, Lindenwood would not release Johnson's grades when I asked the university to corroborate other accounts of his learning. As for his reading ability, Lindenwood counsel Eric Stuhler wrote in an email, "We see no basis for an assertion that Mr. Johnson is functionally illiterate," as "he obviously graduated from high school and completed two years at a community college. If either of these institutions perpetrated a fraud upon our university by falsifying his credentials and transcripts, perhaps you should investigate them."

38 **"harder for Black players to qualify":** Associated Press (@AP), tweet, Twitter, June 2, 2001, 8:49 p.m., https://twitter.com/ap/status/1400162696478265344.

38 **Johnson's former teammates told me:** Anonymous, telephone interview with Steven Thrasher, April, 24, 2014.

39 **the American Medical Association adopted:** "The AMA Adopts a Resolution Opposing HIV Criminalization," The Center for HIV Law and Policy, June 10, 2014, https://www.hivlawandpolicy.org/news/ama-adopts-a-resolution-opposing-hiv-criminalization.

41 **"inner ring suburb of Kinloch":** "Forward Through Ferguson: A Path Toward Racial Equity," The Ferguson Commission, September 27, 2016, https://forwardthroughferguson.org/report/executive-summary/overview/.

42 **Black women—was Ferguson:** "1.5 Million Missing Black Men," interactive graphic, Justin Wolfers et al., *New York Times*, April 20, 2015, https://www.nytimes.com/interactive/2015/04/20/upshot/missing-black-men.html.

2: The Infinite Weight of Zero

44 **"who gets the virus first":** Bill Hutchinson, "Alabama Students Throwing 'COVID Parties' to See Who Gets Infected: Officials," ABC News, July 1, 2020, https://abcnews.go.com/US/alabama-students-throwing-covid-parties-infected-officials/story?id=71552514.

45 **Such contests never happened:** In a separate example of a COVID party moral panic in 2020, a local TV station retracted their reporting on COVID parties. See Neil Fischer (@NeilFischerTV), tweet, Twitter, May 7, 2020, 8:46 p.m., https://twitter.com/NeilFischerTV/status/1258558984522350593. But with the Tuscaloosa story, major news organizations did not address its holes, even after media critics like me, on Twitter and in *Wired*, pointed out the lack of evidence. See Steven Thrasher, tweet, Twitter, July 2, 2020, 10:55 a.m., https://twitter.com/thrasherxy/status/1278703871053963269?lang=en; and Giled Edelman, "'Covid Parties' Are Not a Thing," *Wired*, July 2, 2020, https://www.wired.com/story/covid-parties-are-not-a-thing/.

45 **like CNN:** Faith Karimi and Jamiel Lynch, "Young People Are Throwing Coronavirus Parties with a Payout When One Gets Infected, Official Says," CNN, July 2, 2020, https://www.cnn.com/2020/07/02/us/alabama-coronavirus-parties-trnd/index.html.

45 **CNN and the Associated Press:** "Officials: Students in Alabama Threw COVID Contest Parties," Associated Press, July 2, 2020, https://apnews.com/article/virus-outbreak-tuscaloosa-alabama-us-news-al-state-wire-888ed17ac0e048ba8fdbe248e90cc877.

46 **impoverished than the workforce overall:** "Retail Jobs Among the Most Common Occupations," United States Census, updated September 8, 2020, https://www.census.gov/library/stories/2020/09/profile-of-the-retail-workforce.html.

46 **crisis is to go shopping:** Justin Fox, "Telling Us to Go Shopping," *Time*, January 19, 2009, http://content.time.com/time/specials/packages/article/0,28804,1872229_1872230_1872236,00.html.

46 **story about COVID parties:** City of Chicago (@chicago), "We all know we can do some stupid things in college but . . ." tweet, Twitter, July 2, 2020, 2:11 p.m., https://twitter.com/chicago/status/1278798372091166722.

46 **believing something that wasn't true:** Steven Thrasher (@thrasherxy), "This an OUTRAGEOUS feedback of propaganda!!! City officials in Alabama make unsubstantiated claims without evidence; 'journalists' at @CNN @abcnews @RobinRoberts repeat with no reporting as 'news'; city of Chicago repeats it. ARGGGGH!!!" tweet, Twitter, July 2, 2020, 2:19 p.m., https://twitter.com/thrasherxy/status/1278800524050120707.

46 **advertising, sourcing, flak, and fear:** Noam Chomsky and Edward Herman, *Manufacturing Consent: The Political Economy of the Mass Media* (New York: Vintage, 1995).

50 **about a quarter million deaths:** Harry Atkins, "How Many People Died in the Hiroshima and Nagasaki Bombings?" History Hit, August 9, 2018, https://www.historyhit.com/how-many-people-died-in-the-hiroshima-and-nagasaki-bombings/.

51 **of HIV, HCV, and Ebola:** "Pathogen Research Databases," Los Alamos National Laboratory, 2018, https://www.lanl.gov/collaboration/pathogen-database/index.php.

51 **needing to be stalked and butchered:** Donna Lu, "The Hunt to Find the Coronavirus Pandemic's Patient Zero," *New Scientist* 245, no. 3276 (April 4, 2020): 9.

51 **vilified Gaëtan Dugas:** Gaëtan Dugas is sometimes written as "Gaétan Dugas" or "Gaetan Dugas."

51 **North America since at least 1970:** Michael Worobey et al., "1970s and 'Patient 0' HIV-1 Genomes Illuminate Early HIV/AIDS History in North America," *Nature* 539 (2016): 98–101.

51 **at least hundreds of partners:** Brian Johnson, "How a Typo Created a Scapegoat for the AIDS Epidemic," *Maclean's Magazine*, April 17, 2019, https://www.macleans.ca/culture/movies/how-a-typo-created-a-scapegoat-for-the-aids-epidemic/.

52 **before he died:** Richard A. McKay, *Patient Zero and the Making of the AIDS Epidemic* (Chicago: University of Chicago Press, 2017), 375–76.

53 **"United States to the other":** Randy Shilts, *And the Band Played On: Politics, People and the AIDS Epidemic* (New York: St. Martin's Press, 1993), 439.

53 **once put it to me:** Steven Thrasher, "Why Did It Take So Long for Science to Debunk the AIDS 'Patient Zero'?" *Guardian*, November 1, 2016, https://www.theguardian.com/society/commentisfree/2016/nov/01/patient-zero-aids-hiv-gaetan-dugas.

53 **widely criticized by historians:** Rich Barlow, "How the AIDS Crisis Became a Moral Debate," *BU Today*, December 3, 2015, http://www.bu.edu/articles/2015/anthony-petro-after-the-wrath-of-god.

53 **historians, social scientists:** Steven Epstein, *Impure Science: AIDS, Activism, and the Politics of Knowledge* (Berkeley: University of California Press, 1996), 376–86.

53 **and public health researchers:** Richard A. McKay, "'Patient Zero': The Absence of a Patient's View of the Early North American AIDS Epidemic," *Bulletin of the History of Medicine* 88, no. 1 (Spring 2014): 161–94.

53 **being "outside" California:** Johnson, "How a Typo Created a Scapegoat for the AIDS Epidemic."

54 **"acquired immunodeficiency syndrome in 1984":** McKay, "'Patient Zero,'" 3.

54 **"'Oooh, that's catchy'":** Donald McNeil Jr., "H.I.V. Arrived in the U.S. Long Before 'Patient Zero,'" *The New York Times*, October 26, 2016, https://www.nytimes.com/2016/10/27/health/hiv-patient-zero-genetic-analysis.html?_r=0.

55 **"while circulating compelling content":** Henry Jenkins et al., *Spreadable Media: Creating Value and Meaning in a Networked Culture* (New York: NYU Press, 2013).

55 **an "idea-meme" can mutate:** Richard Dawkins, *The Selfish Gene* (Oxford: Oxford University Press, 1976), 254.

56 **"administration of harmful substances" laws:** "Countries: France," HIV Justice Network, November 2020, https://www.hivjustice.net/country/fr/.

57 **"THEORIES OF AIDS ORIGINS":** John Crewdson, "Case Shakes Theories of AIDS Origin," *Chicago Tribune*, October 25, 1987, https://www.chicagotribune.com/news/ct-xpm-1987–10–25–8703200167-story.html.

57 **was hospitalized at Barnes Hospital:** Crewdson, "Case Shakes Theories of AIDS Origin."

58 **living around the Mediterranean Sea:** Ivanka Temelkova et al., "A Series of Patients with Kaposi Sarcoma (Mediterranean/Classical Type): Case Presentations and Short Update on Pathogenesis and Treatment," Open Access, *Macedonian Journal of Medical Sciences* 6, no. 9 (September 25, 2018): 1688–93.

58 **They were present:** Steve Hendrix, "A Mystery Illness Killed a Boy in 1969: Years Later, Doctors Believed They'd Learned What It Was: AIDS," *Washington Post*, May 15, 2019, https://www.washingtonpost.com/history/2019/05/15/mystery-illness-killed-boy-years-later-doctors-learned-what-it-was-aids/.

58 **"pathogens with each breath":** Carl Zimmer, "Most People with Coronavirus Won't Spread It: Why Do a Few Infect Many?" *New York Times*, June 30, 2020, https://www.nytimes.com/2020/06/30/science/how-coronavirus-spreads.html.

58 **brought "to heel":** C-SPAN, "1996: Hillary Clinton on 'Superpredators' (C-SPAN)," YouTube video, 2:02, February 25, 2016, https://www.youtube.com/watch?v=j0uCrA7ePno&ab_channel=C-SPAN.

58 **"a bag producing Chlamydia":** Crewdson, "Case Shakes Theories of AIDS Origin."

59 **"ignored him instead, neglected him":** Theodore Kerr, video interview with Steven Thrasher, July 21, 2020.

59 **AIDS in the 1970s:** Betty Williams, interview by Sarah Schulman, "ACT UP Oral History Project," August 23, 2008, http://www.actuporalhistory.org/interviews/images/bwilliams.pdf.

59 **"patient in the United States":** "Robert Rayford," National Park Service, October 2017, https://www.nps.gov/people/robert-rayford.htm.

62 **"than in the general population":** Yann Ruffieux et al., "Mortality from Suicide Among People Living with HIV and the General Swiss Population: 1988–2017," *Journal of International AIDS Society* 22, no. 8 (2019), https://www.ncbi.nlm.nih.gov/pmc/articles/PMC6698675/.

64 **net value: $130 billion:** Hillary Hoffower, "A Family Feud over a $400 Million Trust Fund, a Massive Fortune That Left One Heiress with an Inferiority Complex, and a Sprawling Media Empire: Meet the Disney Family," *Business Insider*, December 16, 2020, https://www.businessinsider.com/disney-family-net-worth-fortune-media-walt-2019–6.

64 **net worth: $690 million:** Dominic-Madori Davis, "Bob Iger Will Forgo His Entire Salary This Year as Disney Risks Losing Billions in Revenue: Here's How the Media Titan Makes and Spends His $690 Million Fortune," *Business Insider*, March 31, 2020, https://www.businessinsider.com/disney-ceo-bob-iger-net-worth-life-career-family.

64 **their own venture capital firm:** Steamboat Ventures is the venture capital arm of the Walt Disney Company (steamboatvc.com). See also Ryan Lawler, "With Digital Media on the Rise, Disney Investment Arm Steamboat Ventures Raises $85 Million Fund," TechCrunch, December 21, 2012, https://techcrunch.com/2012/12/21/steamboat-ventures-85m-fund/.

64 **companies like Google and Apple:** Megan Graham, "Oscars Sells Out Ad Inventory Despite Awards Show Ratings Declines," CNBC, April 22, 2021, https://www.cnbc.com/2021/04/22/oscars-sells-out-ad-inventory-despite-awards-show-ratings-declines.html.

64 **woman known as Patient 31:** Youjin Shin, Bonnie Berkowitz, and Min Joo Kim, "How a South Korean Church Helped Fuel the Spread of the Coronavirus," *Washington Post*, March 25, 2020, https://www.washingtonpost.com/graphics/2020/world/coronavirus-south-korea-church/.

65 **a championship game:** "Wild Celebration in Tuscaloosa After Alabama's National Championship Win," WVTM, January 12, 2021, https://www.wvtm13.com/article/massive-crowd-swarms-the-strip-after-alabama-s-national-championship-win/35191070#.

65 **each year from that virus:** "Number of deaths due to HIV/AIDS," World Health Organization, October 11, 2021, https://www.who.int/data/gho/data/indicators/indicator-details/GHO/number-of-deaths-due-to-hiv-aids.

3: Parasite

66 **on the very same day:** Philip Bump, "The Difference in How the Pandemic Has Affected the U.S. and South Korea Remains Staggering," *Washington Post*, December 4, 2020, https://www.washingtonpost.com/politics/2020/12/04/difference-how-pandemic-has-affected-us-south-korea-remains-staggering/.

66 **"'They're very local'":** E. Alex Jung, "Bong Joon-ho's Dystopia Is Already Here: The Korean Director's Ruthless, Bleak New Film *Parasite* Is the Most Fun You'll Have in Theaters This Fall," *Vulture*, October 7, 2019, https://www.vulture.com/2019/10/bong-joon-ho-parasite.html.

67 **war for seven decades:** Erin Blakemore, "The Korean War Never Technically Ended: Here's Why," *National Geographic*, June 24, 2020, https://www.nationalgeographic.com/history/article/why-korean-war-never-technically-ended.

67 **Bong told film writer Kate Hagen:** "The Black List Interview: Bong Joon-ho on *Parasite*," interview by Alci Rengifo, Karen Patterson, and Kate Hagen, Medium, last modified October 11, 2019, https://blog.blcklst.com/the-black-list-interview-bong-joon-ho-on-parasite-5fd0cb0baa12.

67 **bases after World War II:** Mark Harrison and Sung Vin Yim, "War on Two Fronts: The Fight Against Parasites in Korea and Vietnam," *Medical History* 61, no. 3 (June 2017): 401–23.

67 **the 1970s and '80s:** Times Wire Services, "Seoul Police Firing Tear Gas Halt Protests over Student's Torture Death," *Los Angeles Times*, May 24, 1987, https://www.latimes.com/archives/la-xpm-1987–05–24-mn-2581-story.html; and Max Balhorn, "How South Korea's Pro-Democracy Movement Fought to Ban 'Murderous Tear Gas,'" *Jacobin*, June 28, 2020, https://jacobinmag.com/2020/06/south-korea-democracy-movement-protests-tear-gas.

68 **one hundred cities:** K. K. Rebecca Lai et al., "Here Are the 100 US Cities Where Protesters Were Tear-Gassed," *New York Times*, June 18, 2020, https://www.nytimes.com/interactive/2020/06/16/us/george-floyd-protests-police-tear-gas.html.

68 **spraying entire cities with disinfectant:** Hilary Brueck, "China Is Sending Trucks to Spray Bleach on Entire Cities as the Country Struggles to Contain the Wuhan Coronavirus," *Business Insider*, February 6, 2020, https://www.businessinsider.com/wuhan-coronavirus-china-dispatches-bleach-trucks-to-spray-down-cities-2020–2.

69 **"purchased of him":** Karl Marx, "The Working-Day," in *Das Kapital* (Germany: Verlag von Otto Meisner, 1867).

70 **the University of California, Berkeley:** "Prevalence and Predictors of SARS-CoV-2 Infection Among Farmworkers in Monterey County, CA: Summary Report," UC Berkeley School of Public Health, July–November 2020, https://cerch.berkeley.edu/sites/default/files/ucb_csvs_white_paper_12_01_20_final_compressed.pdf.

72 **available in their country at all:** "UNAIDS Calls for Greater Urgency as Global Gains Slow and Countries Show Mixed Results Towards 2020 HIV Targets," UNAIDS, July 16, 2019, https://www.unaids.org/en/resources/presscentre/pressreleaseandstatementarchive/2019/july/20190716_PR_UNAIDS_global_report_2019.

73 **"house is your antiretrovirals":** Zak Kostopoulos et al., *Society Doesn't Fit Me but My Little Black Dress Does* (Athens: Onassis Stegia, 2019), 57.

77 **ever to be eradicated:** "Smallpox Vaccines," World Health Organization, May 31, 2016, https://www.who.int/news-room/feature-stories/detail/smallpox-vaccines.

77 **passing through his filter:** "Dmitry Ivanovsky," *Encyclopedia Britannica*, November 5, 2020, https://www.britannica.com/biography/Dmitry-Ivanovsky.

77 **named the microscopic pathogens *viruses*:** R. M. Krug and Robert R. Wagner, "Virus," *Encyclopedia Britannica*, November 12, 2020; L. Prono, "Martinus W. Beijerinck," *Encyclopedia Britannica*, January 1, 2021, https://www.britannica.com/biography/Martinus-W-Beijerinck.

78 **the world lives with herpes:** Sade Strehlke, "Most of the World Has Herpes—Here's How to Protect Yourself," *Teen Vogue*, October 30, 2015, https://www.teenvogue.com/story/two-third-world-infected-herpes.

79 **on January 20, 2020:** Victor Cha, "A Timeline of South Korea's Response to COVID-19," Center for Strategic and International Studies, March 27, 2020, https://www.csis.org/analysis/timeline-south-koreas-response-covid-19; "CDC Museum COVID-19 Timeline," time line, CDC, August 14, 2021, https://www.cdc.gov/museum/timeline/covid19.html#:~:text=January%2020%2C%202020%20CDC,18%20in%20Washington%20state.

79 **909 daily cases on February 29:** Hyonhee Shin, "South Korea Reports Fewest New Coronavirus Cases Since February 29 Peak," Reuters, March 22, 2020, https://www.reuters.com/article/us-health-coronavirus-southkorea-toll/south-korea-reports-fewest-new-coronavirus-cases-since-february-29-peak-idUSKBN21A043.

79 **13,000 confirmed cases:** "South Korea Coronavirus Cases," graph, Worldometer, n.d., https://www.worldometers.info/coronavirus/country/south-korea/.

79 **130,000 confirmed deaths:** "Coronavirus Disease 2019 (COVID-19) Cases in the US," CDC, https://covid.cdc.gov/covid-data-tracker/#cases_casesper100klast7days.

79 **in the first place:** Kate Gibson, "12 Million Have Lost Employer-Sponsored Health Insurance During Pandemic," CBS News, August 26, 2020, https://www.cbsnews.com/news/health-insurance-coronavirus-pandemic-12-million-lost-employer-sponsored/.

79 **wrote in the *New York Times*:** E. Tammy Kim, "How South Korea Solved Its Face Mask Shortage," *New York Times*, April 1, 2020, https://www.nytimes.com/2020/04/01/opinion/covid-face-mask-shortage.html.

80 **via the U.S. Postal Service:** Julie Mazziotta, "Trump Administration Shut Down US Postal Service Plan to Mail Masks to Every American: Reports," *People*, September 18, 2020, https://people.com/health/trump-administration-shut-down-usps-plan-mail-free-masks/.

80 **culture that is deeply homophobic:** Patrick Strudwick, "LGBTQ People Have Become the New Scapegoats for the Coronavirus," BuzzFeed, May 13, 2020, https://www.buzzfeed.com/patrickstrudwick/coronavirus-lgbtq-scapegoats-south-korea-uganda-hungary.

81 **was infectious or gay:** Victoria Kim, "One of South Korea's Most Reviled Criminal Defendants: A College Student with Covid Who Lied to Contact Tracers," *Los Angeles Times*, August 28, 2020, https://www.latimes.com/world-nation/story/2020–08–28/jailed-for-a-coronavirus-lie-south-korea-brings-the-hammer-down-on-coronavirus-prosecutions.

81 **two additional years in prison:** Josh Smith, "S Korean Accused of Lying to Covid-19 Investigators Sent to Jail," Al Jazeera, October 8, 2020, https://www.aljazeera.com/news/2020/10/8/s-korean-accused-of-lying-to-covid-19-investigators-sent-to-jail.

81 **living with HIV, though rarely:** Bae Ji-sook, "AIDS Fear Spreads in Jecheon County," *Korea Times*, March 15, 2009, http://www.koreatimes.co.kr/www/news/nation/2009/03/117_41317.html.

81 **only three years' imprisonment:** "South Korea," HIV Justice Network, updated March, 2020, https://www.hivjustice.net/country/kr/.

4: Guilty Until Proven Innocent

85 **Long before viral videos:** Tim Stelloh, "Video Shows NYPD Officer Punching Man After Alleged Social Distancing Violation," NBC News, May 3, 2020, https://www.nbcnews.com/news/us-news/video-shows-nypd-officer-punching-man-after-alleged-social-distancing-n1199141.

85 **the COVID-19 pandemic:** Ashley Southall, "Scrutiny of Social-Distance Policing as 35 of 40 Arrested Are Black," *New York Times*, May 7, 2020, https://www.nytimes.com/2020/05/07/nyregion/nypd-social-distancing-race-coronavirus.html.

86 **"the plague and Spanish flu":** Trevor Hoppe, *Punishing Disease: HIV and the Criminalization of Sickness* (Minneapolis: University of Minnesota Press, 2017), 10.

86 **the "pain of death":** Michael Foucalt, "'Panopticism' from *Discipline & Punish: The Birth of the Prison*," *Race/Ethnicity: Multidisciplinary Global Contexts* 2, no. 1 (2008): 1–12.

86 **"retrograde approaches of yesteryear":** Trevor Hoppe, *Punishing Disease*, 9.

87 **frightened the ruling class**: Filio Marineli et al., "Mary Mallon (1869–1938) and the History of Typhoid Fever," *Annals of Gastroenterology* 26, no. 2 (2013): 132–34.

87 **"the presence of bubonic plague":** "A History of Chinese Americans in California: The 1900s," History, November 17, 2004, http://npshistory.com/publications/california/5views/5views3g.htm.

87 **countries have HIV-specific laws:** Roger Pebody, "HIV Criminalisation Cases Recorded in 72 Countries, Including 49 in the Last Four Years," NAM AIDSmap, June 3, 2019, https://www.aidsmap.com/news/jun-2019/hiv-criminalisation-cases-recorded-72-countries-including-49-last-four-years#:~:text=HIV%2Dspecific%20laws%20continue%20to,and%20Central%20Asia%20(18).

88 **conviction rate of 99.74 percent:** Amira Hasenbush et al., "HIV Criminalization and Sex Work in California," The Williams Institute, Los Angeles, October 2017, https://williamsinstitute.law.ucla.edu/wp-content/uploads/HIV-Criminalization-Sex-Work-CA-Oct-2017.pdf.

88 **"they made those comments":** State of Missouri v. Michael L. Johnson, 2016 S.W. ED103217 (2016). Unless otherwise noted, all further quotations from the *State of Missouri v. Michael L. Johnson* are from this same transcript.

90 **up to fifteen years in prison:** "Missouri: Excerpt from CHLP's Sourcebook on HIV Criminalization," The Center for HIV Law and Policy, updated August 2021, https://www.hivlawandpolicy.org/sites/default/files/Missouri%20-%20Excerpt%20from%20CHLP%27s%20Sourcebook%20on%20HIV%20Criminalization%20in%20the%20U.S._0.pdf.

92 **where pathogens are often exchanged:** In November 2015, Groenweghe told me he was just being "precise" about medical terminology.

93 **a paltry $325.31 per case:** "Lack of Adequate Funding Forces Missouri Public Defenders to Shortchange Constitutional Rights," ACLU Missouri, May 17, 2018, https://www.aclu-mo.org/en/news/lack-adequate-funding-forces-missouri-public-defenders-shortchange-constitutional-rights.

95 **might become the accused:** "Probable Cause Statement," PDF, St. Charles Police Department, St. Charles County Prosecuting Attorney, 2013, https://www.documentcloud.org/documents/2580257-police-report-dylan-king-lemons.html#document/p6/a263305.

95 **transmit it to anyone else:** "HIV Undetectable = Untransmittable (U = U), or Treatment as Prevention," National Institute of Allergy and Infectious Diseases, May 21, 2019, https://www.niaid.nih.gov/diseases-conditions/treatment-prevention.

97 **when treated properly:** David Heitz, "Life Expectancy for People with HIV Continues to Improve," Healthline, April 24, 2020, https://www.healthline.com/health-news/hiv-life-expectancy-for-americans-with-hiv-reaches-parity-121813.

97 **"of the general population":** Hasina Samji et al., "Closing the Gap: Increases in Life Expectancy Among Treated HIV-Positive Individuals in the United States and Canada," *PLOS One* 8, no. 12 (December 18, 2013).

99 **with Meredith Rowan:** For clarity, Michael Johnson's friend Meredith is referred to as Meredith Rowan throughout this book, which is her current name. However, she also went by Meredith Mills at the time of Johnson's 2013 arrest and 2015 trial

and is listed as Meredith Mills in some early court documents and in the trial transcripts.

102 **less than 12 percent:** "QuickFacts: St. Charles County, Missouri," United States Census, https://www.census.gov/quickfacts/fact/table/stcharlescountymissouri/PST 120219.

102 **just about 5 percent:** "QuickFacts: St. Charles County, Missouri."

102 **majority of its HIV prosecutions:** "The Criminalization of HIV and Hepatitis B and C in Missouri," Report, Williams Institute, School of Law, UCLA, https://williamsinstitute.law.ucla.edu/publications/hiv-criminalization-mo/.

104 **25.2 years:** Steven Thrasher, "A Black Body on Trial," BuzzFeed News, December 1, 2015, https://www.buzzfeednews.com/article/steventhrasher/a-black-body-on-trial-the-conviction-of-hiv-positive-tiger-m.

104 **David Lee Mangum:** Michelle Friedrich, "Dexter Man Gets 30 Years in HIV-Exposure Case," *Southeast Missourian*, July 23, 2015, https://www.semissourian.com/story/2215743.html.

105 **someone unconscious to do so:** Southall, "Scrutiny of Social-Distance Policing."

105 **had elected to take them:** Joseph Choi, "43 Percent of NYPD Employees Vaccinated: Report," *Hill*, July 22, 2021, https://thehill.com/homenews/state-watch/564392–43-percent-of-nypd-employees-vaccinated-report.

105 **having to get vaccinated:** Craig McCarthy, "New York's Largest Police Union Vows to Sue over Possible COVID Vaccine Mandate," *New York Post*, August 25, 2021, https://nypost.com/2021/08/25/pba-president-patrick-j-lynch-to-sue-nyc-over-covid-19-vaccine-mandate/.

105 **From California:** Richard Winton and Hannah Fry, "Coronavirus Scofflaws Arrested, Criminally Charged as California Cracks Down," *Los Angeles Times*, April 4, 2020, https://www.latimes.com/california/story/2020–04–04/coronavirus-violators-arrested-criminally-charged-california-cracks-down.

105 **criminal matters punishable by arrest:** Phillip Jackson, "Baltimore Police Received 128 Calls for Illegal Gatherings This Weekend as City Extends Coronavirus Restrictions," *Baltimore Sun*, May 18, 2020, https://www.baltimoresun.com/coronavirus/bs-md-ci-cr-stay-at-home-violations-20200518–6mcixyw52jejpofgbqwdmsw7ku-story.html.

106 **no effect on its transmission:** Dini Harsono et al., "Criminalization of HIV Exposure: A Review of Empirical Studies in the United States," *AIDS and Behavior* 21 (September 7, 2016): 27–50.

5: From Athens to Appalachia

107 **health spending by a third:** Roberto Perotti, "The Human Side of Austerity: Health Spending and Outcomes During the Greek Crisis," *National Bureau of Economic*

Research, working paper 24909 (August 2018): E62. Migration was *not* the cause of viral increase, but the expanded size of the viral underclass due to the legacy of European colonialism coinciding with European sanctioned austerity was a disaster.

107 **Suicides increased:** Niki Kitsantonis, "Greece, 10 Years into Economic Crisis, Counts the Cost to Mental Health," *New York Times*, February 3, 2019, https://www.nytimes.com/2019/02/03/world/europe/greece-economy-mental-health.html.

108 **deaths among the aging population:** Perotti, "The Human Side of Austerity," E62.

108 **"prevalence of heroin use":** Alexander Kentikelenis et al., "Greece's Health Crisis: From Austerity to Denialism," *Lancet*, February 22, 2014, https://www.thelancet.com/action/showPdf?pii=S0140–6736%2813%2962291–6#articleInformation.

108 **"to 484 in 2012":** Kentikelenis et al., "Greece's Health Crisis: From Austerity to Denialism."

108 **Greece from 2010 to 2011:** Angelos Hatzakis et al., "Design and Baseline Findings of a Large-Scale Rapid Response to an HIV Outbreak in People Who Inject Drugs in Athens, Greece: The Aristotle Programme," *Society for the Study of Addiction* 110, no. 9 (September 2015): 1,453–67.

108 **from the 28 cases in 2010:** Scott L. Miley, "HIV Cases Down, but Stigma Remains in Scott County," Associated Press, https://apnews.com/article/public-health-health-indiana-indianapolis-archive-d26bf2bd70444154b804fcc3789f9e0f.

108 **to "pray on it" first:** Steven Thrasher, "Mike Pence Is Still to Blame for an HIV Outbreak in Indiana—but for New Reasons," *Nation*, October 4, 2018, https://www.thenation.com/article/archive/mike-pence-is-still-to-blame-for-an-hiv-outbreak-in-indiana-but-for-new-reasons/.

108 **"associated with injecting drug use":** Gregg Gonsalves and Forrest Crawford, "Dynamics of the HIV Outbreak and Response in Scott County, IN, USA, 2011–15: A Modelling Study," *Lancet HIV* 5, no. 10 (September 2018): E569–E77.

108 **sexually transmitted infection (STI) clinic:** Blythe Bernhard, "St. Charles County Shuts Down Its STD Clinic," *St. Louis Post-Dispatch*, November 30, 2017, https://www.stltoday.com/lifestyles/health-med-fit/health/st-charles-county-shuts-down-its-std-clinic/article_bcbad111–72b5–5b20-a6a0–9f25c4fd3fb9.html.

109 **"every cop, every boss, everybody":** James Baldwin and Raoul Peck, *I Am Not Your Negro* (New York: Vintage Books, 2017), 88.

110 **"far-right sympathiser":** Helena Smith, "'Zak's an Icon': The Long Fight for Justice over Death of Greek LGBT Activist," *Guardian*, December 20, 2020, https://www.theguardian.com/world/2020/dec/20/long-fight-for-justice-over-death-of-greek-lgbt-activist-zak-kostopoulos.

110 **the man was reportedly:** Sofia Lotto Persio, "Four Cops Charged for Inflicting Fatal Harm on Gay Activist Zak Kostopoulos," PinkNews, December 5, 2018, https://www.pinknews.co.uk/2018/12/05/four-cops-charges-death-zak-kostopoulos/.

111 **"to service municipal debt":** David Graeber, "Ferguson and the Criminalization of American Life," Gawker, March 13, 2015, https://gawker.com/ferguson-and-the-criminalization-of-american-life-1692392051.

113 **"where people grow new solidarities":** Dean Spade, *Mutual Aid: Building Solidarity During This Crisis (and the Next)* (London: Verso, 2020), 1.

113 **Golden Dawn Party in 2013:** Niki Kitsantonis and Iliana Magra," Golden Dawn Found Guilty of Running Criminal Organization in Greece," *New York Times*, October 7, 2020, https://www.nytimes.com/2020/10/07/world/europe/golden-dawn-guilty-verdict-greece.html.

113 **of Alexandros Grigoropoulos:** Maria Margaronis, "How Police Shooting of a Teenage Boy Rallied the '€700 Generation,'" *Guardian*, December 12, 2008, https://www.theguardian.com/world/2008/dec/13/athens-greece-riots.

113 **work at sea or abroad:** Lori Ioannou, "Imagine a Country Losing All of Its College Grads," CNBC, February 25, 2015, https://www.cnbc.com/2015/02/25/the-real-greek-tragedy-the-worlds-biggest-brain-drain.html.

114 **"tough new austerity measures":** Ioannou, "Imagine a Country Losing All of Its College Grads."

114 **"healthcare systems and social protection":** "IMF Paves Way for New Era of Austerity Post-COVID-19," Oxfam International, October 12, 2020, https://www.oxfam.org/en/press-releases/imf-paves-way-new-era-austerity-post-covid-19.

114 **From Seoul to Ferguson:** "Clashes, Pepper Spray at Rally for South Korea Ferry Disaster," *The Straits Times*, April 16, 2015, https://www.straitstimes.com/asia/east-asia/clashes-pepper-spray-at-rally-for-south-korea-ferry-disaster.

114 **to New York:** Lauren Gambino, "New York City Settles Occupy Wall Street Pepper Spray Lawsuit for $50,001," *Guardian*, July 21, 2015, https://www.theguardian.com/us-news/2015/jul/21/occupy-wall-street-new-york-pepper-spray-lawsuit.

115 **Maria added:** Alexandros Katsis, Nikos Kostopoulos, and Maria Louka, interview with Steven Thrasher, Athens, Greece, February 27, 2020. Unless otherwise noted, all quotations in this chapter from Alexandros Katsis, Nikos Kostopoulos, and Maria Louka are from this interview.

115 **the 2009–10 financial crash:** Kostopoulos, *Society Doesn't Fit Me*, 21.

115 **he wrote:** Kostopoulos, *Society Doesn't Fit Me*, 21.

115 **"girlfriends who really protected me":** Kostopoulos, *Society Doesn't Fit Me*, 21.

115 **"my father's store":** Kostopoulos, *Society Doesn't Fit Me*, 95.

116 **"from hanging out with me":** Kostopoulos, *Society Doesn't Fit Me*, 75.

116 **"signed, sealed and delivered":** Kostopoulos, *Society Doesn't Fit Me*, 25.

116 **"rather than a social one":** Kostopoulos, *Society Doesn't Fit Me*, 25.

116 **"exists even among doctors":** Kostopoulos, *Society Doesn't Fit Me*, 25.

117 **"catching what I had":** Kostopoulos, *Society Doesn't Fit Me*, 25.

117 **"have given up":** Kostopoulos, *Society Doesn't Fit Me*, 91.

118 **"some bad experience I've had":** Kostopoulos, *Society Doesn't Fit Me*, 31.

118 **"to pay the entrance fee":** Kostopoulos, *Society Doesn't Fit Me*, 29.

118 **"not going to get very far":** Kostopoulos, *Society Doesn't Fit Me*, 40.

118 **multimedia investigation by Forensic Architecture:** Eyal Weizman et al., "The Killing of Zak Kostopoulos," Forensic Architecture, September 4, 2019, https://forensic-architecture.org/investigation/the-killing-of-zak-kostopoulos.

119 **"other people who kill you":** Kostopoulos, *Society Doesn't Fit Me*, 91.

120 **COVID-19 coming to Greece:** Daniel Trilling, "Migrants Aren't Spreading Coronavirus—but Nationalists Are Blaming Them Anyway," *Guardian*, February 28, 2020, https://www.theguardian.com/commentisfree/2020/feb/28/coronavirus-outbreak-migrants-blamed-italy-matteo-salvini-marine-le-pen.

121 **trying to destroy it:** Shannon Power, "Homophobic Arsonists Torch HIV Testing Center in Athens," Gay Star News, March 13, 2019, https://www.gaystarnews.com/article/homophobic-arsonists-torch-hiv-testing-center-in-athens/.

121 **sixth century BCE:** Dmitriy Tumanova et al., "The Origin of a Jury in Ancient Greece and England," *International Journal of Environmental and Science Education* 11, no. 11 (2016): 4154–63.

121 **according to the *Guardian*:** Smith, "'Zak's an Icon.'"

122 **off with dynamite:** "Mining in West Virginia: A Capsule History," West Virginia Office of Miners' Health & Safety Training, https://minesafety.wv.gov/historical-statistical-data/mining-in-west-virginia-a-capsule-history/#:~:text=Coal%20is%20reported%20to%20have,in%20the%20following%20two%20decades.

122 **mass to unionize:** "United Mine Workers," National Coal Heritage Area & Coal Heritage Trail, https://coalheritage.wv.gov/coal_history/Pages/United-Mine-Workers.aspx#:~:text=West%20Virginia%20miners%20first%20went,UMWA)%20was%20formed%20in%201890.

123 **"associated with injecting drug use":** Gonsalves and Crawford, "Dynamics of the HIV Outbreak and Response in Scott County," E569–77.

123 **overdose deaths in the country:** "Drug Overdose Deaths," CDC, March 19, 2020, https://www.cdc.gov/drugoverdose/data/statedeaths.html.

123 **a town of just 2,900 people:** Eric Eyre, "Drug Firms Shipped 20.8M Pain Pills to WV Town with 2,900 People," *Charleston Gazette-Mail*, January 29, 2018, https://www.wvgazettemail.com/news/health/drug-firms-shipped-m-pain-pills-to-wv-town-with/article_ef04190c-1763–5a0c-a77a-7da0ff06455b.html.

123 **a total of $84 million:** Dee Carden and Christina Carrega, "West Virginia Lands $37M Settlement Against Pharmaceutical Distributor for 'Massive' Pill Dumping,"

ABC News, May 2, 2019, https://abcnews.go.com/US/west-virginia-lands-37m-settlement-pharmaceutical-distributor-massive/story?id=62781219.

123 **death rate to new highs:** Nabarun Dasgupta et al., "Opioid Crisis: No Easy Fix to Its Social and Economic Determinants," *American Journal of Public Health* 108, no. 2 (2018): 182–86.

123 **led to an overdose:** Walt Bogdanich and Michael Forsythe, "McKinsey Proposed Paying Pharmacy Companies Rebates for OxyContin Overdoses," *New York Times*, November 27, 2020, https://www.nytimes.com/2020/11/27/business/mckinsey-purdue-oxycontin-opioids.html.

123 **"the most overdose deaths":** Michael Kilkenny, video interview with Steven Thrasher, October 7, 2020.

124 **"the poorest state in the nation":** "West Virginia Ranked Poorest State in Country," WVNS TV, October 12, 2018, https://www.wvnstv.com/news/west-virginia-ranked-poorest-state-in-country/.

124 **had peaked decades prior:** "Donald Trump and Coal Mining Jobs: How Far Back Does He Want to Take West Virginia?" Center for Economic and Policy Research, August 20, 2016, https://cepr.net/donald-trump-and-coal-mining-jobs-how-far-back-does-he-want-to-take-west-virginia/.

124 **their governor's veto:** Kurt G. Larkin, "West Virginia Becomes the 26th Right-to-Work State," Hunton Andrews Kurth, March 7, 2016, https://www.huntonlaborblog.com/2016/03/articles/employment-policies/west-virginia-becomes-the-26th-right-to-work-state/.

124 **pass HB 2643:** "H.B. 2643," West Virginia Legislature, https://www.wvlegislature.gov/Bill_Status/bills_text.cfm?billdoc=hb2643%20intr.htm&yr=2015&sesstype=RS&i=2643.

125 **"prosecutors wrote in 2006":** Barry Meier, "Origins of an Epidemic: Purdue Pharma Knew Its Opioids Were Widely Abused," *New York Times*, May 29, 2018, https://www.nytimes.com/2018/05/29/health/purdue-opioids-oxycontin.html.

125 **"conditions can go a long way":** Zachary Siegel (@ZachWritesStuff), "I've been asked multiple times 'what's the best OD prevention policy' and my answer typically has nothing directly to do with drugs or drug use. It's about how we live our lives: Do people feel valued? Jobs, unions, communities—decent life conditions can go a long way," tweet, Twitter, October 25, 2020, 3:18 p.m., https://twitter.com/ZachWritesStuff/status/1320489843391016960.

126 **"godfather of harm reduction":** Chicago Recovery Alliance, "A Tribute to Dan Bigg," September 27, 2018, https://anypositivechange.org/a-tribute-to-dan-bigg/.

126 **research has long shown:** Kris Clarke et al., "The Significance of Harm Reduction as a Social and Health Care Intervention for Injecting Drug Users: An Exploratory Study of a Needle Exchange Program in Fresno, California," *Social Work in Public Health* 31, no. 5 (2016): 398–407.

126 **one hundred and fifty thousand residents:** "QuickFacts: Cabell County, West Virginia," United States Census, July 1, 2019, https://www.census.gov/quickfacts/cabellcountywestvirginia; "QuickFacts: Huntington City, West Virginia," United States Census, July 1, 2019, https://www.census.gov/quickfacts/huntingtoncitywestvirginia.

126 **span across Huntington County:** Joel Massey et al., "Opioid Overdose Outbreak—West Virginia, August 2016," *Morbidity and Mortality Weekly Report* (September 22, 2017): 975–80.

127 **"*you're dirty* . . . Just *degenerate*":** Hayley Brown, video interview with Steven Thrasher, October 7, 2020.

127 **"effort that it takes":** C. K. Babcock, video interview with Steven Thrasher, October 7, 2020.

128 **obtain sterile syringes:** John Raby, "West Virginia Governor Signs Needle Exchange Program Regulations," Associated Press, April 16, 2021, https://apnews.com/article/legislature-legislation-west-virginia-charleston-c26f19aca070b88f8e5f95fd59c01aaf.

128 **"different places, or abandoned houses":** Brown, video interview.

128 **positive with hepatitis A:** Corey Peak et al., "Homelessness and Hepatitis A—San Diego County, 2016–2018," *Clinical Infectious Diseases* 71, no. 1 (July 2020): 14–21.

128 **hepatitis A or HIV:** Dennis Culhane et al., "The Co-occurrence of AIDS and Homelessness: Results from the Integration of Administrative Databases for AIDS Surveillance and Public Shelter Utilization in Philadelphia," *Journal of Epidemiology and Community Health* 55, no. 7 (July 2001): 515–20.

128 **more likely to be arrested:** Tristia Bauman et al., "No Safe Place: The Criminalization of Homelessness in US Cities," National Law Center on Homelessness and Poverty, 2014, https://nlchp.org/wp-content/uploads/2019/02/No_Safe_Place.pdf.

128 **"treated at the same hospital":** Ayae Yamamoto et al., "Association Between Homelessness and Opioid Overdose and Opioid-Related Hospital Admissions/Emergency Department Visits," *Social Science and Medicine* 242 (December 2019).

128 **the risk of overdose death:** Ingrid Binswanger et al., "Release from Prison—A High Risk of Death for Former Inmates," *New England Journal of Medicine* 356 (2007).

128 **camp on public property:** City of Huntington, West Virginia, "Code of Ordinances," in Part Eleven: Health and Sanitation Code, 2014, https://library.municode.com/wv/huntington/codes/code_of_ordinances?nodeId=CO_PTELEVENHESACO_ART1111CAPUPR.

129 **"our outbreak here in 2019":** Hatzakis et al., "Design and Baseline Findings of a Large-Scale Rapid Response to an HIV Outbreak," 1453–67.

129 **anarchy does *not* mean chaos:** Molly Crabapple, "The Attack on Exarchia, an Anarchist Refuge in Athens," *New Yorker*, January 20, 2020, https://www.newyorker.com/news/dispatch/the-attack-on-exarchia-an-anarchist-refuge-in-athens.

6: Borderlands

131 **speaking some 167 languages:** Adam Kaufman and Aaron Wolfe, "Block by Block: Jackson Heights," *New York Times*, November 17, 2015, https://www.nytimes.com/2015/11/17/realestate/block-by-block-jackson-heights.html.

131 **"I was an internet escort":** Cecilia Gentili, video interview with Steven Thrasher, August 11, 2020.

133 **"walking while trans" law:** Amanda Arnold, "A Guide to the 'Walking While Trans' Ban," *Cut*, July 22, 2020, https://www.thecut.com/2020/07/walking-while-trans-law-in-new-york-explained.html.

134 **LGBTQ political brokers ignore:** Jennicet Gutiérrez, video interview with Steven Thrasher, August 3, 2020.

135 **to maintain its coronavirus checkpoints:** "South Dakota Tribe Sues Feds to Keep COVID-19 Checkpoints," Associated Press, June 24, 2020, https://apnews.com/article/9b9fd6f0bd1d4d944ae3b35015d76f05.

136 **"accommodation in train cars":** Nadja Sayej, "'Forgotten by Society': How Chinese Migrants Built the Transcontinental Railroad," *Guardian*, July 18, 2019, https://www.theguardian.com/artanddesign/2019/jul/18/forgotten-by-society-how-chinese-migrants-built-the-transcontinental-railroad.

136 **people in the United States:** Antonio De Loera-Brust, "As the US Exports Coronavirus, Trump Is Blaming Mexicans," *Foreign Policy*, July 14, 2020, https://foreignpolicy.com/2020/07/14/as-the-u-s-exports-coronavirus-trump-is-blaming-mexicans/.

136 **Long before he was known:** Masha Gessen, "Chase Strangio's Victories for Transgender Rights," *New Yorker*, October 12, 2020, https://www.newyorker.com/magazine/2020/10/19/chase-strangios-victories-for-transgender-rights.

137 ***EEOC and Aimee Stephens*:** R. G. & G. R. Harris Funeral Homes Inc. v. Equal Employment Opportunity Commission, No. 18–107 (6th Cir. 2020).

137 **"carceral systems and disability":** Chase Strangio, video interview with Steven Thrasher, July 21, 2020.

137 **"I'll wait three hours":** Strangio, video interview.

139 **Cases of tuberculosis, HIV:** Salome Charalambous and Kavindhran Velen, "Tuberculosis in Prisons: An Unintended Sentence?" *Lancet Public Health* 6, no. 5 (May 1, 2021): E263–64.

139 **HIV, HCV:** Maria Corcorran and Lara B. Strick, "Treatment of HCV in a Correctional Setting," PDF, Hepatitis C Online, https://www.hepatitisc.uw.edu/pdf/key-populations-situations/treatment-corrections/core-concept/all.

139 **and influenza:** L. M. Maruschak et al., "Pandemic Influenza and Jail Facilities and Populations," *American Journal of Public Health* 99, Suppl. 2 (2009): S339–44.

139 **been convicted of any crime:** Jerusalem Demsas, "80 Percent of Those Who Died of COVID-19 in Texas County Jails Were Never Convicted of a Crime," *Vox*, November 12, 2020, https://www.vox.com/2020/11/12/21562278/jails-prisons-texas-covid-19-coronavirus-crime-prisoners-death.

139 **helping more than fifty people:** Daniel Slotnik, "Lorena Borjas, Transgender Immigrant Activist, Dies at 59," *New York Times*, April 1, 2020, https://www.nytimes.com/2020/04/01/obituaries/lorena-borjas-dead-coronavirus.html.

139 **an epileptic seizure in 2019:** Kate Sosin, "New Video Reveals Layleen Polanco's Death at Rikers Was Preventable, Family Says," NBC News, June 13, 2020, https://www.nbcnews.com/feature/nbc-out/new-video-reveals-layleen-polanco-s-death-rikers-was-preventable-n1230951.

139 **hundred thousand admissions a year:** Rosa Goldensohn, "Rikers Population Falls Below 10,000 for First Time in Decades," DNAinfo, June 18, 2015, https://web.archive.org/web/20151222162907if_/http://www.dnainfo.com/new-york/20150618/east-elmhurst/rikers-population-falls-below-10000-for-first-time-decades.

139 **"living with HIV for decades":** The *New Yorker* reported this as well. See Masha Gessen, "Remembering Lorena Borjas, the Mother of a Trans Latinx Community," *New Yorker*, April 2, 2020, https://www.newyorker.com/news/postscript/remembering-lorena-borjas-the-mother-of-a-trans-latinx-community.

140 **medication to treat it:** Ryan P. Westergaard, Anne C. Spaulding, and Timothy P. Flanigan, "HIV Among Persons Incarcerated in the US: A Review of Evolving Concepts in Testing, Treatment, and Linkage to Community Care," *Current Opinion in Infectious Diseases* 26, no. 1 (February 2013): 10–16.

140 **"to go to the bathroom":** Lynly Egyes, video interview with Steven Thrasher, August 2020.

141 **Mexico City in 1960:** Slotnik, "Lorena Borjas, Transgender Immigrant Activist, Dies at 59."

141 **"Mexico at the time":** Queens Public Television, "Queens Stories: The Story of Lorena Borjas: The Transgender Latina Activist," Vimeo video, October 5, 2018, at 10:41, https://vimeo.com/293602593.

142 **who were also trafficked:** Zaira Cortés, "Activista mexicana iniciará nueva vida gracias a indulto de Cuomo," *El Diario*, December 28, 2017, https://eldiariony.com/2017/12/28/activista-mexicana-iniciara-nueva-vida-gracias-a-indulto-de-cuomo/.

143 **other medical and social support:** Kris Clarke et al., "The Significance of Harm Reduction as a Social and Health Care Intervention for Injecting Drug Users: An Exploratory Study of a Needle Exchange Program in Fresno, California," *Social Work in Public Health* 31, no. 5 (2016): 398–407.

144 **On December 26, 2017:** "TLC Wins Rare Governor's Pardon for Celebrated Trans Advocate Lorena Borjas," Transgender Law Center, December 17, 2017, https://transgenderlawcenter.org/archives/14175.

148 **COVID-19 every day:** Madeline Holcombe and Dakin Andone, "At Least 13 Patients Died from Coronavirus over 24 Hours at a New York Hospital," CNN, March 27, 2020, https://www.cnn.com/2020/03/26/health/elmhurst-hospital-new-york-13-deaths/index.html.

148 **could be taken away:** "NYC Setting Temporary Morgues for Surge in Coronavirus Deaths," Fox 5 New York, March 27, 2020, https://www.fox5ny.com/news/nyc-setting-temporary-morgues-for-surge-in-coronavirus-deaths.

148 **move the deluge of bodies:** Arun Venugopal, "One Worker's Experience on the Morgue Overflow Shift," WNYC News, April 16, 2020, https://www.wnyc.org/story/one-mans-experience-morgue-overflow-shift/.

148 **dig mass graves for them:** Ryan Grim, "Rikers Island Prisoners Are Being Offered PPE and $6 an Hour to Dig Mass Graves," *Intercept*, March 31, 2020, https://theintercept.com/2020/03/31/rikers-island-coronavirus-mass-graves/.

148 **COVID-19 vectors in the nation:** Jan Ransom, "Virus Raged at City Jails, Leaving 1,259 Guards Infected and 6 Dead," *New York Times*, May 20, 2020, https://www.nytimes.com/2020/05/20/nyregion/rikers-coronavirus-nyc.html.

148 **"try getting it yourselves":** Jonathan Martin, "Trump to Governors on Ventilators: 'Try Getting It Yourselves,'" *New York Times*, March 16, 2020, https://www.nytimes.com/2020/03/16/us/politics/trump-coronavirus-respirators.html.

149 **COVID-19 in New York City:** "Coronavirus Disease New York, NY Statistics," graph, from the *New York Times*, Google News, March 30, 2020, https://news.google.com/covid19/map?hl=en-US&mid=%2Fm%2F02_286&gl=US&ceid=US%3Aen; archived screenshot of the March 30, 2020, graph, https://drive.google.com/file/d/1z-sRXIi4xkDxZvX6YatiNwfTE7ZLEEyz/view.

150 **"safety of the transgender community":** Alexandria Ocasio-Cortez, "On International Transgender Day of Visibility, we honor our transgender siblings and celebrate our heroes," post, Facebook, March 31, 2020, https://www.facebook.com/repAOC/posts/on-international-transgender-day-of-visibility-we-honor-our-transgender-siblings/694870914594780/.

150 **Spanish American War in 1898:** Bonnie Bertram et al., "Forever Prison," PBS, February 21, 2017, https://www.pbs.org/wgbh/frontline/film/forever-prison/.

150 **ousted in a coup:** Cathy Hannabach, "Technologies of Blood: Asylum, Medicine, and Biopolitics," *Cultural Politics* 9, no. 1 (March 2013): 1–2, https://read.dukeupress.edu/cultural-politics/article-abstract/9/1/22/25908/Technologies-of-BloodAsylum-Medicine-and.

150 **political asylum seekers:** "Convention Relating to the Status of Refugees, Geneva, July 28, 1951," UNHCR, Treaty Series 189, p. 137, https://www.unhcr.org/en-us/5d9ed32b4.

151 **"semipermanent form of birth control":** Hannabach, "Technologies of Blood," 4.

151 **still not ended:** Tina Vasquez, "Exclusive: Georgia Doctor Who Forcibly Sterilized Detained Women Has Been Identified," Prism, September 15, 2020, https://www.prismreports.org/article/2020/9/15/exclusive-georgia-doctor-who-forcibly-sterilized-detained-women-has-been-identified.

152 **overwhelm the impoverished nation:** Melissa del Bosque and Isabel Macdonald, "Exporting the Virus: How Trump's Deportation Flights Are Putting Latin America and the Caribbean at Risk," *Intercept*, June 26, 2020, https://theintercept.com/2020/06/26/coronavirus-ice-detention-deportation-haiti-guatemala/.

152 **yet been vaccinated at all:** Claire Parker and Emily Rauhala, "Twin Epidemics in Haiti, Violence and Coronavirus, Usher in 'Critical Phase' in Wake of Assassination," *Washington Post*, July 8, 2021, https://www.washingtonpost.com/world/2021/07/08/haiti-health-crisis/.

152 **no vaccines in mid-2021:** Jim Wyss, "Haiti Is the Only Country in the Western Hemisphere Without Vaccines," *Bloomberg*, June 8, 2021, https://www.bloomberg.com/news/articles/2021–06–08/haiti-is-the-only-country-in-western-hemisphere-without-vaccines.

152 **expel migrants seeking asylum:** Mary Biekert, "Title 42: The Law Removing Haitians from U.S. Border," Quick Take, *Bloomberg*, September 24, 2021, https://www.bloomberg.com/news/articles/2021–09–24/title-42-the-law-removing-haitians-from-u-s-border-quicktake.

152 **"did in a whole year":** Julian Borger, "Haiti Deportations Soar as Biden Administration Deploys Trump-Era Health Order," *Guardian*, March 25, 2021, https://www.theguardian.com/us-news/2021/mar/25/haiti-deportations-soar-as-biden-administration-deploys-trump-era-health-order.

152 **Haitian refugees seeking asylum:** Jacob Soboroff and Ken Dilanian, "DHS Seeks Contractor to Run Migrant Detention Facility at Gitmo, Guards Who Speak Haitian Creole," NBC News, September 21, 2021, https://www.nbcnews.com/politics/immigration/biden-admin-seeks-contractor-run-migrant-detention-facility-gitmo-guards-n1279886.

152 **"mocks other social constructions":** Kostopoulos, *Society Doesn't Fit Me*, 37.

7: Cages

154 **"saving it for later":** Patrick Grant, *Imperfection* (Alberta, Canada: AU Press, 2012), 82.

154 **"did as Governor of Arkansas":** Bill Clinton and Bob Rafsky, "The 1992 Campaign: Verbatim; Heckler Stirs Clinton Anger: Excerpts from the Exchange," verbal exchange, Manhattan, New York, March 28, 1992, in the *New York Times* archive, https://www.nytimes.com/1992/03/28/us/1992-campaign-verbatim-heckler-stirs-clinton-anger-excerpts-exchange.html.

156 **American lives that year overall:** "Update: Mortality Attributable to HIV Infection Among Persons Aged 25–44 Years—United States, 1991 and 1992," CDC, September 19, 1998, https://www.cdc.gov/mmwr/preview/mmwrhtml/00022174.htm#:~:text=In%201992%2C%20an%20estimated%2033%2C590,or%20equal%20to%2045%20years.

157 **more died at San Quentin:** Brett Simpson, "'Governor Newsom, Save Our Lives: We're Dying in Here'; Demonstrators Plea for San Quentin Inmates' Release," *San Francisco Chronicle*, July 10, 2020, https://www.sfchronicle.com/crime/article/San-Quentin-coronavirus-outbreak-Former-inmate-15398062.php.

157 **hotel rooms for the unhoused:** Anna Bauman, "Protesters Stage 'Die-In' Outside SF Mayor's Home over Hotel Rooms for Homeless," *San Francisco Chronicle*, May 1, 2020, https://www.sfchronicle.com/bayarea/article/Protesters-hold-die-in-outside-Mayor-15239121.php.

157 **COVID-19 hot spot Rikers Island jail:** Nick Pinto, "If Coronavirus Deaths Start Piling Up in Rikers Island Jails, We'll Know Who to Blame," *Intercept*, March 23, 2020, https://theintercept.com/2020/03/23/coronavirus-rikers-jail-de-blasio-cuomo/.

158 **including Harry Truman:** Naomi Murakawa, *The First Civil Right: How Liberals Built Prison America* (New York: Oxford University Press, 2014).

158 **Truman, Lyndon Johnson:** Elizabeth Hinton, *From the War on Poverty to the War on Crime: The Making of Mass Incarceration in America* (Cambridge, MA: Harvard University Press, 2016).

159 **"action to end the AIDS crisis":** ACT UP, last modified 2019, https://actupny.org/.

159 **according to the *New York Times*:** Philip Hilts, "Clinton's Director of Policy on AIDS Resigns Under Fire," *New York Times*, July 9, 1994, https://www.nytimes.com/1994/07/09/us/clinton-s-director-of-policy-on-aids-resigns-under-fire.html.

159 **about fifty thousand in 1995:** "Update: Trends in AIDS Incidence, Deaths, and Prevalence—United States, 1996," CDC, September 19, 1998, https://www.cdc.gov/mmwr/preview/mmwrhtml/00046531.htm#:~:text=The%20estimated%20number%20of%20deaths,1995%20(approximately%2050%2C000%20deaths).

160 **why he was killed by police:** Niall McCarthy, "How Much Do US Cities Spend Every Year on Policing?" *Forbes*, August 7, 2017, https://www.forbes.com/sites/niallmccarthy/2017/08/07/how-much-do-u-s-cities-spend-every-year-on-policing-infographic/#12681d7ce7b7.

161 **"deregulation-mad political landscape":** Avram Finkelstein, *After Silence: A History of AIDS Through Its Images* (Oakland, CA: University of California Press, 2017), 3.

162 **start manufacturing medicine with haste:** Epstein, *Impure Science*.

162 **"rather than coddled with welfare":** Michelle Alexander, "Why Hillary Clinton Doesn't Deserve the Black Vote," *Nation*, February 10, 2016, https://bit.ly/29zrbAC.

162 **future president Joe Biden:** Todd Purdum, "The Crime Bill Debate Shows How Short Americans' Memories Are," *Atlantic*, September 12, 2019, https://www.theatlantic.com/politics/archive/2019/09/joe-biden-crime-bill-and-americans-short-memory/597547/.

163 **"any president in American history":** Serena Marshall, "Obama Has Deported More People Than Any Other President," ABC News, August 29, 2016, https://abcnews.go.com/Politics/obamas-deportation-policy-numbers/story?id=41715661.

163 **"crack versus powder cocaine":** Alexander, "Why Hillary Clinton Doesn't Deserve the Black Vote."

163 **"and the expansion of police forces":** Alexander, "Why Hillary Clinton Doesn't Deserve the Black Vote."

163 **"of incarceration in the world":** Alexander, "Why Hillary Clinton Doesn't Deserve the Black Vote."

163 **"had been in 1983":** Alexander, "Why Hillary Clinton Doesn't Deserve the Black Vote."

163 **a staggering 42 percent:** Alexander, "Why Hillary Clinton Doesn't Deserve the Black Vote."

163 **programs sharply reduce recidivism:** Alexander, "Why Hillary Clinton Doesn't Deserve the Black Vote."

163 **and save governments money:** Lois Davis et al., "Evaluating the Effectiveness of Correctional Education," Rand Corporation, 2013, https://bit.ly/2O2HbL2.

163 **"allocated to food stamps":** Alexander, "Why Hillary Clinton Doesn't Deserve the Black Vote."

164 **"8 to 10 times higher":** Nicholas Freudenberg, "Jails, Prisons, and the Health of Urban Populations: A Review of the Impact of the Correctional System on Community Health," *Journal of Urban Health: Bulletin of the New York Academy of Medicine* 78, no. 2 (June 2001): 316–34.

164 **"sub-Saharan Africa":** Ryan Westergaard et al., "HIV Among Persons Incarcerated in the USA: A Review of Evolving Concepts in Testing, Treatment, and Linkage to Community Care," *Current Opinion in Infectious Diseases* 26, no. 1 (June 2013): 10–16.

164 **"the civilian population":** "Tuberculosis in Prisons," World Health Organization, December 18, 2020, https://www.who.int/tb/areas-of-work/population-groups/prisons-facts/en/.

164 **flourish under certain conditions:** Lauren Lambert et al., "Tuberculosis in Jails and Prisons: United States, 2002–2013," *American Journal of Public Health* 106, no. 12 (2016): 2231–37.

165 **drug testing to receiving benefits:** "Drug Testing of Public Assistance Recipients as a Condition of Eligibility," ACLU, last modified October 18, 2020, https://www.aclu.org/other/drug-testing-public-assistance-recipients-condition-eligibility.

165 **"that continue today in various forms":** Hannabach, "Technologies of Blood," 32.

166 **mere criminal *arrests*:** Alexander, "Why Hillary Clinton Doesn't Deserve the Black Vote."

166 **an inescapable whirlpool of catastrophe:** Bauman et al., "No Safe Place."

166 **the U.S. homeless population:** Jeffrey Olivet et al., "SPARC Phase One Study Findings," Supporting Partnerships for Anti-racist Communities, 2018, https://bit.ly/2uS8odK.

167 **in danger of becoming homeless:** "HIV/AIDS and Homelessness," National Coalition for the Homeless, July 2009, https://www.nationalhomeless.org/factsheets/hiv.html.

167 **people who are housed:** Jennifer Pellowski et al., "A Pandemic of the Poor: Social Disadvantage and the U.S. HIV Epidemic," *American Psychologist* 68, no. 4 (2013): 197–209.

167 **AIDS, homelessness, incarceration, and Blackness:** Culhane et al. "The Co-occurrence of AIDS and Homelessness," 515–20.

167 **race during the Reagan administration:** "The overall cumulative incidences for black and Hispanic adults were 3.1 and 3.4 times, respectively, that for whites (Table 1)." See "Epidemiologic Notes and Reports Acquired Immunodeficiency Syndrome (AIDS) Among Blacks and Hispanics—United States," *MMRW Weekly* 35, no. 42 (October 1986): 655–58, 663–66, https://bit.ly/2O3OceB.

167 **there were no effective drugs:** CDC, "HIV Surveillance Reports," Division of HIV Prevention, National Center for HIV, Viral Hepatitis, STD, and TB Prevention, last modified January 14, 2021, https://www.cdc.gov/hiv/library/reports/hiv-surveillance.html.

167 **"expectancy has ever been":** Elizabeth Wrigley-Field, "US Racial Inequality May Be as Deadly as COVID-19," *Proceedings of the National Academy of Sciences of the United States of America* 117, no. 36 (September 8, 2020), https://www.pnas.org/content/117/36/21854.

168 **at a fundraiser:** Sophia Tesfaye, "I'm Not a Superpredator, Hillary!: Black Lives Matter Protestors Confront Clinton at South Carolina Fundraiser," *Salon*, February 25, 2016, https://www.salon.com/2016/02/25/im_not_a_superpredator_hillary_black_lives_matter_protestors_crash_clinton_south_carolina_fundraiser/.

168 ***New York Times*'s coronavirus tracker:** "Coronavirus in the U.S.: Latest Map and Case Count," graph, *New York Times*, last modified January 14, 2021, https://drive.google.com/file/d/12YyqzSOp5H8TnCsZ8QWqQl3crCui0Yc3/view?usp=sharing and https://www.nytimes.com/interactive/2020/us/coronavirus-us-cases.html#hotspots.

168 **Democratic governor Gavin Newsom:** "Coronavirus in the U.S.: Latest Map and Case Count," *New York Times*, https://www.nytimes.com/interactive/2020/us/coronavirus-us-cases.html#hotspots.

168 **firefighters to smother such blazes:** Dale Kasler et al., "Can California Handle This Many Wildfires at Once? Crews and Equipment Already 'Depleted,'" *Sacramento Bee*, August 19, 2020, https://www.sacbee.com/news/california/fires/article245083025.html.

169 **people convicted of nonviolent offenses:** Alexander Sammon, "How Kamala Harris Fought to Keep Nonviolent Prisoners Locked Up," *American Prospect*, July 30, 2020, https://prospect.org/justice/how-kamala-harris-fought-to-keep-nonviolent-prisoners-locked-up/.

169 **these court-mandated releases:** Nicole Flatow, "California Tells Court It Can't Release Inmates Early Because It Would Lose Cheap Prison Labor," ThinkProgress, November 17, 2014, https://archive.thinkprogress.org/california-tells-court-it-cant-release-inmates-early-because-it-would-lose-cheap-prison-labor-c3795403bae1/.

170 **in Empire State prisons:** Antonia Farzan, "Inmates Are Manufacturing Hand Sanitizer to Help Fight Coronavirus: But Will They Be Allowed to Use It?" *Washington Post*, March 10, 2020, https://www.washingtonpost.com/nation/2020/03/10/hand-sanitizer-prison-labor/.

170 **people killed by COVID-19:** Aimee Picchi, "Texas Inmates Paid $2 an Hour to Move COVID-19 Victims' Bodies," CBS News, November 16, 2020, https://www.cbsnews.com/news/el-paso-covid-body-transport-county-inmates-2-dollars-per-hour/.

171 **"and the next year":** Vito Russo, "Why We Fight," transcript of speech, ACT UP, May 9, 1988, https://actupny.org/documents/whfight.html.

171 **"shit out of this system":** Russo, "Why We Fight."

171 **any president in U.S. history:** Marshall, "Obama Has Deported More People Than Any Other President."

171 **Gutiérrez yelled, "President Obama!":** Democracy Now, "Undocumented Trans Activist Jennicet Gutiérrez Challenges Obama on Deportations at White House Event," YouTube video, June 25, 2015, at 4:16, https://www.youtube.com/watch?v=ER9_M002aQY&ab_channel=DemocracyNow%21.

172 **almost unbearably anxiety inducing:** Steven Thrasher, "Neil Munro of the Daily Caller: Here's the Only Clean Audio of What He Heckled at President Obama [EXCLUSIVE]," *Village Voice*, June 22, 2012, https://www.villagevoice.com/2012/06/19/neil-munro-of-the-daily-caller-heres-the-only-clean-audio-of-what-he-heckled-at-president-obama-exclusive/.

172 **like Roxanna Hernandez:** Tim Fitzsimons, "Transgender ICE Detainee Died of AIDS Complications, Autopsy Shows," NBC News, April 17, 2019, https://www.nbcnews.com/feature/nbc-out/transgender-ice-detainee-died-aids-complications-autopsy-shows-n994836.

173 **Johana Medina from El Salvador:** Rebekah Entralgo, "A Trans Woman Died in ICE Custody on the First Day of Pride Month, Advocates Report," ThinkProgress,

June 2, 2019, https://archive.thinkprogress.org/trans-woman-died-ice-custody-pride-2aec071828ae/.

173 **"domesticity and consumption":** Lisa Duggan, *The Twilight of Equality? Neoliberalism, Cultural Politics, and the Attack on Democracy* (Boston: Beacon Press, 2004), 179.

173 **"the US adult population":** Ilan H. Meyer et al., "Incarceration Rates and Traits of Sexual Minorities in the United States: National Inmate Survey, 2011–2012," *American Journal of Public Health* 107, no. 2 (2017): 267–73.

Act III: Social Death

175 **"return for nothing at all":** Lisa Mare Cacho, *Social Death: Racialized Rightlessness and the Criminalization of the Unprotected* (New York: NYU Press, 2012), 7.

8: One in Two

177 **American Academy of HIV Medicine:** State of Missouri v. Michael L. Johnson, 2016 S.W. ED103217 (2016).

177 **"a trial-by-ambush strategy":** State of Missouri v. Michael L. Johnson.

178 **"until towards the end":** State of Missouri v. Michael L. Johnson.

179 **he'd last been free:** Parker Yesko, "It's Over: Charges Against Curtis Flowers Are Dropped," APM Reports, September 4, 2020, https://www.apmreports.org/episode/2020/09/04/charges-against-curtis-flowers-are-dropped.

179 **HIV-positive in his lifetime:** "Half of Black Gay Men and a Quarter of Latino Gay Men Projected to Be Diagnosed Within Their Lifetime," CDC, February 23, 2016, https://www.cdc.gov/nchhstp/newsroom/2016/croi-press-release-risk.html.

179 **on planet earth:** Linda Villarosa, "America's Hidden H.I.V. Epidemic," *New York Times Magazine*, June 6, 2017, https://nyti.ms/2rZzlKi.

179 **new HIV diagnoses:** Erin Bradley et al., "Disparities in Incidence of Human Immunodeficiency Virus Infection Among Black and White Women—United States, 2010–2016," *Morbidity and Mortality Weekly Report* 68, no. 18 (May 10, 2019): 416–18.

180 **use than our white peers:** Gus Cairns, "Black Gay Men Run Higher Risk of HIV Infection Despite Fewer Partners," AIDSmap, March 6, 2013, https://www.aidsmap.com/news/mar-2013/black-gay-men-run-higher-risk-hiv-infection-despite-fewer-partners.

180 **especially sterilizing vaccines:** Stacey McKenna, "Vaccines Need Not Completely Stop COVID Transmission to Curb the Pandemic," *Scientific American*,

January 18, 2021, https://www.scientificamerican.com/article/vaccines-need-not-completely-stop-covid-transmission-to-curb-the-pandemic1/.

181 **with medical debt:** Lorie Konish, "137 Million Americans Are Struggling with Medical Debts: Here's What to Know If You Need Some Relief," CNBC, November 10, 2019, https://www.cnbc.com/2019/11/10/americans-are-drowning-in-medical-debt-what-to-know-if-you-need-help.html.

181 **bankruptcies in the United States:** Kimberly Amadeo, "Medical Bankruptcy and the Economy," Balance, April 30, 2021, https://www.thebalance.com/medical-bankruptcy-statistics-4154729.

182 **nation on the planet:** Rabah Kamal, Giorlando Ramirez, and Cynthia Cox, "How Does Health Spending in the U.S. Compare to Other Countries?" Health System Tracker, Peterson-KFF, December 23, 2020, https://www.healthsystemtracker.org/chart-collection/health-spending-u-s-compare-countries/#item-spendingcomparison_gdp-per-capita-and-health-consumption-spending-per-capita-2019.

182 **disastrous health outcomes it causes:** Mandy Pellegrin, "How Medical Debt Affects Health," The Sycamore Institute, May 19, 2021, https://www.sycamoreinstitutetn.org/how-medical-debt-affects-health/.

182 **less likely to be raped:** Gregg Gonsalves et al., "Reducing Sexual Violence by Increasing the Supply of Toilets in Khayelitsha, South Africa: A Mathematical Model," *PLOS One* 10, no. 4 (April 29, 2015): e012224.

183 **Jonas Salk and Albert Sabin:** James L. Franklin, "A Cold War Vaccine: Albert Sabin, Russia, and the Oral Polio Vaccine," *Hektoen International* 12, no. 3 (2020).

183 **neither man pursued a patent:** "How Much Money Did Jonas Salk Potentially Forfeit by Not Patenting the Polio Vaccine?" *Forbes*, August 9, 2012, https://www.forbes.com/sites/quora/2012/08/09/how-much-money-did-jonas-salk-potentially-forfeit-by-not-patenting-the-polio-vaccine/?sh=277e94a669b8.

184 **"Could you patent the sun?":** Global Citizen, "Could You Patent the Sun?" YouTube, January 29, 2013, 1:02, https://www.youtube.com/watch?v=erHXKP386Nk&ab_channel=GlobalCitizen.

184 **billions in profits:** "How Much Money Did Jonas Salk Potentially Forfeit by Not Patenting the Polio Vaccine?"

184 **would be eligible:** "The Real Reason Why Salk Refused to Patent the Polio Vaccine," Bio, January 27, 2012, https://www.bio.org/blogs/real-reason-why-salk-refused-patent-polio-vaccine; Jane Smith, *Patenting the Sun: Polio and the Salk Vaccine* (New York: William Morrow and Company, 1990).

184 **have on research and development:** "Chairwoman Maloney Releases Staff Report Showing Pharmaceutical Industry Spends More on Buybacks, Dividends, and Executive Compensation Than on R&D," Press Release, House Committee on Oversight and Reform, July 8, 2021, https://oversight.house.gov/news/press-releases/chairwoman-maloney-releases-staff-report-showing-pharmaceutical-industry-spends.

184 **do with HIV medications:** Christopher Rowland, "Trump Administration Sues Drugmaker Gilead Sciences over Patent on Truvada for HIV Prevention," *Washington Post*, November 7, 2019, https://www.washingtonpost.com/business/economy/trump-administration-sues-drugmaker-gilead-sciences-over-patent-on-truvada-for-hiv-prevention/2019/11/06/68b1cc52–010c-11ea-8501–2a7123a38c58_story.html.

184 **eradicated from the human race:** "Two Out of Three Wild Poliovirus Strains Eradicated," World Health Organization, October 24, 2019, https://www.who.int/news-room/feature-stories/detail/two-out-of-three-wild-poliovirus-strains-eradicated.

186 **some combination of all these:** Bryce Covert, "No, the Unvaccinated Aren't All Just Being Difficult," *New York Times*, August 6, 2021, https://www.nytimes.com/2021/08/06/opinion/covid-delta-vaccines-unvaccinated.html.

186 **Alabama, Mississippi, Louisiana, and Arkansas:** "Tracking the COVID Vaccine: Doses, People Vaccinated by State," graph, *Washington Post*, last updated October 20, 2021, https://www.washingtonpost.com/graphics/2020/health/covid-vaccine-states-distribution-doses/.

186 **poorest states in the nation:** "How Rich Is Each US State?" Chamber of Commerce, n.d., https://www.chamberofcommerce.org/how-rich-is-each-us-state.

186 **highest rates of poverty:** "2019 Poverty Rate in the United States," United States Census, September 17, 2020, https://www.census.gov/library/visualizations/interactive/2019-poverty-rate.html.

187 **"The Vaccinated Class":** Jonah E. Bromwich, "The Vaccinated Class," *New York Times*, January 23, 2021, https://www.nytimes.com/2021/01/23/style/the-vaccinated-class.html.

187 **kinds of prophylaxis:** ChiVaxBot (@ChiVaxBot), "Chicago is currently reporting 32,438 people fully vaccinated: 1.2% of the population," tweet, Twitter, January 25, 2021, 6:01 p.m., https://twitter.com/ChiVaxBot/status/1353885791676739585.

188 **horrifying story from his research:** Brian Mustanski et al., "A Mixed-Methods Study of Condom Use and Decision Making Among Adolescent Gay and Bisexual Males," *AIDS and Behavior* 18 (2014): 1955–69.

188 **abstinence-only education laws:** "Sex Education Laws and State Attacks," Planned Parenthood, September 19, 2017, https://www.plannedparenthoodaction.org/issues/sex-education/sex-education-laws-and-state-attacks.

188 **a form of child abuse:** Sarah McCammon, "Abstinence-Only Education Is Ineffective and Unethical, Report Argues," National Public Radio, August 23, 2017, https://www.npr.org/sections/health-shots/2017/08/23/545289168/abstinence-education-is-ineffective-and-unethical-report-argues.

188 **sexual education of any kind:** Brandon Stratford, "The Majority of Schools in 15 States and DC Offer LGBTQ-Inclusive Sex-Ed Curricula," *Child Trends*, June 26,

2019, https://www.childtrends.org/blog/the-majority-of-schools-in-15-states-and-dc-offer-lgbtq-inclusive-sex-ed-curricula.

188 **viral transmission by the state:** Stratford, "The Majority of Schools in 15 States and DC Offer LGBTQ-Inclusive Sex-Ed Curricula."

190 **be poor, unemployed, homeless, and uninsured:** Nico Quintana, "Poverty in the LGBT Community," Center for American Progress, July 1, 2009, https://www.americanprogress.org/issues/lgbtq-rights/reports/2009/07/01/6430/poverty-in-the-lgbt-community/; Linda Carroll, "LGBT Adults in US Less Likely to Have Jobs, Health Insurance," Reuters, July 26, 2018, https://www.reuters.com/article/us-health-lgbt-employment-insurance/lgbt-adults-in-u-s-less-likely-to-have-jobs-health-insurance-idUSKBN1KG36V; and Adam Romero et al., "LGBT People and Housing Affordability, Discrimination, and Homelessness," Williams Institute, April 2020, https://williamsinstitute.law.ucla.edu/wp-content/uploads/LGBT-Housing-Apr-2020.pdf.

190 **outcomes for queer hearts and lungs:** Mark Hatzenbuehler et al., "Sexual Orientation Disparities in Cardiovascular Biomarkers Among Young Adults," *American Journal of Preventive Medicine* 44, no. 6 (June 1, 2013): 612–21; "Cancer in LGBT Communities," LGBT HealthLink, June 10, 2015, https://www.lgbthealthlink.org/Assets/U/Documents/FactSheets/cancer-lgbt-communities.pdf.

191 **lives to travel for them:** Henrietta D. v. Bloomberg, 331 F.3d 261 (2d Cir. 2003), The Center for HIV Law and Policy, https://www.hivlawandpolicy.org/resources/henrietta-d-v-bloomberg-331-f3d-261–2d-cir-2003.

191 **more likely to contract coronavirus:** Megan Cerullo, "Black and Hispanic Workers Less Able to Work from Home," CBS News, March 23, 2020, https://www.cbsnews.com/news/work-from-home-black-hispanic-workers/.

191 **to practice social distancing:** Conor Dougherty, "12 People in a 3-Bedroom House, Then the Virus Entered the Equation," *New York Times*, August 1, 2020, https://www.nytimes.com/2020/08/01/business/economy/housing-overcrowding-coronavirus.html.

191 **acutely at risk for COVID-19:** Benfer et al., "Eviction, Health Inequity, and the Spread of COVID-19."

191 **"who must die":** J.-A. Mbembé and Libby Meintjes, "Necropolitics," *Public Culture* 15, no. 1 (Winter 2003): 11–40, muse.jhu.edu/article/39984.

9: Disability as Disposability

193 **"write part of Trump's obit":** Ward Harkavy (@WHarkavy), "Former Hot-Metal Printer and Former Newspaperman: Destroyed Both Industries," Long Beach, NY, joined July 2009.

193 **"be made free for everyone":** Bernie Sanders (@SenSanders), "When Jonas Salk developed the polio vaccine 65 years ago, he understood its tremendous benefit

to all of humanity and he refused to patent it. Today, we must put human life above corporate profit. Any coronavirus treatment must be made free for everyone," tweet, Twitter, March 25, 2020, 7:28 a.m., https://twitter.com/SenSanders/status/1242820633412722690.

195 **SARS-CoV-2 to nursing homes:** Luis Ferré-Sadurní and Amy Julia Harris, "Does Cuomo Share Blame for 6,200 Virus Deaths in N.Y. Nursing Homes?" *New York Times*, July 8, 2020, https://www.nytimes.com/2020/07/08/nyregion/nursing-homes-deaths-coronavirus.html.

195 **spell over nursing homes for years:** "Residents at Greater Risk During Flu Season," *Illinois Nursing Home Abuse Blog*, Levin and Perconti Attorneys at Law, October 30, 2018, https://blog.levinperconti.com/nursing-home-flu-season/.

195 **states that did not:** Joaquin Sapien and Joe Sexton, "'Fire Through Dry Grass': Andrew Cuomo Saw COVID-19's Threat to Nursing Homes; Then He Risked Adding to It," ProPublica, June 16, 2020, https://www.propublica.org/article/fire-through-dry-grass-andrew-cuomo-saw-covid-19-threat-to-nursing-homes-then-he-risked-adding-to-it.

196 **pandemic in the United States:** Avik Roy, "The Most Important Coronavirus Statistic: 42% of US Deaths Are from 0.6% of the Population," *Forbes*, May 26, 2020, https://www.forbes.com/sites/theapothecary/2020/05/26/nursing-homes-assisted-living-facilities-0–6-of-the-u-s-population-43-of-u-s-covid-19-deaths/.

196 **residents had died of COVID-19:** Long-Term-Care COVID Tracker, The COVID Tracking Project, https://covidtracking.com/nursing-homes-long-term-care-facilities.

196 **deaths per one hundred thousand people:** "Death Rates from Coronavirus (COVID-19) in the United States as of January 25, 2021, by State (per 100,000 People)," Statista, January 25, 2021, https://drive.google.com/file/d/1zhgTs7m7Q-4oojkWmGD1Wdw4fZfvUfJT/view?usp=sharing.

196 **74,000 beds it once had:** Carl Campanile et al., "New York Has Thrown Away 20,000 Hospital Beds, Complicating Coronavirus Fight," *New York Post*, March 17, 2020, https://nypost.com/2020/03/17/new-york-has-thrown-away-20000-hospital-beds-complicating-coronavirus-fight/.

196 **hospital in Brooklyn:** Ross Barkan, "Cuomo Helped Get New York into This Mess," March 30, 2020, *Nation*, https://www.thenation.com/article/politics/covid-ny-hospital-medicaid/.

196 **funding from the state budget:** Luis Ferré-Sadurní and Jesse McKinley, "N.Y. Hospitals Face $400 Million in Cuts Even as Virus Battle Rages," *New York Times*, March 30, 2020, https://www.nytimes.com/2020/03/30/nyregion/coronavirus-hospitals-medicaid-budget.html.

196 **originally been reported:** Jesse McKinley and Luis Ferré-Sadurní, "N.Y. Severely Undercounted Virus Deaths in Nursing Homes, Report Says," *New York Times*,

January 28, 2021, https://www.nytimes.com/2021/01/28/nyregion/nursing-home-deaths-cuomo.html.

197 **book on his pandemic response:** Jon Campbell, "Andrew Cuomo's COVID-19 Book Sells 11,800 Copies, Lands on Best Sellers List," *Democrat and Chronicle*, October 22, 2020, https://www.democratandchronicle.com/story/news/politics/albany/2020/10/22/andrew-cuomos-book-lands-new-york-times-best-sellers-list/3724407001/.

197 **and was awarded an Emmy:** Dan Schindel, "Andrew Cuomo Got an Emmy for Literally Just Showing Up," *Hyperallergic*, December 8, 2020, https://hyperallergic.com/604761/andrew-cuomo-emmy-award-covid-briefings/.

197 **Royal Free Hospital in 1998:** Jeremy Laurence, "I Was There When Wakefield Dropped His Bombshell," *Independent*, January 29, 2010, https://www.independent.co.uk/life-style/health-and-families/health-news/i-was-there-when-wakefield-dropped-his-bombshell-1882548.html.

197 **"'issue has been resolved'":** Brian Deer, "Andrew Wakefield: The Fraud Investigation," https://briandeer.com/mmr/lancet-summary.htm.

197 **actress Jenny McCarthy:** Jan Hoffman, "How Anti-Vaccine Sentiment Took Hold in the United States," *New York Times*, September 23, 2019, https://www.nytimes.com/2019/09/23/health/anti-vaccination-movement-us.html.

197 **partially retracted in 2004:** Susan Mayor, "Authors Reject Interpretation Linking Autism and MMR Vaccine," *British Medical Journal* 328, no. 7440 (2004): 602, https://www.ncbi.nlm.nih.gov/pmc/articles/PMC381161/.

197 **fully retracted it in 2010:** Gardiner Harris, "Journal Retracts 1998 Paper Linking Autism to Vaccines," *New York Times*, February 2, 2010, https://www.nytimes.com/2010/02/03/health/research/03lancet.html.

198 **medicine in the United Kingdom:** Saad B. Omer, "The Discredited Doctor Hailed by the Anti-vaccine Movement," *Nature*, October 27, 2020, https://www.nature.com/articles/d41586-020-02989–9.

198 **by Thanksgiving of that year:** Priya Chidambaram, Rachel Garfield, and Tricia Neuman, "COVID-19 Has Claimed the Lives of 100,000 Long-Term Care Residents and Staff," Kaiser Family Foundation, November 25, 2020, https://www.kff.org/policy-watch/covid-19-has-claimed-the-lives-of-100000-long-term-care-residents-and-staff/.

198 **"Why I Hope to Die at 75":** Ezekiel Emanuel, "Why I Hope to Die at 75," *Atlantic*, October 2014, https://www.theatlantic.com/magazine/archive/2014/10/why-i-hope-to-die-at-75/379329/.

199 **reaffirmed it in 2019:** Stephen Hall, "A Doctor and Medical Ethicist Argues Life After 75 Is Not Worth Living," *MIT Technology Review*, August 21, 2019, https://www.technologyreview.com/2019/08/21/238642/a-doctor-and-medical-ethicist-argues-life-after-75-is-not-worth-living/.

199 **COVID-19 transition task force in 2020:** Yasmeen Abutaleb and Laurie McGinley, "President-Elect Biden Announces Coronavirus Task Force Made Up of Physicians and Health Experts," *Washington Post*, November 9, 2020, https://www.washingtonpost.com/health/2020/11/09/biden-coronavirus-task-force/.

199 **which are often not working:** Clarisa Diaz, "Infographic: How Much of the NYC Subway Is Accessible?" Gothamist, March 5, 2020, https://gothamist.com/news/infographic-how-much-nyc-subway-accessible.

200 **"at least one disability":** Jennifer Bronson, Laura M. Maruschak, and Marcus Berzofsky, "Disabilities Among Prison and Jail Inmates, 2011–12," Bureau of Justice Statistics, December 2015, https://bjs.ojp.gov/library/publications/disabilities-among-prison-and-jail-inmates-2011–12.

200 **physical, intellectual, or developmental disability:** Erin Vinoski Thomas and Chloe Vercruysse, "Homelessness Among Individuals with Disabilities: Influential Factors and Scalable Solutions," JPMHP Direct, July 24, 2019, https://jphmpdirect.com/2019/07/24/homelessness-among-individuals-with-disabilities/.

200 **a "Kiss-In":** Jim Hubbard, "ACT UP Kiss-In," Jim Hubbard website, April 29, 1988, https://www.jimhubbardfilms.com/unedited-footage/act-up-kiss-in.

201 **died of COVID-19:** Long-Term-Care COVID Tracker.

202 **disability activist and author Alice Wong:** Alice Wong, video interview with Steven Thrasher, August 10, 2020.

203 **Life Care Center of Kirkland:** Jack Healy and Serge F. Kovaleski, "The Coronavirus's Rampage Through a Suburban Nursing Home," *New York Times*, March 21, 2020, https://www.nytimes.com/2020/03/21/us/coronavirus-nursing-home-kirkland-life-care.html.

203 **where thirty-five people died:** Healy and Kovaleski, "The Coronavirus's Rampage Through a Suburban Nursing Home."

204 **"lower staffing and worse care":** E. Tammy Kim, "This Is Why Nursing Homes Failed So Badly," *New York Times*, December 21, 2020, https://www.nytimes.com/2020/12/31/opinion/sunday/covid-nursing-homes.html.

205 **"I'm all in":** Felicia Sonmez, "Texas Lt. Gov. Dan Patrick Comes Under Fire for Saying Seniors Should 'Take a Chance' on Their Own Lives for Sake of Grandchildren During Coronavirus Crisis," *Washington Post*, March 24, 2020, https://www.washingtonpost.com/politics/texas-lt-gov-dan-patrick-comes-under-fire-for-saying-seniors-should-take-a-chance-on-their-own-lives-for-sake-of-grandchildren-during-coronavirus-crisis/2020/03/24/e6f64858–6de6–11ea-b148-e4ce3fbd85b5_story.html.

205 **hospital systems were repeatedly:** Stephanie Innes, "'Do Not Let Your Guard Down': Arizona Hospital Leaders Warn Care May Be Rationed," *Arizona Republic*,

January 13, 2021, https://www.azcentral.com/story/news/local/arizona-health/2021/01/13/medical-officers-governor-doug-ducey-rationing-care/4144224001/; Rhonda Fanning and Caroline Covington, "Rationing Care Is on Horizon if Texas Doesn't Solve Climbing COVID-19 Hospitalizations," *Texas Standard*, January 5, 2021, https://www.texasstandard.org/stories/rationing-care-is-on-the-horizon-if-texas-doesnt-solve-climbing-covid-19-hospitalizations/.

205 **breaking points in Texas:** Marisa Martinez and Carla Astudillo, "Facing a Crush of COVID-19 Patients, ICUs Are Completely Full in at Least 50 Texas Hospitals," *Texas Tribune*, January 22, 2021, https://www.texastribune.org/2021/01/22/coronavirus-texas-hospital-capacity/.

205 **people with learning disabilities:** James Tapper, "Fury at 'Do Not Resuscitate' Notices Given to Covid Patients with Learning Disabilities," *Guardian*, February 13, 2021, https://www.theguardian.com/world/2021/feb/13/new-do-not-resuscitate-orders-imposed-on-covid-19-patients-with-learning-difficulties?utm_term=Autofeed&CMP=twt_gu&utm_medium&utm_source=Twitter#Echobox=1613225875.

205 **"herself to public view":** Sue Schweik, *The Ugly Laws: Disability in Public* (New York: NYU Press, 2009), 294.

206 **how many of them perished:** Joe Sexton, "Not Mentioned in Cuomo's Coronavirus Book: How Many Nursing Home Residents Died in New York," ProPublica, October 23, 2020, https://www.propublica.org/article/not-mentioned-in-cuomos-coronavirus-book-how-many-nursing-home-residents-died-in-new-york.

206 **resign or be impeached:** Steven W. Thrasher, "Andrew Cuomo Should Resign," *Scientific American*, March 4, 2021, https://www.scientificamerican.com/article/andrew-cuomo-should-resign/.

206 **reportedly sexually harassed eleven women:** *Report of Investigation into Allegations of Sexual Harassment by Governor Andrew M. Cuomo*, Office of the Attorney General, Letitia James, State of New York, August 3, 2021, https://ag.ny.gov/sites/default/files/2021.08.03_nyag_-_investigative_report.pdf.

206 **took away his Emmy:** "Statement from the International Academy of Television Arts & Sciences," International Emmy Awards, August 24, 2021, https://www.iemmys.tv/statement-from-the-international-academy-of-television-arts-sciences-2/.

206 **misled the public to believe:** Marina Villeneuve, "New NY Governor Adds 12,000 Deaths to Publicized COVID Tally," Associated Press, https://apnews.com/article/andrew-cuomo-health-coronavirus-pandemic-7312b49695e726eda8d59848e82271c5.

209 **"living with it for years":** Steven Thrasher, "The Pet-Death Business," *Village Voice*, November 10, 2009, https://www.villagevoice.com/2009/11/10/the-pet-death-business/.

10: Ride-Along

211 **Midwest city of about fifty thousand:** "QuickFacts: Bellevue City, Nebraska," United States Census, https://www.census.gov/quickfacts/bellevuecitynebraska.

212 **respiratory problems and headaches:** Heather Smith, "Many Still Living in FEMA's Toxic Trailers, Investigation Finds," *High Country News*, August 28, 2015, https://www.hcn.org/articles/people-are-still-living-in-femas-toxic-katrina-trailers-and-they-likely-have-no-idea.

213 **influenza, mumps, and chicken pox:** Robert Hart, "Report Details 'Shocking' Outbreaks of Mumps, Influenza, and Chickenpox in ICE Detention Centers," *Forbes*, October 30, 2020, https://www.forbes.com/sites/roberthart/2020/10/30/report-details-shocking-outbreaks-of-mumps-influenza-and-chickenpox-in-ice-detention-centers/?sh=1085cc8178f2.

215 **(DPA) in April 2020:** Exec. Order No. 13917, 85 Fed. Reg. 26313 (April 28, 2020), https://www.federalregister.gov/documents/2020/05/01/2020–09536/delegating-authority-under-the-defense-production-act-with-respect-to-food-supply-chain-resources/.

215 **keep slaughterhouses open:** Taylor Telford et al., "Trump Orders Meat Plants to Stay Open in Pandemic," *Washington Post*, April 29, 2020, https://www.washingtonpost.com/business/2020/04/28/trump-meat-plants-dpa/.

215 **Tyson chicken plant in Iowa:** "Coronavirus in the U.S.: Latest Map and Case Count," graph, *New York Times*, January 14, 2021, https://www.nytimes.com/interactive/2020/us/coronavirus-us-cases.html#hotspots.

216 **congregate settings as "trapped":** Wong, video interview.

216 **only to throw them away:** Sophie Lewis, "Farmers Will Have to Euthanize Millions of Pigs as Meat Plants Remain Closed," CBS News, May 15, 2020, https://www.cbsnews.com/news/farmers-euthanize-millions-pigs-meat-plants-close-coronavirus/.

216 **lawsuit against Smithfield Foods alleged:** RCWA & Jane Doe v. Smithfield, 2020 Mo. Ct. App. No. 5:20-CV-06063-DGK (2020).

217 **to incentivize working while sick:** Anonymous, "I Work at Smithfield Foods: I'm Suing Them over Putting Our Lives at Risk for Your Dinner," *Washington Post*, April 24, 2020, https://www.washingtonpost.com/outlook/2020/04/24/smithfield-foods-lawsuit-coronavirus/.

217 **"approximately 19,500 hogs per day":** Fernandez v. Tyson Foods, Inc., 2020 Iowa Ct. App. No. 6:20-cv-02079 (2020).

217 **betting ring at the Waterloo facility:** Laurel Wamsley, "Tyson Foods Fires 7 Plant Managers over Betting Ring on Workers Getting COVID-19," National Public Radio, December 16, 2020, https://www.npr.org/sections/coronavirus-live-updates

/2020/12/16/947275866/tyson-foods-fires-7-plant-managers-over-betting-ring-on-workers-getting-covid-19.

218 **Gilmore calls *organized abandonment*:** Ruth Wilson Gilmore, "What Is to Be Done?" *American Quarterly* 63, no. 2 (June 2011): 245–65.

218 **by the end of the year:** Chris Kirkham and Benjamin Lesser, "Special Report—U.S. Regulators Ignored Workers' COVID-19 Safety Complaints amid Deadly Outbreaks," Reuters, January 6, 2021, https://www.reuters.com/article/us-health-coronavirus-workplace-safety-s/special-report-u-s-regulators-ignored-workers-covid-19-safety-complaints-amid-deadly-outbreaks-idUSKBN29B1FQ?utm_medium=Social&utm_source=twitter.

218 **"died after contracting COVID-19":** Kirkham and Lesser, "Special Report."

219 **bonobo chimpanzees is the same:** Ann Gibbons, "Bonobos Join Chimps as Closest Human Relatives," The American Association for the Advancement of Science, June 13, 2012, https://www.sciencemag.org/news/2012/06/bonobos-join-chimps-closest-human-relatives.

219 **highly gendered, racialized, and ableist:** Sunaura Taylor, *Beasts of Burden: Animal and Disability Liberation* (New York: New Press, 2017).

219 **defined by their beastly bodies:** Londa Schiebinger, "Why Mammals Are Called Mammals: Gender Politics in Eighteenth-Century Natural History," *American Historical Review* 98, no. 2 (April 1993): 382–411.

219 **wrote in the *Conversation*:** Wulf D. Hund and Charles W. Mills, "Comparing Black People to Monkeys Has a Long, Dark Simian History," *Conversation*, February 29, 2016, https://theconversation.com/comparing-black-people-to-monkeys-has-a-long-dark-simian-history-55102.

220 **an ICE detention camp:** Gianna Melillo, "Experts Warn of Child Flu Outbreak in Detention Centers," *American Journal of Managed Care*, February 5, 2020, https://www.ajmc.com/view/experts-warn-of-child-flu-outbreak-in-detention-centers.

220 **found in bats and pangolins:** S. Lau et al., "Possible Bat Origin of Severe Acute Respiratory Syndrome Coronavirus 2," *Emerging Infectious Diseases* 26, no. 7 (2020): 1542–47.

220 **flying nocturnal mammals:** George Arbuthnot et al., "Revealed: Seven Year Coronavirus Trail from Mine Deaths to a Wuhan Lab," *Times*, July 4, 2020, https://www.thetimes.co.uk/article/seven-year-covid-trail-revealed-l5vxt7jqp.

221 **wiped out millions of them:** Heather Pringle, "How Europeans Brought Sickness to the New World," *Science*, June 4, 2015, https://www.sciencemag.org/news/2015/06/how-europeans-brought-sickness-new-world.

221 **more access to it:** Daniel Immerwahr, *How to Hide an Empire: A History of the Greater United States* (New York: Farrar, Straus and Giroux, 2019), 46.

221 **between human workers and shoppers:** Rafi Letzter, "The Coronavirus Didn't Really Start at that Wuhan 'Wet Market,'" LiveScience, May 28, 2020, https://www.livescience.com/covid-19-did-not-start-at-wuhan-wet-market.html.

222 **Smithfield Farms in Mexico:** Tim Philpott, "Swine-Flu Outbreak Could Be Linked to Smithfield Factory Farms," *Grist*, April 26, 2009, https://grist.org/article/2009–04–25-swine-flu-smithfield/.

222 **had sex with monkeys:** Jacob Heller, "Rumors and Realities: Making Sense of HIV/AIDS Conspiracy Narratives and Contemporary Legends," *American Journal of Public Health* 105 (2014): e43–e50.

222 **Democratic Republic of the Congo:** "Origin of HIV & AIDS," Avert, October 30, 2019, https://www.avert.org/professionals/history-hiv-aids/origin.

222 **continent of its resources:** Craig Timberg and Daniel Halperin, "Colonialism in Africa Helped Launch the HIV Epidemic a Century Ago," *Washington Post*, February 27, 2012, https://www.washingtonpost.com/national/health-science/colonialism-in-africa-helped-launch-the-hiv-epidemic-a-century-ago/2012/02/21/gIQAyJ9aeR_story.html.

223 **feces, hog ash, and viruses:** Jen Christensen, Artemis Moshtaghian, and Debra Goldschmidt, "Pig Poop and Coal Ash Are Real Concern in North Carolina Floods," CNN, September 18, 2018, https://edition.cnn.com/2018/09/17/health/hurricane-florence-pig-poop-and-coal-ash-health-concern/index.html.

223 **Thailand, despite its known dangers:** Juarawee Kittisilpa, "Bat Guano Collectors in Thailand Undeterred by Possible Link to Coronavirus," Reuters, March 15, 2020, https://www.reuters.com/article/us-health-coronavirus-thailand-bats/bat-guano-collectors-in-thailand-undeterred-by-possible-link-to-coronavirus-idUSKBN2130L9.

223 **"sustainably invest in its forests":** World Bank South Asia (@WorldBankSAsia), tweet, Twitter, February 13, 2020, 9:00 a.m., https://twitter.com/WorldBankSAsia/status/1227865071164022784.

224 **ten million U.S. homes:** Tommy Andres, "Divided Decade: How the Financial Crisis Changed Housing," Marketplace, December 17, 2018, https://www.marketplace.org/2018/12/17/what-we-learned-housing/.

224 **in cases of West Nile virus:** Nicholas Bakalar, "Patterns: First, Abandoned Pools. Then, West Nile," *New York Times*, November 10, 2008, https://www.nytimes.com/2008/11/04/health/research/04patt.html.

224 **to increased cases of West Nile virus:** Perotti, "The Human Side of Austerity," E62.

225 **dichlorodiphenyltrichloroethane:** Blake Thorkelson, "Smithsonian Scholar Examines Legacy of the U.S.-Mexico Bracero Program," Yale News, November 18, 2016, https://news.yale.edu/2016/11/18/smithsonian-scholar-examines-legacy-us-mexico-bracero-program.

225 **with several titanium teeth:** Brandi Petersen, "Police Dogs Armed with Titanium Teeth," KETV, February 20, 2014, https://www.ketv.com/article/police-dogs-armed-with-titanium-teeth/7644760#.

226 **"person bitten was African American":** *Investigation of the Ferguson Police Department,* PDF, March 4, 2015, United States Department of Justice Civil Rights Division, https://www.justice.gov/sites/default/files/opa/press-releases/attachments/2015/03/04/ferguson_police_department_report.pdf.

226 **where I'd been reporting:** Tyler Wall, "'For the Very Existence of Civilization': The Police Dog and Racial Terror," *American Quarterly* 68, no. 4 (December 2016): 861–82.

11: Release

231 **more white people annually:** "Number of People Shot to Death by the Police in the United States from 2017 to 2021, by Race," Statista, May 3, 2021, https://www.statista.com/statistics/585152/people-shot-to-death-by-us-police-by-race/.

232 **a not-insignificant number:** "Lifetime Risk of HIV Diagnosis," CDC, February 23, 2016, https://www.cdc.gov/nchhstp/newsroom/2016/croi-press-release-risk.html.

232 **before his trial:** Kenneth Pass et al., "An Open Letter to Michael Johnson," *POZ,* May 11, 2015, https://www.poz.com/article/michael-johnson-27220–2596.

233 **"Am I my brother's keeper?":** Genesis 4:9.

234 **to achieve this goal:** Sean Carroll, "At the Height of the Cold War, the US and Soviet Union Worked Together to Eradicate Smallpox," World Economic Forum, July 19, 2016, https://www.weforum.org/agenda/2016/07/at-the-height-of-the-cold-war-the-us-and-soviet-union-worked-together-to-eradicate-smallpox/.

235 **by age twenty-three:** Peggy Binette, "Study: Half of Black Males, 40 Percent of White Males Arrested by Age 23," University of South Carolina, updated February 10, 2015, https://www.eurekalert.org/pub_releases/2014–01/uosc-sho010314.php.

235 **who has been arrested:** Aleks Kajstura, "Women's Mass Incarceration: The Whole Pie 2019," Press Release, Prison Policy Initiative, October 29, 2019, https://www.prisonpolicy.org/reports/pie2019women.html.

235 **eight thousand mostly white people:** "QuickFacts: Boonville City, Missouri," US Census Bureau, July 16, 2018, https://www.census.gov/quickfacts/fact/table/boonvillecitymissouri/MAN450212.

235 **of the surrounding region and state:** "Missouri Incarceration Rates by Race/Ethnicity, 2010," graph, US Census 2010, Prison Policy Initiative, May 2014, https://www.prisonpolicy.org/graphs/2010rates/MO.html.

235 **Mirroring a national dynamic:** "Inmate Race," chart, Statistics, Federal Bureau of Prisons, May 1, 2021, https://www.bop.gov/about/statistics/statistics_inmate_race.jsp.

236 **the state's incarcerated population:** *Profile of the Institutional and Supervised Offender Population, 2019*, Missouri Department of Corrections, March 1, 2020, https://doc.mo.gov/sites/doc/files/media/pdf/2020/03/Offender_Profile_2019_0.pdf.

238 **new generation of Missouri attorneys:** "Heather Donovan," Faculty Directory, Lindenwood University, https://www.lindenwood.edu/about/directories/faculty-staff-directory/details/HDonovan/.

240 **decades of the twenty-first century:** Alfred Lubrano, "Anti-vaccine Parents Are Often White, College-Educated, 'Whole Foods Moms,'" *Philadelphia Inquirer*, April 10, 2019, https://www.inquirer.com/news/middle-class-working-class-vaccine-anti-vaxxers-measles-cdc-20190410.html.

240 **poor country like South Sudan:** Olga Khazan, "Wealthy L.A. Schools' Vaccination Rates Are as Low as South Sudan's," *Atlantic*, September 16, 2014, https://www.theatlantic.com/health/archive/2014/09/wealthy-la-schools-vaccination-rates-are-as-low-as-south-sudans/380252/.

240 **"Mr. Anti-Vax":** Mark Harper, "Conservative Talk Radio Host Who Opposed Vaccinations Dies After 3-Week COVID-19 Battle," *USA Today*, August 30, 2021, https://www.usatoday.com/story/news/nation/2021/08/30/covid-19-host-who-opposed-vaccinations-dies/5658639001/.

240 **"Mr. Anti-Mask":** Mychael Schnell, "Texas Anti-Mask Movement Leader Dies of COVID-19," *Hill*, August 29, 2021, https://thehill.com/homenews/state-watch/569921-texas-anti-mask-movement-leader-dies-of-covid-19.

241 ***Dying of Whiteness*:** Jonathan M. Metzl, *Dying of Whiteness: How the Politics of Racial Resentment Is Killing America's Heartland* (New York: Basic Books, 2019).

241 **"because these were smart people":** Kendall Thomas, interview by Sarah Schulman, "ACT UP Oral History Project," May 3, 2003, https://actuporalhistory.org/numerical-interviews/024-kendall-thomas?rq=kendall%20thomas.

241 **"see it as such":** Thomas, "ACT UP Oral History."

242 **incarcerated again within five years:** Marian Hatcher, "76% of All Inmates End Up Back in Jail Within 5 Years: Here's How I Broke the Cycle," *Vox*, August 8, 2017, https://www.vox.com/first-person/2017/8/8/16112864/recidivism-rate-jail-prostitution-break-cycle.

244 **had died from it:** Katie Moore, "Missouri Inmate, a Man from the Kansas City Area, Dies from the Coronavirus," *Kansas City Star*, April 7, 2020, https://www.kansascity.com/news/coronavirus/article241829391.html.

244 **tested positive for COVID-19:** "Covid-19 Cases in State Adult Institutions," table, Missouri Department of Corrections, August 22, 2020, https://doc.mo.gov/media-center/newsroom/covid-19/data.

244 **prison system had tested positive:** Madison Czopek, "Missouri Lags Behind with Limited Mask Mandate in Prisons," Associated Press, July 24, 2020, https://apnews.com/fbf17e8ad169442f3d4a7cb0967f5a4a.

245 **"Symbol of H.I.V. Criminalization":** Emily Rueb, "He Emerged from Prison a Potent Symbol of H.I.V. Criminalization," *New York Times*, July 14 2019, https://www.nytimes.com/2019/07/14/us/michael-johnson-hiv-prison.html.

245 **"it wasn't in a good way":** Timothy Lohmar, video, Medium.MOV, February 4, 2019, https://bit.ly/2ClF68H.

246 **"just was ignorant":** Lohmar, video.

246 **silent on this issue:** Timothy Lohmar, "Commentary About Michael Johnson Case Was Inaccurate, Misleading," *St. Louis Democrat*, August 15, 2015, https://bit.ly/2TIklyH.

246 **from ten years to three:** Kayla Drake, "Missouri Loosens Laws Criminalizing HIV Transmission After 30 Years of Faulty Assumptions," St. Louis Public Radio/NPR, July 15, 2021, https://news.stlpublicradio.org/government-politics-issues/2021–07–15/missouri-updates-hiv-laws-criminalizing-transmission-for-the-first-time-in-over-30-years.

246 **Illinois in 2021, entirely:** Leanne Fuller, "Illinois Governor Signs Bill Repealing State Statute Criminalizing HIV Transmission," WPSD/NBC, July 27, 2021, https://www.wpsdlocal6.com/news/illinois-governor-signs-bill-repealing-state-statute-criminalizing-hiv-transmission/article_92371b54-ef12–11eb-b200-f713147b9b1a.html.

12: Compound Loss

248 **"his life, contagion or punishment":** Foucault, "'Panopticism.'"

249 **"lose their sleep":** Kostopoulos, *Society Doesn't Fit Me*, 39.

250 **Black feminist Katrina Haslip:** "Katrina Haslip Dies; AIDS Worker Was 33," *New York Times*, December 3, 1992, https://www.nytimes.com/1992/12/03/obituaries/katrina-haslip-dies-aids-worker-was-33.html.

250 **10 percent of the tribe:** Mark Walker, "'A Devastating Blow': Virus Kills 81 Members of Native American Tribe," *New York Times*, October 8, 2020, https://www.nytimes.com/2020/10/08/us/choctaw-indians-coronavirus.html.

251 **tuberculosis, HIV, and malaria:** Apoorva Mandavilli, "'The Biggest Monster' Is Spreading: And It's Not the Coronavirus," *New York Times*, August 3, 2020,

https://www.nytimes.com/2020/08/03/health/coronavirus-tuberculosis-aids-malaria.html.

251 **AIDS deaths worldwide in 2020:** Juan Ambrosioni, José Blanco, and Juliana Reyes-Ureña, "Overview of SARS-CoV-2 Infection in Adults Living with HIV," *Lancet* 8, no. 5 (May 1, 2021): E294–E305.

251 **the opioid addiction crisis:** Zachary Siegel, "The Coronavirus Is Blowing Up Our Best Response to the Opioid Crisis," *New Republic*, July 29, 2020, https://newrepublic.com/article/158645/coronavirus-blowing-best-response-opioid-crisis.

252 **"infections and the outbreak itself":** Lauren Jackson, "A Conversation with Dr. Anthony Fauci," *New York Times*, April 2, 2020, https://www.nytimes.com/2020/04/02/podcasts/the-daily/coronavirus-fauci.html.

252 **hospitalization rates correspondingly rose:** Alexis C. Madrigal, "A Second Coronavirus Death Surge Is Coming," *Atlantic*, July 15, 2020, https://www.theatlantic.com/health/archive/2020/07/second-coronavirus-death-surge/614122/.

252 **the CDC had predicted:** "COVID-19 Pandemic Planning Scenarios," CDC, September 10, 2020, https://www.cdc.gov/coronavirus/2019-ncov/hcp/planning-scenarios.html.

252 **"mattered a lot to me":** Kostopoulos, *Society Doesn't Fit Me*, 27.

253 **"their turn to be vaccinated":** Elliot Kukla, "Where's the Vaccine for Ableism?" *New York Times*, February 4, 2021 https://www.nytimes.com/2021/02/04/opinion/covid-vaccine-ableism.html.

253 **by the *New York Times*:** Slotnik, "Lorena Borjas, Transgender Immigrant Activist, Dies at 59."

253 **the *New Yorker*:** Gessen, "Remembering Lorena Borjas, the Mother of a Trans Latinx Community."

253 **and the *Washington Post*:** Chase Strangio, "LORENA BORJAS," *Washington Post*, April 1, 2020, https://www.washingtonpost.com/opinions/2020/04/01/lorena-borjas-guardian-healer-trans-community-new-york/?arc404=true.

254 **"this message from Greece":** Zak Kostopoulos, "'You've Got This' #HIV Campaign—Zak Kostopolous," YouTube, August 28, 2013, https://www.youtube.com/watch?v=7xhn0d6KUDU. The rest of the quotes in this chapter are from this video.

255 **stars in the universe:** Katherine Wu, "There Are More Viruses Than Stars in the Universe: Why Do Only Some Infect Us?" *National Geographic*, April 15, 2020, https://www.nationalgeographic.com/science/2020/04/factors-allow-viruses-infect-humans-coronavirus/.

Epilogue

258 **in Austin, Texas, went viral:** Marcie Bianco, "COVID-19 Mask Mandates in Wisconsin and Elsewhere Spark 'My Body, My Choice' Hypocrisy," NBC News, August 3, 2020, https://www.nbcnews.com/think/opinion/covid-19-mask-mandates-wisconsin-elsewhere-spark-my-body-my-ncna1235535.

258 **at the Texas State Capitol:** Manny Fernandez, "Conservatives Fuel Protests Against Coronavirus Lockdowns," *New York Times*, April 18, 2020, https://www.nytimes.com/2020/04/18/us/texas-protests-stay-at-home.html.

261 **children living near the airports:** Angel Mak et al., "Lung Function in African American Children with Asthma Is Associated with Novel Regulatory Variants of the KIT Ligand KITLG/SCF and Gene-by-Air-Pollution Interaction," *Genetics* 215, no. 3 (2020): 869–86.

262 **"wretched offspring of pandemics":** Seema Yasmin, *If God Is A Virus* (Chicago: Haymarket, 2021), 26, uncorrected proof.

262 **even just for smog:** Wong, video interview.

263 **Milford, Pennsylvania, population 1,172:** "Milford, PA Profile," 2019 data set, Census Reporter, https://censusreporter.org/profiles/16000US4249400-milford-pa/.

264 **idea into being back in 2011:** Sean Strub, "Prevention vs. Prosecution: Creating a Viral Underclass," *POZ*, October 18, 2011, https://www.poz.com/blog/prevention-vs-prosec.

264 **"and a gay activism":** Sean Strub, interview with Steven Thrasher, Harrisburg, Pennsylvania, September 3, 2020.

265 **friends of Sean's—Deloris Dockrey:** Trenton Straube, "R.I.P. Deloris Dockrey, HIV Activist and Leader Lost to COVID-19," *POZ*, April 28, 2020, https://www.poz.com/article/rip-deloris-dockrey-hiv-activist-leader-lost-covid19.

265 **and Ed Shaw:** Trenton Straube, "R.I.P. Ed Shaw; The Longtime Advocate for Those Aging with HIV Died of COVID-19," *POZ*, May 1, 2020, https://www.poz.com/article/rip-ed-shaw-longtime-advocate-aging-hiv-died-covid19.

267 **"or talk to you":** Thomas Strong, "Sorry in advance. Some of us have lived here for years . . ." post, Facebook, May 14, 2020, https://www.facebook.com/strongthomas/posts/10158461244308980.

Afterword

270 **"loaded with information and energy":** Audre Lorde, "The Uses of Anger: Women Responding to Racism," keynote presentation at the National Women's Studies Association Conference, 1981, https://www.blackpast.org/african-american

-history/speeches-african-american-history/1981-audre-lorde-uses-anger-women-responding-racism.

271 **by federal COVID tax policy:** Christopher Pulliam and Richard V. Reeves, "New Child Tax Credit Could Slash Poverty Now and Boost Social Mobility Later," Brookings Institution, March 11, 2021, https://www.brookings.edu/blog/up-front/2021/03/11/new-child-tax-credit-could-slash-poverty-now-and-boost-social-mobility-later.

271 **set up for early death:** Travis Campbell, Alison P. Galvani, Gerald Friedman, and Meagan C. Fitzpatrick, "Exacerbation of COVID-19 Mortality by the Fragmented United States Healthcare System: A Retrospective Observational Study," *Lancet Regional Health—Americas*, https://www.ncbi.nlm.nih.gov/pmc/articles/PMC9098098.

271 **"should not remain as president":** Agence France-Presse, "Biden: Anyone Responsible for So Many Covid Deaths 'Should Not' Be President," *Barron's*, October 22, 2020, https://www.barrons.com/news/biden-anyone-responsible-for-so-many-covid-deaths-should-not-be-president-01603416304.

271 **"follow the science":** Lev Facher, "Biden Pledged to 'Follow the Science.' But Experts Say He's Sometimes Fallen Short," *Stat*, September 1, 2021, https://www.statnews.com/2021/09/01/biden-pledged-follow-the-science-but-hes-fallen-short.

272 **war with Russia:** Sahil Kapur, Frank Thorp V, and Julie Tsirkin, "Biden's Plans for Ukraine Aid, Covid Relief Jammed Up Over Immigration," NBC News, April 29, 2022, https://www.nbcnews.com/politics/congress/bidens-plans-ukraine-aid-covid-relief-jammed-immigration-dispute-rcna26554.

272 **money and equipment to Ukraine:** Jonathan Masters and Will Merrow, "How Much Aid Has the U.S. Sent Ukraine? Here Are Six Charts," Council on Foreign Relations, May 19, 2023, https://www.cfr.org/article/how-much-aid-has-us-sent-ukraine-here-are-six-charts.

273 **to contain or mitigate:** Apoorva Mandavilli, "Public Health Catastrophe Looms in Ukraine, Experts Warn," *New York Times*, March 23, 2023, https://www.nytimes.com/2022/03/26/health/ukraine-health-tb-hiv.html.

273 **a "quick death" at war:** Andrew Kramer, "'A Quick Death or a Slow Death': Prisoners Choose War to Get Lifesaving Drugs," *New York Times*, April 21, 2023, https://www.nytimes.com/2023/04/21/world/europe/russia-wagner-group-hiv-prisoners-ukraine.html.

273 **Pentagon and the World Trade Center:** White House, "Notice on the Continuation of the National Emergency with Respect to Certain Terrorist Attacks," September 9, 2021, https://www.whitehouse.gov/briefing-room/presidential-actions/2021/09/09/notice-on-the-continuation-of-the-national-emergency-with-respect-to-certain-terrorist-attacks.

273 **of an airborne virus:** Kevin Breuninger, "President Biden Tests Positive for Covid-19, Has Mild Symptoms," NBC News, July 21, 2022, https://www.cnbc.com/2022/07/21/president-biden-tests-positive-for-covid-19.html.

274 **on *hiring more cops*:** Shannon Pettypiece, "Biden Urges Cities to Spend Covid Relief Money on Police, Crime Prevention," NBC News, May 13, 2022, https://www.nbcnews.com/politics/white-house/biden-urge-cities-spend-covid-relief-money-police-crime-prevention-rcna28656.

274 **of every city dollar on police:** Niall McCarthy, "How Much Do U.S. Cities Spend Every Year on Policing?," *Forbes*, August 7, 2017, https://www.forbes.com/sites/niallmccarthy/2017/08/07/how-much-do-u-s-cities-spend-every-year-on-policing-infographic/?sh=13f7ab31e7b7.

274 **pressing public health needs:** Kelly Bauer and Mauricio Peña, "Lightfoot Defends Spending $281 Million of Coronavirus Funding from Feds on Police, Says Criticism Is 'Just Dumb,'" *Block Club Chicago*, February 19, 2021, https://blockclubchicago.org/2021/02/19/lightfoot-defends-spending-281-million-of-coronavirus-funding-from-feds-on-police-criticism-is-just-dumb.

274 **died of COVID election week:** Centers for Disease Control and Prevention Data Tracker, "Trends in United States COVID-19 Hospitalizations, Deaths, Emergency Visits, and Test Positivity by Geographic Area," https://covid.cdc.gov/covid-data-tracker/#trends_weeklydeaths_select_00.

274 **a mass-infection event:** Paul Fahri, "Yes, a Lot of White House Correspondents' Guests Are Testing Positive," *Washington Post*, May 25, 2022, https://www.washingtonpost.com/media/2022/05/05/covid-white-house-correspondents-dinner-guests-positive.

276 **closed in fifteen states:** Marielle Kirstein, Joerg Dreweke, Rachel K. Jones, and Jesse Philbin, "100 Days Post-Roe: At Least 66 Clinics Across 15 US States Have Stopped Offering Abortion Care," Guttmacher Institute, October 6, 2022, https://www.guttmacher.org/2022/10/100-days-post-roe-least-66-clinics-across-15-us-states-have-stopped-offering-abortion-care.

276 **mental, and physical health outcomes:** Diana Greene Foster, "The Turnaway Study," ANSIRH, University of California, San Francisco, https://www.ansirh.org/research/ongoing/turnaway-study.

276 **medical-abortion drug mifepristone:** Erin Doherty, "How a Federal Judge in Texas Became an Obamacare Boogeyman," Axios, April 12, 2023, https://www.axios.com/2023/04/12/obamacare-judge-reed-oconnor-preventive-care-aca.

276 **HIV-prevention medications:** Robert King, "Judge Finds Employers Not Required to Cover HIV Drug, Preventive Service Task Force Unconstitutional," FIERCE Healthcare, September 7, 2022, https://www.fiercehealthcare.com/payers/judge-finds-employers-not-required-cover-hiv-drug-preventive-service-task-force.

278 **as soon as they've opened:** Joe Eskenazi, "SF Cuts and Runs in the Tenderloin—and on Safe-Injection Sites," *Mission Local*, December 12, 2022, https://missionlocal.org/2022/12/san-francisco-fentanyl-tenderloin-safe-injection-drugs-crackhouse-statute.

278 **for those who are counting:** Track Trans Legislation, "2023 Anti-Trans Legislation," https://www.tracktranslegislation.com.

279 **an outbreak in Nigeria:** Michaeleen Doucleff, "He Discovered the Origin of the Monkeypox Outbreak—and Tried to Warn the World," NPR, July 29, 2022, https://www.npr.org/sections/goatsandsoda/2022/07/28/1114183886/a-doctor-in-nigeria-tried-to-warn-the-world-that-monkeypox-had-become-a-global-t.

280 **Denmark for too long:** Joseph Goldstein and Sharon Otterman, "As Monkeypox Spread in New York, 300,000 Vaccine Doses Sat in Denmark," *New York Times*, July 25, 2022, https://www.nytimes.com/2022/07/25/nyregion/nyc-monkeypox-vaccine-doses-denmark.html.

280 **some 32,235 mpox cases:** Centers for Disease Control and Prevention Morbidity and Mortality Weekly Report, "Epidemiologic and Clinical Features of Mpox-Associated Deaths—United States, May 10, 2022–March 7, 2023," https://www.cdc.gov/mmwr/volumes/72/wr/mm7215a5.htm.

280 **4 percent of the world's population:** Centers for Disease Control and Prevention, 2022 Mpox Outbreak Global Map, accessed on May 23, 2023, https://www.cdc.gov/poxvirus/mpox/response/2022/world-map.html.

280 **fell, briefly, to zero:** Demetre Daskalakis (@dr_demetre), White House Deputy Monkeypox Coordinator, "First week of #ZERO #mpox cases reported in the US. We are at risk unless we finish the job vaccinating folks who could benefit from the shot through intentional work supporting people affected by systemic racism, homophobia, and transphobia," tweet, Twitter, April 27, 2023, 1:05 p.m., https://twitter.com/dr_demetre/status/1651633700436598784.

281 **states like Georgia:** Helena Oliviero, "Early Data Shows Monkeypox Disproportionately Affecting Black Men," *Atlanta Journal-Constitution*, August 10, 2022, https://www.ajc.com/news/atlanta-news/early-data-shows-monkeypox-disproportionately-affecting-black-men/D5C6I4VUSVBUZLMBFO75SETFGI/.

281 **and North Carolina:** North Carolina Department of Health and Human Services, "NCDHHS Releases Monkeypox Case, Vaccine and Testing Demographic Report; Shows Vaccine Racial Disparities Within MSM Community," August 10, 2022, https://www.ncdhhs.gov/news/press-releases/2022/08/10/ncdhhs-releases-monkeypox-case-vaccine-and-testing-demographic-report-shows-vaccine-racial.

281 **white men made up less than one-third:** Centers for Disease Control and Prevention, "Mpox Cases by Age and Gender and Race and Ethnicity," updated June 21, 2023, https://www.cdc.gov/poxvirus/mpox/response/2022/demographics.html.

284 **"Hope is a discipline":** Jeremy Scahill, "Hope is a Discipline: Mariame Kaba and the Dismantling of the Carceral State," *Intercept*, March 17, 2021, https://theintercept.com/2021/03/17/intercepted-mariame-kaba-abolitionist-organizing.

284 **largest social protest movement in U.S. history:** Larry Buchanan, Quoctrung Bui, and Jugal K. Patel, "Black Lives Matter May Be the Largest Movement in U.S. History," *New York Times*, July 3, 2020, https://www.nytimes.com/interactive/2020/07/03/us/george-floyd-protests-crowd-size.html.

289 **gassed many of the tens of millions of activists:** K. K. Rebecca Lai, Bill Marsh, and Anjali Singhvi, "Here Are the 100 U.S. Cities Where Protesters Were Tear-Gassed," *New York Times*, June 16, 2020, https://www.nytimes.com/interactive/2020/06/16/us/george-floyd-protests-police-tear-gas.html.

INDEX

THE VIRAL UNDERCLASS DISCUSSION QUESTIONS

1. Before you read *The Viral Underclass*, how did you view the stigma about viruses, especially HIV? Have your views changed now that you've read the book? How?

2. Did reading this book challenge your opinions of "superspreaders" or the idea of "patient zero"? Do you find that you are now blaming different people and entities for the transmission of viruses?

3. Did you watch the movie *Parasite* before reading this book? Have you watched it since? What do you notice now about the movie that you didn't pick up on before?

4. Discuss Michael Johnson's initial thirty-plus-year sentence. What would it take to prevent others in his situation from receiving similar sentences?

5. Do you know anyone who suffers from addiction? Have you witnessed them being treated unfairly? How has reading about the murder of Zackie Oh or what happened in Cabell County affected the way you think about what this person is going through?

6. Discuss the complicated relationship between the U.S. government and workers who are undocumented. In your opinion, what are the biggest hurdles to overcome? You may also want to consider setbacks that have occurred since the publication of this book.

7. While it's easy to blame one political party or the other for the response to COVID-19, what might the federal government have done better during the pandemic? Or during the outset of the AIDS epidemic? Which vectors that make a viral underclass do you think change depending on which party is in office, and which are largely unchanged?

8. What conceptual prophylaxis do you benefit from? Before reading this book, had you ever thought about your privileges

(perhaps money, race, education, access to health care) as being the only things standing between you and infection, addiction, or incarceration? How does this change the way you think about people who don't have your same privileges?

9. Were you surprised to learn that a large factor in the COVID-19 vaccine being offered for free is that the government needed laborers to keep working? Were you surprised to learn that the COVID-19 vaccine's global rollout was so slow partly because of the patent, whereas the polio vaccine has not been patented? How did these realizations make you feel about what you and others went through during this time?

10. Did you know anyone who lived in a nursing home during COVID-19 lockdown? Did their experiences change the way you feel about nursing homes? Do you have any suggestions for alternatives for people who need this kind of care?

11. Did you know anyone who died of COVID-19? Did lockdowns affect how you were able to mourn? What resonated with you while reading this book in thinking about the deaths and lives of those you lost?

12. Discuss the connection that the author makes between the spread of viruses and the meat processing industry. Do you have ideas on how to stop the spread along these vectors? Should people eat less meat? Or are there ways to make working conditions safer?

13. Why do you think the author chose to put himself into the book? What about his decision to explain his ideas through the lens of a handful of specific people? How did these personal stories affect your experience of the concepts discussed in the book?

14. What emotions did you feel while reading *The Viral Underclass*? Did anything in particular make you feel outraged? Did any particular story make you cry? Did any surprising fact cause you to spring into action?

ABOUT THE AUTHOR

STEVEN W. THRASHER, PhD, holds the inaugural Daniel H. Renberg chair at Northwestern University's Medill School, the first journalism professorship in the world created to focus on LGBTQ research. He is also a faculty member of Northwestern University's Institute for Sexual and Gender Minority Health and Wellbeing. His writing has been widely published by the *New York Times*, the *Nation*, the *Atlantic*, the *Journal of American History*, BuzzFeed News, *Esquire*, and *Scientific American*. A recipient of grants from the Ford and Sloan foundations, Dr. Thrasher was named one of the hundred most influential and impactful people of 2019 by *Out* magazine. An alumnus of media jobs with *Saturday Night Live*, the HBO film *The Laramie Project*, and the NPR StoryCorps project, Dr. Thrasher has also been a staff writer for the *Village Voice* and a columnist for the *Guardian*. He holds a PhD in American studies and divides his time between Chicago, New York, and motels at the ends of runways. *The Viral Underclass* is his first book. Twitter and Instagram: @thrasherxy.

Founded in 2017, Celadon Books, a division of Macmillan Publishers, publishes a highly curated list of twenty to twenty-five new titles a year. The list of both fiction and nonfiction is eclectic and focuses on publishing commercial and literary books and discovering and nurturing talent.